Praise for *Premodern Places*

"My Cinderella prize for the year's most underrated book goes to David Wallace, whose Pre-Modern [sic] Places mixes romance and bizarrerie in a study of medieval and Renaissance ideas about geography and locality."

Jonathan Keates, The Spectator 'Book of the Year' feature, 2004

"David Wallace's focus on place enables him to offer a truly innovative approach to writers as diverse as Petrarch and Dante, Columbus and Aphra Behn. The large issues of travel and colonialism, of slavery and race, are approached from unusual directions, always encouraging readers to see familiar territory through fresh eyes. This is one of the sharpest and most imaginative books of literary criticism I've read in many years."

Peter Hulme, University of Essex

"Offering illuminating genealogies for a range of authors and literary texts, *Premodern Places* radically questions many assumptions about historical as well as geographic boundaries. Wallace reveals often surprising interconnections between medieval and early modern periods, and between England, Europe, and the New World. This compelling account of how the 'slaving Mediterranean' moves into the 'black Atlantic' makes it impossible to divide humanism from slavery, or our most cherished literatures from the complex histories of race and colonialism. As such, this book asks both premodernists and postcolonialists to rethink their disciplines and make urgent connections across space and time."

Ania Loomba, University of Pennsylvania

"The postcolonial concept in David Wallace's book lacks the specificity of a historical moment in that it refers to the aftermath of any colonial situation, even when it also defines a privileged theoretical perspective of the present from which he writes. Postcolonial theory as practiced by Wallace, a most brilliant representative of Postcolonial Medieval Studies, has much to teach those of us who working in the context of Latin America get enmeshed in debates over the applicability of postcolonial theory to the colonization of the Americas in the sixteenth century."

José Rabasa, University of California, Berkeley

"Imagine that all the paths between places on our usual cultural map have been obliterated, and strange new paths have been created, some of them linking locales we thought we knew with others we had never heard of. That is the achievement of *Premodern Places*. One of the traditional cultural mappings it obliterates is that between medieval and early modern. Countering Todorov, David Wallace's book shows how splendidly international the supposedly 'insular' Middle Ages already was long before the discovery of the New World. As any voyage into unfamiliar territory should, he offers us surprises at every turn: Chaucer brushing shoulders with the slave trade in Genoa, Dante Alighieri's *Commedia* alive and well in rustic sixteenth-century Somerset, and the love discourse of Abelard and Heloïse in relation to the African speech of Surinam."

Leah Marcus, Vanderbilt University

"In this compelling book, the distinguished medievalist David Wallace takes us far beyond the traditional confines of the Middle Ages to explore relationships between the Old World and the emerging New. Through a series of dazzlingly original case studies, Wallace shows us how European pre- and early-modern literary cultures shaped themselves against the geographical and social other. Chaucer's poetry is illuminated by the lights not just of London but of Calais and Flanders. Dante finds a literary afterlife among provincial English humanists. The slave trade inflects readings of a host of poets, from Petrarch to Spenser, while the drama of Aphra Behn gives voice to what Wallace calls a history of 'Anglophone imagining of white/black relations.' This book synthesizes the best and most provocative of currents in contemporary scholarship, while offering a unique and intimate rereading of texts both familiar and new."

Seth Lerer, Stanford University

Premodern Places

Calais to Surinam, Chaucer to Aphra Behn

David Wallace

Blackwell
Publishing

BLACKWELL PUBLISHING
350 Main Street, Malden, MA 02148-5020, USA
9600 Garsington Road, Oxford OX4 2DQ, UK
550 Swanston Street, Carlton, Victoria 3053, Australia

First published 2004 by Blackwell Publishing Ltd
First published in paperback 2006 by Blackwell Publishing Ltd

1 2006

Library of Congress Cataloging-in-Publication Data

Wallace, David John, 1954–
  Premodern places : Calais to Surinam, Chaucer to Aphra Behn / David Wallace.
    p. cm.
Includes bibliographical references and index.
  ISBN 1-4051-1393-6 (hardcover : alk. paper)
  1. English literature–Foreign influences. 2. English literature–Middle English, 1100 – 1500–History and criticism. 3. English literature–Early modern, 1500–1700–History and criticism. 4. Geography in literature. I. Title.

  PR125.W35 2004
  820.9–dc22

                                                                            2003025594

ISBN-13: 978-1-4051-1393-9 (hardcover : alk. paper)
ISBN-13: 978-1-4051-5152-8 (paperback)
ISBN-10: 1-4051-5152-8 (paperback)

A catalogue record for this title is available from the British Library.

Set in 10.5/13pt Dante
by Graphicraft Ltd, Hong Kong
Printed and bound in the United Kingdom
by TJ International Ltd, Padstow, Cornwall

For further information on
Blackwell Publishing, visit our website:
www.blackwellpublishing.com

CONTENTS

for

Bruce Holsinger
Paul Strohm
Richard Wallace

comites in itinere

ILLUSTRATIONS

INTRODUCTION

I grew up in England, but now live mostly in Philadelphia, a city that transports you suddenly into imagining (inhabiting, it sometimes seems) other times and places. Two blocks west of our house a single-word inscription above the door of a mansion, now an apartment building, proclaims "Meade," designating the gift of grateful Philadelphians after victory at Gettysburg; General Meade died here in 1872. Eight blocks east of our house, opposite my doctor's office, stands the dwelling rented by Joseph Bonaparte, brother of Napoleon, in 1816. And our house itself, which was once a shop (there are still fittings in the floorboards) stands in the Seventh District as surveyed by W. E. B. DuBois for his great, foundational text of modern sociology, *The Philadelphia Negro*; as DuBois saw it in 1896–7, the house was serving the needs of a modest block of middle-class black families.[1] Mention of DuBois keeps us in the frame of European imagining, for he too pursued academic training in Europe and maintained a lifelong interest in transatlantic matters. Erich Auerbach, E. R. Curtius, and Leo Spitzer, those great European Romance philologists whose work subtends Edward Said's hopes for a revitalized humanism, also made this crossing.[2] So while it might seem odd to open discussion of premodern places by evoking transatlantic space, the fact is that this book, as peculiarly the product of Anglo-American training and tradition,[3] has crossed this oceanic divide before it begins; the trajectory of chapters – from Calais to Surinam – simply catches up with what already informs every chapter.[4]

Philadelphia, in many ways, is more European than Europe: there is no finer, unbroken stretch of eighteenth- to nineteenth-century housing, between

the Delaware and the Schuylkill, anywhere in the old world; the equivalent
square miles in the Netherlands and London have been bombed flat. It is
a city of dense sedimentation: at every turn, some bootscraper or gaslight,
African Methodist Episcopal church or synagogue, transports the mind, the
senses, to another time (or, better, an image from that time comes suddenly
to disrupt present preoccupations). Some of these stimuli, such as the "Meade"
inscription, have the force of what Roland Barthes terms the *punctum*: a sign
or detail in a visual field provoking some deep – yet highly subjective –
sense of connectedness with people in the past.[5] Such a potent image, Walter
Benjamin suggests, might be encountered as "that wherein what has been
comes together in a flash with the now to form a constellation."[6] Attempts
to organize experiences of such stimuli, however, can deaden their effects,
as at the wretched, glass-fronted pavilion housing Philadelphia's "Liberty
Bell" (cast at Whitechapel, London, in 1751). And the evocative power of
such symbolization shifts, inevitably, with time. The Philadelphia police
rushed to protect our bell on 9/11, but nothing happened; it clearly no
longer possesses the signifying charge of sites such as the World Trade
Center and the Pentagon. All the places in this book have, in some sense,
disappeared or experienced equivalent losses of symbolic resonance: Calais
and Surinam are no longer English-speaking colonies of key economic importance; Flanders no longer leads the world in technological (hence imaginative) innovation; Somerset is no longer a world-class intellectual center;
Scythia and the Fortunate Islands have receded into mythology; Genoa no
longer rules the waves; and the Guanche no longer rule Tenerife. Their
tales and poetries return, however, to delight and instruct and disrupt. Their
collected imaginings do not evoke the kind of "closed mythopolitical system"
associated by Pierre Nora with the French nation-state and its *lieux de
mémoire*.[7] Narratives of outward expansion and homeward return, of translation and conversion, have designs on these places, but each place interpellates
or buttonholes us with its own images and tales, distracting us from grander
visions of geographical space and historical process.

    The book begins at Calais, or at Calais Gate: a place that at once signals
(for English people such as William Hogarth) where the foreign begins, but
one that is also (as Hogarth notices, to his own epiphanic surprise) a place
where the English (where England) used to be. To imagine English territory
extending into continental Europe – with the Channel as a roadway rather
than a defensive moat – immediately challenges received notions of "insular"
culture; this is obviously – with the advent of the Channel Tunnel and the
ever-impending prospect of the euro – a timely meditation. It was withdrawal from Calais in 1558 – and from the fruitless attempt to extend the

Calais bridgehead into continental empire – that freed English resources for wider exploration and commercial investment. And yet premodern Calais itself in some ways adumbrates later English colonial experiments as Edward III, following its capture in 1347, carries out an extraordinary policy of "repeopling Calais" with "pure English"; and as a border territory, where concepts such as "nation" and "frontier," "race" and "deracination" evolve through complex stages. In Chaucer's encounters with French writing within and across this space, issues of cultural and linguistic hybridity (crucial to his poetic style) assume defining importance.

Hybridity is a subject found by postcolonial studies to be both vexed and indispensable.[8] In some remarkable anticipations of postcolonial dilemmas that English itself will later precipitate, we find English deployed at the Calais border not as a master discourse but as the weaker, ill-bred tongue in a talking war with the civilized world's *lingua franca*: a language and a set of cultural values (French) from which English attempts to escape while yet finding them integral to its own hybrid identity. In the view of the French, as expressed in the long course of the Hundred Years' War, the English cannot constitute a nation. When the English are belatedly granted a *nation* at the council of Constance (1414–18), its fantastical bounds include "Hibernia, which is Scotland [*sic*], the kingdom of Arabia beyond the sea, the kingdom of the Medes, the kingdom of the Persians, the two Indias, the Greater and the Lesser, ruled by Prester John, the kingdom of Ethiopia, where the Moors live, the kingdom of Egypt . . . the kingdom of Nineveh" and, reportedly, "nine other kingdoms . . . beyond Tartary." The French, by contrast, "are a kingdom by themselves . . . to their nation belong merely the lords and cities of their land."[9] Such premodern, continental views of England as a miscegenated, dispersed, and ragbag nation haunt the national imaginary down to Shakespeare's "Falconbridge, the young baron of England," said to have "bought his doublet in Italy, his round hose [puffed breeches] in France, his bonnet in Germany, and his behaviour everywhere."[10]

Premodern Calais is both a contested frontier location and its own distinctive place: for six generations, English soldiery, shipmen, merchants, money-makers, churchmen, musicians, householders, wives, mistresses, and tavern-keepers fashion an intense (and unmistakably hybridizing) local culture. Works of historians, geographers, and economists help fix the parameters of life in such places, but literary (and musical) texts bring us to them with the greatest immediacy. Literature is, after all, the truest history: whereas historians synthesize data to bring us accounts of past places in their own present voices, literary scholars are able (from time to time) to fall silent, bringing us texts from the past in the past's own idiom.[11] Such was the particular genius of Raymond Williams: he was never afraid – in a book such as *The Country and the City* – to let a past text have its own (often quite extended) present moment.[12] Revivifying such voices is surely one of the most pleasurable aspects of literary criticism: to imagine, for example, merchant George Cely singing "Go hert, hurt with aduersite" at Calais in 1479 to the sound of a harp. From ancient times, it has been the dearest and simplest wish of poets that, through their writings, their voices might endure; that, in some sense, they be reembodied (re-membered) by being heard again. The pleasure we take in such recovered voices is inverse to the pain of contemplating voices that have been lost, obliterated, or heavily overlaid (to advert again to a perennial concern of postcolonial studies); acceptance of final loss, however, is to be resisted with every ounce of disciplinary skill at our disposal.[13]

Viewed from this Calais, this continentally English vantage point, Flanders is border country: a place (like many other bordering locations, such as Wales, Scotland, and Ireland beyond the pale) inspiring strong, romantically fantastical, and calculatedly strategic English imaginings. Again, what "Flanders" then meant has to be learned rather than assumed: many intermediate phases, including the Great War, with a record of slaughter that still dominates the landscape (through dozens of military cemeteries), lie between then and now. Premodern Flanders was a place of scant natural resources and poor soils (corn was imported from France, wool from England) that nonetheless created a brilliant urban culture (unrivalled anywhere outside Italy). This was achieved through precocious, highly complex divisions of labor (the abiding preoccupation of Chaucer's *General Prologue*), producing luxurious cloths of peerless quality. And Bruges – as exemplified by Chaucer's *Shipman's Tale* – was the epicenter of European money markets, the medieval Wall Street. It is thus not surprising, then, that surplus capital at Bruges should be absorbed into works or commodities of art (including books, for here Caxton learned his trade); not surprising, either, that the greatest of this artwork – not the overloaded leaves of Flemish Books of Hours (predictable exercises in "added value") – speak to, issue from, new historical anxieties. For the genius of premodern Flanders is to improve upon nature (where the resources of nature are thin, poor, or deficient); and improving upon nature (down to the papal encyclical *Humanae vitae* [1968] and into the present) is always a dangerous, if exhilarating, proposition within Catholic cultures. Much of this ambivalence (exhilaration and anxiety) finds expression by turning to, or upon, the body, as in the Flemish imaginings of Dante and of Chaucer (*Pardoner's Tale*), and in the paintings of Hieronymus Bosch and Gerhard David. Beginning with the Wife of Bath (1. 448), the singular economic success of Flanders also sparks belligerent dreams of English emulation – extending down to Richard Hakluyt and the ministers of Elizabeth I – and, in a move often to be repeated, inspire English designs on another border country: Ireland.

Chapter 3 is called "Dante in Somerset" (rather than plain "Somerset") by way of recording the *punctum*-like instant that sets it in motion. The incredulity or amusement evoked by this title (at least in England) immediately begins the work of "placing," for Somerset today is seen as a deeply rural, backward English county incapable of hosting a phenomenon so furious and all-enveloping as Dante. For Coleridge and Wordsworth, Somerset proved to be an ideal spot for recollecting experiences had elsewhere, but (unlike the Lake District, or Tintern Abbey) Somerset could hardly form the *subject* of Romantic sublime. Again, this naturalized experience of place is shown to seal deliberate phases of historical construction or, better, destruction; for during the time that my "Dante" was to be found at Wells, Somerset housed a literary, scholarly, and indeed musical culture of international range and repute (extending to Constance and Urbino, and serviced by one of the biggest libraries in Britain). Detailed recreation of this milieu suggests that there is nothing in this Somerset to mark out Dante as in any way eccentric, foreign (or out of place). The rustication and ruination of Somerset culture by one set of political, economic, and ideologically driven religious forces – the Reformation – came eventually to serve and disguise the ends of another: the transatlantic slave trade, generative of the wealth that built the neoclassical mansions still dotting the Somerset landscape. Between these moments, the evocative powers of the English countryside – in stages that, even while fixating more intensively on local detail, are unmistakably nationalizing in their effects – are enhanced by suggesting that the body of the English monarch mysteriously folds into, is made identical with, the landscape he rules.

Premodern Genoa, chapter 4 argues, was hardly a place at all: hemmed in by mountains, it crowded down to the sea and, in many senses, was all at sea, for *Genovesi* like Caboto and Colombo lived by transporting the soldiery, luxury goods, and dyestuffs (so essential for Flanders) from place to place.[14] And as Chaucer saw at Genoa in 1373, they also shipped slaves ("Tartars" or "Scythians") across the Mediterranean. A first visualization of Chaucer crossing the lines of the slave trade comes as a shock for which *punctum* seems too weak a term: it messes with every kind of periodizing and disciplinary division that has structured our (my) thinking; Chaucer and slavery have inhabited quite different parts of the English curricular woods. But in coming to Genoa, Chaucer undoubtedly crosses global circuits of trade that had long linked, as Janet Abu-Lughod plainly illustrates, Genoa to Caffa and Alexandria (and, for that matter, Alexandria to Aden, Aden to Calicut, and Calicut to Palembang).[15] In shrinking from such a realization, we rehearse a time-honored reflex, for "Genoa" is a premodern place that has been richly reviled. *Genovesi* are "white Moores" outfacing and outmatching the Jews; they are (according to Boccaccio) "men naturally and voraciously driven by attachment to money." Dante denounces *Genovesi* at the lowest point of his hell and wishes them *del mondo spersi* ("scattered from the world" [*Inferno* 33.157], a brilliant conceit, since Genovesi are scattered *across* the world, probing and extending its known limits). Jacob Burckhardt, in his celebrated *Civilization of the Renaissance in Italy*, insists that Genoa can have nothing to do with his project, since "it took almost no part in the Renaissance."[16] The impulse to disown or revile Genoa meshes with the impulse to separate Renaissance culture from slaving and plantation practices that are migrating steadily across, and then beyond, the Mediterranean. "Genoa" might thus be figured as the premodern id: a name with which to disguise, deny, or repudiate that very energy carrying Europe – for better or for worse – to the New World, the darker complement to the sunnier Renaissance vision (Botticelli's Venus upon the half-shell) of Florence.[17]

Genoese shipmen, inevitably, were the first Christian premoderns to discover the Canaries (long hymned by classical poets as the "Insulae Fortunatae," paradisaical islands at the edge of the world). Chapter 5 opens with the Florentine Giovanni Boccaccio reworking mercantile accounts of the 1341 Genoese expedition to the Canaries into his best protohumanist Latin. The classicizing paradigms laid down by Boccaccio in describing the flora and fauna of these islands and the ways of their near-naked inhabitants prove remarkably durable: when another mercantile humanist, Hieronymus Münzer, encounters Canarians at the slave markets of Valencia in 1494 he clearly thinks (if that is the word) like a Boccaccian disciple. Between these two moments of first encounter and terminal enslavement, just 150 years, the various Canary islands are thoroughly mapped, colonized, and cultivated as premodern places (complete with Gothic cathedrals and sites of Catholic pilgrimage). *Le Canarien* tells how in 1402 a French nobleman threatened by English incursions, Jean de Béthencourt, mounted a Crusade against the Canaries, conquered three islands, and (in a bizarrely belated Norman conquest) moved in his own settler peasantry. The Catalan *Tirant lo Blanc*, composed a little later in the fifteenth century, tells how the King of the Canaries, incensed at depredations of English corsairs in his part of the world, led a Moorish invasion force against England, landing at Southampton. The first of these texts spices up recorded history (Béthencourt is still a name to reckon with in the Canaries), while the second is pure romance (Canarians did not, in fact, know how to sail from one island to the other); but both speak eloquently to the ways in which these colonized Atlantic islands were drawn into the European premodern imaginary long before Columbus left for the Americas.

Cristoforo Colombo, the most famous of premodern *Genovesi*, spent long years haunting European places and sea lanes (considered in the first four chapters) before turning his attention further westward across the Atlantic. And it was from the Canaries that he set out on all four of his famed voyages (just as the Spanish were mounting final campaigns against native Canarians, resistant to conquest for more than a century). Small wonder, then, that when Columbus sees Hispaniola he thinks of the Canaries (and of growing sugar), or that the natives of Guanahani (renamed San Salvador) remind him of *los canarios*. The famous Latin letter telling Europe of his discovery is translated back very easily (in the popularizing work of Giuliano Dati) into the language, idiom, imagining, and poetic form (*ottava rima*) of Boccaccio and his popular successors. Dati's poem is marketed as an account of "new Canary islands," suggesting that the Caribbean and the Americas are to be seen as just the latest staging posts in a steady westward migration demanding no great proclamations of historical rupture: a view sustained by later Catholic mapping (from 1621; figure 25) that finds room for the Americas and the Canaries, St. Brendan and his whale (upon which he celebrates mass) on the same page. It is only in Protestant cultures that the newness of a New World must be proclaimed to coincide with the rejection of an old religion (exemplified by extravagant legends of St. Brendan). In this new view of the world, the inhabitants of St. Brendan's native isle are every bit as pagan, as rebellious to true religion, as the Guanche of Tenerife. In meditating upon Canarian peoples, we intuit that many European perceptions and practices taken to the Americas are first essayed in the Canaries. Throughout this book, we also think often of Ireland, a vital laboratory and stepping stone between England and New England.

"Surinam," my last chapter, stands for what Columbus gazed upon (in sailing by the mouth of the Orinoco river) and which later Europeans actively helped to form. It was to Surinam, famously, that Englishwoman Aphra Behn came, and she came at precisely that period when English and West African forms of language were locked in pressurized processes of daily interaction. It is remarkable that although the English governed Surinam only for a short period (1651–67: it was traded away for Manhattan), it was at this time – rather than during the ensuing three centuries of Dutch rule – that the new language, Sranan, took shape. No scholar of Aphra Behn, to my knowledge, has meditated long on this fact: attention has been focused on what Behn took *from* Surinam – experiences for the memory bank; butterflies for "His Majesties Antiquaries"; feathers for the London stage – rather than what (in the largest sense) she brought to it. My first five chapters have begun addressing this last question; chapter 6 goes further by considering the long, exegetical history of a Scriptural verse – *nigra sum sed formosa, filiae Hierusalem* ("I am black but beautiful, daughters of Jerusalem"). Crucial moments in the history of blackness and whiteness (and associated issues of beauty, abjection, mutuality, being a woman) are aligned with the long trajectory of European slaving. Many aspects of American plantation societies are seen to carry over from European practices, and from Old World representations of peasantry and specific ethnic groups, but there is an acceleration of scale in Surinam (as elsewhere in the Americas) that marks and effects *the* crucial difference. The works of Voltaire (Candide definitively loses faith in Panglossian optimism when confronted with Surinamese slavery), John Stedman, and his engraver William Blake follow after this moment; the work of our Scriptural exegetes (Heloïse and Abelard; Bernard of Clairvaux) precede it; and Aphra Behn's *Oronooko*, her extraordinary narrative of an African prince, enslaved and transported to the Americas – lies on a cusp in between.

Surinam, in every sense, is a difficult place to get to. Today the best flight from Philadelphia reaches Paramaribo airport in the early hours of the morning (following changes in Miami and Trinidad). Evelyn Waugh got to this part of the world, but only with a view to traveling back as quickly as possible (and to making money from telling of his exploits); Aphra Behn and her long train of literary critics follow much the same timetable. The Reverend Isaac Teale dwelt longer in this extended Caribbean space, bordered to the west by Surinam, and in 1801 published his "History of the Sable Venus: An Ode." Here, in this later phase of imagining a woman *nigra sed formosa*, we see again how effortlessly the humanist classicism inaugurated by Boccaccio and Petrarch sustains the core classical practice of enslavement; and how well certain aspects of medieval poetics travel in its service. Teale, and Waugh after him, model white *otium*: the notion of *being* in a place, profiting from it, yet remaining uninvolved; the fantasy of clean separation between imperial center (which, in a sense, every civilized traveler brings with him) and far-flung outpost. For Waugh, the greatest horror imaginable (that of *A Handful of Dust*) is to be stuck *out there*, with no hope of return. In the work of Indian, West Indian, Guyanese poet and novelist David Dabydeen, however, and in the Sranan poetry of Trefossa, such differentiations of *here* from *there* have no purchase. Indeed, it is precisely through encounters with premodern (and specifically medieval) literary forms in Europe that their powerful new poetries are shaped, or shaken loose; the book ends with the raw, "broke" language of Dabydeen's Guyanese *Slave Song* and with Trefossa's joyful Italianate Surinamese sonnet, *Humor in èksèlsis*.

The reading of premodern texts might be regarded, as it is by the Secretary of State for Education and Skills in the 2003 English Labor government, as an activity of questionable utility, as, perhaps, nostalgia-driven rather than future-oriented.[18] There is, I think, something magical in the business of bringing past texts, voices from forgotten places, into the present: a magic akin to the beguiling art of W. G. Sebald, whose (unabashedly Eurocentric) narratives of place and travel spin out from seemingly random textual remainders such as train tickets, official forms, and old photographs.[19] I know little of the future, but remain convinced that the informing and unsettling effects of premodern texts educate in the most basic sense (in leading us away from present-day self-absorption). The ways in which historically minded literary criticism deploys linkages between past and present, however, have recently been scrutinized to searching and bracing effect by postcolonial critics. "To critique historicism in all its varieties," Dipesh Chakrabarty remarks, "is to unlearn to think of history as a developmental process in which that which is possible becomes actual by tending to a future that is singular. Or, to put it differently, it is to learn to think the present – the 'now' that we inhabit as we speak – as irreducibly not one."[20] There is much worth pondering here and elsewhere in Chakrabarty's *Provincializing Europe*.

Works of Marxist historicism have certainly favored robustly developmental titles: Perry Anderson's *Passages from Antiquity to Feudalism* was designed to preface *Lineages of the Absolutist State* and thus form "a single argument."[21] Anderson's long account of peasants succeeding slaves as the chief energy source for expanding empires and states retains its value – certainly as a prior text of this book – despite its elevated and impersonal viewpoint (Anderson rarely observes from ground level); and his account of the plural lineages of absolutism (a political form never fully realized in any country, especially not in England) is distinguished both by its meticulous localism and its concern with eastern as well as western Europe (and also with Japan). In this body of work, economics (above all) and reasons of state do indeed precede and determine choices in culture and religion. As Simon Gikandi observes, Benedict Anderson's more modestly proportioned *Imagined Communities* has proved greatly more influential than Perry's monumental sequence both in analyzing *nation* rather than *state* and in engaging with aspects of personal and collective desire.[22] Tracking the desires and imaginings that inform a richly complex premodern concept such as *nation* is indeed crucial: but deployment of the term "nation" itself *as* a medieval or premodern term, insulated from the forward definitional pull of later centuries, has proved extremely tricky (for medievalists and postcolonialists alike).[23] Weberians have made noteworthy efforts to expand conventionally Eurocentric frames of analysis; Randall Collins' comparative account of Chinese and western European precapitalist cultures is particularly illuminating.[24] There remains, nonetheless, a powerful pull within Weberian analysis to assume the way of the West as the standard against which other developmental paths are mapped. Much the same is true of Immanuel Wallerstein, whose account of an evolving world economy bespeaks a notion, as Hendryk Spruyt observes, of "unilinear historical progress."[25] Spruyt himself proves exemplary in resisting the notion of the *inevitable* rise of the sovereign, European territorial state: the Hanseatic League and the Italian city-states function as organizational models alternative to (and indeed simultaneous with) the sovereign, territorial model first strongly exemplified by Capetian France (987–1328). This resonates in part with Chakrabarty's implicit appeal for a non-teleological, multiple model of historically minded criticism. How might such a practice, seeking to escape prior insular limits and delimited, period-specific timespans, develop elucidating power without suggesting an only-one-outcome, view-of-the-victors *modus agendi*? How do recent historicist practices, particularly those dedicated to the premodern period, hold up?

New Historicism, the most influential recent avatar of historicist critique, tends always to have thrown in the towel *as* a historicism by eschewing diachronic analysis (any account of historical change) in favor of lateral movement (across rather than through time) from archival fragment to literary text: a curious form of freeze-frame analysis characterized by Wai Chi Dimock as "Newtonian literary studies," regulated by (in her wonderful phrase) a "nonbiological clock."[26] It is no accident that this mode of synchronic thick description (adapted from anthropology) was first developed by Renaissance specialists in English departments, for the "New" here stands in for (is happily and silently complicit with) those acts of cultural erasure – the destruction, fragmentation, or reallocation of books and manuscripts; the abolition or attenuation of self-determining, local associational forms such as guilds, *compagnyes*, *felaweshipes* – with which the English state affirmed (imperfectly and impossibly) its separation from Rome and continental Europe. In writing of and from this brave new world, now increasingly identified as the *fons et origo* of the English literary tradition (or at least of the taught canon), Renaissance critics can at least consider themselves free of the taint of Hegelian historicist determinism (since in this critical enclave there is no past and future; just the present-world of the suddenly and silently modernized text). Medievalists, by contrast, continue to insist on the linguistic and cultural differences of their texts (thus widening the gulf between themselves and everyone else). If for Renaissance scholars the past is always now, for medievalists (dedicated decryptors of a ruined and fragmented culture) the end is always nigh.[27] Thus medievalist readings of literary texts tend to be colored by knowledge of what happens next (Anne of Bohemia dies; Archbishop Arundel returns; John Badby is burned in a barrel; Prince Arthur yields to Prince Henry). We know (adverting to another key insight of postcolonial studies) that *multiple* temporalities course through every literary text; sometimes, under the pressure of local readings, we tend to forget.[28]

It is in part in an attempt to escape the peculiar eddying (and indeed mutually antagonistic) force fields of "medieval" and "Renaissance" that the term "premodern" is adopted in this book. This immediately concedes that my *longue durée* is actually of short duration. Scholars (such as Copeland, Carruthers, and Baswell) whose analyses run from classical antiquity to the late Middle Ages complement my time scheme.[29] The dazzling internationalisms of Anglo-Saxon England, particularly of Wearmouth–Jarrow and Lindisfarne, compare in cultural richness with any place explored in this volume. The spices bequeathed by Bede on his deathbed and the objects buried with Cuthbert (complemented by the startling researches of Michael McCormick) suggest extraordinarily fluid patterns of movement between Irish, Northumbrian, Indian, African, and Arabian places.[30] There are, in short, other premodern places – further removed from us in time and language, hence more difficult to retrieve – every bit as singular and astonishing as those explored here.

In fourteenth-century Italy, I have argued elsewhere, republican Florence and despotic Milan fought out ideological conflicts traditionally associated with the guild-minded Middle Ages and the princely Renaissance: "their dates are the same," as Perry Anderson has it, "their times are different."[31] This succinct formulation, while brilliantly suggestive, also misleads, for no earlier social formation (city, colony, nation) ever moves *tout entière* in the tracks of another. Postcolonial theory understands this particularly clearly in deploying the term *medieval*, for the medieval is that from which modernity develops (the germ of modernity being always contained in the medieval, for without it the modern could not come into being); yet the medieval can never be entirely absorbed into, become identical with, the modern. While medievalists have been scandalized by postcolonialist representations of the

Middle Ages as an infantile or indeed prehistorical phase of European development, considerable conceptual potential opens up with this formulation
(which must, in any event, be preferable to the time-honored definitions of
medium aevum formulated by Renaissance paradigm-making).[32] As modern
medievalism decrypts texts from a distant past that challenge presentist,
self-coincident assumptions, so postcolonial critique considers texts and voices
whose residually medieval, unmodern ways of thinking and being mark
them as alien to the metropolitan center (although they may, in fact,
form part of the modern metropole).[33] Such kinship in critical thinking owes
something to the fact, as Bruce Holsinger demonstrates, that the pioneers of
subaltern studies were diligently attentive to *Annales* school accounts of
medieval European peasant economies.[34] While it would be opportunistic
and misleading to superimpose or exchange the understanding of things
"medieval" in postcolonial and medieval studies scholarship, there is at least
the assurance that the term "medieval" need not be swallowed up into –
become a subset of – the Renaissance when we speak of the "premodern";
the medieval (by this postcolonial definition) is unassimilable.

  The *Annales* school, in typically attending to exceptionally long stretches
of time, has attempted to render accounts of human life and development
without (in Hegelian fashion) according sequential temporalities the power
of determinative or necessary force. It has also eschewed narrowly regnal or
political versions of history by opening itself to the fullest range of human
activities (sailing and trading, traveling and crusading, planting and reaping,
writing and reading).[35] Such attempts do not always succeed: but this *longue
durée* historicism has (at its best) proven able to consider general socioeconomic trends while remaining forever cognizant of locally experienced
differences. It is thus possible to trace the development of trading and slaving practices across and beyond the Mediterranean – one of the chief concerns of this book – while yet observing the intensely localized conjunctions
of social, economic, legal, and linguistic practice that make (say) Haiti, Cuba,
and Jamaica such distinctively different places. A commitment to locally
contingent but endlessly exfoliating processes is difficult to manage in writing this kind of book. But the struggle seems preferable to reliance on those
paradigms, or notions, more readily and typically favored by literary critical
method, such as *rupture* and *crisis*. *Rupture*, a notion at the heart of medieval
and Renaissance paradigm-making, generally indicates an unwillingness to
think through or into a particularly intense phase of political activity (such
as the 1530s); the notion that there *is* a break or rupture in historical time is
itself generally an ideological propagation issued by interested parties within
that time.[36] The associated invitation to imagine certain key figures of such

moments, such as Petrarch, *escaping* time by embodying rupture (within themselves: hence anguished, self-divided poetics) distracts attention from the very concrete acts of social and political destruction with which such individuals may be complicit. *Crisis*, while seeming to speak of flux and uncertainty, is actually a stabilizing, reassuring notion, for it suggests that diverse strands of complex historical development come conveniently knotted together in a single instant (thus rendering themselves amenable to analysis, like a well-wrought urn).[37]

Terms such as *rupture* and *crisis*, then, encountered as part of apologetics that figure as organic (both are bodily metaphors) sharp adjustments in policy, wealth distribution, or religious practice excogitated by the state itself, inspire skepticism. As a *descriptor* of certain kinds of human experience, however, *rupture* seems too weak a term, particularly that of being taken from the place where you live, separated from your language community, shipped thousands of miles, and set to work with no hope of return. If there is a still-defining *break* in history, as the term *pre*modern implies, it comes as this individual tragedy (driven by an economic imperative growing ever more anonymous, founding itself on difference of skin color) replicates on a scale of millions. The term *crisis* is also too feeble and indeed optimistic[38] to encompass this, unless employed in the modern Italian sense of *la crisi*: an intolerable state of affairs that has become an accepted way of living.

Praxes of feminism, over the last half-century, have proved powerfully instructive in moving between paradigmatic articulations and particular, local acts. Patriarchy, when first described, seemed sometimes to assume the lineaments of an unquestionable, universalist force (far outstripping its possible performative capacities); more recent accounts, accentuating constructed rather than ontological traits, treasuring historicity while disavowing historicism,[39] have found greater room for imaginative maneuver. It is now possible to ask, even as a man in the classroom, how, *given circumstances that were far from favorable*, premodern women might have found self-expression, self-realization, and enjoyment. The italicized part, of course, is not be leapt over lightly; and there are texts that form limit cases, driving us deep into hermeneutics – such as *Ancrene Wisse*. It is possible to read this text, written by a male cleric for enclosed female religious, as devising to keep women (in every sense) fully enclosed; and it is possible to imagine this same text (once handed through the anchorhold window) being crossed and traversed by pathways of female reading never contemplated by the original author.[40]

But to what extent is it possible to move from anchorhold to slavehold and apply the same question? To ask how, *given circumstances that were far from favorable,* African people found resources to sustain identity during the middle passage, seems reckless: not a question yet to be posed by a white teacher in any classroom I know of. It is not an impossible question, just an untimely one, for writers such as Toni Morrison and Saidiya Hartman are beginning to enter that desperate, undocumented space of "catastrophic rupture," lending it voice through imaginative acts envisioned as reparative justice.[41] The danger for white scholars who write of the enslavement of black people is that remorse – expressed through determined detailing of every last horror and outrage – ironically invests this trade with the Hegelian force of something having to happen. This compounds with assumptions of absolute black/white difference still structuring modern consciousness, especially in the United States: a phenomenon both parodied and confirmed by the black/white tableaux of Kara Walker. Again, it is through artistic exploration that some wiggle or breathing space is first won for these over-powering topics, as in Walker's black paper silhouettes on white grounds, depicting scenes from the old south at once familiar and (looking more closely) deranged.[42] The stark representational simplicity of Walker's figures neatly complements the definition of *race* essayed by Michael Omi and Howard Winant as "a concept which signifies and symbolizes social con-flicts and interests by referring to different types of human bodies."[43] Here again, *longue durée* approaches prove resistant and instructive in suggesting how, when, and why such "conflicts and interests" are projected onto par-ticular bodies (and to suggest a time before all this was fully achieved, or even dreamed of). In many of the premodern places considered in this book, European peasants are treated and described (physiognomy is particularly important) in ways later applied to black slaves. In others, the phenomenon of skin color is regarded not as *the* but as *a* constitutive personal trait (and as by no means the sole sign of freedom or unfreedom). And in many texts (see chapter 6), the status of being black and female is something that medieval white men are eager to claim for themselves. All this might help-fully contextualize the work of critics such as Paul Gilroy and Brent Edwards, mindful that their material "does not fit unambiguously into a time-consciousness derived from and punctuated exclusively by changes in the public, urban worlds of London, Berlin, and Paris."[44]

Place is my organizing category of choice. Some readers, following Michel de Certeau, might favor *space* over *place*, *espace* over *lieu* (although the concepts are in constant interrelation, as in Certeau's formulation *space is a practiced place*).[45] *Place*, which for Aristotle was one of the ten indisputable categories of every substance, has been increasingly assimilated to *space*; and *space*, as Edward S. Casey argues, "has become a cosmic and extracosmic Moloch that consumes everything in its path."[46] Time, particularly since

Huygens invented his "no. 1 chronometer" (1735), has been a category of yet more absolute importance ("the formal a priori condition of all appearances whatsoever," according to Kant): for in order to know your place at sea, it was necessary to look to the clock; to know *"where* one was," as Casey puts it, "became equivalent to *when* one was."[47] Anna-Teresa Tymieniecka, however, speaks of "the esoteric passion for place," illustrating her point by pointing to "the dog that digs in the soil projecting in space its indefinable striving to discover or to hide precious bones in a safe depository."[48] It is difficult to know whether the "esoteric passion" here applies to canine digger or female author, but the image captures something specific to place, namely heightened states of emotion: the pleasures of being fully in place; the pains and travails of being out of it.[49] One thinks of Ulsterman Seamus Heaney, digging his native sod (sort of) to claim patrilinear identity; also of Raymond Williams, happy to imagine a post driven down by his house "for a new wire fence" striking a cobbled road, a thousand years old. The emotional charge of such a direct and simple act is heightened, for Williams, by its borderline location: having told of his upbringing "under the Black Mountains, on the Welsh border," he then situates us just outside Cambridge, his workplace, seen as a glow of lights on the nocturnal horizon. Ulster, too, is border country.[50]

Such liminal, emotional, and indeed erotic locational resonances are well understood by premodern texts; the most memorable gesture in Middle English love poetry, one from which a royal protagonist will never recover, registers a claim to place (within the most famed medieval place of all): "What, may I nat stonden here?"[51] It is further understood that such limits and resonances change (as Troy will fall). For Aristotle, a *topos* is a mental place where an argument can be found. A rhetor may choose a geographical place (such as Troy) as *topos*, remembering that emotions inhere not in the place itself but in what any given articulation excites in a particular audience (pity, delight, rage).[52] Eustache Deschamps, in his vast French poetic corpus, works hard to establish English-occupied Calais as a place whose very naming excites outrage; the territory of France, "the nation-state par excellence, and by seniority" (as Pierre Nora has it), cries out for conquest or rescue.[53] Tartary – Scythia, in Petrarchan and Spenserian usage – that vast, unknowable space that loomed over the exiled Ovid (so far from the Roman center) – marks the extreme Eurasian limit of the western world. In the course of the fourteenth century, this limit is breached and Tartar slaves begin flowing toward the European center; so too does the Black Death. Meanwhile, the Insulae Fortunatae – those islands so long dreamed of beyond the pillars of Hercules – are actually (in the form of the Canary Islands) being "discovered":

how do European visitors make sense of their experience in crossing the time-honored limits of locational myth? How do such myths endure or mutate as their places are added to the map? The locales in this book, then, are both geographic sites and ideas, dreams, and feelings about places. Such feelings, while never repeating, migrate and are refined as socioeconomic forces demand changes of location: thus, in a sequence of widening watercourses, Bruges–Antwerp–Amsterdam. More interesting, however, are unlikelier isomorphic plottings of feelings about place: Flanders–Venice–Los Angeles. Readers of this book feel strongly and differently about places they have never seen: the Bronx and Baghdad, Calcutta and Cheltenham Spa, Jerusalem and (to end with a premodern place featured in chapter 4) Nuremberg. All the emotions, past and present, attaching to such names represent more than colorings or flavorings or accidental properties of history; they form part of its substance (to persist with the scholastic figure) in that they condition, drive, and compel historical acts of greater and lesser importance. Although we may seek to separate our own feelings about a particular place from those of these premodern texts, it will never be possible to perfect such detachment, to fully distinguish their Jerusalem from ours.

NOTES

1 W. E. B. DuBois, *The Philadelphia Negro*, introduction by Elijah Anderson (Philadelphia: University of Pennsylvania Press, 1998). First published in 1899.

2 See Said, *Orientalism*, with a new preface (London: Penguin, 2003; first published in 1978); see further *Literary History and the Challenge of Philology: The Legacy of Erich Auerbach*, ed. Seth Lerer (Stanford, Calif.: Stanford University Press, 1996).

3 In attending my first lectures at the University of York, England, in fall or autumn 1973, I heard Derek Pearsall plot modern Chaucer studies between (something like) "the Scylla of D. W. Robertson and the Charybdis of Talbot Donaldson"; Charles Muscatine featured as a sort of Rock of Gibraltar. All these critics lived and worked in the USA.

4 Naturally it is desirable to try and think to and beyond the limits of this tradition, and to engage with (listen to) those speaking from elsewhere; but it would be otiose not to acknowledge such situatedness at the outset.

5 See Roland Barthes, *La Chambre claire: note sur la photographie* (Paris: Gallimard, 1980); *Camera Lucida*, trans. Richard Howard (New York: Hill and Wang, 1981).

6 *The Arcades Project*, trans. Howard Eiland and Kevin McLaughlin (Cambridge, Mass.: Belknap Press, 1999), p. 463.

7 *Rethinking France: Les Lieux de Mémoire*, vol. I, *The State*, trans. Mary Trouille (Chicago: University of Chicago Press, 2001), p. xxi. See further Nora et al.,

Realms of Memory: Rethinking the French Past, trans. Arthur Goldhammer, 3 vols. (New York: Columbia University Press, 1996–8).

8   See Robert Young, *Colonial Desire: Hybridity in Theory, Culture, and Race* (London: Routledge, 1995); Ania Loomba, *Colonialism/Postcolonialism* (London: Routledge, 1998), pp. 173–83; Paul Gilroy, *The Black Atlantic: Modernity and Double Consciousness* (London: Verso, 1993), pp. 72–110, 199; Jeffrey Jerome Cohen, "Hybrids, Monsters, Borderlands: the Bodies of Gerald of Wales," in *The Postcolonial Middle Ages*, ed. Cohen (New York: St. Martin's Press, 2000), pp. 85–104 (pp. 85–6).

9   All this according to the chronicle of Ulrich Richental, citizen of Constance: see *The Council of Constance: The Unification of the Church*, trans. Louise Ropes Loomis, ed. John Hine Mundy and Kennerly M. Woody (New York: Columbia University Press, 1961), pp. 200–465 (p. 317); John Scattergood, "*The Libelle of Englyshe Polycye*: the Nation and its Place," in *Nation, Court and Culture; New Essays on Fifteenth-Century Poetry*, ed. Helen Cooney (Dublin: Four Courts, 2000), pp. 28–49 (pp. 45–6).

10 *The Merchant of Venice*, 1.2.62–4; the speaker is the Venetian Portia. References to Shakespeare follow *The Norton Shakespeare. Based on the Oxford Edition*, ed. Stephen Greenblatt, Walter Cohen, Jean E. Howard, and Katherine E. Maus (New York: W. W. Norton, 1997).

11 For the last 20 years or so we have tended to accentuate how every text from the past comes densely mediated by the conditions of its transmission (in manuscripts and printed editions); without in any way repudiating all this, it is perhaps time to emphasize (to hear again) the phenomenality of voice.

12 Raymond Williams, *The Country and the City* (London: Chatto and Windus, 1973).

13 See the exemplary meditations of Gary Tomlinson, "Unlearning the Aztec *cantares* (preliminaries to a postcolonial history)," in *Subject and Object in Renaissance Culture*, ed. Margreta de Grazia, Maureen Quilligan, and Peter Stallybrass (Cambridge: Cambridge University Press, 1996), pp. 260–86; Nicholas Watson, "Desire for the Past," *Studies in the Age of Chaucer* 21 (1999), 59–97.

14 Genoese monopoly of trade in alum, the substance that made colors bite into fabric, was guaranteed through possession of Phocaea and Chios (at the far eastern end of the Mediterranean): see Lisa Jardine, *Worldly Goods: A New History of the Renaissance* (London: Papermac, 1997), pp. 114–15; on Columbus' work at Chios, see chapter 4 below.

15 *Before European Hegemony: The World System A.D. 1250–1350* (New York: Oxford University Press, 1989), p. 34, figure 1.

16 *The Civilization of the Renaissance in Italy*, 15th edn., trans. S. G. C. Middlemore (London: Harrap, 1929), p. 106.

17 For an important attempt "to inscribe 'the darker side of the Renaissance' into the silenced space of Spanish/Latin American and Amerindian contributions to universal history," see Walter D. Mignolo, *The Darker Side of the Renaissance: Literacy, Territoriality, and Colonization* (Ann Arbor: University of Michigan Press, 1995), p. xi.

18   Charles Clarke allegedly told a gathering at Worcester College, Oxford, that "I don't mind there being some medievalists around for ornamental purposes, but there is no reason for the state to pay for them." In an official transcript released some days later, Mr. Clarke muses on why the state should fund "the medieval concept of the university as a community of scholars seeking truth," while urging universities to think more about benefiting the economy (Jeevan Vasagar and Rebecca Smithers reporting, *The Guardian*, May 10, 2003). On medievalism as "an interesting limit case in contemporary discourses of utility," see Louise Fradenburg, "'So that We May Speak of Them': Enjoying the Middle Ages," *New Literary History* 28 (1997), 205–30 (p. 210).

19   See, to begin with, *The Emigrants*, trans. Michael Hulse (London: Harvill, 1996); *The Rings of Saturn*, trans. Michael Hulse (London: Harvill, 1998).

20   *Provincializing Europe: Postcolonial Thought and Historical Difference* (Princeton, NJ: Princeton University Press, 2000), p. 249.

21   Perry Anderson, *Passages from Antiquity to Feudalism* (London: New Left Books, 1974), p. 7; *Lineages of the Absolutist State* (London: New Left Books, 1974).

22   *Maps of Englishness: Writing Identity in the Culture of Colonialism* (New York: Columbia University Press, 1996), p. xvii.

23   My chief reservation about Thorlac Turville-Petre's fine book *England the Nation: Language, Literature, and National Identity, 1290–1340* (Oxford: Clarendon Press, 1996) concerns its dedicated attempt to show English *growing into* and largely fulfilling definitions of nationalism set by later centuries: "The underlying contention of this book is that it is the similarities between medieval and modern expressions of national identity that are fundamental, and the differences that are peripheral" (p. v). There is thus an excessive reliance on regnal-based chronicling and a downplaying of local and dialectal differences; the book ends by analyzing the Harley lyrics "as a demonstration of the triumphant emergence of English as the language of the national culture" (p. vii). Benedict Anderson's account of the Middle Ages as (in Kathleen Davis' words) "*both* a primitive or infant stage incapable of thinking the mature nation, *and* as the source, or origin, of the nation-people's characteristics" offers a view symmetrically opposite to that of Turville-Petre (while, ironically, sharing its progressivist logic): see Davis, "National Writing in the Ninth Century: A Reminder for Postcolonial Thinking about the Nation," *Journal of Medieval and Early Modern Studies* 28 (1998), 581–637 (p. 613).

24   *Weberian Sociological Theory* (Cambridge: Cambridge University Press, 1986), pp. 45–76.

25   *The Sovereign State and Its Competitors: An Analysis of Systems Change* (Princeton, NJ: Princeton University Press, 1994), p. 18; Wallerstein, *The Politics of the World Economy* (Cambridge: Cambridge University Press, 1984).

26   "Nonbiological clock: Literary History against Newtonian Mechanics," *South Atlantic Quarterly* 102 (Winter 2003), 153–77 (p. 157).

27 On this and related forms of medievalist enjoyment, see Fradenburg, "'So That We May Speak of Them.'"

28 Thus our reading of Christine de Pisan's joyful poem on Joan of Arc might be overshadowed by knowledge of Joan's burning by the English on 30 May, 1430: a knowledge completely foreign to the poem itself. See *Le Ditié de Jehanne d'Arc*, ed. Angus J. Kennedy and Kenneth Varty (Oxford: Society for the Study of Mediaeval Literatures and Language, 1977); *The Selected Writings of Christine de Pizan*, ed. and trans. Renate Blumenfeld-Kosinski and trans. Kevin Brownlee (New York: W. W. Norton, 1997), pp. 252–62. For an exemplary account of multiple temporalities structuring one premodern poem, see Paul Strohm, "Chaucer's *Troilus* as Temporal Archive," in *Theory and the Premodern Text* (Minneapolis: University of Minnesota Press, 2000), pp. 80–96. For timely meditations upon "the possibility of contact between linguistic fragments across time," see Carolyn Dinshaw, *Getting Medieval: Sexuality and Community, Pre- and Postmodern* (Durham, NC: Duke University Press, 1999), p. 54; see further Wai Chi Dimock, "Literature for the Planet," *PMLA* 116 (2001), 173–88.

29 See Rita Copeland, *Rhetoric, Hermeneutics and Translation in the Middle Ages: Academic Traditions and Vernacular Texts* (Cambridge: Cambridge University Press, 1991); *Pedagogy, Intellectuals, and Dissent in the Later Middle Ages: Lollardy and Ideas of Learning* (Cambridge: Cambridge University Press, 2001); Mary Carruthers, *The Craft of Thought: Meditation, Rhetoric, and the Making of Images* (Cambridge: Cambridge University Press, 1998); Christopher Baswell, *Virgil in Medieval England: Figuring the* Aeneid *from the Twelfth Century to Chaucer* (Cambridge: Cambridge University Press, 1995).

30 See McCormick, *Origins of the European Economy: Communications and Commerce A.D. 300–900* (Cambridge: Cambridge University Press, 2001).

31 *Chaucerian Polity. Absolutist Lineages and Associational Forms in England and Italy* (Stanford, Calif.: Stanford University Press, 1997), p. 1; Anderson, *Lineages*, p. 10.

32 See Wallace, *Chaucerian Polity*, pp. xiv–xvii.

33 Chakrabarty, meditating on contemporary India, remarks that "the peasant as citizen keeps looking like the relic of another time, although we know that he belongs squarely to the same present as the modern citizen" (*Provincializing Europe*, p. 249).

34 "Medieval Studies, Postcolonial Studies, and the Genealogies of Critique," *Speculum* 77 (2002), 1195–1227. Holsinger offers a revelatory account of "the tremendous political, psychological, and ideological diversity the [subaltern studies] group finds in the medieval epoch" (p. 1216).

35 For a succinct overview, see Peter Burke, *The French Historical Revolution: The Annales School, 1929–89* (Cambridge: Polity Press, 1990); for more exhaustive coverage, see *The Annales School: Critical Assessments*, ed. Stuart Clark, 4 vols. (London: Routledge, 1999); and see further Holsinger, pp. 1195–6.

36   A point grasped and copiously illustrated by James Simpson, *Reform and Cultural Revolution. The Oxford English Literary History,* vol. 2, *1350–1547* (Oxford: Oxford University Press, 2002). Simpson's literary history begins by focusing in exemplary fashion upon those very specific acts of destruction (the spoliation of monastic libraries; Somerset's demolition of the painted cloister at St. Paul's) accompanying proclamations of newness in religious and political life; his deployment of the term "revolution" thus assumes a concreteness generally lacking in popular usage.

37   See Randolph Starn, "Historians and *Crisis,*" *Past and Present* 52 (August 1971), 3–22; Cleanth Brooks, *The Well-Wrought Urn: Studies in the Structure of Poetry* (London: D. Dobson, 1949).

38   As Starn explains, the Greek-derived medical term *crisis* implies a feverish illness that, within a matter of days, eventuates in death or cure.

39   See *Premodern Sexualities,* ed. Louise Fradenburg and Carla Freccero, with the assistance of Kathy Lavezzo (New York: Routledge, 1996), p. xvii.

40   For a reading tending to the first alternative here, see Christopher Cannon, "Enclosure," in *The Cambridge Companion to Medieval Women's Writing,* ed. Carolyn Dinshaw and David Wallace (Cambridge: Cambridge University Press, 2003); for one tending to the second, see chapter 5 below. For a reading set within wider, multilingual contexts of female literacy, see Elizabeth Robertson, "'This Living Hand': Thirteenth-Century Female Literacy, Materialist Immanence, and the Reader of the *Ancrene Wisse,*" *Speculum* 78 (2003), 1–36.

41   Gilroy, *Black Atlantic,* p. 197.

42   See "Slavery! Slavery! Presenting a GRAND and LIFELIKE Panoramic Journey into Picturesque Southern Slavery or 'Life at Ol' Virginny's Hole (sketches from Plantation Life).' See the Peculiar Institution as never before! All cut from black paper by the able hand of Kara Elizabeth Walker, an Emancipated Negress and leader in her Cause" (1987, cut paper and adhesive on wall, 12 × 85 feet); Kara Walker, *Narratives of a Negress,* ed. Ian Berry et al. (Cambridge, Mass.: MIT Press, 2003), pp. 106–7.

43   *Racial Formation in the United States: From the 1960s to the 1990s,* 2nd edn. (New York: Routledge, 1994), p. 55. Omi and Winant move in exemplary fashion between the twin temptations of thinking of race as *essence* and as mere *illusion.* See further *The House That Race Built,* ed. Wahneema Lubiano (New York: Vintage Books, 1998).

44   See Gilroy, *Black Atlantic,* p. 197; Brent Hayes Edwards, *The Presence of Diaspora: Literature, Translation, and the Rise of Black Internationalism* (Cambridge, Mass.: Harvard University Press, 2003).

45   *The Practice of Everyday Life,* trans. Stephen Rendall (Berkeley: University of California Press, 1984), p. 117.

46   *The Fate of Place: A Philosophical History* (Berkeley: University of California Press, 1997), p. x.

47 *Getting Back into Place: Toward a Renewed Understanding of the Place-World*
(Bloomington: Indiana University Press, 1993), p. 6. "Space and time are absolute for Newton," Wai Chi Dimock argues, "not only in the sense that they are
objective and immutable but also in the sense that they are fixed numbers,"
expressible as "absolute places." In this scheme, "space provides the mental
image for time; space dictates the ontology of both" ("Nonbiological Clock,"
p. 155).

48 *Passion for Place, Book II: Between the Vital Spacing and the Creative Horizons of
Fulfilment*, ed. Tymieniecka, *Analecta Husserliana* 51 (1997), p. xii.

49 See Edward W. Said, *Out of Place: A Memoir* (London: Granta Books, 1999). *"Out
of Place,"* Said writes, "is a record of an essentially lost or forgotten world"
(p. xi).

50 Heaney, "Digging," in *Death of a Naturalist* (London: Faber, 1966), p. 13; Williams,
The Country and the City, pp. 4, 5. Williams' book is all about borders or, as
Gikandi astutely observes, "the function of peripheries in the making of cultural
hegemony" (*Maps of Englishness*, p. 6).

51 *Troilus and Criseyde*, 1.292.

52 See Aristotle, *On Rhetoric*, trans. George A. Kennedy (New York: Oxford University Press, 1991), esp. pp. 122–62.

53 *Rethinking France*, p. xxi.

CHAPTER ONE

AT CALAIS GATE

In 1749, William Hogarth painted "The Gate of Calais, or O the Roastbeef of Old England" (figure 1). We see, at left, the artist – Hogarth – practicing his art; above him we notice English coats of arms, picked out by a dramatic, diagonal shaft of light that leads us back down to the artist;[1] and at the center we see a drama played out around the massive, newly arrived, English joint of beef that supplies the painting's subtitle. All this conspires to remind us that Calais stood upon English ground, or under English rule, for better than 200 years, which is to say from 1347 to 1558, a period taking in the lives of Chaucer, Margery Kempe, Sir Thomas Wyatt, and the recent cultural memory of Shakespeare. La Manche, or the English Channel, has come to assume a mythic role in English self-imaginings since the sixteenth century; but how did the sense of national identity differ for English writers when this seaway – between the white cliffs of Dover and the *pas de Calais* – formed in effect an extension of the highway from London to Canterbury? How did this strongly fortified English presence in continental Europe (boldly represented by the Gough map, ca. 1360, figure 2) affect those living on French or Flemish territory beyond this new frontier? How does their frontier experience (the term "frontiere" is often employed by Eustace Deschamps) compare with that of those living on either side of "St. George's Channel" (that is, in Ireland and Wales)? And how does the history, culture, and literary production of the Calais colony align with greater and longer narratives of English global movement?

1 William Hogarth, *The Gate of Calais*. Cambridge University Library.

Channel Crossings

Such questions cannot be answered by a simple, precipitate leap back to the fourteenth century. We need, rather, to *work* our way back through time, since strong and complex muddled emotions accrete, century by century, round this prospect of an English Channel. The prospect continues to change. Until the summer of 1999, one in three people in Calais at any given time was English: duty-free shopping drew thousands across the Channel to hypermarkets lying just inland from the ferry terminals. The European age of duty-free goods came to an end in July, but the ferry companies, attempting to maintain their profits, have dropped the prices of their onboard merchandise to duty-free levels. The day-trip return fare from Dover to Calais now costs just six pounds; English shoppers – not permitted to shop until they have left English territorial waters – are reminded that they must actually disembark at Calais and touch French soil before traveling home again. They might wait at the Lighthouse pub (figure 3), which serves London

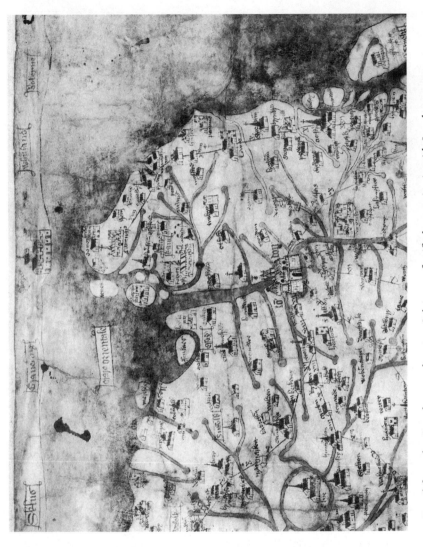

2 Detail from the Gough map, showing Calais as a fortified town (top), with London at center. Bodleian Library, Oxford.

3 Looking south from the Channel, Calais: foreground, The Lighthouse Pub; background, the often-restored Tour du Guet (known by the English occupiers as "The Watch Tower"). Photograph by David Wallace.

Pride; on your way in you can just see the tower from which *Calaisiens* learned of Edward III's terms and conditions.

The Channel crossing today, then, is typically an unheroic, short-lived expedition in search of cheap tobacco and booze. And yet, as the white cliffs recede, many English voyagers are clearly or obscurely moved. Several years ago the most demonstrative travelers were teenage girls, hanging over the rails with their arms wide open, proclaiming "I'm the king of the world!" But there were also, as ever, knots of football fans in distinctive liveries muttering – as we approached the French coast – "fucking French peasants." Such aggression, traditionally acted out by English soccer thugs going continental, taps deep historical roots. The Channel Tunnel, which emerges into sunlight several miles from Calais, clearly promises to change all this. But it was interesting to note, as the giant Japanese tunnelling machine broke through the last thin crust of French soil on April 27, 1989, that here too minds ran to earlier phases of cross-Channel history: to the Field of the Cloth of Gold, when Henry VIII met the French King Francis I between Ardres and Guines. This famous meeting was commemorated by giant, 20–foot polystyrene figures of the monarchs ranged either side of the tunnel.[2] Such Styrofoam history is hardly propitious: Francis and Henry, who met only twice, thoroughly disliked and distrusted one another. Within weeks, Henry was plotting an alliance with the Holy Roman Emperor, Charles V of Spain. Charles actually came to visit Henry in London in 1522; Spanish and English monarchs then traveled to Winchester, where they contemplated Henry VIII as King Arthur (freshly painted on the famous Round Table).

The tendency to exaggerate and racialize the divide between England and the continental landmass was brought to a peak of acuteness by French as well as English writers in the nineteenth century. Hippolyte Taine, in opening his influential *History of English Literature*, imagines himself making the crossing as an early Germanic invader: *pays rude et brumeux*, he says: "a rude and foggy land, like their own, except in the depth of its sea and the safety of its coasts, which one day will call up real fleets and mighty vessels; green England – the word rises to the lips and expresses all."[3] "What impression," he muses, "must such a land have made on the men of the South, the Romans of Caesar!" (I, p. 25). And how, later, might the Saxons have adapted to this island?

> Il leur fallait vivre en chasseurs et en porchers, devenir, comme auparavant, athlétiques, féroces et sombres. Mettez la civilisation en moins sur ce sol. Il ne restera aux habitants que la guerre, la chasse, la mangeaille et l'ivrognerie. L'amour riant, les doux songes poétiques, les arts, la fine et agile pensée sont pour les heureuses plages de la Méditerranée. Ici le barbare, mal clos dans sa chaumière fangeuse, qui entend la pluie ruisseler pendant des journées entières sur les feuilles des chênes, quelles rêveries peut-il avoir quand il contemple ses boues et son ciel terni? (I, p. 6)

> They must have lived as hunters and swineherds; grown, as before, brawny, fierce, gloomy. Take civilization from this soil, and there will remain to the inhabitants only war, the chase, gluttony, drunkenness. Smiling love, sweet poetic dreams, art, refined and nimble thought, are for the happy shores of the Mediterranean. Here the barbarian, ill housed in his mud-hovel, who hears the rain rustling whole days in the oak leaves – what dreams can he have, gazing upon his mud pools and his somber sky? (I, pp. 25–6)

Anglo-Saxonism, Taine suggests, cannot be leavened into Englishness without the sunny, civilizing powers of Gallicism.[4] Constructions of the north and west – Scythia, Anglia, Hibernia – as gloomy and unknowable (from the normative perspective of "middle earth," Mediterranean culture) extend back beyond Ovid in exile.[5] Perverse acknowledgment of such notions might be read in the studied, self-conscious boorishness adopted by elements of the English proletariat in crossing to Calais; they might be read, too, in the pragmatic, anti-theoretical, "I refute it thus" attitude maintained by elements of the English professoriate against the sophistications and abstractions of French theory. Once again (as this quotation suggests),[6] the eighteenth century demands attention as a crucially determinative period for the formation of such attitudes. Consider this famous account of a Channel crossing, published in 1768:

> – They order, said I, this matter better in France –
> – You have been in France? said my gentleman, turning quick upon me with the most civil triumph in the world. –
> Strange! quoth I, debating the matter with myself, That one and twenty miles sailing, for 'tis absolutely no further from Dover to Calais, should give a man these rights – I'll look into them: so giving up the argument – I went straight to my lodgings, put up half a dozen shirts and a black pair of silk breeches – "the coat I have on, said I, looking at the sleeve, will do" – took a place in the Dover stage; and the packet sailing at nine the next morning – by three I had got sat down to my dinner upon a fricassee'd chicken . . . incontestably in France.[7]

This passage, which opens *A Sentimental Journey*, Laurence Sterne's last novel, is both conventional and outrageous. Mr. Yorick, the narrator, begins by assuming the superiority of French manners. Challenged to substantiate this conventional, unexamined claim, he pragmatically elects to go to France. It is the sheer unthinking rapidity of his passage to Calais that is, by the standard of post-1558 Channel-crossing narratives, so outrageous: the notion that one can move from lodgings in London to eating fried chicken in Calais on a whim and with no regard to the crossing of borders. Cultural otherness soon asserts itself with the arrival of a figure chosen, it seems, to embody the very essence of un-Englishness: a Franciscan mendicant monk, begging for his convent. For this ingenuous English traveler, we deduce, there may be trouble ahead.

In 1829, a writer of negligible talent called James Albany published a slim volume entitled *The Englishman's Guide to Calais*.[8] Albany was evidently a great admirer of Sterne. He absorbs whole pages of *A Sentimental Journey* into his narrative and, once landed in Calais, endeavors to track Sterne down: at Dessin's Hotel he finds a room with "STERNE'S CHAMBER" painted on the door and an engraved portrait of his hero over the fireplace (pp. 22–3). But his crossing to Calais could hardly be more different. Progress is premeditated and slow rather than heedlessly rapid. Three pages of "directions for travellers" tell us of the various applications and visas that must be obtained at London, Calais, and Paris before attempting further explorations; the short water-crossing itself seems thrillingly momentous:

> I had never touched foreign ground, and gazed on the opposite and then distinctly visible coast of France with the feelings one may suppose to be excited in the breast of a Mahometan pilgrim at the first glimpse of Mecca. (p. 15)

Albany is here standing on the beach at Sandgate, gazing out over what (as Sterne has reminded us) is little more than a 20-mile stretch of water. Yet his anticipated crossing seems to threaten, promise, or imply a change of religion, an exotic flight from the familiar self. Such promise heightens when his ship – called, it seems inevitably, the *Crusader* – comes in view of Calais:

> For some time previously my eyes were fixed on the town glittering in the Sun and on the French hills in its vicinity, which are very sterile and ugly. Nevertheless, they were viewed by me with more interest than would have been created by the finest English scenery. Such is the effect of novelty, under whose magic influence we may be induced to prefer Picardy to Kent or Surrey. (p. 16)

Such alternating play between seduction and repulsion – a sense of sterility and ugliness, and a suspicion of magic – continues throughout Albany's narrative. This makes it consonant, of course, with many English colonial narratives of this period written much further east of Sandgate beach. Like colonizing Englishmen everywhere, he finds familiar comforts abroad: an English newspaper called the *Pas de Calais*, published twice weekly and distributed to all parts of France; a series of English *cabarets*, such as the "Brittania [sic] Tavern and Coffee House," and "a paltry cabaret y'clept *Robin Hood and Little John*" (p. 36). At the same time, he is titillated and amused by sights turned exotic by his own imaginings, such as what he calls "shrimp girls": walking around the ramparts, he glimpses "between twenty and thirty shrimp girls, with naked feet, who came scampering towards us with mirthful importunity" (pp. 61–2).[9] And in Catholic churches he notes "females of the poorer classes" praying to images:

> These images in question are rudely carved in wood, and painted in a tawdry manner, resembling those placed at the head of ships. Upon that of the Virgin Mary, I noticed pieces of ribbon, chaplets of flowers, &c. (p. 46)

Albany frequents Calais churches and Calais theaters alternatively, almost interchangeably, in his search for spectacle and entertainment. In viewing a statue of the Virgin he shows no sense or knowledge of an English past continuous with this culture: one that was fond of tying ribbons and flowers to devotional objects, and of fitting little gold shoes or shawls to the statues of saints.[10] And yet, of course, the very power which draws him to these continental objects might speak to, issue from, an encrypted English past (however dimly apprehended). His conscious frame of reference is unmistakably that of the English present, which sees the figureheads of English ships nosing into all corners of the globe to extend networks of commerce and – after Trafalgar – naval dominance. Even his view and taste of foodstuffs is colored by an intense (albeit humorous) anti-Catholic, anti-Gallic vein of nationalist sentiment. On a *jour maigre*, he notes, "the repast was not deficient in heretical viands" (p. 28). Some of the offerings at table – such as the spinach – are delicious, but others are outrageously awful, especially the mustard: "the mustard," he notes, is "detestable, being strongly impregnated with garlic" (p. 28). What we have here, of course, amounts to more than adulterated condiments: it suggests cultural cross-contamination, miscegenation of the kind that Hippolyte Taine sees as integral to the evolution of the English character. For in England, garlic was (and in certain quarters still is) associated with smelly-breathed Catholic Europe; and mustard is the condiment chosen to dress "the roast beef of Old England," the heroic viand that dominates the front and center of Hogarth's *Gate of Calais*.

The Gate of Calais

Albany's anti-Gallicism is most immediately rooted in memories of the Revolutionary Terror and the Napoleonic wars: he regrets that the English had not possessed Calais in 1793 (hence offering a launch-site for counter-revolution); he notes with satisfaction, on Calais pier, a foot-shaped bronze plate commemorating the first footfall of the returning monarch, Louis XVIII (pp. i–ii, 21). Hogarth's anti-French animus is immediately fuelled by memories of the Jacobite Rebellion of 1745 and the invasion of England from Scotland, which got as far south as Derby. The destitute Highlander at the bottom right of *The Gate of Calais*, fled from the failed rebellion and spared the vengeance of Culloden, balances out the three ecstatic women or nutty nuns at left who, it seems, have discovered a new Veronica (Christ's facial image) on the flank of a fish. Through the gateway we glimpse the poor of Calais, on their knees, fed by a Catholic eucharist; above them the dove of

the Holy Spirit flies (but only as painted on a pub sign). Partially obscuring
the view into the city, the slavering corded friar lays one hand on his belly
and his other on (or into, by way of *assay*) the English beef; the thin broth
intended for the feeding of the Calisian poor, termed by Hogarth "the Kettle
of soup meager," is carried off to the right.[11] And observing all this, framed
by musket and pike, is Hogarth himself: the heroic English artist/artisan,
recording the follies and hypocrisies of this foreign, once-English world for
native English consumption.

The hand clapped upon Hogarth's shoulder in *The Gate of Calais* suggests
that our artist-hero is about to be arrested; it also authorizes this image as a
celebrated, if much elaborated, personal and historical event. In October
1747, the English Channel fleet won a decisive victory against the French off
Cape Finisterre; the War of the Austrian Succession – eight years of continental and colonial conflict that killed half a million people to no conclusive
end – was wound down the following year. In the summer of 1748, Hogarth
took advantage of the reopening of France to English travelers. At the time
of his traveling, England and France quite literally followed different models
of time: France, having switched to the Gregorian calendar in 1582, was
now 11 days ahead. England did not catch up until 1752, when the day after
September 2 became September 14.[12]

By all accounts, Hogarth proved recklessly free and "clamorously rude"[13]
in his criticism of all things French. His companions managed to get him
back to the Channel, but at Calais he took inordinate pleasure in the fact
that the gate was, "it seem[s] built by the English, when the place was in our
possession."[14] Having whipped out his sketch book, he settled to record the
scene, but even as he sketched he was nabbed from behind and carted off to
face charges as an English spy. Nearly 60 years earlier, in 1690, the playwright and architect Sir John Vanbrugh had been arrested at Calais in similar circumstances for (according to one report) studying the fortifications.[15]
Vanbrugh spent some 18 months in French prisons, including a spell in the
Bastille in Paris. Hogarth was also rumored to have been "clapt into the
Bastille": but he was, in fact, merely put under house or hotel arrest before
being bundled onto the next packet-boat bound for England. Nonetheless,
the profile of Hogarth in tricorn hat from the *Gate of Calais* soon became –
along with the famous portrait of the artist with his pug dog – a favorite
personal emblem; the "Hogarth's head" was subsequently adopted as a
trade sign by printsellers in Cheapside and Fleet Street and by other trades-
men (such as tailors) elsewhere.[16] Released as a print in 1749, *At Calais Gate*
proved to be hugely successful.[17] Tobias Smollett's *Peregrine Pickle* (1751)
features an English painter called Pallet who does time in the Bastille, a "tall,

long-legged, meagre" cook encountered on the road from Calais to Boulogne (clearly wandered from his beef-carrying duties in Hogarth's print), and some sad-eyed English Jacobins. Exiled for "their adherence to an unfortunate and ruined cause," these melancholy men go down to the seaside every day "to indulge their longing eyes with a prospect of the white cliffs of Albion, which they must never more approach."[18]

The immense success of Hogarth's *Calais Gate* among English printmakers, museum directors, and a commercially minded public might be attributed to its suggestive theme of buying British, in art as in beef: a sentiment that resonates down the decades to Mrs. Thatcher and mad cow disease.[19] The superiority of English product is attested by the singing Frenchman in the ballad or "Cantata" that often accompanied Hogarth's print (very likely published, Nichols tells his eighteenth-century audience, "under the sanction of our artist"):

> Ah, sacre Dieu! Vat do I see yonder,
> Dat looks so tempting, red and white?
> Begar I see it is de *Roast Beef* from *Londre,*
> O grant to me one letel bite.
>
> *(p. 292)*

Following further famished apostrophes to the "Sweet Beef" by a Hibernian and others ("How sweet it would gang down"), a brief recitative, meditating on England as a place where "chains, and racks, and tortures are not known," leads to the allegory of the *Ox* and the *Frog.* Elucidation soon follows:

> Then, *Britons,* be valiant; the moral is clear:
> The *Ox* is *Old England,* the *Frog* is *Monsieur,*
> Whose puffs and bravadoes we need never fear.
> *Oh, the Roast Beef,* &c.
>
> *(p. 295)*

Hogarth's print and its companion "Cantata" mix much humor and some nastiness with immense complacency. This inconsequential skirmish at the gateway to the continent is to be enjoyed as a garnish to knowledge of continuing English triumphs, east and west (India and North America). It confirms, above all, the wisdom and utility of English insularism; for, as Hogarth remarked (in his characteristically agrammatical way):

> The first time anyone goes from hence to France by way of Calais he cannot avoid being struck with the Extreem different face things appear with at so

little distance as from Dover a farcical pomp of war, parade of riligion, and
Bustle with little with very little bussiness in short poverty slavery and Insol-
ence (with an affectation of politeness) give you even here the first specimen
of the whole country . . .[20] (p. 463)

Hogarth's casual mention of "slavery" here – in tacit opposition to English
"liberty": this at the apogee of English global slave-trading – finds plentiful
echoes in English public discourse in this period.[21] And the more particular
differences noted here by Hogarth recall those registered by eighteenth-
century Englishmen traveling far beyond the Channel: colorful but inferior
military traditions; egregious religious practices; insufficient grasp of sound
business principles. Hogarth's view of Calais, of course, busily fabricates
rather than passively discovers cultural difference, something that the painting, in portraying the artist at work within it, seems tacitly to acknowledge.
Viewed diachronically, the painting reads as a defiant generic anti-type held
up against the dominant prior discourse that had long surrounded Calais
Gate: that of historical romance. Froissart, whose assiduously translated and
oft-printed history was held in the highest regard in England until the mid-
nineteenth century,[22] unfolds a life-and-death liminal drama before Calais
Gate, featuring an irate king, a pregnant queen, six courageous burghers,
and the fate of a town; Hogarth gives us one scene, featuring stereotypical
comic characters and an outsized joint of meat, which must end with the
expulsion of himself, the English painter. The whole painting works to
endorse the logic of this expulsion, for there is nothing in it to suggest a
genuine desire to make contact with, to comprehend, an English past. Such
contact would compel acknowledgment of common ground between the
English past and the French present of the painting, something that Hogarth,
in this giant blown raspberry of a painting, is loath to admit. His canvas
works to widen, rather than to bridge, the gap between England and continental Europe. Viewed within the context of eighteenth-century national
rivalries, the discovery of English arms upon French ground seems less like
a desire to revive the past than a taunting reference to current global conditions: we, the English, have always already been there, done that, claimed
this as our own.

And yet, however much Hogarth revises or exaggerates differences and
distances from the continental past in this painting, his original moment
of inspiration (the painting's chief subject, as all else flows from it) works
in the opposite direction, as the past floods in to dominate the present.
The painting's *punctum* is undoubtedly the fourteenth-century coat of arms,
seen beaming down to the artist along a shaft of light; all other details (the

ecstatic nuns, the fat friar) might be read as gestures of appeasement, belatedly resisting this moment of collapsed time. Ironically, then, Hogarth both dissuades and persuades us to a reading of Froissart, the most powerful originator of Calais as a site of mythic, national struggle. Froissart's account greatly appealed to English audiences during later, imperially inclined centuries; the placing of Rodin's famed burghers of Calais (surrendering to Edward III) under the shadow of Big Ben, just outside the Houses of Parliament, Westminster, in 1915 caps Froissart's extraordinary run as a classic of English classroom history.[23] Most romancers and historiographers before Froissart tell of Britain's colonization by diasporic Romans and Trojans;[24] Froissart, in telling of outward English expansion, offers later centuries a new narrative (in what seems a Renaissance-like strategy) of beginning and forgetting.

Repeopling Calais

Froissart himself was neither French nor English: he was from Hainault, an independent county (now part of northeast France) with a distinctively internationalist culture.[25] Born ca. 1337, Froissart crossed the Channel in 1361 to serve Philippa of Hainault, Queen of England and wife to Edward III, as *clerc de chambre*. In 1365 he toured lowland and highland Scotland in the train of King David II; he also visited Severnside and the Welsh Marches with Edward Despenser. He was part of the English party that descended on Milan for the marriage of Lionel, Duke of Clarence, to Violante Visconti. On hearing of the death of Philippa while he was at Brussels, he elected to remain in the Netherlands. Here he first served Robert of Namur, a member of the family of the Count of Flanders who had married a sister of Queen Philippa. Robert, pro-English, commanded a ship in King Edward's fleet at the battle of Winchelsea; it was for Robert that Froissart began writing his *Chronicles* (in or shortly after 1369). Froissart's later patrons were both pro-French: Wenceslaus of Bohemia, son of the blind King John who fell at Crécy, and Guy de Châtillon, Count of Blois, who had extensive holdings in the Netherlands. Froissart's later journeying included a visit in 1388 to Foix and Béarn, a small principality on the north side of the Pyrenees. On Christmas Day of that year he sat down to dinner with his famously blond-haired, hunting-obsessed host, Gaston Phoebus (author of *Le Livre de la chasse*), with two Urbanist and two Clementist bishops, and with Sir William Willougby (sent from John of Gaunt, then reportedly at "Lerbone," Lisbon).[26] In 1395 he made a second visit to England, where – on the very day that he presented

Richard II with a copy of his "book" – he heard and recorded an amazing
tale of a seven-year captivity in Ireland from one Henry Crystède.[27]

Froissart's extensive, lifelong movements across Europe suggest remarkable continuities of culture. And his career profile – offering instructive points
of comparison with those of Chaucer and Boccaccio – suggests that clerkly
or writerly skills could be turned to chivalry, religion, and business (or any
combination of the above). Froissart's family were business people and money-
lenders: his chronicle-writing characteristically blends feeling for chivalry
with a sense of competent accounting. Good accounting, material and spiritual, was as much appreciated in clerics as in courtly chroniclers: having
finished Book I of his *Chroniques*, Froissart took holy orders and became
parish priest of Estinnes-au-Mont in Brabant. As chivalric historian – a vocation he never renounced – Froissart was sought out by courtiers (like Henry
Crystède, unknown to history outside Froissart) wishing to preserve their
deeds for posterity. But as a necessary complement to eyewitness testimony,
Froissart was obliged to rework prior accounts (particularly those by the
worldly canon of Liège, Jean le Bel).[28] This process, necessarily most pronounced in Book I, again invites comparison with Chaucer and Boccaccio,
particularly their accounts of historical or epical romance. It also proved
inviting to later authors, such as John Bourchier, Lord Berners, whose
Englishing of the *Chroniques* was very promptly published by Richard Pynson,
"printer to the kinges moost noble grace" (volume I in 1523; volume II in
1525).[29] Berners also translated the romance *Huon de Bordeuxe* from the French
(thereby introducing Oberon, king of the fairies, to English literature). He
also Englished *Petit Artus de Bretayne*, although professing himself unnerved
by its "many unpossybylytees."[30] But Froissart too was a romancer: his verse
Méliador (containing the lyrics of his patron Wenceslaus) wanders widely
over Scottish, English, Irish, and Breton territories (with an extended visit to
the Isle of Man).[31] The remarkable longevity of romance as a defining literary genre[32] provides just one more reason for viewing the period of English
presence in Calais, 1347–1558, as a coherent historiographical phase. There
was, of course, continuity of religion, too: when Pynson first published
Berners's Froissart, Henry VIII was in good papal odor as *defensor pacis*. And,
in this instance, there was continuity of place: Lord Berners, present at the
Field of the Cloth of Gold, was appointed deputy of Calais in December
1520; he died at Calais in March 1533.[33]

The account of the siege and capitulation of Calais in Froissart and Berners
is figured chiefly as a struggle between two distinct forms of polity: the will
of a town, collectively represented through its six burghers, and the will of
a prince.[34] The episode possesses a mythic charge in coinciding with the

period of Edward's foundation of the Order of the Garter.[35] Edward is incensed because the city has held out against him for almost a full year (allowing the Scots to invade England from the north). Sir Walter de Manny, English military commander at Calais, reasons with the king, but the king is absolute, requiring the absolute surrender of the town to his will and pleasure. Manny relays the bad news to the Governor of Calais, messires Jehans de Viane (Sir John de Vienne), who has requested that his starving people be allowed to depart in safety. "Saciés que," Manny declares (sounding like a public proclamation):

> ce n'est mies se entente que vous en peuissiés aler ensi que vous avés ci dit; ains est sa volonté que vous vos metés tous en se pure volenté, ou pour rançonner chiaus qu'il li plaira, ou pour faire morir. (p. 639)

> Surely knowe for trouth it is nat his mynde that ye nor they within the towne shulde departe so, for it is his wyll that ye all shulde put your selfes into his pure wyll, to ransome all such as pleaseth hym and to putte to dethe suche as he lyste. (I, p. 329)

Manny shuttles back to the king, who restates his intention of enforcing an absolute surrender "to his pleasure" (I, p. 329; p. 641 in French). Finally, however, Edward makes his famous proposal: that the six most prominent *Calaisiens* should leave the town bareheaded and barefoot, with halters around their necks and the keys of town and castle in their hands. A bell summons the people of Calais, men and women, to the market square; the assembly is asked for its collective opinion. At this point the richest citizen of the town, Eustache de Saint-Pierre, stands up and speaks:

> "Signeur, grans pités et grans meschiés seroit de lassier morir un tel peuple qui ci a, par famine ou autrement, quant on y poet trouver aucun moiien. Et si seroit grant aumosne et grant grasce à Nostre Signeur qui de tel meschief les poroit garder. Je, endroit de moy, ay si grant esperance d'avoir grasce et pardon envers Nostre Signeur, se je muir pour ce peuple sauver, que je voeil estre li premiers." (p. 642)

> "Sirs, great and small, great myschiefe it shulde be to suffre to dye suche people as be in this towne, other by famyn or otherwyse, whan there is a meane to save theym: I thynke he or they shulde have great merytte of our Lorde God that myght kepe theym fro suche myschiefe: as for my parte, I have so good truste in oure Lorde God, that if I dye in the quarell to save the residewe, that God wolde pardone me; wherefore, to save them, I wyll be the first to putte my lyfe in jeopardy." (I, p. 330)

Eustache here shapes a powerfully symbolic role for himself as savior, almost redeemer ("ce peuple sauver") of his people; five other burgesses soon elect to join "my gossyppe Ewstace" (I, p. 330). Accompanied by the cries and lamentations of men, women, and children, the six pass through the gate of Calais and kneel before the English king:

> "Gentilz sires et gentilz rois, ves nous chi six, qui avons esté d'ancisserie bourgois de Calais et gran marceans. Si vous aportons les clés de le ville et dou chastiel de Calais, et les vous rendons à vostre plaisir, et nous mettons en tel point que vous nous veés, en vostre pure volenté, pour sauver le demorant dou peuple de Calais." (pp. 644–5)

> "Gentyll kyng, beholde here we sixe, who were burgesses of Calays and great marchantes: we have brought to you the kayes of the towne and of the castell and we submyt our selfe clerely into your wyll and pleasure, to save the resydue of the people of Calays." (I, p. 331)

The French text, which had earlier told of the English king fiercely glaring at and intensely hating the *Calaisiens* – "car moult haoit les habitans de Calais" (p. 644) – goes on to tell of the momentary, rage-induced paralysis effected in the king by this last speech:

> Li rois regarda sus yaus très ireusement, car il avoit le coer si dur et si espris de grant courous que il ne peut parler; et quant il parla, il commanda que on leur compast les tiestes tantost. (p. 645)

> The king glared at them most fiercely, for his heart was so hard and swollen with anger that he could not speak; and when he spoke, he ordered that their heads should immediately be struck off.

Princely incapacitation through momentary rage – familiar as a nightmarishly recurrent moment in Chaucer – finds no place in the Englishing of Berners (servant to the princely and irascible Henry VIII). But Berners rejoins Froissart (albeit preferring hanging to beheading) for the famous scene of queenly mediation. This begins with Edward's rejecting the last appeal for the burghers by his tireless military commander, Sir Walter de Manny:

> A ce point se grigna [ground his teeth] li rois et dist: "Messire Gautier, souffrés vous, il ne sera aultrement, mès on fece venir le cope teste. Chil de Calais ont fait morir tant de mes hommes, que il convient chiaus morir ossi."
> Adonc fist la noble royne d'Engleterre grant humilité, qui estoit durement enchainte, et ploroit si tenrement de pité que on ne le pooit soustenir. Elle se

jetta en jenoulz par devant le roy son signeur et dist ensi: "Ha! gentilz sires, puis que je apassai le mer par deçà en grant peril, si com vous savés, je ne vous ay riens rouvet ne don demandet. Or vous pri jou humlement et requier en propre don que, pour le fil sainte Marie et pour l'amour de mi, vous voelliés avoir de ces six hommes merci."

Li rois attendi un petit de parler et regarda la bonne dame sa femme, qui moult estoit enchainte et ploroit devant lui en jenoulz moult tenrement. Se li amolia li coers, car envis l'euist couroucie ens ou point là où elle estoit; si dist: "Ha! dame, je amaisse mieulz que vous fuissiés d'autre part que ci. Vous me priiés si acertes que je ne le vous ose escondire; et comment que je le face envis, tenés, je les vous donne: si en faites vostre plaisir." La bonne dame dist: "Monsigneur, très grans merci."

Lors se leva la royne et fist lever les six bourgois, et leur fist oster les chevestres d'entours les colz, et les amena avoecques lui en sa cambre, et les fist revestir et donner à disner tout aise; et puis donna à çascun six nobles, et les fist conduire hors de l'ost à sauveté. (pp. 645–6)

Than the kyng wryed away fro hym, and commaunded to sende for the hangman, and sayd, They of Calys had caused many of my men to be slayne, wherfore these shal dye in likewyse. Than the quene beynge great with chylde, kneled downe and sore wepyng, sayd, A gentyll sir, syth I passed the see in great parell, I have desyred nothyng of you; therfore nowe I humbly requyre you, in the honour of the Son of the Virgyn Mary and for the love of me that ye woll take mercy of these six burgesses. The kynge behelde the quene and stode styll in a study a space, and than sayd, A dame, I wold ye had ben as nowe in some other place, ye make suche request to me that I can nat deny you: wherfore I gyve them to you, to do your pleasure with theym. Than the quene caused them to be brought into her chambre, and made the halters to be taken fro their neckes, and caused them to be new clothed, and gave them their dyner at their leser; and than she gave ech of them six nobles and made them to be brought out of thoost in savegard and set at their lyberte. (I, pp. 331–2)

Here, as so often, Berners prunes out Froissart's more affect-laden details: his king does not experience a softening of the heart in contemplating his wife's pregnant condition ("ou point là où elle estoit"). But it is remarkable how neatly both writers shape the narration of this liminal episode to the generic expectations of romance. We have the irate monarch, exercising his will in haste but with absolute force; the weeping, mediating queen asking – by the rules of courtliness, tacitly understood – for her *don*, or favor; the king, momentarily caught in that suspensive "study" so familiar from Chaucer; the surrender of kingly will to queenly pleasure; the gracious reception of the captives. Froissart and Berners were both, we have noted, authors of romance; the scene has the comforting finality of conventional romance closure. And yet when the next scene opens, the king soon voices a new ambition, a new *diktat*: all men, women, and children must leave Calais,

> "car je voeil la ville repeupler de purs Englès." (p. 646)

> "for I wolde repeople agayne the towne with pure Englysshmen." (I, p. 332)

This menacing, enigmatic (perhaps incomprehensible) statement troubles the lingering spell of romance with suggestions that our enjoyment of narrative closure was premature. Such a jolt to our reading pleasure compares remarkably with that experienced toward the end of Chaucer's *Melibee*: the moment when Prudence – another dedicated wifely protector and mediatrix – enquires of her spouse what is to become of those enemies that he had (so it seemed) delivered into her hands:

> "Certes," quod he, "I thynke and purpose me fully/to desherite hem of al that evere they han and for to putte hem in exil for evere." (7.1834–5)

The grimness of Edward's resolution in Froissart suggests that his hatred of "chil de Calais" has never abated, and that he has never lost sight of the greater *agon* in which he and they are embroiled. Eustache de Saint-Pierre, we have noted, declared himself unwilling to see "un tel peuple" perish; he is willing to sacrifice himself "pour ce peuple sauver" (p. 642). The implicit hope or assumption here is that Calais will survive *as* its people, whatever becomes of the six burghers. But Edward, having honored or weathered the protocols of queenly mediation, delivers a devastating counter that turns substantive to verb: the burghers aim to save the *peuple*, but the monarch (by sheer force of will) will *repeupler* the town. Such repeopling, staged within the ancient urban fabric, means that those locked out in exile will lose their collective identity as *Calaisiens*. Rather than being held to ransom, then, or subjected to foreign rule, the town of Calais is straightforwardly colonized. The model of proposed settlement differs markedly from that of classical narrative such as the *Aeneid*, from the Norman Conquest of 1066, or from the later colonialisms of Portugal and Spain. All these involve miscegenation (invading males marrying native women) and cultural admixture. Edward, however, proposes wholesale evacuation of native space and the importation of uncontaminated Englishness ("purs Englès"): an ideological modeling of non-interactive colonizing that would inspire Henry V at Harfleur and prove prescient of English activity further afield in centuries to come.[36]

Edward's putative repeopling of Calais "with pure Englysshmen" is enigmatic and self-contradictory *and thus* (postcolonial theory might suggest) characteristic of the modalities of colonizing discourse. What can "purs Englès" hope, expect, or pretend to mean? Can the notion of purity refer to those born on English soil? Hardly: the sons of Edward III (and the sons of his sons) were often born on campaign, at places like Antwerp, Ghent, and Bordeaux; his queen, "qui moult estoit enchainte," is about to give birth again.[37] Might then "purs Englès" refer to those of pure, blue, or royal English blood? This too is problematic: the English queen, like so many before or since, is of French-speaking stock. Can Edward be invoking an inchoate, evanescent sense of English nationhood? Perhaps. But it is worth noting that the only usage of the term *nation* in this narrative – and the only convincing exemplification of it – is applied not to England or France, but to Calais itself: "ceuls de la nation de Calais," Edward declares (in the Rome manuscript), "on fera morir, car bien il l'ont deservi."[38] The term *nation* here evokes close bonds of kinship, family, and personal ties rather than more abstract notions of political entity; its values are those of medieval *trouthe*, which are quite different from the more universalizing implications of modern *truth*.[39] The point is brilliantly made by the chronicling of the *Brut*, which tells how the besieged *Calaisiens*, "for defaute of vitailles and & of refresshyng . . . eten hors, houndes, cattes & mys, *for to kepe her trouthe* as long as they myghte" (emphasis added).[40] Edward, having conquered the town, co-opts such language by proclaiming his Calais cathection a matter of flesh and blood: Calais, he declares, is "the thynge in this worlde that I love best, next my wyfe and chyldren" (I, p. 336).[41] Such passion seems less than all-consuming, however. Edward, having returned to Westminster, is here upbraiding the military commander to whom he has entrusted his much-loved city. This man, a soldier of fortune called Aymeris de Pavie, has been caught attempting to sell Calais to the French; French overtures were encouraged by the fact that "this Aymeris was a Lombard, and Lombards are by nature covetous."[42]

Having returned to London, Froissart and Berners tell us, Edward had indeed initiated his plan "repeupler le ville de Calais" (the phrase is repeated, p. 649): 36 prosperous English burghers are sent out with their wives and children, plus more than 400 others of lesser "estat" (p. 649). Numbers increased daily, we are told, "for the kynge graunted there suche lyberties and franchysses, that men were gladde to go and dwelle there" (I, p. 333; p. 649). At this moment of modular shift from romance to urban chronicle in Froissart and Berners, it is worth asking how their accounts square with the greater historical record. Within days of entering Calais, it seems, Edward had proclamations read in the north and east of England, promising liberties and commercial privileges to would-be Calais residents. About 190 such tenures were registered in the Patent Rolls of 1347, followed by analogous concessions in the French Rolls; other agreements, oral rather than written, may be inferred. Weak and unproductive people, "bouches inutiles," had been expelled from Calais by the *Calaisiens* themselves in the course of the siege. A document in the French Roll ordains the expulsion of all remaining *Calaisiens*, excepting those expressly granted royal permission to stay. All "Calais clerks and chaplains" were driven out during the period of repopulation; in 1351, a new Augustinian house was established, to be inhabited exclusively by English friars. All chronicles agree that most citizens were forced to leave; legal traces of refugee *Calaisien* communities were left at St. Omer (a favored destination) and at towns as far afield as Carcassonne.[43]

The English victory at Poitiers in 1356 (featuring the capture of the French King John) and the treaties of Brétigny and Calais in 1360 effectively transformed the English presence in those parts from de facto occupation to consolidated juridical suzerainty; English holdings now included the territory of Marck and three-quarters of the county of Guines. But excessive attention paid to the military and chivalric record – Froissart is particularly difficult to resist – often obscures (as R. R. Davies suggests) the true complexity of colonizing processes.[44] Indeed, much that Davies and his colleagues have to say about English infiltration of Scotland, Ireland. and Wales bears fruitful comparison with the experience of Calais and its marches. Calais might now be added to the list of "border communities" studied as constituent parts of the British Isles; the kinds of literature favored and produced there might also be read as "history on the edge," joining and refining long-established traditions of British "border writing."[45]

The entrepreneurial and commercial skills of foreign settlers (as Gerald of Wales recognized) could prove more difficult to resist than straightforward military domination, especially if such newcomers helped revitalize the local economy. On the other hand, a medieval state (such as England) might become so engrossed in the business of holding together constitutive colonies, palatinates, principalities, and dominions that it finds itself overextended and thus prone to internal collapse.[46]

Calais, we should note, appeared in the twelfth century only as a little fishing village in the territory of Marck.[47] By the early thirteenth century the town had evolved away from Marck; in 1330 it is designated subject to the duke of Burgundy, count of Artois. Guillaume de Machaut, who was (despite his age) pressed into military service to defend the sacred and royalist city of Reims against English attack in the winter of 1359–60, contemptuously refuses to name this two-bit village full of foreigners in his *Fonteinne amoureuse*.[48] Following the 1360 treaty of Brétigny, Jean, duc de Berry (third son of King Jean II of France and Machaut's patron) has been forced to accept exile in England in order to release his captive father; as the poem winds down, poet and patron surrogates approach the "ville petiote" without enthusiasm:

> En cest estat nous chevauchames
> Tant que sus la mer nous trouvames
> En une ville petiote,
> De barat pleinne et de riote.
> Or la nommez se vous volez,
> Car il y a moult d'avolez.
>
> *(ll. 2807–12)*

> In this way we rode along
> Until we found ourselves near the sea
> In a very small village,
> A place full of uproar and license.
> Now you name the town if you like,
> For the town is full of strangers.

In 1363, however, the Wool Staple was transferred to Calais: a move that enhanced its reputation for "riote" in France while decisively transforming its fortunes and international significance. Calais became what Bruges and Anvers once had been: the principal seat of English merchants in continental Europe. And it thereby attracted a great deal of capital to itself. The large military garrison needed to be fed and provided for: most provisions were imported from England, and the cost of maintaining the garrison was always high. In 1371–2, a particularly quiet period, no fewer than 1,112 regular men of arms were in English service "dans l'enclave calaisienne."[49] Eventually a mint was established in the town – still remembered in John Skelton's time a hundred years later – which led to complex, mutually dependent arrangements between mercantile entrepreneurs, soldiery, townspeople, town authorities, and customs officials.[50]

It is naive to suppose, then, that Calais survived after 1347 in a kind of Babylonian exile, severed from its motherland, awaiting the return of its true French king (although Deschamps – as we shall see – worked hard to disseminate such a view).[51] *Calaisien* identification with the kingdom of France was not, of course, as intense in the Middle Ages as later mythologization would have us believe; and besides, after Poitiers the French king spent

4 Auguste Rodin, *The Burghers of Calais* outside the Flemish-style Town Hall, Calais. Photograph by David Wallace.

much of his time as a prisoner in England. Symbolic reclamation of Calais is eloquently expressed by the placement of Rodin's magnificent sculptural group of six burghers, *Les Bourgeois de Calais*, immediately outside the Town Hall (figure 4). General De Gaulle, famously resistant to further English invasions of French-dominated space (the "Common Market"), actually married a local *Calaisien* girl at "l'église Notre-Dame" (figure 5): his wedding

5 Church of Notre Dame, Calais. Photograph by David Wallace.

reception was held in the Town Hall, where – between sips of *champagne brut imperial* – he might have admired the stained-glass windows commemorating the recapture of Calais from the English in 1558. But it is worth noting that the Town Hall itself had been rebuilt in fifteenth-century Flemish style in 1910, and that the medieval church doorway through which De Gaulle and his bride appeared on April 7, 1921, is unmistakably of English design (figure 5).[52] So rather than pressing the point that Calais might be regarded – for essential economic and political purposes – as an English invention, we might rather propose that Calais has always been a place of striking cultural hybridity.

Imagining Calais

In 1377 Edward III died and a new and more effective French king – Charles V – oversaw an invasion that pinned the English back into Calais; English overlordship would henceforth be restricted to the town itself and its immediate rural hinterland. In 1379, following the papal schism, ecclesiastical loyalties were transferred from the diocese of Thérouanne to that of Canterbury (a transfer that was never reversed). Thereafter, for six generations of English merchants, ecclesiastics, and soldiers, Calais became part of the accepted nexus of trade and preferment; a stopping place *en route* to continental Europe or to higher benefices or political places back home.[53] The peculiarly intense urban energy of Calais – with its volatile admixture of merchant capital, military might, royal dignity, and native provisioning – is glimpsed in a number of the Cely letters but fully exploited in the sixty-second tale of the Burgundian *Cent nouvelles nouvelles*.[54] This is set in July 1439, at the time of ransom negotiations for hapless Charles d'Orléans, who had been a prisoner of the English since Agincourt, 1415.[55] The male principles of the tale are John Stotton, squire and carver, and Thomas Brampton, cupbearer to the cardinal of Winchester; the female lead is the Dutch wife of the hotel-keeper Richard Fery. This wife, unnamed, serves (in narrative terms) to test the mutual devotion of the two young Englishmen, which is intense: they dress alike and carry weaponry and military gear of identical design; they usually share a bedroom and a bed. No harsh or angry words pass between them; they love each other as much or more than would two natural brothers ("se entreaymoient autant ou plus que pourroient faire deux freres germains ensemble," p. 181). In reading this *novella*, one senses that the intensity of their relation is somehow epiphenomenal of that informing the town: a thought that often occurs in reading Boccaccian *novelle*, particularly those set in Florence. Crucial narrative details – the timing of watch-duty, the crucial mediation of a merchant – recall urban mechanisms employed in the *Decameron*. Italian literary precedent is acknowledged by the book's dedication to the duke of Burgundy, although the places featured here (we are told) are first and foremost northern European.[56] As a sharply delimited urban space containing such an overcapitalized, overmilitarized, and (it seems) oversexed mix of social elements, then, Calais seems fraught with imaginative potential.

Such potential is under-exploited (but not entirely neglected) by English writers. Sir Thomas Wyatt, who served as a military captain at Calais, mentions the town in one short and intense poem. All Wyatt's poems are intense, but the intensity here springs not from Calais, but from the thought of accompanying Anne Boleyn, his putative lover, across the Channel in the company of Henry VIII: he travels, he tells us, "from Dover to Calais against my mind" (LIX, 4).[57] Calais, most probably the place where Anne finally decided to have sex with Henry, features here only as a geographical marker; the Channel seems like a well-worn road. Much the same can be said for the town's appearance in *The Book of Margery Kempe*: Calais, for Margery, is a nice place for a sit-down after laborious traveling. The overland approach to Calais, Margery pointedly observes, is full of sand and short of good lodging: an accurate characterization of the Calais Marches (reminding us of their proximity to Flanders).[58] More pointedly, the town of Calais itself offers the comforts of home: a return to English ground and an end to the epical journeyings of Book II. Chaucer (to complete this theme) was intensively involved with Calais in all phases of his many careers as soldier, squire, letter-carrier, and controller of customs; he did business at Calais, worked with merchants from Calais, and set off from Calais on many European adventures. Yet he mentions Calais not at all. We might imagine that Calais, for Chaucer, was a place equivalent to Heathrow airport (Terminal Three): a place to pass through, but not to dwell upon; a place at which to fear unforeseen delays; a place familiar, but not loved.

There is, of course, a degree of complacency in all this, a complacency that sets the seal on, is the proof of, successful colonial expansion. And it is in the course of one of his most charmingly complacent pilgrim portraits that Chaucer actually maps the space of Calais, as it were, in silhouette. His youthful, curly-haired, bubble-headed Squire – who spends his days singing and piping, jousting and dancing – has performed war service, we are told, "in chyvachie / In Flaundres, in Artoys, and Pycardie" (1.85–6): that is, in those regions immediately surrounding Calais and its Marches. Such a short list of campaigns shrivels beneath the lengthy roll call of battles undertaken by his father, the Knight (1.151–66). The sense is that they represent a reasonable beginning for one so young; greater things may follow, and his lady (for one) might be favorably impressed (1.187–8). The father, then, commands admiration for extending the limits of the faith at the remote frontiers of Christendom; the son merits less attention for his skirmishing immediately beyond English borders (a domain shared, perhaps, with the tail-rhyme hero Sir Eglamour).[59] And the Yeoman bowman who completes this opening triad (1.101–17) attracts no notice as a fighting man; he has typically been regarded as a rural estate manager. But it is possible to view this group quite differently, as, in fact, representative of the basic English military unit of the Hundred Years' War. The old Knight lends his lineage and crusading prestige to the campaign; the son carries out the ruinous English tactic of "chyvachie" (1.85), *chevauchée* (involving the wholesale burn-ing and destruction of villages, towns, and rural settlements); the yeoman fires the arrows that so often (to the secret chagrin of the English mounted classes) proved decisive in pitched battles (and sometimes, as at Agincourt, amounted to technological slaughter).[60]

Chaucer's recurring historical presence at Calais, then, suggests knowledge of the costs of war comparable to that confined by Theseus (in his *Knight's Tale*) to the temple of Mars. "Costs" here is the operative metaphor, for *chevauchées* of the kind essayed by Chaucer and company before his capture early in 1360 (somewhere, he recalled in 1386, in the vicinity of Réthel)[61] were primarily a tactic of economic warfare: "the defenders' means of pro-duction (crops, fishponds, mills, barns) were among the prime targets for destruction," Christopher Allmand writes, "so that their economic capability was seriously undermined."[62] Later that year, Chaucer served as a letter-carrier from Calais to Westminster, thus playing a minor role in the treaty-making process that decisively enlarged English holdings in France (while, as a byproduct of the peace, cutting loose – rather than shipping home – thousands of soldiers who would terrify the pope at Avignon before descending into Italy and wreaking havoc – they and their descendants – for the next 200 years).[63]

Italy might have been spared much unpleasantness had Edward III heeded the arguments of Langland's Lady Meed: for a king should give "mede to men" who serve him, including "aliens."[64] Events leading to and ensuing from the treaties of Brétigny and Calais in 1360 are addressed by the A and B texts of *Piers Plowman* as matters of considerable topical urgency.[65] On the Sunday after Easter, 1360, an English army approaching 10,000 stood arrayed for battle outside Paris. On the following day, April 13, there was a terrifying hailstorm. When it seemed, as Froissart tells it, that the end of the world was nigh, Conscience (according to Langland's Meed) "crope into a cabane for cold of thi nayles."[66] Interpreting such natural signs as divine command, the royal conscience was moved to the treaty table: and all, Meed says, through fear of a downpour ("and dreddest to be ded for a dym cloude" [B 3.193; see also A 3.180]). In retreating to Calais, the English army performs its usual feats of pillaging or *chevauchée*, robbing poor men of their brass (coins or utensils):

Withouten pite, pilour, povere men thow robbedest
And bere here bras at thi bak to Caleis to selle

(B 3.195–6)[67]

Meed goes on to berate Conscience for being excessively money-conscious: for "a litel silver" (some 3,000,000 écus), Edward was persuaded "to leven his lordshipe" (B 3.207), that is – such was the provision of Brétigny – to renounce his claim to the French throne.[68] Such renunciation was retracted long before Langland undertook the last major revision of his poem.[69] It is fascinating to note, however, that while the C-text drops some of the topical 1360s references, it actually expands meditation on the rights and constraints governing kings in disposing of conquered territory. For that which has been won through common enterprise, involving the efforts of fighting men under royal direction, cannot just be sold off for profit:

Unconnynge is that Conscience a kyndom to sulle,   *Unentitled*
For that is conquered thorw a commune helpe, a kyndom or ducherie,
Hit may nat be sold sothliche, so many part asketh
Of folk that fauht therfore and folwede the kynges wille.

(C 3.243–6)

Such an appeal to the rights of common soldiers, as in some sense co-inheritors of conquered land, brings us far from Froissart, but it does suggest that the ideological territory of Langland's Westminster – of which Froissart formed part through the 1360s – extends out to Calais.[70] For in each of these intense and pressurized localities we find commercial and royal calculation, profiteering, merchandising, war-mongering, merchant business, and the minting of coin (in the Tower as at Calais); such a heady mixture suggests a whiff of sexual opportunism memorably embodied by Mrs Richard Fery (the Dutch wife in the French *nouvelle*) and by Lady Meed. There is no evidence that Langland ever went to Calais, but (I am suggesting) there is every indication that he knew what went on there. At the very least, we know for sure – from all three versions of his poem – that he treated news from the French front, as purveyed by "mynstrales and messagers," with extreme skepticism.[71]

The debate over the ethics and opportunities of continental warfare staged between Conscience and Meed is remarkable, especially when the King's kinswoman seems to be winning the debate ("By Crist," the King exclaims in A and B, "Mede is worthi the maistrie to have!").[72] For robustly unambiguous endorsement of Edward's campaigns we may turn to the delimited

corpus of Laurence Minot (11 poems celebrating English border victories –
against French and Scots – from the Battle of Halidon Hill, 1333, to the
conquest of Guines, 1352). Minot's taunting poem on the siege of Calais,
addressed to "Calays men," reads like an appalling antiromantic riposte to
Froissart; a whole stanza is taken up by the starving citizenry's accounting of
animals eventually eaten.[73] The poem on the English capture of Guines
taunts and challenges "men of St Omers" (XI.31, the chief resort of *Calaisiens*
in exile) and John, the new French King:

> Say now Sir John of France,   how saltou fare   *shall you*
> that both Calays and Gynes   has kindeld thi care?
> If thou be man of mekil might   lepe up on thi mare   *great*
> take thi gate unto Gines   and grete tham wele thare.   *your way*
>   *(XI.25–8)*

"No notion in France," Pierre Nora observes, "is so filled with memory as
that of the 'borders'."[74] This particular challenge to retake lost cities is taken
up, on the French side, with career-long intensity by the poet known to us
as Eustache Deschamps.

Brulé des Champs and the English *frontière*

Deschamps feels the loss of Calais with particular sharpness; one of his
pastourelle refrains emphasizes that there can be no peace so long as the
English remain in occupation:

> Paiz n'arez ja s'ilz ne rendent Calays.[75]

This remarkable poem, written in August 1384, views political affairs from
the perspective of peasants, men and women, who are gathering in the
harvest some 40 miles south of Calais. This is a dangerous location. In 1370,
Robert Knolles had set out on a march from Calais with 55 named criminals,
all granted royal pardons: 43 were murderers and the rest rapists and thieves.
In the Pas de Calais, as in Vietnam, there were complex systems of tunnels
or *souterrains-refuges* that allowed the peasantry, quite literally, to sink below
the earth.[76] Fat Margot is the first to swear (by her distaff) that there will
never be peace until the English give up Calais (344.10). Berthelot is so
frightened that he hardly dares get out of bed in the morning, "pour les
Anglois qui nous sont destruisans" ("on account of the English, who go

about destroying us"). Guichard the brown, born at Seclin in French Flanders, believes that the English harbor the evil design ("mal engin," 43) of forever hanging on to Calais (despite projected peace talks); all agree, in the envoy addressed directly to "princes," that a peace settlement leaving Calais in English hands would be a filthy disgrace ("orde et meschans," 54).

There is a double mystique at work in this poem: that of the immediate bond between peasants and princes (cutting out all politicial middlemen), and that of the land, the tilled and harvested ground itself. The first such mystique had proved potent in England just three years earlier; the second, while stronger in 1381 than in later English centuries, proved especially potent in France (which enjoyed a "long Middle Ages").[77] Deschamps, in such poems, speaks primarily not as a royal apologist (or critic) but as one who owns, loves, and lives by the land. The point is convincingly if cheekily made in a *ballade* that dedicates a month to each of the poet's patrons or "seigneurs," beginning with the king in January and ending with December for the duke of Burgundy. The months from July to October, however, are dedicated to nobody since (so says the refrain) a man must see to his needs:[78] for he who wishes to maintain social estate ("qui veult estat tenir," 19) must look to his meadows, gather in his corn, and pluck his grapes (17–21). While this poem may double nicely as a courtier's excuse for absenteeism,[79] there is no doubting that Deschamps' sense of personal identity is intimately bound up with his landholding: indeed, his very name, or change of name, speaks to this. In official documents before 1389 the poet is referred to as Eustache Morel or Eustache Morel de Vertus.[80] A letter of 1370 locates him at "Maison des champs," an estate at Vertus; in 1380 this property and its environs were razed by an English *chevauchée*. "Now I am burned," says ballade 835, "so my name is changed: / from now on I'll have the name Burned-out[81] of the Fields":

> Or sui tous ars, s'est mon nom remué:
> J'aray desor a nom Brulé des Champs.
> *(835.7–8)*

In 1388 Charles VI granted the poet funds to rebuild Maison des champs; the official adoption of the name "Deschamps" shortly thereafter likely marks his elevation to noble status.[82] His very name, then, carries marks or memories of the endless Anglo-French conflict that structured both his identity and his deepest anxieties. Another of his properties was sacked in 1383, this time by Burgundians. And in ballade 1124 he looks back over 50 years of "universel guerre," fuelled by "le debat de France et d'Angleterre" (8–9): in

such a world, he reflects, nothing can be truly or securely possessed ("nul
n'en a vraie possession," 13). When peace seems within reach, he takes the
occasion to upbraid the kings of France and England alike (1171). For more
than 50 years temples, towns, castles, and cottages have been destroyed
or defaced by burning; the earth is fruitless and unworked; some places are
uninhabited (as people at Calais, Ardres, and Guînes – towns just south
and west of Calais – know all too well, 34–9). You are of one blood, he tells
the French and English kings; your lust for power has shed the blood of
100,000 men:

> Cent milles hommes sont mors pour vo pouoir
>
> *(1171.33)*

Elsewhere Deschamps singles out individuals from this host of dead warriors for more particular lamentation. People "in Flaundres, in Artoys, and
Pycardie" – the three territories that host the brief and cheerfully narrated
excursions of Chaucer's Squire (1. 86) – are here called to regret the death of
a good knight:

> Picardie bien plaindre le devroit;
> Therouenne, Saint Omer et aussi
> Flandre et Artois, et chascun qui congnoit
> Le bon prodhomme et chevalier Sampy.
>
> *(13.24–7)*

> Picardy should well lament his passing;
> So too Thérouanne, Saint Omer and also
> Flanders and Artois, and each person who knew
> The good man of valor and knight, Sempy.

"Sempy" is thought to be one Jean de Sempy, knight of Artois, who spent
most of his life fighting the English (and occasionally the Flemings); following his death, his wife married another knight (who died at Agincourt). But
the ballade might just as well have been written for his father, also Jean de
Sempy, who was well-known in the environs of Calais (14) and "maintefoiz
les Anglois desconfy" (16).[83] There is no doubting the subject of ballade
1366, however: Enguerrand de Coucy, who died as part of the crusader
force defeated at Nicopolis in September 1396.[84] As a French prisoner of war
in England, Enguerrand had married Isabella, the oldest daughter of Edward
III; he was admitted to the Order of the Garter and created earl of Bedford.
In 1377, however, Enguerrand surrendered his garter to Richard II, returned

to France, and then returned Isabella and her young daughter to England.[85] Deschamps' account of the life, death, and geographical range of his patron Enguerrand evokes a figure of the grandest dimensions: one famed in Lombardy (where, at Pavia, he founded the chivalric "Ordre de la couronne") and feared in Barbary (where, like his "anceserie" on the first crusade, he fought the Turks).[86] Yet he was ever wise and full of largesse (12): a "beau chevalier" (13), merciful to vanquished enemies and full of "douçour" (23). All this reminds us of the "verray, parfit gentil knyght" of Chaucer's *General Prologue* (1.72): yet it is instructive to note that Deschamps' listing of military campaigns makes no distinction between far-off and neighboring territories, the domains of Chaucerian Knight and Squire, father and son:

> Osteriche sentit bien son levain,
> Flandres, Guerle, Savone et Barbarie,
> La frontiere de Calais, Picardie,
> D'Angolesme, de Guyenne environ
> *(1366.25–8)*

> Austria felt the force of his levy,
> [So too] Flanders, Gueldre, Savone and Barbary,
> The frontier of Calais, Picardy,
> Angoulême, the environs of Guyenne

The application of the term "frontiere" to Calais here – and elsewhere in Deschamps[87] – balances curiously against the term used earlier to evoke Enguerrand's movement into Barbary; all noble hearts, we are told, should lament

> La mort et fin d'Enguerrant le baron,
> Qui trepassa pour la foy en Turquie;
> Prions a Dieu qu'il li fasse pardon!
> *(1366.8–10)*

> The death and end of the baron Enguerrand,
> Who passed over for the faith in Turkey;
> Let us pray to God that God might pardon him!

The verb *trespasser* in Old French implies the sense of movement from one sphere or domain to another. So it is that the phrase *trespasser de cest siecle* can mean *to die*; Enguerrand thus crosses one border in Turkey while attempting to invade another. From the evidence of this poem (and from much else in Deschamps' vast corpus), little distinction is made between eastern and western frontiers, the Pas de Calais and the limits of Christendom: both entail matters of life, death, and lifelong struggle. In Froissart's *Meliador*, too, there is a sense that struggles at Scottish, Welsh, and Irish borders compare with those ongoing in "Prusse" (at the eastern limits of Christendom).[88] All this differs, of course, from the English experience of reading Chaucer, where matters of war play out far away or long ago, not on native, or insular, ground.

Chaucer and Deschamps develop from places that look remarkably alike. In registering such commonalities, however, we are ultimately led to grasp profound divergences between the polities and cultures each served. They were born within years of each other: just in time to weather, as infants, the Black Death that carried off (as the English were repeopling Calais) one in three. Each was of humble ancestry: the name of Chaucer suggests descent from makers of *chauceure*, footwear or hose; Deschamps, late in life, was taunted as a *savetier*, a cobbler, by pedigree-minded nobles.[89] Each became attached to noble and then royal households, where they held the rank of *écuyer* or squire; each showed competence in a range of administrative tasks and served as juror and estate manager. Both fought in the Hundred Years' War. Chaucer started and gave up young, whereas Deschamps began campaigning somewhat later and was still in the saddle when he was approaching 50.[90] Each married a French-speaking woman who eased access to enlarged circles of courtly acquaintance. Each began (and indeed continued) writing in a French lyric tradition that was profoundly indebted to Guillaume de Machaut: Chaucer's earlier verse, in particular, shows massive absorption of Machaut; Deschamps' bond to the great French poet who "nourished" him ("qui m'a nourry," 447.5) was so tight that he was long rumored to be his nephew. Each poet developed (in part from Machaut) a fine sense of self-deprecating humor that broadened into skillful deployment of estates satire; each courted orthodoxy by putting into the vernacular the *De miseria condicionis humane* of Lotario dei Segni (later Pope Innocent III).[91] And each developed an impressive range of international contacts, through travel or acquaintance, that extended to Bohemia[92] and Italy.

When Deschamps travelled to Italy, however, he visited Milan and Pavia, but not Florence. His sense of connectedness with the Visconti, rulers of Lombardy, was an intimate, cradle to grave affair. Deschamps was born, he tells us, in the county of Vertus in Champagne (ca. 1340); his first known appointment was as juror of the Count of Vertus (1367). The count in question was Gian Galeazzo Visconti, who had acquired his title by paying 300,000 florins for the hand of Isabelle, daughter of King John (strapped for ransom money in 1360). In 1387 Valentina, daughter of Gian Galeazzo and Isabelle, contracted a marriage with Louis d'Orléans (younger brother of Charles VI); Deschamps had served Louis, he tells us, since his birth in 1372.[93] When he eventually visited Gian Galeazzo at his Francophile Pavian court in 1391, then, Deschamps brought with him a 50-year accumulation of personal, cultural, and territorial ties. Ballade 1037, which finds Pavia "tresbeau," manages to work in the Vertus connection (22) while commending the quality of wine and court life. In 1396, when Louis decided to have Valentina exiled as a witch, Deschamps defended her orthodoxy and royal lineage in a spirited ballade. Its refrain features the motto that Gian Galeazzo had inherited from Isabelle and made his own, "à bon droyt":

A bon droit n'est d'elle un cuer plus loyal.[94]

Chaucer's Visconti connections started quite early, too: his first master, Lionel, duke of Clarence, traveled to Lombardy in 1368 to marry Bernabò Visconti's daughter Violante (and died several months thereafter).[95] Ten years later Chaucer was himself dispatched to Milan to enlist the aid of Bernabò and Sir John Hawkwood, an English mercenary captain, to the English cause against France. His subsequent poetic accounts of Lombardy – testing the rhyming possibilities of *Lumbardye* and *tirannye* – suggest an unfavorable view of Viscontian polity: a view that accords with that vigorously promulgated by Florentines in their perennial struggle, ideological and military, against their northern neighbors. Florence is a city that Deschamps chose never to visit or praise. The name of "Florence" appears just twice in his vast verse corpus: once as a city comparing unfavorably with the French capital ("Riens ne se puet comparer a Paris," 170.10, 20, 30) and once as the eponymous heroine of *Florence de Rome*, the French romance.[96] Modalities of artistic production in Florence – emanating from a republican regime that had exiled the nobility from public office – are inimical to the aesthetic of Deschamps: whereas the Frenchman produced a *Livre de memoire* (a versified chronicle of noble doings in verse, now lost), Florence produced the *Decameron*. And London and Westminster, of course, produced the *Canterbury Tales*, a text that has always invited comparison with its Boccaccian antecedent. Juxtaposition of Chaucer and Deschamps, then, can but accentuate the peculiar hybridity of English writing, itself epiphenomenal of peculiar socioeconomic complexities. For Chaucer was dispatched not just to Lombardy, but to Genoa and Florence too: cities involved in networks of commerce that kept Chaucer employed for long stretches of his career. These networks included the precocious cities of Flanders.

As large urban and banking centers with highly complex divisions of labor, Florence and the great textile-making cities of Flanders – Ghent, Bruges, and Ypres – had much in common. To the aristocratic outsider, such complexity spelled chaos: the Florentine regime of 1343–78 was eventually toppled by unemployed wool-workers; the Flemish cities fought one another and were wracked internally by dissent between weavers, fullers, and other trades. Deschamps, who rode wearily through several campaigns in Flanders, expressed his contempt for the region in a ballade beginning "Orgueilleuse, desloial, tricheresse" ("Proud, disloyal, treacherousness," 18.1) that continues simply to pile up of terms of abuse: it is as if the very thought of Flanders jams the delicacy, wit, and syntactic intelligence of his courtly *forme fixe*.[97] Perhaps the most telling line is the characterization of the Fleming as "Envieuse subjuguer de noblesce" ("envious subjugator of nobility," 19). Deschamps, as we have seen, had raised himself from humble origins to become the devoted servant of noble patrons. His wish to serve, praise, and commemorate nobility runs deep; deeper still is a desire to *perform* nobility, season by season, by demonstrating control of a self-sufficient land he can call his own. The presence of the English at Calais troubles this aesthetic in several ways. First, and most obviously, his much-loved country estates might be ruined by *chevauchée* at any time. Second, the development of trade at Calais, involving extensive contacts with Flemish and Italian cities, brings commercial and monetary practices to French territory that might contaminate the pure aristocratic ethos. All this, I would suggest, feeds the anger, contempt, and derision Deschamps feels for Calais, feelings most memorably registered by an actual visit to the town.

In August or September 1384, while negotiations with the English were going on at Boulogne, Deschamps was dispatched by Charles VI to inspect French defenses in Picardy.[98] It was very likely at this time that he decided, or was persuaded, to slip into Calais; the inevitable ballade report opens thus:

> Je fu l'autrier trop mal venuz
> Quant j'alay pour veir Calays;
> J'entray dedenz comme cornuz,
> Sanz congié; lors vint .II. Anglois,
> Granson devant et moy après,
> Qui mi prindrent parmi la bride:
> L'un me dist: "dogue," l'autre: "ride";
> Lors me devint la coulour bleue:
> "Goday," fair l'un, l'autre: "commidre."
> Lors dis: "Oil, je voy vo queue."
>
> *(893.1–10)*

The other day I was miserably received
When I went to see Calais;
I entered the town like a fool,
Without permission; two Englishmen came up
(Granson riding in front and I behind)
And seized me by the bridle:
One said to me "dog," the other "ride";
My coloring then turned pale:
"Good day," said one, the other: "come hither."
I said to them: "Yes, I see your tails."

We do not expect Deschamps, of all people, to turn macaronic by featuring *English* words in a French ballade; such contamination neatly emblematizes the anomalous space of the French-founded, English-peopled town that he has just entered. The first of these thickly accented words, "dogue," perhaps supplies the cue for Deschamps' refrain: it is the English who – following a long-lived Anglo-Norman and French tradition – are tailed creatures (more probably devils than dogs).[99] This opens to the wider conceit of Calais Gate as hell mouth (with the English, across the water, in deeper states of damnation). Deschamps, though he does not yet know it, has been betrayed ("trahi," 17). He is to be imprisoned, the most ill-schooled of the Englishmen tells him, and held forfeit ("vous estes forfais," 14). Oton de Granson, his traveling companion, refuses to vouch for him ("Pas ne l'adveue," 18). Things look bleak for Deschamps at the close of the second stanza: Granson is his fellow poet, but he has long sided with the English as a retainer of both Richard II and John of Gaunt. When he speaks to the soldiers, Granson adopts their native tongue ("en Anglois dist," 18).

Deschamps now "stretches his talons" (21) and prepares to fight. There is every evidence to suppose that Deschamps was a tough nut: he long held the rank of "huissier d'armes" under Charles VI, was employed by Louis d'Orléans as a sort of aristocratic repo man, and sometimes imposed his will over his rivals by sheer force.[100] At this delicate point in the proceedings, however, Granson extends a restraining hand, smiles, and then agrees to vouch for him. Deschamps and the English exchange final dog-and-tail insults before he is discharged to his escort, Granson:

"Chien, faisoit l'un, vez vous vo guide?"
Lors dis: "Oil, je voy vo queue."
(29–30)

"Dog," said one of them, "do you see your guide?"
I said to them: "Yes, I see your tails."

Deschamps' discomfiture in this episode is neatly summed up by the line immediately following the one in which Granson (not yet having vouched for his safety) smiles: "from such love," he says, "I thought to have died."[101] Such disorientation is sustained by the remarkable *rondeau* that recalls other aspects of this Calais visit. The insomniac unease here seems almost Joycean ("I hear an army charging upon the land"), although the last line drops us to Joyce in a lower register:

> Et, d'autre part, oir la grant mer bruir,
> Et les chevaulx combatre et deslier?
> C'est a Calys; Granson, veillés jugier:
> Est cilz aise qui ne se puet dormir
> Et qui ne fait toute nuit que viller,
> Puces sentir, oyr enfans crier?
>
> *(596.8–14)*

> And, somewhere else, to hear the great sea crash,
> And the horses fighting and breaking off?
> That is [so] at Calais: Granson, judge my nights:
> Is he at ease who cannot sleep,
> Who cannot do anything all night but stay awake
> Bitten by fleas, hearing infants cry?

For Deschamps, memories of lying awake at night on the English *frontière* are clearly strange and estranging, particularly when shared with the English-speaking knight who mock-betrayed him. Granson is indeed the perfect border knight: his family, from Savoy, had developed close ties in England since the thirteenth century (when Peter of Savoy's niece, Eleanor of Provence, married Henry III).[102] John of Gaunt's London manor, known as the Savoy (and sacked in 1381), had been willed to his ancestors by Peter; the name of Granson often shares space in John of Gaunt's Register with the less illustrious, less remunerative name of Chaucer.[103] Froissart, who names Chaucer but once, speaks approvingly of Granson throughout his *Chroniques*; and Chaucer, who never names Deschamps at all, speaks of his struggle to follow, "word by word . . . Graunson, flour of hem that make in Fraunce" (81–2).[104] Chaucer's Englishing of Granson's triple ballade as *The Complaint of Venus* may have been inspired as much by ties of Lancastrian affinity as by poetic admiration. It is possible that similarly complex calculations inform Deschamps' celebrated missive to Chaucer, ballade 285: a poem thought to date from the period when Philippa of Lancaster was (as we learn from *chanson royale* 765) under active consideration as a possible match for Charles

VI. These two poems, in turn, have been assigned to a period close in time to Deschamps' Calais adventure, namely 1384. But such datings are precarious, and attempts to fix poems to specific events come unglued rapidly because events themselves (as poets themselves seem well aware, even in the act of writing) shift with alarming speed. Deschamps' acclamatory ballade to Chaucer needs to be read, then, in light of the whole Anglo-French nexus adumbrated by this chapter so far, rather than as an isolated *pièce d'occasion*.[105]

Read within such a nexus, then, the ballade might be considered as a spirited act of reverse or returned colonization. The first stanza acclaims Chaucer as a Socrates, a Seneca, an Aulus Gellius, and an Ovid in the island kingdom of Aeneas, the Giants, and "Bruth"; but the only actual poetic work going on is that of planting "the rose-tree for those who are ignorant of French," namely Chaucer's translating of *Le Roman de la Rose*. Contemplation of the French Rose on English ground ("de la rose, en la terre Angelique") is continued through the mock-etymology of *Anglia*, a name supposedly derived "from the Saxon lady Angela" ("d'Angela saxonne"). Chaucer's translation of the *Rose* has been executed "En bon anglès"; but "bons anglès" can never be that of a "purs Englès" (the mysterious dream of Edward III) since this island race was conceived through acts of miscegenation. At the Council of Constance, some 30 years later, the French were to argue that the English nation "should be placed back in the German nation, of which it is really a part and joined directly to it"; England does not merit or constitute a nation in its own right.[106] Chaucer, intent on establishing an orchard, thus does well to seek saplings "De ceuls qui font" ("from those who make": in France, of course): "Grand translateur," the ballad refrain teasingly runs, "noble Geffroy Chaucier."[107]

In the third stanza, Deschamps represents himself as paralyzed or paralytic in Gaul ("en Gaul seray paralitique") until he receives a drink from Chaucer's Helicon. Such a stream, of course, is likely to refresh or reassure a Gallic poet, for Chaucer's verse will be either in French, or in an English springing from the transplanted *Rose*. Deschamps now names himself – "Eustaces sui" – and assures Chaucer that Sir Lewis Clifford will be bringing over some of his poems for planting ("de mon plant aras"). Having named a knight, Deschamps signs off (by way of envoy) by commending "noble" Chaucer as "glory of the esquires" (a non-noble rank Deschamps shared, but left behind in the late 1380s). He ends oddly by declaring that, in Chaucer's garden, he would fit in no better than a stinging nettle ("ne seroye qu'ortie"); "bear in mind," he continues, "what I said first of your noble plants," and do write back, "Grant translateur, noble Geffroy Chaucier." There is no evidence that Chaucer ever did write back.

Deschamps, himself the victim of a practical joke orchestrated by Granson at Calais, was himself something of a joker; it is thus not out of character for him to adopt such a joshing tone with Granson's fellow poet, Chaucer. And Deschamps' praise for Chaucer as rhetorician, Ovidian, and Helicon-dweller compares closely with terms he had applied to Machaut.[108] But such talents would be misapplied (this poem seems to suggest) when turned from the international nexus of French courtly making and exercised on English ground in the English tongue. The disdain for the island territory of England that peeps through in this ballade receives more overt expression elsewhere in Deschamps. Ballade 211, for example, opens thus:

> Selon le Brut de l'isle des Geans
> Qui depuis fut Albions appelée,
> Peuple maudit, tardis en Dieu creans,
> Sera l'isle de tous poins desolée.
>
> *(211.1–4)*

> According to the *Brut* of the isle of Giants
> (That was later called Albion) –
> A people accursed, slow to believe in God –
> The island will be utterly destroyed.

The prophet pressed into service here is Merlin, "leur prophete" (6); now that the territory is governed by a child-king ("gouvernée d'enfans," 11), destruction is nigh ("Destruiz serez, Grec diront et Latin," 19). "Greeks and Latins agree": once again, England is isolated as an island of impure, miscegenated stock; Chaucer, as hybridizing *makere*, can hardly hope to escape these limits. His chief value, as "grant translateur" of French texts, may be to help facilitate the more full-blooded act of *translatio* that Deschamps is urging in this period (the mid-1380s): a full-scale French invasion of England. Ballade 211, dating from 1387, urges that French victory in Brittany may be followed by a crossing of the Channel; other poems cheer the active preparations for invasion that began at Sluys in August 1386. When French resolve wavers Deschamps castigates the troops, figured as 10,000 rats (plus accompanying mice) who are afraid to start swimming (1040.4–8) or as rodents (again) who are daunted by the task of belling the cat.[109] Calais, for Deschamps, remains the sticking point; for although nearby towns may have been recaptured from the English, "Forty years of singing *Requiem*" (as one ballade begins) cannot end until the English are expelled. This may entail moving beyond Calais ("d'oultre Calais," 12) to England itself:

Passons la mer, ou, j'apperçoy trop bien,
Sanz paix avoir, nous aurons guerre, guerre.

(48.27–8)

Let us cross the sea or, I see only too well,
Not having peace, we shall have war, war.

Deschamps had no interest in a new French conquest of England; he was simply outraged by the English presence in France and would support anything that might bring it to an end. His outrage is rooted, I would suggest, in a sense of nobility that would seek deep roots in the land that bore its name; to lie abed in Calais and hear English hoofs drumming over this territory was more than he could stand. France, in the imagining of ballade 1139, is alienated or displaced from itself by the very presence of the English:

France, tu es Jherusalem: se sente
Et puet sentir estrange nascion,
Qui tant as eu de paine et de tourmente
Par les gens Bruth ...

(1139.17–20)

France, you are Jerusalem: you feel yourself
And may well feel yourself to be an estranged nation
Since you have received so much punishment and torment
From the people of Brut ...

This is apparently the only time that Deschamps applies the term *nation* to the sum total of people living in the kingdom of France.[110] Invasion and occupation – as in the case of Scotland – may speed the need for integrationist metaphors, although it is worth noting that (as with Froissart on Calais), the term *nation* is applied (here metaphorically) to a town or city rather than to a kingdom. And if France, like Jerusalem, is an "estranged nation," the English are like infidels, like those "Saracen" invaders who, as Margery Kempe was to discover, controlled the holiest sites of Christendom.[111] The author of *Arthour and Merlin* simply concedes that if Arthur's Britons are truly English, then the Anglo-Saxons are Saracens: such are the complexities and loose ends of English foundational myth that Deschamps was able to exploit.[112]

It is perhaps surprising to learn that Deschamps, so wedded to his country estates, was prone to praise cities.[113] But there are good cities – like "Jherusalem" – and bad. A good and orderly city loves and submits to her prince; she prospers in his presence, accepts his largesse, and laments his absence. Bad cities, denounced by Deschamps through many a poetic *vituperatio loci et populi*, rebel against their prince and imagine themselves able to manage without him. Calais thus stands as a Babylon on French soil, embodying everything despicable about England, for it is a heady, unpedigreed admixture of military prowess and merchant calculation, knighthood and commerce, *otium* and *negotium*. Even when attempting to compliment Chaucer as the great translator of England, Deschamps barely conceals his contempt for the mishmash of Saxonism, gigantism, and derivative Gallicism over which "Chaucier" rules. Although English-speaking critics have been tempted to imagine that Chaucer's verse might have received an appreciative audience across the Channel, there is little in Deschamps to encourage such a view.[114] Indeed, the appearance of a fragmentary English lexicon within a ballade of Deschamps – "dog, ride, good day, come hither," 893 – seems as calculatedly outlandish as the rude irruption of plebeian English names amid the measured Latinity of Gower's *Vox Clamantis*.[115]

Deschamps' land-locked poetics, fixated on nobility, might be read as epiphenomena of a localized, high-volume, low added-value economy, that of a primarily agricultural region with limited interest in intensive industrialization. Movement of commercial products through such terrain was difficult, since local toll stations occurred with great frequency. Florence and the Flemish cities, by contrast, are moderate-volume, high added-value economies, producers of cloths and other intensively worked commodities that could be shipped long distances for profit.[116] These economies are intensively urban, relying on highly complex divisions of labor. England, characteristically, is attracted by both models of economy: excellent local soils facilitate an agriculture which manages (for the most part) to feed the population and to export fleeces abroad. Flanders, by contrast, must depend upon England for its wool and France for its grain. The precocious successes of Flanders and Florence in manufacturing, and in necessary adjunct enterprises such as moneylending, stir English dreams of emulation; they also expedite a peculiar alliance of Crown and commercial interests that grows more urgent as the demands and rewards of continental campaigning complicate the equation. Chaucer's career was defined, to a very considerable extent, by movements within this Flemish/Italian/ English nexus of capital, warfare, and wool.[117] Calais, flanked by Flanders, Artois, Picardy, and the open sea, at once English and continental, military, mercantile, and (even) ecclesiastical, might be considered epiphenomenal of a Chaucerian poetic: for if Chaucer is to be imagined as the "poet of England," this is what his England looked like in its most intense and concentrated form.

The hybridity imputed by Deschamps to Chaucer's England and egregiously exemplified by Calais does become, ultimately, the salient feature of Chaucer's literary opus. Chaucer's earliest writing does indeed conform to the pattern envisaged by Deschamps: the translation of the *Rose*, the steady absorption of French lyric and narrative models, the unremitting exaltation of courtly and aristocratic ideals. Such attachments survive Chaucer's first visit to Italy. The *Troilus* is certainly possessed of a new generic diversity, but its concerns remain chiefly aristocratic. And when Chaucer comes to incorporate a rare gem of a Petrarchan sonnet into his poetic fabric, he chooses to translate the 14-line Italian sonnet into 21 lines of English, which is to say, he aligns it – a gem in its appropriate setting – with the ballade tradition of Granson and Deschamps.[118] In Boccaccio, however, he discovers a poet of undoubted cultural hybridity: a poet attached with equal passion to the French-derived court culture of Angevin Naples (hence the *Decameron*'s rotating monarchy) and the mercantile ingenuities and streetsmarts of Florence (hence Day VI). This emboldens him to recognize the peculiarities of his own social condition and so explore hybridities of class, style, and gender through the extraordinary compiling of his *Canterbury Tales*.

Such adventures in hybridity extend, however, to form: for whereas Boccaccio repeats himself through one hundred *novelle*, Chaucer compiles (his word) an extraordinary range of genres and registers, sacred and secular. In this, finally, he does seem (for all his continental encounters) English: more like the *compilator* of Harley Manuscript 2253 (or of other, similarly eclectic collections) than, say, the presiding spirit of University of Pennsylvania, MS French 15.[119] English, but not insular (and here the Calais of Deschamps' imagining seems to place him most suggestively). To the one side lies Flanders: the territory narrated by Chaucer's Pardoner, the pilgrim who (so the next chapter argues) undoes all assumptions about the natural, the profitable, the pleasurable. To the other side lies France,[120] domain of an aristocratic ethos aspiring to a condition of pure art: "the note, I trowe, imaked was in Fraunce."[121] In between lies Calais: an intermediate zone of imagining that was to become, over the next 150 years, essential to the staging of Englishness within and as part of Europe.

Keeping Calais: Music, Sex, and Reformation

From 1400 to 1558 Calais remained both a familiar and an exceptional part of English experience: it continued to function within extended circuits of trade, military calculation, diplomacy, and ecclesiastical preferment; it was

increasingly used as a "staging post" to signal English designs to greater
Europe. Anxiety about the "keeping of Calais" sounds throughout this period:
the Emperor Sigismund, who allied with Henry V in 1416, urged the English
monarch to maintain Dover and Calais as the twin eyes of his kingdom:

> "Kepe these too townes sure to youre mageste
> As youre tweyne eyne to kepe the narowe see."[122]

A high percentage of English military expenditure was, in fact, dedicated to
Calais. Control of the town thus became a matter of considerable importance during the Wars of the Roses; the Calais garrison was the closest thing
to a standing army medieval English kings ever had.[123] It is thus not surprising that between 1457 and 1460 an anonymous "parson of Calais" should
have chosen to translate the treatise on war, *Epitoma rei militaris*, by Vegetius
(ca. 383–450 CE). The first vernacular translation of this work had been into
Anglo-Norman, intended for "Lord Edward" (the future Edward I or Edward
II of England); the Calais parson, siding against Edward IV, dedicates his
work to Henry VI.[124] His *Knyghthode and Batayle*, which survives in three
manuscripts, offers a very loose rendition of the Latin original (eschewing
French intermediaries), with frequent digressions supporting the Lancastrian
cause. The parson poet, who favors stanzas of eight lines in his "Proemium"
and of seven in the poem proper, apostrophizes himself early on:

> Now, person of Calais, pray euery Seynte
> In hevenys & in erthe of help Thavaile.   *To avail you of help*
> It is, That in this werk nothing ne feynte,   *grows weak*
> But that beforn good wynde it go ful sayle
>
>   (33–6)

The metaphor of sailing out in beginning a literary work is thoroughly
conventional – the Calais parson owes much to Chaucer – and yet is here,
we later learn, peculiarly apt. Late on in the poem we are treated to an
imagining of an unruly sea, developed from slight hints in Vegetius. Anyone
caught on board a ship in such a storm – "Heryn beleve me," 2692 – fears
for his life as the winds shake their chains:

> Sum varyaunce of tyme will refreyne
> Her cruelous & feers rebellioun,   *Their*
> A nothir helpith hem to shake her cheyne   *Another [wind]*
> As all the firmament shulde falle adoun
> And Occian lepe ouer Caleys Toun;

And after in a while it is tranquylle
And playne & calme, as who seith "husht, be stille!"

(2693–9)

In the last lines of the poem proper (before the "Epilogus" or "Recapitulatio"), Calais itself is apostrophized as a port desired as journey's end, but currently barred to the author (who remains all at sea, or, in his own terms of imagining, seasick):[125]

Hail, port saluz! with thi pleasaunt accesse,
   Alhail Caleis! ther wolde I faynest londe;
That may not I [-] oo, whi so? for thei distresse   *happen constrain*
   Alle, or to deye or with her wrong to stonde.   *either*
That wil I not, to wynne al Engelonde!
   What might availe, a litil heer to dwelle,
   And worlde withouten ende abide in helle.

(2980–6)[126]

At the beginning of the stanza, Calais is greeted as the longed-for, suggestively salvific port ("saluz"); by the end it is disavowed as a hell-mouth (recalling imagery previously employed by Deschamps).[127] The reason for this unhappy change is the Yorkist occupation; the poem proper ends with the Calais parson mourning for the house he calls his own, like a mid-Victorian having home thoughts from the sea:[128]

O litel case, o pouere hous, my poort   *shelter*
   Saluz thou be, vntil that ayer amende,   *may you remain well*
That is to sey, vntil an other soort   *fortune / group of people*
   Gouerne there, that by the kynge be sende.

(2987–90)

King Henry VI did indeed send forces to recover Calais for the Lancastrian cause during 1459–60, but they were not successful.[129] Calais remained a Yorkist outpost (and platform for invasion), which is why it features only intermittently in the earlier Paston papers.[130] In 1452 we have a letter from Calais by John Paston's servant, Osberne Mundeforde, promising John that if he comes to Calais with the King he "shul haue a stope of bere to comforte you aftere your trauaille of the see" (II.79); in 1457 John is told how the earl of Warwick, the captain of Calais, has thanked the people of Canterbury and Sandwich for "her gode hertes and vytaillyng of Calix" (II.172).[131] We find John's son, John II, entertaining thoughts of traveling to Calais in 1472; on

November 6, 1473, he feels more urgently impelled to go, remarking to his
brother John III that "it were better for me to be owt off syght" (I.469). John
II here refers to his soured romance with Anne Haute: he has employed
more than one "Rome-rennere" to try and dissolve the engagement (he tells
John III on November 22, I.471). A little later in the same letter he asks
his brother to retrieve "myn instrumentys" from a chest in his chamber
at Norwich: "Thys most be had," he adds, "to avoyde jdelnesse at Caleys"
(I.472). The appeal of Calais as a bolt hole or remedy for soldierly fortunes
had already occurred to John III, finding that "argent me fawlt" in 1469: "I
preye yow remember Caleys," he tells the older John, "for I am put owt of
wagys in thys contré" (I. 551). In 1473 he was hoping to drop by Calais on
his way back from pilgrimage to Compostella (I.465).

Once settled in Calais, John II looked to amuse himself and traveled out
to Bruges to be measured for a new suit of armor; a letter of August 28,
1473, from Martin Rondelle, "Armurier de Monsire le Bastart de Bourgogne,"
tracks him down following "nouvelles" from several "marchans de Calais"
(II.409). Four years later other attractions of Bruges are joshingly evoked in
another letter to John II at Calais, this time from one John Pympe (who
shows impressive knowledge of the term *frowe* – which passed into Middle
English from Middle Dutch *vrouwe*, thus betokening a woman of the Low
Countries and hence often, in England, a prostitute):[132]

> Mary, we have herd sey that the frowys of Brvggys wyth theyre hye cappys
> have gyven sum of yow grete clappys, and that the fete of [her] armys doyng
> is such that they smyte al at the mowthe and at the grete ende of thyeh; but
> in feith we care not for yow, for we know well that ye be gode ynowh at
> defence. But we here sey that they be of such corage that they gyve yow moo
> strokys than ye do [to] them, and that they strike sorer than ye also. But I
> thynke that the English ladyes and jantylwomen, and the pore also, can do as
> well as they and lyste not to lerne of them no thing . . . (II.414)

Pimp and *clap* do not acquire their current sexual connotations until the
seventeenth century (a medieval *pympe* is a flock of chickens), but this is still
quite racy (and Pympe goes on in this vein for ten more lines). John II was
vulnerable to such innuendo, since he had fled to Calais from Anne Haute
(and at the time of Pympe's letter was still not legally free of her). And of
course, Calais was a garrison town and Bruges[133] catered to foreign visitors:
a copy of Valerius Maximus' *Faits et dits mémorables* produced at Bruges ca.
1475 (figure 6) contains a sumptuous depiction of a bathhouse; following a
good meal in a large communal bathtub, men are led away to beds by
women wearing nothing but elaborate headgear, the "hye cappys" evoked

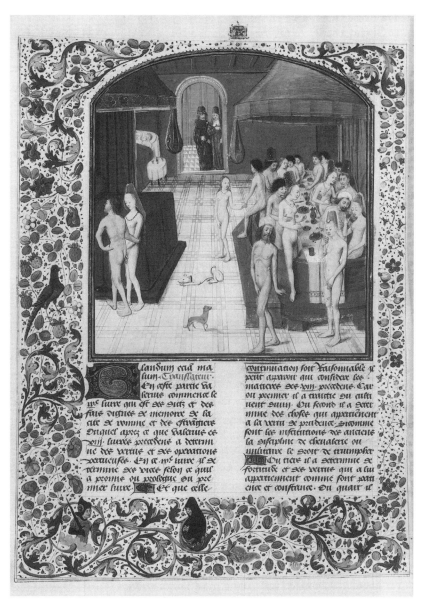

6 Bordello scene in a public bath, Valerius Maximus, *Facta et dicta memorabilia* (produced at Bruges, ca. 1475). Bibliothèque Nationale de France, Paris, MS fr. 289, volume II, folio 414v.

by John Pympe.[134] The wool-stapler George Cely, who also arrived at Calais in 1473, had a series of mistresses before settling down with Margery Rygon in 1484. (She was the widow of a London draper who was sole heir to his property in Calais and its marches.) George's Calais career thus ended better than that of his wastrel brother Robert: having been given 30 shillings to pay for his lodging (brother Richard tells George, writing from Calais to Bruges), "he has playd hyt at dys, euery farthing"; plans are laid to bail him out of prison and ship him back to London.[135]

It seems that John II did not much care for Pympe's insinuations: Pympe wrote him six times in 1477 and yet (so the last letter tells us) received no reply. His final effort to rouse his erstwhile friend sees him resorting to verse; Pympe now represents himself as the abandoned lover, forgotten by the foreign adventurer:

> Fresh amourouse sihtys of cuntreys ferre and straunge
> Have all fordoone yowr old affeccioun.
> In plesurys new yowr hert dooth soore and raunge
> So hye and ferre that, like as the fawcon
> Which is a-lofte tellith scorne to loke a-down
> On hym that wont was her federys to pyke and ympe,
> Ryht so forgotyn ye have yowr pore Pympe
>
> *(II.417)*

Pympe carries on in this vein for four more stanzas. Better verse was read and sung at Calais by George Cely, such as this:

> Go hert, hurt with aduersite,
>   And let my lady thi wondis see;
> And sey hir this, as y say the:
> Far-wel my Ioy, and wel-com peyne,
> Til y se my lady Agayne.[136]

George paid Thomas Rede, a Calais harper, 20 pence for the teaching of this song; he learned others in English, French, and Italian. These included "O rosa bella," deemed "one of the most famous songs of the century" and associated with the Este court of Ferrara (which correctly attributes its composition, in the best manuscript copy, to Englishman John Bedyngham, 1422–60) and "Votre tres douce" by Binchois (Gilles de Bins).[137] Cely also took harp and lute lessons, paid for instruction in the playing of 40 dances, and learned dance steps by employing "bills of footing"; he mastered new ways of tuning his harp and took refresher courses "to amende all my davnsys a3en."[138] He also seems to have combined singing, *daliaunce*, and French lessons at one point, to judge from some jottings on the back of a business letter sent to him in 1479.[139] John Paston III also appreciated the value of multilingualism in this part of the world: in 1476 he wrote to Lord Hastings, Lieutenant of Calais since 1471, recommending a young protégé:

> He is well spokyn jn Inglyshe, metly well in Frenshe, and verry parfit in Flemyshe. He can wryght and reed. Hys name is Rychard Stratton. Hys moder is Mastress Grame of Caleys. (I.600)

Since virtually everything had to be shipped to or foraged for outside Calais – "ther is non hey to gete at Caleys," complains John III (I.598) – the Pastons often ranged quite far afield. On January 17, 1475, John II planned to seek new horse and harness in Flanders and was hoping to see Charles the Bold, Duke of Burgundy, besieging Neuss "iff I have tyme" (I.482). Neuss is on the Rhine, some 10 miles from Dusseldorf: it is not surprising that his next letter to his mother Margaret, dated February 22, 1475, is full of aches and pains (I.485). He promises "to daunce atendaunce" upon his mother just as soon as he can: but for now he is preoccupied by the labors that have taken him "nowe in-to Fraunce warde" (I.485). Such prolonged absences made Margaret, famously, a very full participant in this family enterprise. Their sense of territory, as a perennially traveling, minor East Anglian dynasty, was genuinely cross-continental. Some years after his return to England, the Calais connections of John III are recognized by an invitation for him to spy on "a soudiour of Caleis called John Jacob, of olde tyme dueling in Lynne."[140]

On February 18, 1492, William Paston III (the youngest surviving brother to Johns II and III) wrote excitedly of his plans "to goo to Caleys to purvey me of harneys and suche thyngys as I schall need besides hors" (I. 660). William clearly thought that in forming part of Henry VII's invasion force he might remedy his fortunes. In 1477 the family matriarch, Margaret, had refused to pay his debts at Eton (I.379–80); two years later, he is looking into marriage prospects but is unwilling to leave school until he has perfected his poetry ("I lake no-thynge but wersyfyynge," I.651). However, when Henry eventually set sail for France – at about the time Columbus was first sighting the New World – William was too sick to travel; by 1503 or 1504 he was so "troubelid with sekenes and crasid in his myndes" that his patron, the Earl of Oxford, sent him home to John III (II.486). In 1520, however, another William Paston sailed with a King Henry to Calais. This time it was William IV, son of John III; he was to attend Henry VIII at the famous Field of the Cloth of Gold.[141]

Henry VIII saw his meeting with the French king Francis "within our dominion, pale, and marches of Calys" as momentous, since it marked the first time (so a letter from Henry claims) that a French monarch had explicitly acknowledged English "preheminence" in this region.[142] The following year saw Cardinal Wolsey, who had served as chaplain to the deputy of Calais earlier in his career, busily organizing the Calais conference designed to reconcile Francis and Charles V; Skelton satirically advises "Seigneour Sadoke" – who has taken the great seal of England with him "over the fome" – to come home "From Calys to Dovyr, to Caunterbury in Kent."[143] In 1532, Henry met with Francis at Calais again, hoping to agree on a policy that would speed his divorce from Katherine of Aragon and marriage to Anne Boleyn. Elizabeth Barton, a nun of St. Sepulchre's (just outside Canterbury, on the Dover road), had a vision which saw her mysteriously transported to the English-built "Churche of our Lady" (where General De Gaulle was married: figure 5) "at Caleis": Henry was denied sight of "the blessed Sacrament in forme of breade, for it was takyn away from the Prest . . . by an angel, and mynystered to the seid Elizabeth then being there present and invisible."[144] Elizabeth Barton was dragged the five miles from the Tower of London to Tyburn on April 20, 1534 (on a hurdle, with her hands roped into an attitude of prayer). Henry VIII, having employed his coronation oils to cure a little Calais boy of scrofula and (like the Wife of Bath before him) having offered to Our Lady of Boulogne, left Calais on November 13, 1532.[145] The 25 parishes of Calais assumed increasing importance throughout Henry's reign as, in Diarmaid MacCulloch's words, "an English listening post for the burgeoning variety of Continental Reformation," and also as "a showcase to bewildered foreigners for the latest religious intentions of the king of England."[146] Calais, with its now traditionally volatile mix of royal, mercantile, and military interests, saw a succession of struggles between Protestant evangelicals and conservatives, which got Cranmer's full attention.[147] The 1,000-strong garrison, containing a high proportion of East Anglians and Welshmen, proved a potent site for disseminating ideas that might then be carried back to remoter corners of the realm.

In 1533 Lord Lisle, illegitimate son of Edward IV, succeeded Lord Berners as Governor of Calais and took up residence in the Staple Inn; a superb cache of letters gives a vivid, cumulative picture of this turbulent period up to 1540 (when Lisle died in the Tower of London).[148] Calais was by now no longer the plum posting it had been in earlier times (since the Staplers were in decline and there were ever-expanding civil-service opportunities at Westminster); Lisle informed Thomas Cromwell shortly after his arrival that the royal servants of Calais "were never so poor since it was first English" (I.548).

French and Flemish "strangers" began to predominate, although Lisle found it difficult to get his most wayward son, James, properly educated in French.[149] Sir Francis Bryan (recipient of Wyatt's famous *Satire*) was appointed Lisle's deputy: "I perceive that in Calais," he wrote Lisle on October 24, 1533, "that ye have sufficient of courtezans to furnish and accomplish my desires."[150] Intense disputes raged between the long-established mayoral family of the Whethills and the come-lately Lisles, climaxing in Lady Whethill railing at Lady Lisle in church (as Lord Lisle complains to Henry VIII) "in Pilates' voice" (III.337). More conventional dramatic entertainment was provided (in 1538) by "an interlude which is called Rex Diabole"; Lisle, who had officiated at Anne Boleyn's coronation banquet, was able to assist Henry in the affecting drama of her beheading (by shipping him an expert swordsman from Calais).[151]

We might expect the Lisle letters to differ from those of the Paston and Cely collections through their focus on royal and courtly, rather than mercantile, matters. Lisle certainly devotes considerable energy to building up an impressive network of friends, informants, and spies. His best man at court was Henry Norris: in 1533, Norris tells how Henry, having taken a great fancy to a spaniel given by Lisle to Robert ap Reynold, took it from the Welshman (I.597); three years later, however, Norris was "judged to be drawn, hanged and quartered" as a supposed lover of Anne Boleyn (III.360). Wheels of patronage are greased in the Lisle letters by a steady flow of gifts: Lady Lisle's famous homemade marmalade and conserves, ornamental toothpicks, every conceivable item of clothing, and an endless parade of fish, birds, and animals (which might be kept as pets or eaten – or both, in succession) pass through Calais.[152] All this, of course, depends upon networks of trade which could stretch extremely wide, as when the Admiral of France presents Lady Lisle with "certain small beasts, the which are come from Brazil" and which are said to eat "only apples and little nuts, or almonds" (II.316–17). Lisle himself traded across the Mediterranean to the Levant through his ship *Mary Plantagenet*; his ship-man John Cheriton tells lurid tales of Genoese betrayal at sea ("Jenevayes," III.308) and of being "taken with Turks slave into Barbary" (V.40).

In 1535 Lisle was keen to convince Cromwell that he was working diligently with "the King's Highness' commissioners" in assessing "the yearly value of all the spiritual benefices and promotions on this side the sea"; he was, however, berated for not certifying Sandingfield priory and "the House of the Sisters by the walls of Calais."[153] When Mary succeeded Edward VI in 1553 there was, of course, great consternation in Protestant quarters at the prospect of Calais returning to Catholicism. In 1557, the exiled English

Protestant Robert Pownall raged – in his pamphlet *An admonition to the towne of Callays* – at the prospect of Calais being now again subject to "papistical pigges" and their stinking doctrines; the "backslydinge Towne" was urged to return to the true religion, or it was surely doomed.[154] In 1558, the following year, the town did indeed fall to the French: "well might Queen Mary exclaim," James Albany exclaimed in his dim-witted *Guide to Calais* of 1829, "that Calais would be found engraven on her heart. If her sister Elizabeth had then occupied the throne," Albany continues, "perhaps Calais would at the present time have constituted a part of the dominions of George IV" (p. i). Albany knows, as every nineteenth-century English Protestant Sunday schoolboy knew, that Mary died with Calais "engraven on her heart" because John Foxe says so in his *Book of Martyrs*; vilification of Mary quickly became folded in with her "losing" of Calais.[155]

Losing Calais: Braudel and Shakespeare

It is perhaps otiose to point out, against such a mighty tide of historiographical tradition, that the "losing" of Calais was as much an accident as the "finding" of it. In the summer of 1346, Edward III had landed in Normandy and marched south, east, and north before deciding to besiege Calais. In 1557 the French had assembled a sizable army in Picardy in case Philip II decided to march on Paris. Once it became clear that Philip had no such intentions the French army decided to redeem a disappointing year by embarking upon some "enterprise": Calais was first mentioned on December 6 and by January 7 the town, poorly garrisoned and expecting no such threat, had surrendered.[156]

Earlier in 1557, the Venetian ambassador to London had recognized the importance of Calais to England as a "second frontier" (the first being against the Scots) and argued that, without Calais, England "would consequently lose what is essentially necessary for the existence of a country."[157] There was certainly a good deal of hankering for Calais throughout the Elizabethan period: Harley Manuscript 283 (in the British Library), for example, contains a "certyffycate" listing "persones dwelling in Callyce and Hames, as be well affected to the English Natyon."[158] Richard Hakluyt, in thinking of people who might be fed by cultivating land discovered by Martin Frobisher's "Northwest discouerie" of 1578, thinks "of a towne as big as Calice."[159] And it is worth noting that the Calais region long remained one of the strongholds of Protestantism in northern France.[160] But no serious plans for reconquest were laid and, as it turned out, the Venetian ambassador was quite wrong to suppose that without Calais, England "would not only be shut out from the continent, but also from the commerce and intercourse of the world" (p. xxv). Indeed, when viewed from longer historiographical perspectives, the losing of Calais may be read as integral to the rise of English fortunes. For as Braudel suggests, the *Calaisien* foothold forever enmeshed the English in the temptations of gigantism, those perennial battles against fellow European territorial powers that had absorbed so much blood and so many resources over two centuries (and would still be raging when Hogarth came to Calais). Once England had become (in Braudel's famous formulation) "an island," it was left to consolidate its own identity by attending to its other "borders" – Scotland, Wales, Ireland – and by expanding the reach of its sealanes south and west.[161] By 1589 Richard Hakluyt felt emboldened to boast that the English, "in searching the most opposite corners and quarters of the world, and to speake plainly, in compassing the vaste globe more than once, haue excelled all the nations and people of the earth."[162] Catholic Mary, the notorious "loser," might thus be rehabilitated – if we are still keeping score – as the only begetter of England as a global and imperial power: Duessa beats out Gloriana.[163]

But it is Shakespeare rather than Spenser who deserves the last word in this account of Calais and its historical importance. The plays in which Calais figures most prominently are *Henry V* and (perhaps a little more surprisingly) *Richard II*. It is in Calais (glossed by the Norton editor as "French port town") that Nim and Bardolph, "sworn brothers in filching," think to steal "a fire shovel."[164] More instructive, however, is the way that Shakespeare holds Calais and England punctiliously apart – we will proceed "to Calais," the victorious Henry V declares, "and to England then" (4.8.119) – and the way he stumbles at the Channel. Such stumbling – more pronounced in the would-be Shakespearean *Edward III* – is evidenced by the egregiously lengthy Prologue that opens Act V. "Now we bear the King," the Chorus says, "Towards Calais" (5.0.6–7). Once there, we are to immediately imagine him (for six full lines) crossing the Channel, to be acclaimed by "men, maids, wives, and boys." Once landed, he is brought to Blackheath and thence to London, where he enjoys the kind of triumph reserved for a conquering Roman emperor (and perhaps for a conquering English hero, Essex, about to return from Ireland with "rebellion broachèd on his sword," line 32). We are then to imagine the King in London (line 35); then engaged in a hurried "back-return again to France" (42); then finally – after fully 46 lines, back where we started, in France. All this is very odd and, of course, thoroughly undramatic; it suggests that the foreign victories of an English monarch can no longer be registered until they are, quite literally, brought home to an English public.

In *Richard II*, Calais is bad news, bad news structuring a play about political disaster: Acts I and IV (the first and second halves of most productions) begin with trials and challenges to combat over malfeasance – corruption and murder – committed just across the Channel. In Act I, Bolingbroke accuses Mowbray of embezzling 8,000 nobles, intended for payment of the garrison at Calais, which he has spent on "lewd employments, / Like a false traitor and injurious villain" (1.1.90–1). At the opening of Act IV, in proceedings now governed by Bolingbroke, Bagot accuses Aumerle of having boasted that his arm "reacheth from the restful English court / As far as Calais," where it chops off Gloucester's head (4.1.10–12). The insular logic informing all this is entirely consistent with the famous sentiments of the dying John of Gaunt: England will do well to conceive of itself as a "sceptred isle," as a "fortress built by nature for herself," as a "little world," a "precious stone set in the silver sea, / Which serves it in the office of a wall, / Or as a moat defensive to a house / Against the envy of less happier lands" (2.1.40–9). Calais – very likely the place where England's Virgin Queen was actually conceived – should, by this logic, be left to its own continental devices: a logic strengthened by the fact that from 1596 to 1598, Calais was in the hands of the Spanish. Whether through short-term calculation or visionary genius, then, Shakespeare views Calais as a hot spot needing to be dumped in pursuit of ambitions at once more local and global. Such logic harmonizes sweetly with Braudel's account of the loss of Calais as an accident, historically speaking, needing to happen.

The closing scene of Shakespeare's *Henry V*, which negotiates the union between the victorious English monarch and the French princess, looks both backwards and forwards. Peace, according to the Duke of Burgundy, has been too long absent from "this best garden of the world, / Our fertile France" (5.2.36–7). "Alas," he continues,

> ". . . she hath from France too long been chased,
> And all her husbandry doth lie on heaps,
> Corrupting in it own fertility.   *its*
> Her vine, the merry cheerer of the heart,
> Unprunèd dies; her hedges even-plashed
> Like prisoners wildly overgrown with hair
> Put forth disordered twigs; her fallow leas
> The darnel, hemlock, and rank fumitory
> Doth root upon, while that the coulter rusts
> That should deracinate such savagery."[165]
>
> *(5.2.38–47)*

This is a remarkably revisionary assessment of the ills of fifteenth-century France. For, as we have seen, the French countryside suffered not so much from the neglect of its landowners, riding to battle, as from the systematic destruction imposed by English *chevauchées* as a policy of war. Northern France has always been admired by the English (and by all Europe) as a fertile land; the idea that it needs the touch of a firm, seigneurial hand to be fruitful is a fanciful extravagance.[166] But such a notion is applied to other parts of the globe by the English after the loss of France: there are, it is imagined, fertile places whose fruitfulness can be realized by cultivated hands only through deracination of native "savagery." The verb *deracinate* appears only twice in Shakespeare: here it looks directly to its etymological root in *radix*, suggesting organic ties to the soil, while glancing sideways at other, complex, evolving senses of *race* (denoting differences of gender, descent, or status between various groups of living things).[167] Some Shakespearean usages of the term evoke medieval senses of *nacioun* or family tie, as in speaking of "the Nevilles' noble race" (*2 Henry VI*, 3.2.215); others drift between familial, ethnic, and statist terms of reference. But such a drift is not so great that Edward III's desire to *repeupler* the town of Calais and Burgundy's formula for deracinating the fields of France escape affiliation, for each sees *nativi* displaced or subjected to governing principles (and physical bodies) brought over from England. Except that, as we have noted, the fertile and unruly France of *Henry V*'s last act now stands in for territories and ambitions further afield. And here again, certain continuities of experience will link the "vile race" commanded by Prospero (and his historical surrogates) with medieval peasantry, the native people of the *vill*.[168]

Notes

1   What we see, precisely, are English leopards or *lions léopardés* and French fleurs-de-lys on separate escutcheons above the center gate, and the same motifs halved on escutcheons left and right. Edward III, conqueror of Calais, was the first monarch to quarter the Royal Arms of England with the French fleurs-de-lys: see *Historical Poems of the Fourteenth and Fifteenth Centuries*, ed. Rossell Hope Robbins (New York: Columbia University Press, 1959), p. 268.

2   See the photograph by Tim Bishop in *The Times*, April 28, 1989; Sidney Anglo, *Images of Tudor Kingship* (London: Seaby, 1992), p. 2. See further Eve Darian-Smith, *Bridging Divides: The Channel Tunnel and English Legal Identity in the New Europe* (Berkeley: University of California Press, 1999).

3   See H. A. Taine, *Histoire de la littérature anglaise*, 2nd edn., 4 vols (Paris: Hachette, 1866), I.5; Taine, *History of English Literature*, trans. H. Van Laun, 2 vols. (New York: Holt and Williams, 1871), I.25.

4   "It is the conception of the binding core of the English nation as the Anglo-Saxon race," Kwame Anthony Appiah writes, "that accounts for Taine's decision to identify the origins of English literature not in its antecedents in the Greek and Roman classics that provided the models and themes of so many of the best-known works of English 'poesy,' not in the Italian models that influenced the drama of Marlowe and Shakespeare, but in *Beowulf*, a poem in the Anglo-Saxon tongue, a poem that was unknown to Chaucer and Spenser and Shakespeare" ("Race," in *Critical Terms for Literary Study*, ed. Frank Lentricchia and Thomas McLaughlin, 2nd edn. (Chicago: University of Chicago Press), pp. 274–87 (p. 285). On "the need to emphasize the essentially Germanic origins of the English people and its institutions" that drove the accounts of nineteenth-century English historians, see Rees Davies, *The Matter of Britain and the Matter of England* (Oxford: Clarendon Press, 1996), p. 21.

Seamus Heaney, having meditated on northernness in his collection *North* (Oxford: Oxford University Press, 1976), later impishly laid his Celtic hands on the Ur-text of Saxonism: see *Beowulf*, trans. Seamus Heaney (London: Faber and Faber, 1999).

5   See chapter 4 below, p. 191.

6   The stone-kicker is, of course, Samuel Johnson.

7   Laurence Sterne, *A Sentimental Journey through France and Italy By Mr. Yorick*, ed. Ian Jack (Oxford: Oxford University Press, 1998), p. 3.

8   James Albany, *The Englishman's Guide to Calais, and thence by the route of Beauvais and Amiens to Paris, including an essay on colloquies and extracts from Froissart's Chronicles* (London, St. Paul's Churchyard: Hurst, Chance, 1829).

9   Hogarth's *The Shrimp Girl*, it is perhaps worth noting, is one of his most sensuous and vibrant paintings; it looks back to and extends established "street cries" traditions of English and European painting. See Jenny Uglow, *Hogarth: A Life and a World* (London: Faber and Faber, 1997), pp. 53, 408–9 and plate X.

10 On this past, see Eamon Duffy, *The Stripping of the Altars: Traditional Religion in England c.1400–c.1580* (New Haven: Yale University Press, 1992), pp. 166–9.

11 For an account of Hogarth behaving badly in France and Calais, see John Nichols, *Biographical Anecdotes of William Hogarth with a Catalogue of His Works*, 3rd edn. (London: John Nichols, 1785), pp. 49–50; Uglow, *Hogarth*, p. 464.

12 See "Calendar" in *Encyclopaedia Britannica*, 15th edn. (Chicago: Encyclopaedia Britannica, 2002), 15.417–34 (pp. 430b–432b). There was considerable sectarian resistance to this long-anticipated change: see for example John Willes, *The Julian and Gregorian Year, or, The difference betwixt the old and new-stile shewing, that the reformed churches should not alter their old-stile, but that the Romanists should return to it* (London: Printed for Richard Sare, 1700).

13 Nichols, *Biographical Anecdotes*, p. 50.

14 "There is," Hogarth continues, "a fair appearance still of the arms of England upon it" (quoted in Ronald Paulson, *Hogarth*, vol. 2, *High Art and Low, 1732–1750* (New Brunswick, NJ: Rutgers University Press, 1992), p. 353.

15 See Laurence Whistler, *Sir John Vanbrugh, Architect and Dramatist* (New York: Macmillan, 1939), pp. 22–3; Paulson, *High Art and Low*, pp. 445–6, n. 55.

16 See Paulson, *High Art and Low*, p. 55.

17 The painting was exhibited and reexhibited: in 1814, for example (the year of Napoleon's exile to and escape from Elba) it was on view at the British Gallery: see John Bowyer Nichols, *Anecdotes of William Hogarth, Written by Himself: with Essays on His Life and Genius*, etc. (London: J. B. Nichols and Son, 1833), p. 359.

18 *The Adventures of Peregrine Pickle*, ed. James L. Clifford (London: Oxford University Press, 1964), pp. 194, 195.

19 "An English historical painting," Iain Pears has argued, "challenged the public to live up to their patriotic words and pay as much for domestically produced works as for foreign ones" (*The Discovery of Painting: The Growth of Interest in the Arts in England, 1680–1768* (New Haven: Yale University Press, 1988), p. 125; see also Ronald Paulson, *Hogarth*, vol. 3, *Art and Politics, 1750–1764* (New Brunswick, NJ: Rutgers University Press, 1993), pp. 321–2. Hogarth resisted efforts to establish an Academy for painting in England; English painters (his canvas argues) have no need of such French-inspired affectations.

20 William Hogarth, *The Analysis of Beauty*, ed. Joseph Burke (Oxford: Clarendon Press, 1955), pp. 227–8.

21 See Suvir Kaul, *Poems of Nation, Anthems of Empire: English Verse in the Long Eighteenth Century* (Charlottesville: University Press of Virginia, 2000).

22 James Albany's *Englishman's Guide to Calais* (cited above) advertises (in its title) "*Extracts from Froissart's Chronicles.*" The extent to which Froissart's *Chronicles* shaped English views of European medieval history through countless schoolboy editions can hardly be exaggerated. F. Carruthers Gould, in his *Froissart's Modern Chronicles* (London: T. Fisher Unwin, 1902), gives an illustrated account of the battle for Irish Home Rule featuring Sir Stuart de Parnell and Sir Gladstone Le Grand.

23 The copy of Rodin's statue may still be found in Victoria Tower Gardens, close by statues of Emmeline (1930) and Christabel (1959) Pankhurst.

24 See *The Historia Regum Brittaniae of Geoffrey of Monmouth*, ed. Acton Griscom (London: Longmans, 1929); Lawman, *Brut*, trans. Rosamund Allen (London: J. M. Dent, 1992); Andrew Galloway, "Writing History in England," in *The Cambridge History of Medieval English Literature*, ed. David Wallace (Cambridge: Cambridge University Press, 1999), pp. 255–83.

25 "As the westernmost tip of the Empire adjoining France," Juliet Vale writes, "Hainault's geographical position helped ensure widespread diffusion of French literary and artistic influences within the county" (*Edward III and Chivalry: Chivalric Society and its Context, 1270–1350* [Woodbridge: Boydell Press, 1982],

p. 44). "While [Froissart's] birthplace lay near to territory ruled by the Kings of France and his language was French," Geoffrey Brereton remarks, "his nationality was not" ("Introduction" to Froissart, *Chronicles*, ed. and trans. Brereton [Harmondsworth: Penguin, 1968], p. 10).

26 See Jean Froissart, *Voyage en Béarn*, ed. A. H. Diverres (Manchester: Manchester University Press, 1953), p. 112; Anthony Goodman, *John of Gaunt: The Exercise of Princely Power in Fourteenth-Century Europe* (New York: St. Martin's Press, 1992), pp. 193–4.

27 Conveniently available in Froissart, *Chronicles*, trans. Brereton, pp. 409–17.

28 See Peter F. Ainsworth, *Jean Froissart and the Fabric of History: Truth, Myth, and Fiction in the* Chroniques (Oxford: Clarendon Press, 1990), pp. 38–47, 87–90, 296–7 (the "Calais Gate" episode); Paule Mertens-Fonck, "Un chroniqueur Liègois sur la route de Canterbury," *Bulletin de la Société Royale le Vieux-Liège* 13 (1997), 707–18. The well-dressed canon satirized for his knightly and venereal inclinations by Jacques de Hemricourt's *Le Miroir des Nobles de Hesbaye* resembles Le Bel and, Merten-Fonck shows, compares suggestively with the Monk of Chaucer's *General Prologue*.

29 *The Chronicle of Froissart. Translated out of French by Sir John Bourchier, Lord Berners*, ed. William Paton Ker, 6 vols. (London: David Nutt, 1901–3), I, p. xv. Unless otherwise indicated, translations from Froissart follow the text of Berners (a text of considerable literary interest in its own right, not to be mistaken for a literal translation). Textual relationships between various manuscripts of Froissart are complex; unless otherwise indicated, my citations follow *Chroniques. Livre I (première partie, 1325–1350) et Livre II. Rédaction du manuscrit de New York Pierpont Morgan Library M. 804*, ed. Peter F. Ainsworth and George T. Diller (Paris: Le Livre de Poche, 2001).

30 "Translatour's Prologue," from *The hystory of the moost noble and valyaunt knyght Arthur of lytell britayne*, published ca. 1534 (probably by Wynkyn de Worde) as cited in Froissart, *Chronicle*, introd. Ker, p. xviii. Berners also made several translations from Spanish texts.

31 See Jean Froissart, *Méliador. Roman comprenant les poésies lyriques de Wenceslas de Bohême, duc de Luxembourg et de Brabant*, ed. Auguste Longnon, Société des anciens textes français, 3 vols. (Paris: Firmin Didot, 1895–9); Peter F. Dembowski, *Jean Froissart and his* Meliador: *Context, Craft, and Sense* (Lexington, Kentucky: French Forum Publishers, 1983). On Froissart's debt to antecedent traditions of romance, chronicle, and history, see Ainsworth, *Fabric of History*, pp. 23–50.

32 See Helen Cooper, "Romance after 1400," in *The Cambridge History of Medieval Literature*, ed. Wallace, pp. 690–719; Andrew King, *The* Faerie Queen *and Middle English Romance: The Matter of Just Memory* (Oxford: Clarendon Press, 2000).

33 It is worth remembering that the Order of the Garter, *the* model for future chivalric orders, evolved during the period between Crécy and the taking of Calais: see Juliet Vale, *Edward III and Chivalry: Chivalric Society and its Context 1270–1350* (Woodbridge: Boydell and Brewer, 1982), pp. 81–2.

34 Analogous conflicts were, of course, acted out between London and Westminster throughout this period: it would be rash to assume that the sym-
pathies of Londoners were necessarily invested in the English king.

35 See Vale, *Edward III and Chivalry*, pp. 76–91. Almost all the founding Garter
knights had fought at Crécy, the great English victory immediately preceding
the siege of Calais (p. 86).

36 Henry V cleared the townspeople, recruited English immigrants, and (so
fifteenth-century sources claim) burned the muniments of the town and its
inhabitants' title deeds in the market place; according to Jacques du Clerq,
some 1,500 English inhabitants left (not all returning to England) when the
town passed to the French king 35 years later: see Paul Strohm, *England's
Empty Throne: Usurpation and the Language of Legitimation, 1399–1422* (New
Haven: Yale University Press, 1998), pp. 1–2. For the argument that the
"stuffing" of Calais with a substitute English population provided a precedent
for Henry V's policies at Harfleur, see C. T. Allmand, *Lancastrian Normandy:
The History of a Medieval Occupation* (Oxford: Clarendon Press, 1983), pp. 50–1.

37 To a daughter, called Margaret of Calais (1347–69).

38 Froissart, *Chroniques. Début du premier livre. Edition du manuscrit de Rome Reg.
lat. 869*, ed. George T. Diller (Geneva: Droz, 1972), p. 840; Ainsworth, *Fabric of
History*, p. 298.

39 For a superb account of the shift "from a truth that resides in people to one
located in documents," see Richard Firth Green, *A Crisis of Truth: Literature
and Law in Ricardian England* (Philadelphia: University of Pennsylvania Press,
1999), pp. 41–164 and *passim*.

40 *The Brut. Edited from MS Rawlinson B 171*, ed. Frederick W. D. Brie, Part II,
Early English Text Society, os 136 (London: EETS, 1908), p. 300.

41 "Tu scès," Edward tells Aymeris, "que je t'ay donnet en garde la riens ou
monde que plus ayme apriès ma femme et mes enfans, le chastiel et le ville de
Calais" (p. 654).

42 "Et s'i enclina, pour tant que cilz Aymeris estoit Lombars, et Lombart sont de
leur nature convoiteus" (p. 654).

43 See John Le Patourel, "L'occupation anglaise de Calais au XIVe siècle," *Revue
du Nord* 33 (1951), 228–41 (pp. 228–30); Dorothy Greaves, "Calais under Edward
III," in *Finance and Trade under Edward III* (Manchester: Manchester University
Press, 1918), pp. 313–50 (pp. 314–15, 337); Henri Platelle and Denis Clauzel,
*Histoire des provinces françaises du Nord, II: Des principautés à l'empire de Charles-
Quint* (Dunkirk: Westhoek-Editions, 1989), pp. 150–4.

44 "The English diaspora within the British Isles may have been seignorially led,"
Davies remarks, "but it was demographically and economically determined"
(*The First English Empire: Power and Identities in the British Isles 1093–1343*
[Oxford: Oxford University Press, 2000], p. 149). See further *The British Isles
1100–1500: Comparisons, Contrasts and Connections*, ed. R. R. Davies (Edinburgh:
John Donald, 1988).

45 Michelle Warren, *History on the Edge: Excalibur and the Borders of Britain* (Minneapolis: University of Minnesota Press, 2000), p. 3. For a brief but cogent comparison of events in Calais with impositions of English communities in Wales and southern Scotland, see Allmand, *Lancastrian Normandy*, pp. 50–1.

46 Calais is thus configured with the palatinates of Chester, Durham, and Lancaster; with the dominions of Gascony and the Channel Islands; with the principality of Wales and its Marches; with Ireland, and the Isle of Man. For the argument that tensions between the English center and these peripheral territories had much to do with the Wars of the Roses, see Ralph A. Griffiths, "The Provinces and the Dominions in the Age of the Wars of the Roses," in *Estrangement, Enterprise and Education in Fifteenth-Century England*, ed. Sharon D. Michalove and A. Compton Reeves (Stroud, Gloucestershire: Alan Sutton, 1998), pp. 1–25.

47 See Alain Derville, "Une ville vers 1300: Calais," *Revue du Nord* 72 (1990), 737–56. Derville estimates the population of Calais to have been between 13,000 and 15,000 by 1300; this made it the third largest town in Artois (and a very large town by contemporary English standards): see Derville, "Calais avant 1347: La vie d'un port," *Revue du Nord*, special extra-series volume, 1 (1986), 189–213 (p. 190). Alain Joblin estimates a population of approximately 15,000 for the region made up by Calais, Gravelines, and Guînes around 1700; Calais itself had 5,000 inhabitants ("Le protestantisme en Calais aux XVIe–XVIIe siècles," *Revue du Nord* 80 (July–December 1998), 599–618 (p. 600).

48 Text and translation follow Machaut, *The Fountain of Love (La Fointeinne amoureuse)*, ed. and trans. R. Barton Palmer (New York: Garland, 1993). See also Jacques Le Goff, "Reims, City of Coronation," in Nora et al., *Realms of Memory*, 3.193–251.

49 Platelle and Clauzel, *Histoire*, p. 151. The head count includes Calais and its satellite towns: some 320 men at Ardres and others at places such as Guines, Marck, and Sangatte. Such numbers "font de Calais un phénomène presque unique de concentration des troupes en Europe" (p. 151).

50 See the remarkable collection of essays in *Les champs relationnels en Europe du Nord et du Nord-Ouest des origines à la fin du Premier Empire: 1er Colloque Européen de Calais*, ed. Stéphane Curveiller (Calais: La Municipalité de Calais, 1994). In "The Bowge of Court," Ryote swears [by] "The arms of Calyce, I have no coyne nor crosse!" (John Skelton, *Poems*, ed. Robert S. Kinsman [Oxford: Clarendon Press, 1969], line 398); fifteenth-century English coins, Kinsman notes, were often marked with a cross on the reverse side (p. 142). Countenance swears "By the arms of Calais" in *Magnificence*, line 675 (ed. Paula Neuss [Baltimore, Md.: Johns Hopkins University Press, 1980]).

51 Alain Derville writes of Calais before 1347 as "le centre actif et peuplé d'une petite région riche et populeuse"; after 1347 it becomes "une ville coloniale, une ville de garnison tremblant de peur au côuer d'un pays dépeuplé, parfois devasté, toujours manacé." And yet between 1347 and 1558, he continues (in

comparable hyperbolic vein), Calais becomes a town to reckon with across Europe: "l'histoire de Calis, c'est d'abord l'histoire générale de l'Europe" (*Histoire de Calais*, ed. Derville and Albert Vion [Dunkirk: Westhoek, 1985], p. 55).

52   See Geneviève Moll, *Yvonne de Gaulle: L'Inattendue* (Paris: Éditions Ramsay, 1999), p. 37 (for the wedding reception menu); Christine Clerc, *Les de Gaulle: Une famille française* (Paris: NiL éditions, 2000) (featuring the epigraph, from a 1916 letter from Charles to his father Henri, "Notre chère et vaillante famille, parcelle de nostre glorieuse patrie"); Philippe Ratte, *De Gaulle: La vie, la légende* (Paris: Larousse, 2000), p. 29.

53   It is remarkable to note, for example, how continuously well informed the Benedictines at York were about various aspects of Calais. In 1376, a knight visiting their chapter house speaks of (assumes their prior knowledge of) "lestaple des layns et autres marchandys . . . a Kalays": see *The Anonimalle Chronicle, 1333 to 1381. From a MS. Written at St. Mary's Abbey, York*, ed. V. H. Galbraith (Manchester: Manchester University Press, 1970), p. 81, but see *passim* too.

54   See *Les Cent Nouvelles Nouvelles*, ed. Pierre Champion (Geneva: Slatkine Reprints, 1977), pp. 180–5; *The One Hundred New Tales (Les Cent Nouvelles Nouvelles)*, trans. Judith Bruskin Diner (New York: Garland, 1990), pp. 234–8.

55   See *Charles d'Orléans in England, 1415–1440*, ed. Mary-Jo Arn (Rochester, NY: D. S. Brewer, 2000); A. E. B Coldiron, *Canon, Period, and the Poetry of Charles of Orleans* (Ann Arbor: University of Michigan Press, 2000).

56   The tales to come, we are told, are set in "parties de France, d'Alemaigne, d'Angleterre, de Haynau, de Brabant et aultres lieux."

57   Sir Thomas Wyatt, *The Complete Poems*, ed. R. A. Rebholz (New Haven: Yale University Press, 1981), LV.4 (p. 96); Kenneth Muir, *Life and Letters of Sir Thomas Wyatt* (Liverpool: Liverpool University Press, 1963), pp. 23–4.

58   See *The Book of Margery Kempe*, ed. Sanford Brown Meech and Hope Emily Allen, Early English Text Society, os 212 (London: Oxford University Press for EETS, 1940), pp. 239–41 (and see chapter 2 below, pp. 95–6).

59   The Middle English *Sir Eglamour*, a tail-rhyme romance dating from the late fourteenth century, has no discernible French antecedents. "Artois" is not viewed as an exotic or indeed exotic-sounding location in this poem: indeed, it rhymes with *was* and *place* and the manuscript evidence suggests it should properly be entitled *Eglamour of Artas*. See *Sir Eglamour of Artois*, ed. Frances E. Richardson, Early English Text Society, os 256 (London: Oxford University Press for EETS, 1965), pp. ix–xliii. The father of Chaucer's Sir Thopas was born not far from here: see chapter 2 below.

60   See John Keegan, *The Face of Battle* (London: Jonathan Cape, 1976). Archers are celebrated in a broadside entitled "Agincourt, or the English Bowman's Glory": but this dates from 1665, a much later phase of the complex afterlife of the 1415 battle. See Anne Curry, *The Battle of Agincourt: Sources and Interpretations* (Woodbridge: Boydell Press, 2000), pp. 302–4. In his *History of the Battle*

of Agincourt (London: Johnson, 1832), Sir Harris Nicholas, K. H., includes an extensive listing of retinues, pp. 331–404.

61   See *Chaucer Life-Records*, ed. Martin M. Crow and Clair C. Olson (Oxford: Clarendon Press, 1966), pp. 23–8.

62   *The Hundred Years' War: England and France at War c.1300–c.1450* (Cambridge: Cambridge University Press, 1988), p. 56; *Chaucer Life-Records*, p. 27. See further the excellent account of Nicholas Wright, *Knights and Peasants: The Hundred Years' War in the French Countryside* (Woodbridge: Boydell Press, 1998), pp. 68–9. It is argued that a typical radius of burning and destruction was five leagues (about 20 kilometers) either side of the main body of the army. Such an army "depended almost entirely on its foragers" (p. 69).

63   Chaucer was to meet up with some of this soldiery during his two visits to Italy in the 1370s.

64   William Langland, *The Vision of Piers Plowman. A Critical Edition of the B-Text based on Trinity College Cambridge MS B.15.17*, 2nd edn., ed. A. V. C. Schmidt (London: Everyman, 1995), B 3.210–11. I here prefer the reading "mede to men" to Schmidt's "[men mede]"; the former reading appears in all B MSS. For texts of A and C, I follow *Piers Plowman: The A Version. Will's Vision of Piers Plowman and Do-Well. An Edition in the Form of Trinity College Cambridge MS R.3.14 Corrected from Other Manuscripts, With Variant Readings*, ed. George Kane, rev. edn. (London: Athlone Press, 1988); William Langland, *Piers Plowman. An Edition of the C-text*, ed. Derek Pearsall (London: Edward Arnold, 1978).

65   The question of Langland's attitude to the continental campaigns deserves further reflection. Even if (as a poet finely attuned to the delicate mechanisms of the rural economy) Langland knew little of the English ruination of the French and Flemish countryside, he would have known of the wide-ranging royal agents who raised money and supplies, and of "the demobilized troops who often continued the habits of violence and pillage picked up on active service in enemy territory" (W. M. Ormrod, "The Domestic Response to the Hundred Years' War," in *Arms, Armies and Fortifications in the Hundred Years' War*, ed. Anne Curry and Michael Hughes [Woodbridge: Boydell Press, 1994], pp. 83–101 [p. 86]).

66   See Froissart, *Chronycle*, trans. Berners, II.59 ("suche a tempest of thonder, lyghtnyng, rayne, and hayle, in the kinges oost, that it semed that the worlde shulde have ended" (a translation very close to the wording of French sources); *Piers Plowman*, B 3.191; see also A 3.178. By all contemporary accounts (Jonathan Sumption cites seven), this was a spectacular storm: the English army was caught in open country; many men and horses died (Sumption, *The Hundred Years' War*, 3 vols. (Philadelphia: University of Pennsylvania Press, 1990–), II.443, 623 n. 73; see further Andrew Ayton, "English Armies in the Fourteenth Century," in *Arms, Armies*, ed. Curry and Hughes, pp. 21–38 (pp. 21–2).

67   These lines are not present in A. Bennett surmises that B 3.194–202, referring to a later phase of continental pillaging, were inserted during revision. See Langland, *Piers Plowman. The Prologue and Passus I–VII of the B Text as found in*

Bodleian MS. Laud Misc. 581, ed. J. A. W. Bennett (Oxford: Clarendon Press, 1972), p. 139.

68 King John II of France, imprisoned in London, signed the Treaty at a banquet in the Tower on June 14, 1360. He was transferred to Calais on July 8, but was only released – following slow French fund-raising efforts – on October 24 (when the Treaty of Brétigny, with amendments, was ratified by Kings Edward and John). See John Palmer, "The War Aims of the Protagonists and the Negotiations for Peace," in *The Hundred Years' War*, ed. Kenneth Fowler (London: Macmillan, 1971), pp. 59–60; Sumption, *Hundred Years' War*, II.445–54.

69 Hostilities broke out again in 1369. Putative dates for the composition of *Piers Plowman* seem to be getting earlier: in 1978, Pearsall had A "still being revised and rewritten in 1369–70," with B "mainly assigned to the 1370s" and C "probably complete by 1387" (*Piers Plowman*, p. 9).

70 Conversely, we might meditate further on how the military and economic practices of the continental war return to trouble the rural settings of Langland's poem. See Ormrod, "The Domestic Response to the Hundred Years' War," in *Arms, Armies*, ed. Curry and Hughes, p. 86.

71 "Mynstrales and messagers," it is said, once met up with Lyere "And [with]helden hym half a yeer and ellevene days" (B 2.229: here I accept Schmidt's emendation, since the term *withholden* can imply the joining of a household and the taking of a livery). See further A 2.185–90 ("And withheld him"); C 2.237–8. Half a year and eleven days measures the exact duration of Edward III's French campaign, from his landing on October 28, 1359, to the signing at Brétigny on May 8, 1360: see J. A. W. Bennett, "The Date of the A-text of *Piers Plowman*," *PMLA* 58 (1943), 566–72.

72 B 3.228; see also A 3.215–16. Anna P. Baldwin, in reviewing past accounts of Langland's poem as moral critique, asks some good questions: "Why is Meed a noblewoman, the kinswoman of the king, if she represents only a moral threat? Why does her own defence of her activities to Conscience in Passus III have so much to do with war?" See *The Theme of Government in Piers Plowman* (Cambridge: D. S. Brewer, 1981), p. 25.

73 Oure horses, that war faire and fat,
    er etin up ikone bidene;   *everyone together*
    have we nowther conig ne cat   *rabbit*
    that thai ne er etin and hundes kene.   *fearless dogs*
    All er etin up ful clene;
    es nowther levid biche ne whelp–   *left bitch nor pup*
    that es wele on oure sembland sene– *seen by our appearance*
    and thai er fled that suld us help.

Text (and most marginal glosses) from *The Poems of Laurence Minot, 1333–1352*, ed. Richard H. Osberg (Kalamazoo, Mich.: Medieval Institute Publications, 1996), p. 58 (lines 73–6).

74 *Rethinking France*, p. xxxviii.

75 Eustache Deschamps, *Oeuvres complètes*, ed. Auguste Henri Edouard Queux de Saint-Hilaire and Gaston Raynaud. Societé des Anciens Textes Français, 11 vols. (Paris: Firmin-Didot, 1878–1903), item 344, lines 10, 20, 30, 40, 50, 56. All references will be given from this edition in this format. Volume 11 of this edition contains a useful "Vie de Deschamps" (pp. 9–99). Navigation of the Deschamps corpus has been greatly eased of late, however, by the excellent biographical essay of I. S. Laurie, "Eustache Deschamps: 1340?–1404," in *Eustache Deschamps, French Courtier-Poet: His Work and his World*, ed. Deborah M. Sinnreich-Lévi (New York: AMS Press, 1998), pp. 1–72. See further, for an anthology of Deschamps' work with excellent commentary, *Eustache Deschamps en son temps*, ed. Jean-Patrice Boudet and Hélène Millet (Paris: Publications de la Sorbonne, 1997).

76 See Nicholas Wright, *Knights and Peasants*, pp. 69, 101. A stairway leading from the church tower at Hermies (Pas-de-Calais) leads to a vast complex of some 300 subterranean cells.

77 On the endurance of "the feudal mode of production in which agriculture is still the basis of production" into the French eighteenth century, see Pierre Vilar, "Constructing Marxist history," in *Constructing the Past: Essays in Historical Methodology*, ed. Jacques Le Goff and Pierre Nora (Cambridge: Cambridge University Press, 1985), pp. 47–80 (p. 65). As the essays in this volume demonstrate, French historiography contemplates many different cycles and timescales at work (to different social and economic effects).

78 "Les autres mois vueil faire ma besonge" (1047: 8, 16, 24, 28).

79 A suspicion neatly anticipated by the poem's *envoy* (lines 25–8).

80 See Laurie, "Deschamps," pp. 1–2.

81 Thomas Kelly suggests that Deschamps is here riffing on his name, Eustache Morel, "Eustache the Moor," a name accorded to him "on account of his dark complexion": "Deschamps, Eustache," *Dictionary of the Middle Ages*, ed. Joseph R. Strayer, 12 vols. (New York: Scribner's, 1982–9), 4.163–4 (p. 163).

82 See Laurie, "Deschamps," p. 19.

83 The ballade thus floats between three chivalric generations, all killed in the Anglo-French conflict. See Froissart, *Oeuvres*, 1.330–2.

84 On the "crushing" Christian defeat and its long-term consequences, see Norman Housley, *The Later Crusades: From Lyon to Alcazar, 1274–1580* (Oxford: Oxford University Press, 1992), pp. 75–8 (p. 77). Enguerrand actually died in captivity in February 1397 as his ransom was being arranged; see John Bell Henneman, "Enguerrand VII of Coucy (1340–1397)," in *Dictionary of the Middle Ages*, ed. Strayer, 4.490–1.

85 See May McKisack, *The Fourteenth Century. 1307–1399* (Oxford: Clarendon Press, 1959), p. 268; Malcolm Vale, *War and Chivalry: War and Aristocratic Culture in England, France, and Burgundy at the End of the Middle Ages* (Athens: University of Georgia Press, 1981), p. 34.

86   On the founding of this order on April 26, 1390, see ballade 212, rondeaux 655, 656, and Laurie, "Deschamps," p. 22; on the famed origins of the Coucy family arms in the first crusade, see Maurice Keen, *Chivalry* (New Haven: Yale University Press, 1984), p. 131.

87   See ballade 883 (which opens with a typical roundup of towns encircling Calais): "Guynes, Hames, Merc, Sangattes, Calays, / Oye et Puille, qui nous faittes frontiere, / Finerons nous de guerroier jamais? / Tout est destruit en plain et en costiere" (1–4). Usage of the term *frontière* in Deschamps (and Froissart) seals a shift from the more concrete sense of the thirteenth century (indicating a "front d'une armée" or a particular fortified place, facing the enemy) to a more abstract sense of territorial limit or boundary.

88   Such is the argument of Dembowski, *Jean Froissart*, pp. 139–44. The Knight of Chaucer's *General Prologue*, famously, had been honored in "Pruce" and "reysed" (gone raiding) in Lithuania and Russia (1.53–4).

89   See Laurie, "Deschamps," p. 2 and ballades 803, 1199; *Eustache Deschamps*, ed. Boudet and Millet, p. 10. Ballades 772, 773, and 803 tell how, on a different occasion (possibly the failed invasion of England), Deschamps was beaten, paraded backwards on a horse, and put in irons by young nobles resenting the excessive cheek of his satire.

90   See ballades 128, 191. Deschamps later jousted at a Prague tournament in 1397 when he was well into his fifties (and managed to pick up an eye injury); on this "grotesque" exercise, see Laurie, "Deschamps," and rondeau 1321.

91   On estates satire, see Deschamps, *Oeuvres*, 804, 908, 909, 910, 912, 913, 1022, 1205, 1217, 1285, 1389, 1404, 1492; Jill Mann, *Chaucer and Medieval Estates Satire* (Cambridge: Cambridge University Press, 1973). Deschamps presented his *De miseria* translation as *Double lay de la fragilité humaine* to Charles VI on April 18, 1383: see Deschamps, 309, and Laurie, "Deschamps," pp. 14 and 47 n. 65. On Chaucer's (lost) translation of this text, see *Legend of Good Women*, G 414–15 and Lotario de Segni, *De miseria condicionis humane*, ed. and trans. Robert E. Lewis, Chaucer Library (Athens: University of Georgia Press, 1978).

92   Deschamps was dispatched on a diplomatic mission to Bohemia and Moravia in 1397; his experiences at Prague and elsewhere are described in 11 poems (see Laurie, "Deschamps," pp. 25–6). On Chaucer's Bohemian connections, see Alfred Thomas, *Anne's Bohemia: Czech Literature and Society, 1310–1420* (Minneapolis: University of Minnesota Press, 1998); David Wallace, *Chaucerian Polity* (Stanford, Calif: Stanford University Press, 1997), pp. 357–64.

93   See Laurie, "Deschamps," pp. 1–6, 21; Wallace, *Chaucerian Polity*, p. 45. The marriage was not celebrated until 1389; Valentina processed into Paris on August 22, 1389.

94   Ballade 771.10, 20, 30. The motto "à bon droyt" is boldly employed by the artists of the celebrated *Visconti Hours*: see Wallace, *Chaucerian Polity*, pp. 45–51 (and plate 2d).

95   Chaucer "passed at Dover" on July 17, 1368, and could have been out of the
     country for up to 106 days. He might have gone only as far as Calais, where
     Henry le Scrope had recently assumed governorship, or he might (easily, in
     this time frame) have traveled to Italy. See *Life-Records*, ed. Crow and Olson,
     pp. 30–1.

96   See ballade 170.14; ballade 1274.8.

97   For alternative terms of abuse heaped on Flanders by Deschamps, see ballades
     16, 17, 19. On 16.4, which associates the "mauvais pueple" of Flanders with
     the sins of Sodom and Gomorrah; see p. 112 below.

98   It is worth noting, with Kenneth Fowler, that more than half the years
     between 1337 and 1453 saw periods of truce. 1360–9 saw the period of incom-
     pletely ratified peace following Brétigny; between 1337 and 1400 there were
     29 years of general and 7 of local truce, and 18 years of major campaigns. See
     "Truces," in *The Hundred Years' War*, ed. Fowler, pp. 184–215 (p. 184).

99   The phrase *Angli caudate* is found in twelfth-century Latin texts; in the first
     continental redaction of *Bueve de Hantone*, tailed English children issue from
     the union of the French giant Açopart and an English bride. See Peter Rickard,
     "*Anglois coué* and *l'Anglois qui couve*," *French Studies* 7 (1953), 48–55 (pp. 48–9);
     Rickard, *Britain in Medieval French Literature 1100–1500* (Cambridge: Cambridge
     University Press, 1956), pp. 165–6. Deschamps makes further use of this tradi-
     tion in rondeau 671 and (to obscene effect) ballade 868.

100 In 1382 Deschamps was accused of exploiting his powers as "huissier d'armes"
     to prevent a rival in a property claim from entering the courts. Shortly there-
     after he persuaded or coerced the inhabitants of Fismes into making him
     the master of the local leprosarium. In 1393, following the death of Blanche,
     duchess of Orléans, Deschamps went on a tour to secure properties for the
     widowed duke. See Laurie, "Deschamps," pp. 11, 13, 23.

101 "De tel amour ma mort me cuide" (27).

102 Oton de Granson was in the service of John of Gaunt from 1374 to 1386. He
     seems likely to have met Deschamps in the spring of 1375 during a phase
     of knightly feasting that saw Deschamps deliver a presentation copy of
     Machaut's *Voir Dit* to Louis de Mâle at Bruges. See Joyce Coleman, "The Text
     Recontextualized in Performance: Deschamps' Prelection of Machaut's *Voir
     Dit* to the Count of Flanders," *Viator* 31 (2000), 233–48 (pp. 235–6).

103 See Haldeen Braddy, *Chaucer and the French Poet Graunson* (Baton Rouge:
     Louisiana State University Press, 1947), pp. 22–3; *The Riverside Chaucer*,
     p. 1081. The work of Arthur Piaget, *Oton de Grandson: Sa vie et ses poésies*
     (Lausanne: Payot, 1941) is still valuable.

104 This compliment is rendered by the closing line of the poem known as *The
     Complaint of Venus*, a translation of a triple ballade by Granson (that was some-
     times treated by medieval scribes as a continuation of the poem known as *The
     Complaint of Mars*). For the best text of Granson's poem, see James I. Wimsatt,
     Chaucer and the Poems of "Ch" (Cambridge: D. S. Brewer, 1982), pp. 69–74. On

the Granson/Chaucer relationship, see Wimsatt, *Chaucer and His French Contemporaries: Natural Music in the Fourteenth Century* (Toronto: University of Toronto Press, 1991), pp. 234–41.

105 For a fine account of this ballade (as "a valuable contribution to our understanding of Chaucer's social and literary world"), see Glending Olson, "Geoffrey Chaucer," in *The Cambridge History of Medieval English Literature*, ed. Wallace, pp. 566–88 (p. 566). For a fine analysis of Deschamps' ballade, viewed within a full account of Deschamps' poetic corpus, see Wimsatt, *French Contemporaries*, pp. 242–72.

106 From the diary of Cardinal Guillaume Filastre (*licenciatus in legibus* at the University of Paris, 1382; dean of Reims cathedral, 1392) in *The Council of Constance*, trans. L. R. Loomis, ed. J. H. Mundy and K. M. Woody (New York: Columbia University Press, 1961), pp. 200–465 (p. 317).

107 For the view that Chaucer "must have made the first move" in this exchange, see William Calin, "Deschamps' 'Ballade to Chaucer' Again, or the Dangers of Intertextual Medieval Comparatism," in *Deschamps*, ed. Sinnreich-Lévi, pp. 73–83 (p. 76). All translations from the text of this ballade follow the text of Calin (p. 75).

108 See Wimsatt, *French Contemporaries*, p. 251; Ardis Butterfield, *Poetry and Music in Medieval France: From Jean Renart to Guillaume de Machaut* (Cambridge: Cambridge University Press, 2002), pp. 291–2.

109 On "belling the cat" as a metaphor for the French invasion of England, see Deschamps 58 (where the refrain runs "Qui pendra la sonnette au chat?"); 1085.13–15. For other poems associated with French invasion plans in this period, see 8, 48, 58, 62 (a morale-boosting ballade for the fleet, now embarked), 211, 228, 445, 822, 847, 848, 854, 1040, 1059, 1060, 1145; and see Laurie, "Deschamps," pp. 17–19.

110 See *Eustache Deschamps*, ed. Boudet and Millet, p. 162.

111 See *The Book of Margery Kempe*, ed. S. B. Meech and E. H. Allen, Early English Text Society, os 212 (London: Oxford University Press for EETS, 1940; reprint, Woodbridge: Boydell and Brewer, 1997), pp. 66–73.

112 See Derek Pearsall, "The Idea of Englishness in the Fifteenth Century," in *Nation, Court and Culture*, ed. Helen Cooney (Dublin: Four Courts Press, 2000), pp. 15–27 (p. 25).

113 "Deschamps est le premier grand poète français de la ville" (*Eustache Deschamps*, ed. Boudet and Millet, p. 165, with acknowledgment of the work of Jacqueline Cerquiglini-Toulet).

114 It is quite reasonable to anticipate that Chaucer himself (as a fluent French speaker, deeply read in French courtly tradition) would have been warmly welcomed into the company of French poets anywhere. It is perhaps worth noting that when Charles d'Orléans left England, having labored for so long on poems in English and French, he took the French poems with him and left the English ones behind. See Mary-Jo Arn, "Two Manuscripts, One Mind:

Charles d'Oréans and the Production of Manuscripts in Two Languages (Paris, BN MS fr. 25458 and London, BL MS Harley 682)," in *Charles d'Orléans in England*, ed. Arne (Cambridge: D. S. Brewer, 2000), pp. 61–78 (p. 76).

115   See David Aers, "*Vox populi* and the literature of 1381," in *The Cambridge History of Medieval English Literature*, ed. Wallace, pp. 432–53 (pp. 441–2); Steven Justice, *Writing and Rebellion: England in 1381* (Berkeley: University of California Press, 1994), chapter 5.

116   See Spruyt, *The Sovereign State and its Competitors: An Analysis of Systems Change* (Princeton, NJ: Princeton University Press, 1994), pp. 61–7; Michael M. Postan, "The Trade of Medieval Europe: the North," in *The Cambridge Economic History of Europe*, vol. II, 2nd edn., *Trade and Industry in the Middle Ages*, ed. Postan and Edward Miller (Cambridge: Cambridge University Press, 1987), pp. 168–305 (p. 183); Jacques Bernard, "Trade and Finance in the Middle Ages, 900–1500," in *The Fontana Economic History of Europe*, vol. I, *The Middle Ages*, ed. Carlo M. Cipolla (Hassocks: Harvester Press, 1976), pp. 274–338 (p. 299).

117   See Wallace, *Chaucerian Polity*, pp. 11–40, 62–4.

118   See Wimsatt, *French Contemporaries*, pp. xi–xii.

119   The Penn MS contains 310 neatly copied French lyrics: see Wimsatt, *Poems of "Ch"*. On the altogether more eclectic British Library MS Harley 2253, see Derek Pearsall, *Old English and Middle English Poetry* (London: Routledge and Kegan Paul, 1977), pp. 120–32.

120   Deschamps actually wrote a rondeau on the subject of crossing the border – formed by the river Lys – between Flanders and "ce doulz pais de France" (548.3).

121   *The Parliament of Fowls*, 677. If there is a questioning of this ethos in Chaucer, it is surely most forcefully supplied by Chaucer's Franklin, a character of indeterminate social status floating somewhere below aristocratic *otium* and above mercantile activity. His tale is set in ancient times, yet plays out across a territory – Brittany – that was being fought over by French and English forces even as Chaucer wrote (see Deschamps, ballades 211, 822). One male protagonist, a knight, feels the need to travel to England to test his prowess; this precipitates a crisis of *trouthe* requiring the kind of fairytale ending that the tale's genre allows (but that the tale's practically minded narrator, the English Franklin, clearly does not believe in). For a poem expressing the regret of a lady at the departure of her husband, who is about to cross the sea and seek renown in England, see Deschamps, ballade 1040: "De son retour suy en trop grant doubtance," 1040.7.

122   *The Libelle of Englyshe Polycye: a poem on the use of sea-power, 1436*, ed. Sir George Frederic Warner (Oxford: Clarendon Press, 1926), lines 20–1.

123   Ayton, "English Armies," p. 37; David Iain Grummitt, *Calais 1485–1547: A Study in Early Tudor Government and Politics*, University of London Ph.D. thesis (February 1997), pp. 33–48.

124 See *The Earliest English Translation of Vegetius' De Re Militari, from Oxford MS Bodl. Douce 291*, ed. Geoffrey Lester, Middle English Texts, 21 (Heidelberg: Carl Winter, 1988), pp. 9–17; *Knyghthode and Battle*, ed. R. Dyboski and Z. M. Arend, Early English Text Society, os 201 (London: Oxford University Press for EETS, 1935), "Proemium." The Anglo-Norman translation antedates the influential translation of Jean de Meun (1284) by some 30 years.

125 "See seke am I, fulfayn o lande I wolde!" (line 2979). The term "Epilogus" appears in MS Pembroke College, Cambridge 243 (chosen as base text by Dyboski and Arend); "Recapitulatio" is favored by MSS BL London, Cotton Titus A XXIII and Bodleian Oxford, Ashmole 45.

126 Lines 2982–5 differ somewhat in the two other MSS. Dyboski and Arend report the other two MSS thus:

> That may nat Joo. whiso. for they distresse
> All or to deye or with her werke to stonde
> That dar to right go wynne all Engelonde
> What myght availe, a lite in errour dwelle

The reading "That may nat joo" seems preferable, given the precedent of *Troilus and Criseyde*, 3.33 ("Whan they" [folk] "kan nought construe how it may jo [Hrl: Ioo]"): *Middle English Dictionary*, jo.

127 See above, p. 55. The term *saluz*, employed twice here by the poet, relates to the Middle English verb *salusen*, to greet, while resonating more precisely with Latin *salus*, "a wish for one's welfare (expressed by word of mouth or in writing), a greeting, salute, salutation (the state of being safe and sound, in whole condition, in safety" (*A Latin Dictionary*, ed. Charlton T. Lewis and Charles Short [Oxford: Clarendon Press, 1987 [first published in 1879]), *salus*, I (B).

128 Browning's "Home-Thoughts from the Sea," located further south, also entail mooning over a passing English colony (Gibraltar); the poem closes as "Jove's planet rises yonder, silent over Africa" (*Poems by Robert Browning*, introd. Richard Garnett [Ipswich: Boydell Press, 1973], p. 83).

129 See Anthony Goodman, *The Wars of the Roses: Military Activity and English Society, 1452–97* (London: Routledge and Kegan Paul, 1981), pp. 22–40.

130 See G. L. Harris, "The Struggle for Calais: an Aspect of the Rivalry Between Lancaster and York," *English Historical Review* 75 (1960), 30–53.

131 Citations follow *Paston Letters and Papers of the Fifteenth Century*, ed. Norman Davis, 2 vols. (Oxford: Clarendon Press, 1971–6).

132 "Frowe" thus appears as a female surname in English records associated with prostitution: while less spectacular than surnames such as "Clatterballock," "Frowe" is nonetheless (like other Middle English surnames) suggestive of a specialist trade. See Ruth Mazo Karras, *Common Women: Prostitution and Sexuality in Medieval England* (New York: Oxford University Press, 1996), pp. 56–7, 745.

133   On brothels at Bruges, see chapter 2 below.

134   See André Vandewalle, *Hanze@Medici: Bruges, Crossroads of European Cultures*
      (Oostkamp: Stichting Kunstboek, 2002), p. 18; this manuscript is now in
      the Bibliothèque Nationale de France, Paris. Caxton's edition of Anthony
      Woodville, Earl Rivers' translation from the French text of Valerius Maximus,
      was very likely the first book printed in England (November 18, 1477); William
      Caxton worked in Bruges (where the first books in English were printed,
      1474–5). See *The Dicts and Sayings of the Philosophers: The Translations made
      by Stephen Scrope, William Worcester and an Anonymous Translator*, ed. Curt F.
      Bühler, Early English Text Society, os 211 (London: Oxford University Press
      for EETS, 1941), p. ix; Seth Lerer, "William Caxton," in *The Cambridge History
      of Medieval English Literature*, ed. Wallace, pp. 720–38.

135   *The Cely Letters*, ed. Alison Hanham, Early English Text Society, os 273
      (London: Oxford University Press for EETS, 1975), p. 29 [August 27?] 1478.

136   *Secular Lyrics of the XIVth and XVth Centuries*, ed. Rossell Hope Robbins, 2nd
      edn. (Oxford: Clarendon Press, 1955), p. 150 (from MS Ashmole 191). The
      lyric in the Ashmole MS is set for three voices (p. 275). See further Douglas
      Gray, "Fifteenth-century Lyrics and Carols," in *Nation, Court and Culture*, ed.
      Helen Cooney, pp. 168–83 (p. 172).

137   Reinhard Strohm, *The Rise of European Music, 1380–1500* (Cambridge: Cambridge
      University Press, 1993), pp. 392, 393.

138   Alison Hanham, "The Musical Studies of a Fifteenth-Century Wool Merchant,"
      Review of English Studies 8 (1957), 270–4.

139   George had a French-speaking mistress called Clare at about this time; the
      jottings make up a dialogue in French between male and female parts.

140   This letter is dated "probably after 1479, not after June 1483" (II,441).

141   See *Paston Letters*, ed. Davis, p. lxiv. William Paston IV died in 1554.

142   BL MS Cotton Caligula D. vii f. 227 as cited in *The Chronicle of Calais, in the
      Reigns of Henry VII and Henry VIII*, ed. John Gough Nichols, Camden Society
      (New York: AMS Press, 1968), pp. 78–9 (p. 78). *The Chronicle of Calais* was
      written by Richard Turpyn, a garrison soldier at Calais whose son became a
      herald. See Anne Curry, *The Hundred Years' War* (London: Macmillan, 1993),
      p. 19.

143   "Speke, Parrot," in *Poems*, ed. Kinsman, lines 302, 304, 340.

144   *Statutes of the Realm*, 25 Henry VIII c. 12 (1533–4), "An Acte concerning the
      Attaynder of Elizabeth Barton and Others."

145   See Alan Neame, *The Holy Maid of Kent: The Life of Elizabeth Barton, 1506–1534*
      (London: Hodder and Stoughton, 1971), pp. 177, 331–6; *Canterbury Tales*, 1.465.
      The cathedral of Notre Dame at Boulogne-sur-Mer, destroyed during the
      French Revolution, housed a statue of the Virgin Mary that had been washed
      up on the shore. Edward II married Isabella of France here in 1308. See James
      Bentley, *The Gateway to France: Flanders, Artois and Picardy* (London: Viking,
      1991), p. 16.

146 *Thomas Cranmer: A Life* (New Haven: Yale University Press, 1996), p. 111.

147 See Joblin, "Le protestantisme en Calais," pp. 600–1.

148 *The Lisle Letters*, ed. Muriel St. Clare Byrne, 6 vols. (Chicago: University of Chicago Press, 1981). See further *The Lisle Lettres: An Abridgement*, ed. Byrne, selected by Bridget Boland, foreword by Hugh Trevor-Roper (Chicago: University of Chicago Press, 1983).

149 James' tutor Thomas Rainolde, educated at Oxford and Paris, clearly despaired of his pupil: "by my advice," he informs Lady Lisle, "he should be utterly from the company of English men, or else it will hinder the learning of the tongue very much" (III.122; see further III.108).

150 I.596; see Seth Lerer, *Courtly Letters in the Age of Henry VIII* (Cambridge: Cambridge University Press, 1997), pp. 161–83.

151 For "Rex Diabole," see V.238 (October 5, 1538). See also V.428 (with talk of "players' garments" plucked from a shipwreck "upon Margate"); V.437 (on the safe arrival of the rescued garments, "which with much ado are received"). Henry VIII composed a tragedy for the occasion of Anne's beheading which he would take from his pocket for people to read: see Wallace, *Chaucerian Polity*, p. 384.

152 See Trevor-Roper, "Foreword," in *Lisle Letters Abridgement*, ed. Byrne, pp. xiv–xv.

153 II.505 (June 5, 1535); II.609, 610 (October 28, 1535).

154 STC 19078 (BL C.38.c.32); the text declares itself written "From Exile the. 12 of April 1557."

155 See David Loades, *The Reign of Mary Tudor*, 2nd edn. (London: Longman, 1991), p. 300.

156 See Loades, *Mary Tudor*, pp. 316–17. The words of Mary Tudor, here attributed to Holinshed, conclude what is perhaps the most poignant account of English occupation, Marcel Denquin, "Calais sous la domination Anglaise." Poignancy in this case is afforded by the date of this address, delivered by Marcel Denquin, Président d'Honneur des Rosati de Calaisis on February 19, 1939 (Cambridge University Library 9560 c.1, author's presentation copy).

157 Cited in *The Chronicle of Calais*, ed. Nichols, p. xxv.

158 *The Chronicle of Calais*, ed. Nichols, p. xxx.

159 Richard Hakluyt, *Principall Navigations . . . (1589)*, photo-lithographic facsimile, introd. David Beers Quinn and Raleigh Ashlin Shelton, 2 vols, Hakluyt Society, Extra Series, 39 (Cambridge, Mass.: Hakluyt Society and Peabody Museum of Salem, 1965), pp. 636, 638. Hakluyt thus correctly remembers Calais as an infertile outpost, in need of continuous supply.

160 Huguenot members of the newly installed French garrison carried out acts of iconoclasm at Calais in 1560: See Joblin, "Le protestantisme en Calais," p. 606.

161 See Fernand Braudel, *Civilization and Capitalism, 15th–18th Century*, trans. Siân Reynolds, 3 vols. (Berkeley: University of California Press, 1992), III.353–6. The retreat from Calais coincides with the period of English withdrawal from

the Mediterranean: see Braudel, *The Mediterranean and the Mediterranean World·
in the Age of Philip II*, trans. Siân Reynolds, 2 vols. (continuous pagination),
I.615–21.

162   Hakluyt, *Principall Navigations (1589)*, "The Epistle Dedicatorie," p. 2b. Earlier
in his "epistle," dedicated to Walsingham, Hakluyt acknowledges that he has
"heard in speech, and read in books other nations miraculously extollèd for
their discoueries and notable enterprises by sea, but the English of all others
for their sluggish security" (p. 2a). Hakluyt's work thus knowingly sets out to
chronicle a global mission yet to be achieved: see chapter 2 below.

163   England was actually offered a new foothold on continental Europe in 1658
when Cromwell was awarded Dunkirk for the loan of 8,000 Ironsides; Charles
II, however, promptly sold the town back to Louis XIV for 5,000,000 livres.
See Bentley, *Gateway to France*, p. 3.

164   *Henry V*, 3.2.42 in *Norton Shakespeare*, ed. Greenblatt et al.

165   The *coulter* is the iron blade of the plough (rather than just, as the Norton has
it, the "plow") fixed in front of the share to cut the furrow; a *coulter* is warmed
by Gervaise the Blacksmith in the *Miller's Tale*.

166   "Both within France and without, French soil has enjoyed an unshakeable
reputation for being rich, fertile, productive, [and] ardently sought after"
(Armand Frémont, "The Land," in Nora, *Realms of Memory,* 2.3–35 (p. 17)).

167   The other usage of deracinate is at *Troilus and Cressida*, 1.3.99. Scotsman William
Dunbar, in speaking of "bakbyattaris of sindry racis" (1508), has been identified as the first person to employ *race* in something like its modern sense; his
usage is perhaps too broadly generic to deserve this distinction: see Michael
Banton, *Racial Theories*, 2nd edn. (Cambridge: Cambridge University Press,
1998), p. 17. *Race* is a term that is foreign to the *Middle English Dictionary*,
except as denoting a narrative or story (from Old English *racu*; not attested
after 1225) or (after 1450) the root of ginger. See further *Race and Ethnicity in
the Middle Ages*, ed. Thomas Hahn, a special issue of the *Journal of Medieval and
Early Modern Studies* 31 (Winter 2001).

168   See *The Tempest*, 1.2.361; the phrase, glossed by Norton as "hereditary nature,"
is Miranda's. For more on such linkages, see the last two chapters below; for
earlier conflations between the terms *vill* and *vile*, see especially p. 250.

CHAPTER TWO

IN FLAUNDRES

dat woeste land.
Bavaria Herald, **Wereldkroniek.**

Margery Kempe, in the *secundus liber* of her *Book*, makes much of her epical overland traveling from Stralsund to Wilsnack (for the Holy Blood) to Aachen and thence to Calais. Such a feat, especially for a medieval woman of around 60, is certainly remarkable; Margery affords us every opportunity to experience the aches, pains, and travails of her journeying. It is all hard, but the final leg, "to-Caleysward," is worst of all; it sees her and her accompanying friar

> goyng wery weys & greuows in dep sondys, hillys, & valeys tweyn days er thei comyn thedyr, suffreryng gret thrist & gret penawns, for ther wer fewe townys be the wey that thei went & ful febyl herberwe. (p. 241, 3–7)

The barrenness of this landscape, accentuating her sense of "sufferyng gret thrist," feeds nocturnal fears. Perhaps, she reflects, it was the work of her "gostly enmy, for sche was euyr a-ferd to a be rauischyd er defiled" (8–10). At any event, she was always happy to meet up with groups of "maidenys" and to go to bed with "a woman er tweyn" (14–16). "Sche was so wery," she tells us,

> & so ouyrcomyn wyth labowr to-Caleysward that hir thowt hir spirit xulde a departyd fro hir body as sche went in the wey. Thus wyth gret labowrys sche cam to Caleys . . . (p. 241, 17–20)

Margery's relief on reaching Calais is palpable, for here "this creature had good cher of diuers persons, bothyn of men & of women"; (26–7). After a few days she boards ship for Dover and busies herself in comforting her fellow passengers as they puke and vomit their way across the Channel (p. 242, 21–7). This crossing is not, for Margery, fraught with liminal danger; for her, the true borderland experience had come in crossing Flanders. This landscape was indeed barren – a bleak outer expression of inner spiritual fears – and fraught with sexualized danger (patrolled by soldiery under the regent Duke of Bedford, whose yeomen accused Margery of being "Cobham's daughter," whose troops burned Joan of Arc).[1] It is through such imagining of borders that notions of *nacioun* and nation begin to work themselves out. The firm demarcation and patrolling of limits with or within Ireland, Scotland, and Wales absorbed much English energy at this time. Such imaginary lines in the dirt, projecting onto foreign places anxieties experienced at home, help delineate notions of English distinctiveness throughout this period. Premodern Flanders, as a territory (like Scotland or Wales) immediately adjoining – or blending into – England, plays a vital role in this highly wrought, contradictory process of *naciounal* differentiation.

Views of Flanders from England have changed since 1558. After World War I Flanders betokened mud, death, poppies, and a postwar shortage of eligible men. The landscapes of the Hundred Years' War, and their imaginative connotations, have been thickly overlaid by commemorations of twentieth-century battles (with dozens and dozens of tidy, well-maintained grave sites). Whereas Flemish-speaking territory now finds itself divided between Belgium, France, and Holland, "Flanders" survives in England chiefly as a state of feeling, as a term full of ill-defined, sodden, but poignant pathos. Such feelings may be fading as the last surviving veterans die out, yet it is interesting to note the highly traditional, affect-laden approach to Flemish art assumed by Englishman Alan Hollinghurst's novel, *The Folding Star*. In entering an "austere Town Museum," somewhere in Flanders, the narrator feels himself "a little out of step among those chaste northern saints and inward-looking Virgins – there wasn't one of them that welcomed you or held your gaze as the dark-eyed Italian gods and holy men so often did."[2] Such a museum experience is colored by loneliness and channeled by a polarizing of northern and southern styles effected by nineteenth-century European art history. Such assumptions concerning the division of the Italian from the Flemish are continuously disrupted in Flanders. The early Gothic Onze Lieve Vrouwekerk at Bruges frames Michelangelo's *Virgin and Child* within a baroque interior. This statue forms part of Flemish culture: it was acquired by Jan van Moescroen, merchant of Bruges, in 1505.[3] Two-way connections and collaborations between the Mediterranean world and premodern or "primitive" Flanders (another pejorative term from art history) were powerful and definitive in ways that the greater European world is still slow to appreciate.[4]

Flanders and Italy form two corners of a trading triangle that flourished for centuries during the Middle Ages; the third corner is England, or that southeastern quadrant of England running from East Anglia to Southampton. The continental staple for English wool (the royal-designated site of trade) was first established at Bruges in 1297; English merchants gained major civic privileges at Bruges in 1359 (which they continued to enjoy after the staple first moved to Calais four years later). This network is peculiarly the space of Chaucer's mature business and professional life. It is not *the* international space of late medieval England: the places traveled in the *Book of Margery Kempe*, particularly those of the second book, are typically reached from Lynn (now King's Lynn), a town that looks northward and eastward toward Prussia, the Hanseatic ports, and the Baltic.[5] Where Margery sails to Danzig, Chaucer crosses to Calais. And yet, as we have seen, Margery does come to traverse Flanders by descending upon it from German territory. This was a well-traveled route, for merchants from the German Hanse, like their counterparts in London or Paris, must needs come to Bruges. Chaucer and Margery thus meet in meditating upon the barren, sandy landscapes of Flanders that they both, as a matter of historical record, traversed. And yet (as Chaucer, in particular, knew) extraordinary pockets of complex and sophisticated urban culture had been built upon such unpromising foundations.

There is a distinct discourse of Flanders (as a place, as a way of being) in Chaucer, whereas a discourse of France proves – in every sense – difficult to find. Eustache Deschamps, whom we have seen confecting a discourse of bastard Englishness in writing to Chaucer,[6] knows that French has long ruled over the Channel as the voice of prestige or prestige-hungry culture. Wealthy London merchants, at the beginning of the fourteenth century, gathered to hear *chansons* sung in French "for the renown of London"; John Gower, a century later, affirmed national allegiance by proclaiming "Je sui Englois."[7] And the huge, 1,400-ton warship built at Southampton for Henry V – the monarch seen as a stalwart champion of English – was named *Grace Dieu*.[8] Choice of language has not yet, in Chaucer's time, become synonymous with the proclaiming of nationality.[9] But more fundamentally, Frenchness cannot yet be externalized or figured foreign as a discourse because it remains essential to the self-understanding of English civic and courtly life. This is perhaps why Chaucer's discourse of Frenchness remains formal, poetic, and the matter of dreams.[10] In approaching *The Romaunt of the Rose*'s walled garden, the dreamer finds more singing birds (fellow poets?) "Than ben in all the rewme of France" (A 495); resolved to join them and finding "noon to teche me," he resolves to break in via "hole" or "ladder" (A 515, 523–4). Once within this *locus amoenus*, this Englished garden, he is moved to meditate upon certain linguistic differences setting apart usage "in Fraunce" from "oure usaunce" (A 683–4; see further A 1455–7).

The discourse of France in Chaucer, such as it is, seems chiefly a matter of art, aristocracy, and "natural music."[11] The ways in which Chaucer writes of and imagines himself "in Flaundres" (the phrase recurs) are altogether more ingenious, tortuous, and exhilarating. The great cities of Flanders, from which he has half-escaped, though still half-mesmerized by aristocratic tutelage and French domination, see dizzying exchanges – *commercium* – between languages and habits of religion and trade. And they go beyond this, improving upon (rather than obediently observing) limits hitherto regarded as *natural*. In thus suggesting social and gendered relations of uncharted complexity, they further suggest new possibilities for poetic voices and visual art (to stimulate pleasures of both beguilement and repudiation).[12] Such a powerful *agon*, involving something more complex than the *medieval* straining to transmogrify within the carapace of the premodern, goes on and changes ground long after Chaucer is dead. But the very intensity and persistence of his engagement with all that "Flaunders" entails demands close attention (and hence temporary recourse, for some pages, to a slower-lane diachronic method).[13]

Cloth, Clothing, Tapestry: England and Flanders

At about the time Chaucer was born, in 1343, his father John received a royal permit allowing him to ship merchandise from his home town of Ipswich to Flanders.[14] Ipswich is on the estuary of the Orwell, a key reference point for the Merchant of the *General Prologue*, who "wolde the see were kept for any thing / Bitwixe Middelburgh and Orewelle" (1.276–7).[15] Middelburgh, in Zeeland, was home to the English wool staple between 1384 and 1389.[16] Chaucer's Merchant "wolde the see were kept," since piracy was rife (and the French, in 1386, had commandeered the Flemish fleet with a view to invading England).[17] This Merchant, said to be expert at exchanging *sheeldes*, a fictional money of account sold at London and redeemed at Bruges, wears "a Flaundryssh bever hat" upon his head (1.272).[18] Foreign merchants at Bruges, while generally lodging with fellows of their own *nation* (country, trading alliance, or city-state), enjoyed frequent and intense contacts with the local populace: they joined their guilds, took part in their festivals, and sometimes married locals. And they cooperated openly with local authorities (rather than, like the Genoans in the Mediterranean and the Crimea, keeping within their own *fondaco*).[19] Some 2,000 foreign merchants were to be found in medieval Bruges at the high point of its prosperity, plus an even greater number of non-Flemish artisans and workers.[20] Exchanges between England and Flanders included both luxury items and certain staples of everyday life: beer, apples, onions, garlic, and the pears that were to make Poperinge famous.[21] The return journey from England to Bruges took only 12 days; England to Paris and back (in favorable conditions) took 31.[22]

When the Chaucers of Ipswich became vintners of London their links with Flanders persisted.[23] Royal servant Geoffrey had occasion to travel "versus partes Flandrie" as a diplomat or messenger, involved with Anglo-French peace negotiations, Anglo-French marriage plans, and reparation for war damage suffered by Flemish cities.[24] But even from the vantage point of Calais, which was at the northern tip of Artois (hence "closely nudging the weaving towns of Flanders")[25] Chaucer could see how Flemings were caught between the rock of France and the hard place of the invading English. It was Edward III's wish to make the garrison at Calais self-financing that precipitated the transfer of the staple for English wool from Bruges to Calais in 1363. The wool will pay for the war; the warriors will protect the merchants.[26] This policy was sealed in 1363 with the foundation of the Calais mint. Flemings were now expected to travel to English territory to buy English wool with English-minted coin to finance the war that was their ruin.

The wool business had made the economies of Flanders and England interdependent for more than two centuries before Chaucer took up his position as Controller of Wool Custom at the port of London in 1374, a post he held until 1386.[27] Before 1270, Flemings dominated the business of exporting wool from England; after this date, however, Italians gradually displaced Flemings in shipping and financing.[28] These arrangements continued to work well for the Flemings so long as they could obtain a steady supply of high-grade English wool, convert it into cloth, and send it on for export.

The Flemish textile industry was dominated by three major cities: Ypres, Ghent, and Bruges. Flanders and Holland, plus the cities of northern Italy, were the most intensively and precociously urbanized cities in Europe. Flemings were proud of having created so much out of so little. They knew their natural resources to be poor: local polders, loam, or sand plain – fit only for a light scratch plough – could not sustain much of a population;

inferior grassland yielded scrawny sheep.[29] Urban ingenuity was hence sub-
stituted for natural plenty: corn was imported from France, wool from England, and labor from the rural hinterland; water, vital for the textile industry,
was channeled through the digging of canals. Textile manufacture dominated all other industries: at Ghent in 1356–8, it occupied some 63 percent of
the professionally active population.[30] Weavers and fullers were the two
largest textile guilds. Division of labor was highly complex: 53 non-textile
guilds have been discovered at Ghent, plus no fewer than 146 other non-
textile trades denied rights of organization.[31]

The guild-governed cities of Flanders present a peculiar evolutionary variant in political form, in that they strive toward the independence achieved
by German and Tuscan cities, while owing allegiance to the count of Flanders, himself a fief of the French crown. All but the last of these counts
spoke French but not Flemish; they presided loosely and often distantly over
what we might term a bastard feudalism.[32] These guild-governed cities have
much in common with their Italian counterparts.[33] Urbane values of im-
provisation and quick wit were admired in Reynard the Fox, as in Boccaccio's
Decameron. Urban spectacle and drama were precociously developed; it is no
coincidence that most surviving Middle English drama is found in towns
and districts linked by trade with Holland and Flanders.[34] And given the
fact that Flemings in London were associated with prostitution and beer-
making, it is not surprising to discover that Herry Bailey's wife, Goodelief,
has a Flemish name. Saint Godelief, virgin and martyr, is the local and
patron saint of Ghistelles (between Bruges and Nieupoort). Murdered by
her husband in 1070, she has been dubbed "the patient Grissel of the north."[35]
Such a title is hilariously ill-applied to Goodelief Bailey, whose *fabliau*-like[36]
fomenting of extreme, tavern-based violence raises prevalent notions of
Flemish civic behavior to a dedicated sublime: "By Goddes bones," says the
Southwark innkeeper (reacting to the violent *Tale of Melibee*),

> . . . whan I bete my knaves,
> She bryngeth me the grete clobbed staves,
> And crieth, "Slee the dogges everichoon,
> And brek hem, bothe bak and every boone!"
> *(7.1897–1900)*

The urban culture of Flanders was, and knew itself to be, precocious and
precarious. It is always a precarious undertaking in Catholic cultures to
propose improving upon nature: the Vatican was nervous of gas-lighting in
the nineteenth century and feared contraception in the twentieth. Intensive

urbanization subjected the constitutive parts of the urban body politic, in Flanders as in Italy, to severe new pressures. One source of relief for the city was to unify all social classes by beating up on the countryside.[37] The "White Hoods of Ghent" spent much time terrorizing rural populations.[38] An anti-peasant song, beginning "Wi willen van den Kerels zinghen," mocks peasant lineage, peasant dress, peasant labor, weaponry, and dancing (to pipers). Its chorus singles out peasant diet and peasant gluttony for repeated ridicule: "broot ende caes," "bread and cheese."[39]

The most precarious aspect of Flemish polity concerned its balancing of allegiances between England and France, suppliers of wool and grain. Generally speaking, the cloth-producing cities inclined toward the English and the counts favored France, but there were many factional variations.[40] At the beginning of the Hundred Years' War, the Flemish count, Louis of Nevers, followed a pro-French policy that infuriated Edward III of England and, following English reprisals, plunged the Flemish textile industry into depression. Jacob van Artevelde, a Ghentian broker and merchant, developed an alliance with England. In January 1340, Edward III entered Ghent and was proclaimed King of France; his son, John of Ghent – John of Gaunt – was born just a few months later.[41] Bruges and Ypres resented the new preeminence of Ghent, and Ghentian weavers fought Ghentian fullers in a bloody battle on the Friday market; Jacob van Artevelde was killed soon after. Louis of Male, the new count of Flanders, invaded Flanders in September 1348. Weavers were banned from assembly and government in all Flemish cities, provoking a steady stream of emigration that added a timely boost to the emergent English textile industry.

This buoyant native industry was clearly in the ascendant during Chaucer's years at the Customs House, years that saw its long-established counterparts in Florence and Flanders in catastrophic decline. In 1378, while Chaucer – financed by the War Funds – was courting despots and mercenaries in Lombardy, the government of Florence was overthrown by the Ciompi, wool-workers in an industry made desperate by the lack of English wool. In 1379, Flanders was engulfed by civil war. The century in Flanders between 1270 and 1385 has been summarized as "a numbing list of virtually annual foreign attacks or serious internal violence"; the six-year civil war at the end of this period has been assessed "a total disaster."[42] In December 1381, Philip van Artevelde (son of Jacob, and pensioner of the English crown) took power at Ghent, took control of the city records, and hunted down the eldest male relative of anyone implicated in his father's death.[43] Ghent seized Bruges in May 1382; in November, the French slaughtered the second Artevelde and his army in a swamp. In the summer of 1383, Richard II sent a "crusade" to

Flanders under the command of the Bishop of Norwich; having destroyed the unfortified suburbs of Ypres, the English returned safely home. Weavers from Ypres, who worked in these suburbs, soon joined the trail of emigrants to England.[44]

There is no doubt that English textiles, deemed by Walter Prevenier "sans tradition de réputation" before 1350,[45] benefited on international markets from difficulties suffered by Florentines in 1378 and by Flemings after 1379. Two of Chaucer's pilgrims may be directly associated with this upturn in English fortunes; here is the first who comes to mind:

> A good Wif was there of biside Bathe,
> But she was somdel deef, and that was scathe.
> Of clooth-makynge she hadde swiche an haunt
> She passed hem of Ypres and of Gaunt.
>
> *(1.446–9)*

It is notable here how the name of the English city (the place the Wife is wedded to) bumps up against the names of the two most famous weaving towns of Flanders;[46] naming is power, as the Shipman's merchant says.[47] The English name that mattered most in Flanders before 1350 was "Cottswold," designating the first-grade raw material from which Flemish textiles were made. In the 1380s, Cotswold wool was more likely to support native English industry than the fullers and weavers of Flanders; Bath might be the coming name to drown out talk "of Ypres and of Gaunt."

The Wife's riding posture is at once comfortable and militant: she ambles, but wears sharp spurs; she laughs and carps (beneath a hat of shield-like dimensions). The second pilgrim in the *General Prologue* set in hostile relation to Flemish territory is similarly characterized through a mix of militant and companionable registers: the Squire, who

> . . . hadde been somtyme in chyvachie
> In Flaundres, in Artois, and Pycardie.
>
> *(1.85–6)*

The discovery of "Flaunders" here, round the corner of the couplet, surely aims to raise a snicker from Chaucer's first audience. Mention of "Flanders," in the 1380s, would stir memories of the recent and humiliating bishop's "crusade" to Ypres: an undertaking so disastrous that it persuaded Gaunt to abandon "the way of Flanders" and to pursue the "chemin de Portyngale."[48] Mention of "chyvachie" draws attention to the unheroic mode of combat employed by the English in this and other campaigns. The aim of *chevauchée*, as we have noted, was *not* to engage the enemy in battle, but rather to cut a wide swathe of havoc, damage, and destruction through their territory. Such distinctively English tactics saw the lower echelons of military society – squires, yeomen, and below – do most of the decisive fighting (burning and demolition).[49]

Our second citation of "in Flaundres," like the first, evokes suggestions of chivalric lineage compromised by considerations of Flemish provenance: the father of Sir Thopas is said to be

> Yborn. . . in fer contree,
> In Flaundres, al biyonde the see,
> At Poperyng, in the place.
> *(7.718–20)*

Again, the uncovering of "In Flaundres" sounds a retreat from an epic regis-ter: "al biyonde the see" / "In Flaundres" – 40 miles from Dover. Critics have argued that "Poperyng," too, conduces to mirth, since it sounds funny.[50] Ypres and Ghent certainly find no place in *Sir Thopas*, since they were pow-erful names with unfunny associations. Poperinge, however, was a *respect-able* name (at least until Skelton toyed with it): the town headed up the secondary tier of Flemish cloth-producers and became well-known for its pears.[51] It could never be more than middling, since it was landlocked and lay too close to Ypres; when Poperinge got ideas above its station, Ypres sent out the militia to smash up its machinery.[52]

The middling status of Poperinge befits Sir Thopas, a middling kind of knight and a distinctively Flemish one. I have yet to find a Flemish Sir Thopas: the closest I have come so far is Simon Saphir of Ghent, demesne wool-merchant of the King of England.[53] It is worth noting, however, that Chaucer's Sir Thopas wears Flemish-made stockings:

> Of Brugges were his hosen broun,
> His robe was of skylatoun,
> That coste many a jane.
> *(7.733–5)*

These stockings might be regarded as Flemish-speaking as well as Flemish-fabricated, since Chaucer's meter here – as in all other deployments of "Brugges" – requires a disyllabic articulation suggestive of Flemish (rather than of French or of modern English usage). "Brugges" is much more than a middling name, famed not for retailing luxury socks but rather as the Wall

Street of late medieval Europe. The Genoese were prominent in such business at Bruges, although the "jane" was not one of their more sought-after
coins: it was worth about one English halfpenny. Collocation of Bruges and
the "jane" serves to remind us, however, of the Flemish–Italian–English and
trade–finance–war triangles so familiar to Chaucer. John de Mari, citizen of
Genoa, was employed by Edward III to hire Genoese mercenaries and made
payments at Bruges in 1373; in this same year, this same John de Mari led
Chaucer and company to Genoa on the king's "secret business."[54]

The middlingness of *Sir Thopas* is most eloquently suggested by its "drasty"
tail-rhyme "ryming," which offered lower to middling audiences econom-
ical accounts of great Anglo-Norman ancestral heroes (such as "Beves and
sir Gy [of Warwick]," 7.899). Evocation of Flanders accords with all this just
perfectly, for it suggests, to Chaucer's audience, the vigorous imitation of
nobility in the land of the non-noble. The fundamental non-nobility of the
Flemish may be readily deduced from their buildings, for "in contrast to
Italy," Wim Blockmans notes, "the nobility of these regions did not dwell
in the cities and thus did not impose its magnificent architecture in the
urban space."[55] Most urbanized space in Flanders serves the needs of merchants and artisans. Whereas Italian aristocrats built high, non-functional
towers to the glory of their family name, Flemings built belfries. Adapted
from the feudal *donjons* of Picardy, Flemish belfries assumed purely civic
functions in accommodating the watch, housing the city archives, and in
sounding the hours of the working day. The most exquisite craftsmanship
at Bruges was reserved for the iron grillework (figure 7) protecting the city
seal and documents high up in the belfy that still dominates the main city
square.[56]

At the battle of Courtrai on July 11, 1302, the craftsmen of Bruges had
defeated the army of France. This was the first major battle in which urban
infantry had defeated cavalry commanded by nobles; some 500 pairs of
golden spurs were taken from fallen French aristocrats and housed in a
Flemish church.[57] Deschamps perhaps remembers this moment, or others
since, when he upbraids the Fleming as "envious subjugator of nobility."[58]
This legendary triumph did not, however, dispel the allure of French culture
in Flanders. In ballade 127, Deschamps tells Machaut how he read "Vostre
Voir Dit" at Bruges before Louis III, count of Flanders.[59] In the Middle
Dutch *Reinaert*, the Flemish bourgeoisie was invited to laugh at the obses-
sive cultivation of French by Flemish nobles: the little dog Courtois,
"Courtier," speaks French "in and out of season."[60] But these same Flemish
urbanites were themselves avid consumers of French or French-derived chivalric adventures; such "romances of prys" (as *Sir Thopas* terms their English

7 Iron grillework by Nicolaas Grootwerc, 1300, protecting the seal and documents in the belfry at Bruges. Photograph by David Wallace.

equivalents, 7.898) became the favored form of fantasy literature, in Bruges as in London, for the town-bound business and mercantile classes.

J. M. Manly has surmised that the English audience of Chaucer's *Sir Thopas* was accustomed "to poke fun, not without a little resentment, at the efforts of the Flemish bourgeoisie to ape the manners of the English and French aristocracy, and with their new-found wealth to compete in dress, in manners, and in exploits on the battlefield with the ancient chivalry of France and England."[61] Manly was not English, but there is no doubt here that disciplinary loyalty leads him to unite French and English culture against that of the upstart Flemish. It is true that English royal blood was not willing to ally itself, in the twelfth, thirteenth, or fourteenth centuries, with that of Flanders or its counts.[62] It is also true that throughout this period, England was much indebted to industrial and moneymaking technologies pioneered by the Flemish; it was, as Caroline Barron says, "the junior partner" in such ventures.[63] In the field of vernacular literature, however, Flemish and English were as peas in a pod: retarded, west Germanic, country cousins in the kingdom of the French. Chaucer, in assigning himself *Sir Thopas*, embraces that which Manly cannot contemplate.

Florence, Flanders, and London – places strongly connected in Chaucer's trade-related experience of Europe – hosted emergent vernacular traditions attempting to make their way forward, out from under French domination. Italy, following Brunetto Latini's transplanting of the *Roman de la Rose* in the 1260s, had made significant progress by the mid-Trecento; Flemish and English, by contrast, were still feeling and theorizing their way out from under French and Latin models of authority and use.[64] Italian is closely related to the pedigreed languages of Latin and French; Flemish and English, by contrast, are hybridized languages lying along the shifting borderline of Romance and Germanic tradition. In this sense, to write in English in the 1380s is broadly equivalent to writing "in Flaundres"; by insisting that Flemish "sounds funny," English can be distanced from the realization that, to the rest of the premodern world, it could be difficult to distinguish Flemings from Englishmen. Chaucer's grandfather was in fact known as "Robert Malin le Chaucer." The original family name of the Chaucers, according to Derek Pearsall, "is likely to have been Malyn"; "Malines" is the French name for the Flemish Mechelen, a town acquired by the Count of Flanders ca. 1333 and said to be "strongly Flemish in character."[65] .

The Fleming Sir Thopas, the hero whose adventures Chaucer chooses to tell *as* the pilgrim Chaucer, wears "hosen broun . . . of Brugge." Periodically, by way of encouraging the emergent English textile industry, common or middling people would be forbidden to wear alien cloth.[66] At the same time, their social superiors were all too keen to lay their hands on foreign textiles, especially "arras" or tapestries. Richard II, in particular, was a tapestry aficionado, boosting the royal collection from 7 in 1377 to no fewer than 50 by 1399. Magnates, such as the earl of Warwick, were also keen to acquire sets (depicting, for example, the adventures of Guy of Warwick).[67] Such luxury items, Scott McKendrick has argued, "served a prominent role in the king's general projection of his great personal wealth and power." Where the campaigning Julius Caesar had taken portable floors into Gaul to impress guests and rivals in hosting banquets, so Richard traveled with tap-estries.[68] There is a clean disassociation here between the exigencies of kingly status projection and any sense of loyalty to native (English) industry. Why should kingly power wish to stage itself surrounded by the fruits of foreign, artisanal labor? *Sir Thopas* lifts the lid on such paradoxes, honoring "roial chivalry" (7.902) while acknowledging the workaday exigencies of small foreign coins and hungry horses needing "good forage" (7.783). Its themes are precisely those favored by royal and magnate purchasers of *arras*: scenes from romances, hunting, battles, decorative natural description, and courtly "love-likynge."[69] Chaucer's *Sir Thopas* is, in short, a genuine Flemish tapestry.

Coming to Bruges: Poetry and Painting, Faith and Business

In Chaucer's *Shipman's Tale*, Flanders looms large. We spend just five lines securely *in* Flanders, but much energy and calculation is dedicated to the business of getting there: "whan youre housbonde is to Flaundres fare" (199); "To Flaundres wol I go" (239); "wel I see to Brugges wol ye go" (258); then, finally:

> The morwe cam, and forth this marchaunt rideth
> To Flaundres-ward; his prentys wel hym gydeth
> Til he came into Brugges murily.
>
> *(7.299–301)*

The trajectory traveled by the Shipman's monk and merchant forms a strongly articulated triangle: Seint-Denys, Bruges, Paris. Such triangles, in-volving the shifting of credit notes, coin, and merchandise, were often traveled by those in the wool business eager to avoid customs dues or brokerage fees, or to buy on leveraged capital; Chaucer, as a customs officer, was expert in such matters. A merchant might buy English wool in the Cots-wolds on credit, sell it at Venice for cash, lend the cash in Flanders at high interest, and then (finally) pay off the cost of the Cotswold wool. England, Italy, and Flanders – that triangle we have associated with Chaucer – is the classic configuration for such enterprise, although there were variants.[70] An Exchequer enquiry of 1383 revealed that one Hugelin Gerard had bought wool at Westminster, faked a sale at Calais, then sent on the merchandise to Bruges.[71] Flanders, and specifically Bruges, thus figures in the *Shipman's Tale*

as a vortex inexorably sucking in a merchant protagonist before, following a
brief and hectic interval, propelling him out again. Time within Bruges,
described as "the commercial emporium of western Europe," as "*the* commercial metropolis of the west,"[72] is spent as follows:

> Now gooth this marchant faste and bisily
> Aboute his nede, and byeth and creaunceth.   *obtains credit*
> He neither pleyeth at the dees ne daunceth,
> But as a marchaunt, shortly for to telle,
> He let his lyf, and there I lete hym dwelle.   *led*
>
> *(7.302–6)*

Foreign merchants had plenty of opportunity for dicing and dancing at Bruges:
taverns, bath-houses, brothels, and gambling-houses lay within easy reach of
their lodgings along Vlamingstraat, just north of the market square. English
merchants worked very close to such distractions, weighing their commodities on the street – Engelsestraat – still bearing their name.[73] The merchant
of Chaucer's *Shipman's Tale* ignores such temptations: yet he is, of course,
consumed by a greater gambling game, since (as the Man of Law suggests)
merchants are professional rollers of the dice, medieval crap-shooters hoping for a six-and-five (and fearing one-and-one).[74] English, Scots, and other
foreign merchants at Bruges held their meetings at the Carmelite monastery. In 1344, the English had a chapel dedicated to St. Thomas Becket built
in the Carmelite church; friars were to celebrate mass there daily and, once
a week, sing a special mass in honor of the English saint. The Scots followed
suit in 1369 by commissioning a chapel dedicated to St. Ninian.[75] Such over-
laying of religious and national spaces and timetables tacitly recognizes
that commercial dealings of the kind essayed in the *Shipman's Tale* maintain
precarious relations to Christian doctrine, since they entail mysterious
vanishings of value bordering on usury.[76] At Bruges they are conducted with
"sheeldes," that imaginary unit of exchange: to redeem the loan of 20,000
"sheeldes" extended to him by the Italian bankers at Bruges, the merchant
must scare up real coin from his associates and pay the Italians at their Paris
branch.[77]

    Bruges of the *Shipman's Tale* can be seen, then, as the eye or aporia of a
vortex where agreements escape, for a moment, secure material referents.
On the home front, however, the husband's vanishing into Flanders cues
more material forms of exchange, of "frankes" for "flankes" (7.199–203).
The merchant's wife, contemporary English audiences might have thought,
finds her own way of traveling "in Flaundres," since Flemish women followed

the trade routes with the cloth and were prominent as prostitutes in both Florence (at the municipal brothel) and London.[78] But there is a complex exchanging of roles in this tale between professional merchant and professional religious, which sees the wife, moving between men, performing an invaluable crossover function; she is hence the knowing avatar of a newly fused, sacred and secular, *businesse*. Her husband, before setting out on his mercantile travels, "up ariseth" on the third day

> And on his nedes sadly hym avyseth,
> And up into his countour-hous gooth he
> To rekene with hymself, wel may be,
> Of thilke yeer how that it with hym stood,
> And how that he despended hadde his good,
> And if that he encressed were or noon.
> His bookes and his bagges many oon
> He leith biforn hym on his countyng-bord.
>
> *(7.76–83)*

While the monkish merchant reckons with himself, shutting "his countour-dore" so that "no man sholde hym lette," his *cosyn* monk walks back and forth below, reading from his portable Book of Hours ("portehors," 135). It is in this public space framed for recreation and delight – "the gardyn" (90, 93) – that the monk encounters the merchant's wife and conceives the "frankes" / "flankes" exchange. The exchange of roles within "cosynage" (36) between merchant and monk is accentuated by a later husbandly speech, or sermon, on the mysteries of his profession:

> "Wyf," quod this man, "litel kanstow devyne
> The curious bisynesse that we have.
> For of us chapmen, also God me save,
> And by that lord that clepid is Seint Yve,
> Scarsly amonges twelve tweye shul thyrve
> Continuelly, lastynge unto oure age."
>
> *(7.224–9)*

Given such slim chances of survival (endurance, salvation), the merchant must perennially "avyse" himself "Upon this queynte world" (236).

Implicit in all this is the recognition that religious and secular spheres press upon one another as what we now call *business* (a term itself emerging from religious practices, as in the Second Nun's "leveful bisynesse" of translating, 8.5) evolves. Monks, particularly English monks, had long proved indispensable to the economy that cycled its money through Bruges. The ransom value of Richard I, King of England, had been assessed at one year of the Cistercian wool-clip (plus that of two minor orders); English monasteries were household names in Flanders. Monkish wool-growers were pioneering many of the business techniques – such as double-entry bookkeeping, and factory-style, class-based divisions of labor – that established preconditions for later capitalist expansion.[79] It is thus not surprising to find the merchant in Chaucer's tale sitting monk-like among "his bookes and his bagges" as he contemplates a trip to Bruges; and that once there, he sets about *creauncing* (another word transferred from religious registers, meaning literally "faithing," or as we would say – sustaining the moral vocabulary – affirming credit-worthiness).[80] Such half-acknowledged minglings of secular and sacred registers – essential to the emergence of capitalism – were productive both of high humor (as in the *Decameron* and the *Shipman's Tale*) and high anxiety. Flemish painting worked at both ends of this scale, while occasionally attempting to balance between extremes.

In Quinten Massys' first surviving "secular" picture, *The Moneychanger and His Wife* (1514; figure 8), we find many of the narrative elements of the *Shipman's Tale*. The husband, at left, is in part withdrawn from us (his face partly obscured by shadows). He is thoroughly or "sadly" (in the *Shipman's Tale* sense of 7.76) absorbed in a task that is secular, and yet suggestive of religious devotion: as Chaucer's merchant proceeds to "rekene with hymself," so Massys' deploys scales (that might be deployed on him come Judgment Day).[81] At right we have his wife – his red cuff-bands neatly picked up by her red gown – set to read her portable Book of Hours (or *portehors*). She is thus securely situated within religious terms of reference – except that her left hand holds a leaf suspended in mid-turn as her gaze moves from her domain of religious instruction to his world of commerce. Here again, as with Chaucer's merchant wife, the mediating movement of a female protagonist proves vital both to the artistic project (the painting, the poem) and to ideological possibilities beyond the frame.

Quinten Massys joined the St. Luke guild of painters at Antwerp in 1491 and reportedly died in a Carthusian house in the outskirts of the city in 1530. Antwerp grew in prosperity as Bruges declined, helped by an agreement of 1496 that established the city as the continental outlet for the sale of English cloth. Interestingly, Massys chose to dress his moneychanging couple in fifteenth-century costumes associated with Jan Van Eyck and Petrus Christus, great Bruges-based painters of the earlier, prosperous time. His 1514 painting borrows from the representation of St. Eloy executed by Christus for a guild of goldsmiths in 1449.[82] Here again we have a suggestive mix of sacred

8 Quinten Massys, *The Moneychanger and His Wife* (1514), Musées Royaux des Beaux-Arts de Belgique, Brussels. Photograph © Erich Lessing/Art Resource, NY.

and secular elements (figure 9); and here again, a woman supplies a vital narrative linkage between two men (her intended spouse and the goldsmith saint who is about to weigh her wedding ring in his scales).[83] Saint Loy is the favorite saint of Chaucer's most secular religious, the Prioress: she swears by him (1.120) while sporting "a brooch of gold ful sheene" (160) engraved with a particularly famous straddling of spiritual and worldly terms: *Amor vincit omnia* (162).

Massys' ambition to locate a mercantile marriage on secure ideological ground is sustained through two narrative inserts. The mirror on the *counting-bord* shows a man engaged in solitary reading, presumably of a religious cast (given the cross formed by the window frame and the church spire glimpsed beyond); the door open to the street – behind the wife's left shoulder – shows a leathery old man gossiping with a young man in a hat.

9 Petrus Christus, *Saint Eloi* (1449), The Metropolitan Museum of Art, New York. Robert Lehmann Collection, 1975.1.110.

Neither excessively pious and world-shunning, nor too gregarious and addicted to words on the street, Massys' couple thus seems exemplary. Such delicate, negotiated positioning was particularly crucial for Flemings and Florentines, since their urban class structures were effectively severed from subservience to nobility (and hence from nobility's monopolistic hold over ethical discourse).[84] Such confident cross-hatching of sacred and secular terms of reference, however, is not frequently achieved by Flemish painting of this period; more common is an impulse to explore the polarized extremes of Massys' two vignettes. His later representations of moneychanging push toward grotesquerie; copies of his 1514 painting secularize the scene (as the Book of Hours becomes a book of accounts).[85] Such splitting, troubling, or polarizing of registers delivers us to our third, final, and most enigmatic Chaucerian articulation of "in Flaundres."

Bettering Nature and Breaking Bodies

The phrase, "In Flaundres," opens the *Pardoner's Tale*, but after this opening no reference is made to anything specifically Flemish. In the *Shipman's Tale*, the merchant asks "Quy la?" (7.214) and the monk swears "by Seint Denys of Fraunce" (7.151), reminding us that the tale indeed opens at Seint-Denys in France; but in the *Pardoner's Tale*, nothing. We can hunt for localizing details: the land is plague-ridden; Flanders suffered most acutely from plague *after* the European pandemic of 1348–9 (although it is worth remembering that plague was interpreted as divine punishment for deviant or unruly sexuality).[86] Flemings were famous drunks: Ghentians invaded Bruges during the procession of the Holy Blood in 1362 because they counted on "the wholesale inebriation" of the population. Tavern life was dangerous: a man sitting in a pub in Eeklo in 1373 was hit in the head with a battle-axe; fortunately, he was wearing an iron helmet at the time.[87] Such anecdotes, while usefully exemplifying discourses of Flanders, actually lead us away from what happens "in Flaundres," as the Pardoner tells it, for whereas anecdotes bring the assurances of familiar literary form, the Pardoner's narrative at once disintegrates into listing and troping:

> In Flaundres whilom was a compaignye   *once*
> Of yonge folk that haunteden folye,   *addicted to*
> As riot, hasard, stywes, and tavernes,   *dicing, brothels*
> Where as with harpes, lutes, and gyternes,
> They daunce and pleyen at dees bothe day and nyght,   *dice*
> And eten also and drynken over hir myght,   *beyond*
> Thurgh which they doon the devel sacrifise
> Withinne that develes temple in cursed wise
> By superfluytee abhomynable.
>
>   *(6.463–71)*

It is not clear whether "that develes temple" is to be imagined as a tavern, or as the human body itself. Perhaps both at once: Hieronymus Bosch can imagine a tavern within the giant body of a man (see figure 10).[88] Bosch also isolates and amplifies many of the objects found in the Pardoner's opening passage to create fantastic new landscapes of damnation: dice and gaming-tables; naked people impaled on stringed instruments; wind instruments protruding from every human orifice. Bosch provides us with important clues as to what is going on "in Flaundres": he projects a landscape where natural cycles are arrested, where nature is used up, compromised, or

10 Hieronymus Bosch, detail from right (Hell) panel, *Garden of Delights* triptych, Prado, Madrid. Photograph © Scala/Art Resource, NY.

destroyed; where human beings, at once crowded together and isolated from one another, are tortured by artifacts of their own devising.

As in Bosch, so in the *Pardoner's Tale*; we encounter both the disintegration of symbolic representation and the reconstitution of shattered discursive form through the employment of the most traditional religious schemata: the Seven Deadly Sins; the exemplum; the Biblical citation; the oath. In the

Pardoner's hands, this process is both satisfying and suspect, as religious narrative is reduced to its most basic elements and then reconstituted through a brilliant tour de force of storytelling. Such brilliance cannot be denied, but the Pardoner can finally be repudiated as a purveyor of counterfeits: shitty trousers proffered as "the relyk of a seint" (6.949); the shoulder-bone of "an hooly Jewes sheep" sold to cure "pokkes," "scabbe," and animal diseases (6.350–60). The Pardoner speaks of counterfeiting just before launching into his tale – "I wol noon of the apostles countrefete," he says (6.447). Talk of counterfeiting offers some contemporary resonance with the Flemish setting of his tale. In 1385, the first Burgundian count of Flanders, Philip the Bold, forced Flemings to renounce an alliance with England; in 1388 he backed the minting of counterfeit English nobles. These debased Flemish coins were so skillfully manufactured that they circulated in England as legal tender, thereby undermining the English economy while insulting, *disparaging*, the honor system that English nobles supposedly imaged forth.[89] The *Pardoner's Tale* was written ca. 1390–5.[90]

Discussion of the natural and the counterfeit, meshed with anxieties about nativeness and passing as native, bring us to questions of sexuality. Recent engagements with the Pardoner's sexuality have been shadowed by the recognition (unconscious or unspoken) that the figure of the Pardoner is, historically speaking, marked for extinction.[91] Other pilgrim types will disappear during the Henrician revolution; monks, nuns, and friars will walk the Shakespearean stage (if not, at least not openly, the streets of London). Pardoners, however, will become the *particular* target of anti-Catholic polemic. Chaucer's representation of the Pardoner certainly helped sustain this sixteenth-century discourse of ridicule, vilification (and homophobia). But what were the well-springs of such a discourse for Chaucer in the fourteenth century, and of what anxieties do they speak?

In the fifteenth canto of his *Inferno*, Dante meets Brunetto Latini, his sometime teacher, at a place where fire rains from the skies, the earth is barren, and nature runs backwards: the circle of the sodomites. This place is delimited by a series of walls; their architect is said to build:

> Quali Fiamminghi tra Guizzante e Bruggia
> temendo 'l fiotto che 'nver' lor s'avventa,
> fanno lo schermo perché 'l mar si fuggia . . .
> $$(15.4–6)^{92}$$

> Just as, between Wissant and Bruges, the Flemings,
> fearing the tide that rushes in on them,
> make the bulwark to drive back the sea . . .

Hell's builder is actually said to be *less* ambitious than the Flemings: his walls are said to be "né sí alti né sí grossi," "neither so high nor so thick" (15.11). The Flemings, we have noted, were proud of having built such great urban cultures upon land recovered from marsh and sea, employing ingenuity and technical cunning where nature proved deficient. They were pressured by the knowledge, passed on by Dante's *Inferno*, that the business of improving upon nature is perilous for those seeking salvation within Catholic cultures. They were further oppressed by suggestions that the marshy desolation of Flemish landscapes bespoke unnatural resistance to the claims of noble blood; for Bavaria Herald (who had traveled to the English court in 1390) the waste land ("dat woeste lant") of Flanders could only be redeemed by the healing touch of knightly rule.[93] Eustache Deschamps (in many poems) agrees: for him the cursed land of Flanders ("la terre maudite") is to be compared, for its God-defying presumption, to "Sodom et Gomorre" (16.4–5). And yet, as the Flemish cities told their count, Flanders could not and would not be different: "Flanders is a sterile country, infertile in itself, completely founded on the fact and course of merchandise, densely populated with foreigners, merchants, and others."[94]

Chaucer's Pardoner, assumed incapable of natural reproduction, also proves skilled in generating wealth from sterile conditions: where his genitals should be, "in his lappe," he carries a wallet full of pardons. There is convergence here between that which the Pardoner embodies, or unembodies, and the land of which he speaks. And of course, inasmuch as antisemitic discourse is not *about* Jews (it is, rather, about the anxieties of gentiles),[95] so this discourse of "in Flaundres" is not about Flemings (or those whose sexuality is considered sterile). Although the *Pardoner's Tale*, following its opening phrase, finds not a single Flemish referent, it does touch down in London: once in Fish Street, and twice in "Chepe." It was in Cheapside that the dizzying effects of a highly complex division of labor, serving local and international markets, was most acutely registered. The "fumositee" of Spanish wine drunk in "Chepe" (with the Pardoner) transports us to "Spaigne" (6.565–72), to similarly phantasmagoric scenes in Bosch, but most directly to Langland, Cheapside's poet laureate, whose B Prologue dissolves in street cries and a roll call of specialized employment: wool weavers and weavers of linen, tailors and tinkers and toll-collectors, and so on (220÷3).[96] This litany is amplified five Passus later, when Glutton enters a tavern (not a million miles from the *Pardoner's Tale*) to find Pernele of Flanders, a Cheapside scavenger, and more than two dozen other people pursuing highly specialist trades.

Langland reprises the articulation of a highly complex division of labor in Passus V of the C text, in which the awakened dreamer is subjected to searching vocational interrrogation by Resoun. Set within the London district of Cornhill – ill-famed for its pillories, stocks, vagabonds, and market for stolen clothes – the dreamer figures himself as a tradesman who has "ay loste and loste" (95), but hopes one day to win and thus justify his self-appointed calling (presumably by completing his poem).[97] In his *General Prologue*, which is about the division of labor, Chaucer eschews models of authorly and poetic identity borrowed from French and Italian precedents to subject himself to Langlandian scrutiny. In a meditated act of authorial signature – evoking those continental texts he here parts company with – he aligns himself with the Pardoner as part of a group Derek Pearsall calls "miscellaneous predators."[98] As such, Chaucer writes "in Flaundres" in two senses: first, as purveyor of a funny-sounding mother tongue that would command little respect in Florence, Avignon, Paris (or even, as yet, parts of Westminster). Second, as a poet struggling to assess the possibilities of a complex, commercial, urbanizing, aggressive, post-bastard feudal society pioneered by those cities north of Calais. Through the Pardoner, his most brilliant and ambivalently embodied rhetor, he tastes the exhilaration and the terror of a world that, finding nature deficient, exhausted, or all used up, dares to improve upon nature.[99] It is here that historicist and psychoanalytic approaches might unite to explore prehistoric – or, better, medieval – traces of "the ego's era."[100] Technological innovation, craft specialization, and increasing urbanization will open new social and economic possibilities *and* incubate new forms of psychic disturbance, fragmentation, and disequilibrium *while* identifying newly projected threats to personal and social well-being. New senses of spatial constriction will fuel the drive to outward-bound territorialization, nation-making, and empire-building while at the same time, paradoxically, demanding fixed boundaries of selfhood, nationality, and sexuality.

The most famous explorations of such contradictory, expansive, and restrictive anxieties are by Hieronymus Bosch. The wasted and fruitless landscapes of his Last Judgment scenes are lit by lurid flames from distant cities (generated by war or by industrial processes run out of control). In the central panel of the Bruges Judgment (figure 11), musical instruments double as instruments of torture; bestial troops and demons wield weapons of assured destruction – one of them employed to open a gigantic Flemish *mossel* – or goad naked humans to every kind of excess.[101] In a serious of ferociously local, myopic engagements, naked human beings either work gigantic machines – devised by some absent technological genius – or are processed, dismembered, and consumed by them; Christ floats in judgment above all this, safe and clean within his bio-spheric bubble.

11 Hieronymus Bosch, *Last Judgment*, Groeninge Museum, Bruges. Photograph © Scala/Art Resource, NY.

Bosch, as Michel de Certeau suggests, defeats decoding and defies comparisons.[102] Yet very many paintings still found at Bruges – the Groeninge Museum rates as one of Europe's most harrowing collections – share Bosch's compelling contemplation of disintegrating human bodies, set within frameworks of retributive justice, *in extremis*. Gerhard David's *The Judgement of Cambises* sees a corrupt judge, Sisamnes, being arrested (left panel) and then being skinned alive (figure 12). At left a dog scratches himself; under the table we have a fine array of fashionable footwear (including the judge's

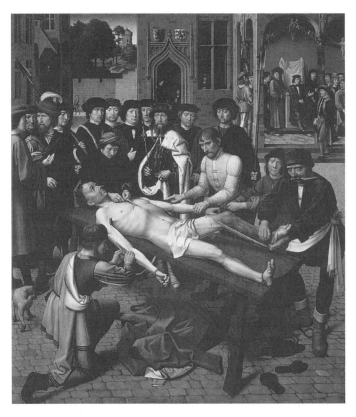

12 Gerhard David, *The Judgment of Cambises* diptych, oil on panel, 1498.
Right panel, known as "The flaying of Sisamnes." Groeninge Museum, Bruges.
Photograph © The Bridgeman Art Library International.

discarded slippers); at top right we see the judge's son and heir dispensing
justice from a seat upholstered with his father's skin. This very large diptych
– best not viewed on a full stomach – was painted in 1498 to hang in the
Council Chamber of Bruges Town Hall. It thus both issues from and speaks
to the heart of civic power, fashioning and reflecting the anxieties of alder-
men charged with administering justice. Judicial torture, first recorded at
Bruges in 1258–60, spread rapidly in Flanders through the fourteenth century; by the time Gerhard David set to work it was commonplace, an
accepted part of everyday procedure.[103]
   Such compulsive contemplations of human bodies being skinned, processed, or broken, I am suggesting, express anxious apprehensions of communities no longer observing traditional limits of rank and religion; nobility

no longer rules, and human ingenuity (through newly intensive divisions of labor) improves upon nature, prospers, and grows rich in, or in spite of, "dat woeste land." English ruling classes, as I argued in chapter 1, looked to France for models of aristocratic value and deportment, wedded to (almost epiphenomenal of) the fruitful soil of an agrarian economy. And yet everything here summarized as "Flanders" is gaining some purchase on English imagining. Even as possibilities for an English industry were being explored through immigrant Flemish weavers (Bath might really surpass Ypres or Ghent), so writers such as Langland and Chaucer – while uncertain of their standing in this emergent social order – begin to dream. In the unprecedentedly complex social orders of Langland's *Visio* and Chaucer's *General Prologue*, we find tremors of anxiety and fears of transgression attending unmistakably exuberant apprehensions of new imaginative possibilities. All such feelings, I am suggesting, are projected onto the body that would situate us (lead us into) "in Flaundres." This, for the notional leader of Chaucer's pilgrim *compagnye*, is a body that invites both kissing and castration (7.951–68). Such a project – to spell it out in historical terms – requires the English to become Fleming-like while repudiating all things Flemish.

The denatured, or ambiguously natured, character of the Pardoner is insisted upon at his first appearance, in the *General Prologue*, and reasserted through that threat of castration as he ends his speaking. This last attack on the Pardoner's personhood concedes that his language (his entire bodily performance) *is* beguiling, so very like our own, and yet not. The urge to isolate the Pardoner from the social collectivity at the end of his verbal performance "in Flaundres" again returns us to that uneasy English/Flemish borderline. Interest in differentiating discourses at permeable linguistic or territorial boundaries is rarely benign: witness Bosnia. Trevisa, in his famous survey of languages, speaks of Flemings "in the west syde of Wales" moderating their "strange speche."[104] Chaucer's Cook, the most disorderly of low-life Londoners, shows himself familiar with the sayings and inflections of Flemings ("'sooth pley, quaad pley,' as the Flemyng seith," 1.4357); his fellow Londoner and drinking companion, the Manciple, has "the Flemyng" say that little talking causes less trouble.[105] In 1381, a Southwark brothel managed by Flemings was attacked; in London, some 30 or 40 Flemings were massacred at the church of St Martin, Vintry. All chronicles note this massacre; one of them reports that linguistic inflection proved crucial in isolating Flemings: "And many fflemmynges loste hir heedes at that tyme, and namely they that koude nat say Breede and Chese, but Case and Brode."[106]

Caroline Barron has said that "no-one was executed by mob violence or lynch law on the streets of London between 1381 and Cade's Revolt in

1450."[107] This remarkable assertion cannot dispel unease about those lines in the *Nun's Priest's Tale* that would compare the chasing of a fox to the shrill shouts let out by "Jakke Straw and his meynee," when "they wolden any Flemyng kille" (7.3394–6). It is the naturalized complacency of these lines that makes them so disturbing; their accommodating of targeted homicide within the familiar confines of classroom exercise or barnyard fable. Their effect compares with that of Chaucer's most dangerously freighted antisemitic line, spoken within the comfortable confines of a saint's legend: "Whoso that troweth *nat* this [namely, Christian revelation; my emphasis] a beest he is" (*Second Nun's Tale*, 8.288). In the complex history of antisemitic discourse after 1100, Miri Rubin has written, "those who could never aspire to eucharistic wholesomeness became more clearly distinguished as different, as not belonging."[108] And the more the eucharistic cult came to predominate – literally taking over the streets – in Western Europe, the more unease was felt "about the Jew's proximity to it within Christian spaces."[109] Perhaps it is not surprising, then, that it is in the language of the unwhole or unwholesome Pardoner that we find gobbets of eucharistic discourse afloat in a sea of random, fragmentary (but brilliantly articulated) religious discourse that holds us all spellbound. And here perhaps is one last historical intuition (that the text of Chaucer cannot know): that the magic of the transformed eucharist will itself migrate, with time, to the mystery of the commodity.[110]

Cunning Cosmography and Preposterous Desire

In 1435, Philip, duke of Burgundy and count of Flanders, abandoned his alliance with England, sided with the French, and (in the summer of 1436) joined the siege of Calais. This act of royal and noble calculation soon unleashed an accumulated fund of "national" stereotyping about ignoble Flemings. The English crown circulated letters throughout England urging subjects to come to the defense of Calais, recognizing "how grete a jewel the seide towne with his marchies is to us"; prayers and processions were ordered (by archiepiscopal mandate) in support of the besieged city.[111] Having duly relieved Calais, Humphrey, duke of Gloucester, proceeded to west Flanders and burned Poperinge. In London, houses of Flemish merchants were sacked by the mob and 400 Lowlanders hurried forward to renew their oaths of allegiance. Four surviving English poems, in what Pearsall terms "an outbreak of Englishness," describe the siege of Calais.[112] Two of them survive in copies of the *Brut*, supplementing the chronicle account; one of them, edited as "Mockery of the Flemings," mocks Flemings for fighting "fersli as lyons of Cotteswold" (thus equating them with the English sheep that support their cloth-making).[113] There is even a poem in Latin hexameters by the Ferrarese Titus Livius Frulovisi, an author of "desperate incompetence" who subsequently joined Duke Humphrey's household as his personal "poeta et orator." This poem, the *Humfroidos*, sees Flemings strung from trees, in the course of Humphrey's *chevauchée*, like grapes on a vine.[114]

Shortly after all this, someone in London or Westminster, close to the inner circles of power, wrote a poem called *The Libelle of Englyshe Polycye*.[115] Lydgate too wrote of Humphrey's triumph at Calais (as about most everything else),[116] but the *Libelle* poet – a writer of formidable intelligence – drew inspiration directly from Chaucer. Some of this simply recycles commonplaces glimpsed in the *Pardoner's Tale*: "ye have herde," he says, that Flemings go nowhere without first drinking beer (282–7), and then (he says) "Undre the borde they pissen as they sitte" (288); the English, he says, made them shit in their breeches when they ran home from Calais (290–2).[117] Shitty breeches are invoked just once in Chaucer: the Host attributes them to the narrator who has just led the *compagnye* through an imaginary Flanders (6.948–50). Elsewhere, the influence of Chaucer (and specifically of the *Pardoner's Tale*) is registered more directly.[118] Flanders trades with Spain: why not territorialize this sea, keep it under English control, and stop the commons of Flanders, that sterile land, from living off of our superior native product?

> Thus, if the see be kepte, then herkene hedere,   *listen here*
> Yf these ij. londes comene not togedere,
> So that the flete of Flaundres passe nought,
> That in the narowe see it be not brought
> Into the Rochelle to feche the fumose wyne,
> Nere into Britoune bay for salt so fyne,   *nor*
> What is than Spayne, what is Flaundres also?
> As who seyth, nought; there thryfte is alle ago.
> For the lytell londe of Flaundres is
> But a staple to other londes iwys,
> And all that groweth in Flaundres, greyn and sede,
> May not a moneth fynde hem mete or brede.   *month*
> What hath thenne Flaundres, be Flemmynges leffe or lothe,
> But a lytell madere[119] and Flemmyshe cloothe?
> By draperinge of oure wolle in substaunce
> Lyvene here comons, this is here governaunce.
>
>   *(108–23)*

The *Libelle* poet argues that the English should pursue their expansionist ambitions by following the logic of their coin: the noble, which images forth "kyng, shype and swerde and pouer of the see" (35). Such ambitions are thwarted, however, chiefly by Flemings, who continue to counterfeit our coin and contest our naval superiority. The *Libelle* poet deploys his inherited anti-Fleming rhetoric to energetic effect: but Flanders can no longer be rolled over quite so easily, since it forms part of Burgundy, allied with France. What to do? In the second half of the poem, attention drifts westward. Ireland abounds with "commodities" (listed at some length, 658–64); and since the king called *rex Anglie* is *"dominus* also *Hibernie"* (666–7), Ireland should help England "to kepe well aboute the see" (673). Ireland, furthermore, is fertile in ways that are wasted on its rude and unskillful native inhabitants:

> It is fertyle for thynge that there do growe
> And multiplyen, loke who so lust to knowe,
> So large, so gode and so comodyouse
> That to declare is straunge and merveylouse.
> For of sylvere and golde there is the oore
> Amonge the wylde Yrishe, though they be pore,
> For they ar rude and can thereone no skylle;
> So that, if we had there pese and gode wylle
> To myne and fine and metal for to pure,   *refine*
> In wylde Yrishe myght we fynde the cure.
>
> *(682–91)*

The "cure" here proposed, of course, is counterfeited from Flanders: just as the Flemish have done to us – take a raw native product, export it, transform it through superior technology – so we will do to the Irish. Care must be taken, therefore, that Yrelonde not "be shente" (707), lost to some deformed native creature ("wylde Yrishe wyrlynge," 716). English holdings in Ireland have shrunk to no more than "a lytell cornere," 727). No "grounde" in Christendom is as good as Ireland – "So large, so gode, so plenteouse, so riche" – that "me semyth" (the poet says) "that ryght were and not wronge / To gete that lond" (742–6). And so the poet concludes with a modest proposal: just one year's expenses sustained in the war with France

> Myght wynne Yrelond to a fynall conquest
> In one sole yere, to sett us all in reste.
> *(770–1).*[120]

The *Libelle* proved popular with powerful people: owners of manuscripts include Lord Burghley (chief minister to Elizabeth I) and Samuel Pepys

(Secretary to the Admiralty); in one manuscript, presented as a gift in 1471 by a William Caston, the poem is renamed "The *byble* of Englyshe polecie."[121] The *Libelle* poet had promised to write another "lytell boke," detailing how the Irish "cure" might be effected (775). This book does not survive, but its imaginative enterprise is carried forward in the next phase of English westward expansion by Richard Hakluyt. The Americas, for Hakluyt, like Ireland for the *Libelle* poet, are imagined as fabulous repositories of natural resources (as English representations of the "wild Irish" are being mapped forward onto the native inhabitants of "New England").[122] English merchant adventurers are struggling to revive their continental trade in unfinished cloth; the queen is disturbed by the "pitifull outecryes" of unemployed cappers, knitters, and spinners.[123] What then, if instead of bringing to England finished commodities, "as wee bringe nowe the commodities of Fraunce and Flaundres," we were to bring "substaunces vnwroughte" [from the Americas] "to the ymployment of a wonderfull multitude of the poore subiectes of this Realme" (p. 32)? England again, in short, might do to wild and primitive peoples what Flanders has done to England.[124]

The *Libelle of Englyshe Polycye* does not appear in the first, 1589 edition of Hakluyt's *Principall Navigations, Voiages and Discoveries of the English Nation.* In the second edition, however, Mandeville's *Travels* and Pliny are out,[125] and the *Libelle* is in – and so too is that "cunning Cosmographer," Geoffrey Chaucer. Certain themes of the *Libelle*, which appears in its entirety,[126] harmonize well with Hakluyt. Steady emphasis is placed upon the need for naval domination; the "grete karrekkis" of the Genoese, freighted with "wollene clothe of ours," are watched with a jaundiced eye as they "aventure, as ofte it dothe byfall, / Into Flaundres" (332–40).[127] And the tendency to associate national character with commodities characteristic of the nation – fully developed in Hogarth – is already evident. Whereas the "best chaffare" of England may be stated with robust simplicity – "Clothe, woll, and tynne" (375–6) – Venetians and Florentines hoodwink the English with their "thynges of complacence":

> Apes and japes and marmusettes taylede,
> Nifles, trifles, that litell have availed,
> And thynges wyth whiche they fetely blere oure eye,   *cleverly*
> Wyth thynges not endurynge that we bye.
>
> *(348–51)*

In the preface to Hakluyt's second edition (1598–1600), Chaucer shares a short paragraph with Henry of Derby and Thomas of Woodstock. Derby, "afterward king of England," is celebrated for his journeys "into Prussia & Lithuania, with a briefe remembrance of his valiant exploits against the Infidels there."[128] "Then," Hakluyt continues,

> mention is made also of Tho of Woodstock his trauel into Pruis, and of his returne home. And lastly, our old English father Ennius, I meane, the learned, wittie, and profound Geffrey Chaucer, vnder the person of his knight, doeth full iudicially and like a cunning Cosmographer, make report of the long voiages and woorthy exploits of our English Nobles, Knights, & Gentlemen, to the Northren, and to other partes of the world in his dayes. ("Preface," p. 8)

Thus in Hakluyt's long history of English navigation, which follows an inexorable westward telos, we find Chaucer as the chronicler of a royal class pushing north and east at the borders of Christendom. Later in his volume Hakluyt prints "verses of Geofrey Chaucer in the knights Prologue" (under the heading *The English Knights Prologue*); the account ends at 1.66, with the Knight fighting "Heathen in Turkie." The imaginative supposition here compares with Bavaria Herald's: that a waste land, or a pagan land, can be redeemed or rendered fruitful by the touch of noble hoofprints. Such harping upon purity of lineage and motive touches on the anxious apprehension, earlier confessed by Hakluyt to Philip Sidney, that more recent English travelers have "been led with a preposterous desire of seeking rather gaine than Goddes glory": a complex anxiety – sexual, territorial, and religious – earlier excited by or projected onto Chaucer's Pardoner.[129] The preposterous, according to George Puttenham, is a trope bordering on those deemed "notoriously indecent"; acts of "preposterous Venus," once associated with the admired and reviled territory of Flanders, are now (Jonathan Goldberg demonstrates) to be discovered in the New World.[130]

Hakluyt's drive to the east – his *Voyages, Navigations, Traffiques, and Discoueries of the English Nation* leaves Chaucer's Knight in the eastern Mediterranean – seems to be laying a pedigreed prehistory for the westward turn that occupies most of the volume, except that, for Hakluyt, the drive north and east might just bring us westward. Pliny and Mandeville, expunged from Hakluyt's second edition, were much concerned with Scythia and Tartary. Mandeville tells of the war between Scythia and the Amazons (first edition, 46), and (elaborating upon Pliny) of women in Scythia with two pupils in each eye (first edition, 78). He also has much to say about Tartars, a subject of enduring interest to Hakluyt: for there remains the tantalizing possibility that "Scythians, and Tartarians" might "haue found the way to America, and entered the same" (first edition, 599): expeditions north and east might ultimately emerge in the west. Chaucer's Knight, of course, tells a tale of Scythia, and his son of Tartary. Although Hakluyt takes pains to deny the possibility of a northeast passage to America, he is nonetheless able to honor Chaucer as a "cunning cosmosgrapher," chronicling the best and most audacious aristocratic intuitions of his age. It is important to grasp, with Richard Helgerson, that when Hakluyt began writing in 1580, "England did not control a square inch of territory outside the British Isles."[131] Hakluyt writes proleptically, fashioning a vision of English global reach that the nation itself has yet to grow into.

Hakluyt's citation of Chaucer's crusading Knight immediately precedes a switch from military to mercantile matters, announced by the following title: "The original, proceedings and successe of the Northren domestical and forren trades and traffiques of this Isle of Britain from the time of Nero the Emperour . . . vntil this present time" (second edition, 124). This transition from matters of war to trade is made without great fanfare (two-thirds down the page), suggesting that all this forms part of one continuous history. And in this history, the winning and keeping of Calais now assumes newly mythic proportions, although the space mapped no longer cuts into continental Europe, but is England herself. Starting at p. 118 (and extending to p. 120) we find "the roll of the huge fleete of *Edward* the third before Calice, extant in the kings great wardrobe in London, whereby the wonderfull strength of *England* by sea in those dayes may appeare." The roll itself is accorded lavish space and two distinct typefaces (figure 13); the placenames themselves unfurl to map a proud island space: "Sandwich, Dover, Wight, Wincelsey, Waymouth, Lyme, Seton, Sydmouth, Exmouth" (and four more "-mouths"), "Loo, Yalme, Fowey, Bristol . . . Poole, Warham, Swanzey, Ilfercombe . . . Bamburgh, Newcastle, Walerich, Hertilpoole, Hull, York . . . Goford, Herwich, Ipswich . . . Boston, Swinhumber, Barton." This is very like the island-ringing music that still lulls many Brits to sleep every night (and inspires at least one Irish poet): the Shipping Forecast.[132]

By the time Hakluyt set to work, Flanders was once again a battleground for foreign armies: Germans, English, Scots, and French supporting the States General; Spaniards, Italians, and Germans on the royalist and Catholic side. In August 1585 Antwerp fell to the Spanish; in 1586 General Ralph Lane found his hopes for immediate rescue from Virginia confounded by "the doings in England for Flanders."[133] "Flanders" itself resonates less powerfully for Hakluyt and succeeding English generations than it does for Chaucer. In the steady migration of financial and artistic power from Bruges to Antwerp to Amsterdam, and in the emergence of the Dutch as a major naval power by 1650, much of the peculiar mystique of Flanders – embodied by those

The great fleete of Ed.3. Traffiques, and Discoueries. 119

Place	Ships	Mariners	Place	Ships	Mariners	
Sandwich	22.	504.	Hithe	6.	122.	
Douer	16.	336.	Shoreham	20.	329.	
Wight	13.	220.	‡Soford	5.	80.	‡Or,Seford.
Winchelsey	21.	596.	Newmouth	2.	18.	
Waymouth	15.	263.	Hamowl-hooke	7.	117.	
Lyme	4.	62.	Hoke	11.	208.	
Seton	2.	25.	Southhäpton	21.	576.	
Sydmouth	3.	62.	Leyming-ton	9.	159	
Exmouth	10.	193.	Poole	4.	94.	
Tegmouth	7.	120.	Warham	3.	59.	
Dartmouth	31.	757.	Swanzey	1.	29.	
Portsmouth	5.	96.	Ilfercombe	6.	79.	
Plimouth	26.	603.	‡Patricke-stowe	2.	27.	‡Or,Padstow.
Loo	20.	315.	Polerwan	1.	60.	
Yalme	2.	47.	Wadworth	1.	14.	
‡Fowey	47.	770. ‡Or,Foy.	Kardife	1.	51.	
Bristol	22.	608.	Bridgwater	1.	15.	
Tenmouth	2.	25.	Kaermar-then	1.	16.	
Hasting	5.	96.	Cailechef-worth	1.	12.	
Romney	4.	65.	Mulbrooke	1.	12.	
Rye	9.	156.	Summe of the Southfleete	493	9630	

The North fleete.

Place	Ships	Mariners	Place	Ships	Mariners
Bamburgh	1.	9.	Newcastle	17.	314.

Walcrich

13 "Roll of the huge fleete of Edward the third before Calice," in Richard Hakluyt, *Voyages, Navigations, Traffiques, and Discoveries of the English Nation*, second edition, I.119. Cambridge University Library.

great, precocious, polder-defying cities – gets lost. Lingering associations between Flanders, prostitution, and cloth-making are powerfully exploited by Defoe.[134] But the electrifying sense of a culture essaying an edgy, unmapped relationship to nature (under the shadow of violence, and through unprecedentedly complex divisions of labor) no longer endures; or it has, perhaps, migrated. No place and time, of course, replicates another, but we might conclude by just nominating two places – east and west – where something of "in Flaundres" survives. The first, as the far-sighted *Libelle* prompts us to realize (344–95) and Renaissance drama confirms, is Venice: another city precariously reclaimed from the sea, devoid of agriculture, dedicated to commerce, luxury "nifles" and "trifles," slick finance, and living on its wits; and imaginatively associated with sterility, usury, sodomy, artfulness, and death. The second is Los Angeles, or its "urban galaxy," extending its gridlocked freeways across a desert reclaimed through an "ecology of evil":[135] a city of infinite possibility, hybridity, and waste, where nature is improved upon (through a million cosmetic operations) and dreams are made and beamed to the world; a place endlessly watched, with fascination and repulsion, as or as if the way of the future. Whatever happens, apocalyptic and/or entertaining, happens here first, in LA, as once "in Flaundres."

NOTES

1 See *The Book of Margery Kempe*, ed. Sanford Brown Meech and Emily Hope Allen, Early English Text Society, os 212 (London: Oxford University Press for EETS, 1940; reprint Woodbridge: Boydell and Brewer, 1997), p. 132 ("Combomis dowtyr"). Joan of Arc was burned on May 30, 1431; Margery journeyed from Wilsnack to Calais in the late summer of 1433. John, duke of Bedford, became regent of France on the death of Henry V in 1422.

2 *The Folding Star* (London: Chatto and Windus, 1994), p. 9. For Hollinghurst's narrator, the "austere Town Museum" functions as a gay pick-up joint.

3 See Bernard McDonagh, *Belgium and Luxembourg*, Blue Guide (New York: W. W. Norton, 1993), pp. 167–8.

4 As "Cultural Capital of Europe, 2002," Bruges was at pains to emphasize its identity as an internationalist hub in both art and trade. The phenomenal art exhibit thoroughly dismantled the north/south divide implicit in the famous "Flemish primitives" show staged at Bruges in 1902: see Till-Holger Borchert et al., *The Age of Van Eyck: The Mediterranean World and Early Netherlandish Painting, 1430–1530* (Ghent and Amsterdam: Ludion, 2002), p. 6. And the *Hanze@Medici* exhibit, spread over four sites, explored the uniquely complex networks of trade and finance centered on Bruges: see André Vandewalle, *Hanze@Medici. Bruges: Crossroads of European Cultures* (Oostkamp: Stichting

Kunstboek, 2002); *Les Marchands de la Hanse et la banque des Médicis. Bruges, marché d'échanges culturels en Europe*, ed. Vandewalle (Oostkamp: Stichting Kunstboek, 2002).

5 The northward and eastward orientation of King's Lynn is in part determined by the peculiar geography of the Wash. The basic Baedeker for Margery is hence T. H. Lloyd, *England and the German Hanse, 1157–1611* (Cambridge: Cambridge University Press, 1991), rather than (as for Chaucer) T. H. Lloyd, *The English Wool Trade in the Middle Ages* (Cambridge: Cambridge University Press, 1977).

6 See chapter 1 above, pp. 56–61.

7 See Ardis Butterfield, "French Culture and the Ricardian Court," in *Essays on Ricardian Literature: In Honour of John Burrow*, ed. A. J. Minnis, Charlotte Morse, and Thorlac Turville-Petre (Oxford: Clarendon Press, 1997), pp. 82–120 (pp. 88, 119–20).

8 The *Grace Dieu*'s only known voyage ended in mutiny off the Isle of Wight. This great ship – one of the largest English vessels afloat before the seventeenth century – was subsequently moored in the River Hamble; its remains are still visible at very low tides. The three other large ships built for Henry V between 1413 and 1420 – again, the names are instructive – are the *Trinity Royal* (rebuilt from the old *Trinity*), the *Holigost* (rebuilt from a Spanish ship), and the *Jesus*. See Ian Friel, "Winds of Change? Ships and the Hundred Years' War," in *Arms, Armies and Fortifications in the Hundred Years' War*, ed. Anne Curry and Michael Hughes (Woodbridge: Boydell Press, 1994), pp. 183–93 (pp. 190–1); Susan P. Rose, "Henry V's *Grace Dieu* and Mutiny at Sea: Some New Evidence," *Mariner's Mirror* 63 (1977), 3–7; A. J. Holland, *Ships of British Oak: The Rise and Decline of Wooden Shipbuilding in Hampshire* (Newton Abbot: David and Charles, 1971), pp. 67–9. On Henry V's championing of English, see John H. Fisher, "A Language Policy for Lancastrian England," *PMLA* 107 (1992), 1168–80; Paul Strohm, *England's Empty Throne: Usurpation and the Language of Legitimation, 1399–1422* (New Haven: Yale University Press, 1998).

9 A point powerfully and extensively made by Derek Pearsall, "The Idea of Englishness in the Fifteenth Century," in *Nation, Court and Culture: New Essays on Fifteenth-Century Poetry*, ed. Helen Cooney (Dublin: Four Courts Press, 2000), pp. 15–27.

10 And nonetheless, for all that, historical in impact. The rest of this paragraph owes much to the proddings and concrete suggestions of Bruce Holsinger.

11 See James I. Wimsatt, *Chaucer and His French Contemporaries: Natural Music in the Fourteenth Century* (Toronto: University of Toronto Press, 1991).

12 For a sophisticated guide to the latter, see Aranye O. Fradenburg, *Sacrifice Your Love* (Minneapolis: University of Minnesota Press, 2002).

13 The terms "Flaunders," "Flaundryssh," and "Flemyng" are used somewhat loosely by Chaucer (as by his contemporaries). Flemings and Brabantines were keen to distinguish themselves from one another. In London, Fleming and

Brabantine weavers organized themselves into separate guilds; there is no evidence that such separation saved alien workers from the massacre at St. Martin Vintry in June 1381. Chaucer refers ten times to Flanders or things Flemish, makes no reference to Brabant, and speaks once of "Pipers of the Duche tonge" (*House of Fame*, 1234). Citation of "Flaundres" in Chaucer hence works in ways comparable to the naming of "Lombardy." "Lumbardye" evokes both the historical territory ruled by northern Italian despots or tyrants, an imaginative terrain explored by Fragment 4 of the *Canterbury Tales*, and an alarming set of possibilities for English polity under Richard II: see David Wallace, *Chaucerian Polity: Absolutist Lineages and Associational Forms in England and Italy* (Stanford, Calif.: Stanford University Press, 1997), pp. 31–54, 261–387.

14   This same permit warned him against attempting to smuggle any wools, hides, or wool-fells out of the country without paying customs duties. See *Chaucer Life-Records*, ed. Martin M. Crow and Clair C. Olson (Oxford: Clarendon Press, 1966), p. 4.

15   The Orwell is a river and not, as *The Riverside Chaucer* suggests, a coastal town.

16   West Flanders was under French control at this point, rendering Calais difficult of access from Bruges.

17   "In three successive years from 1385 to 1387," J. J. N Palmer writes, "England was faced with invasion from massive armadas concentrated at Sluys" ("English Foreign Policy 1388–99," in *The Reign of Richard II*, ed. F. R. H. Du Boulay and Caroline Barron [London: Athlone Press, 1971]), p. 82. On Deschamps' enthusiastic hopes for a French invasion, see chapter 1 above, p. 58.

18   "English bills for Bruges in Flanders," Kenneth S. Cahn writes, "were quoted in English sterling against the shield or *ecu* (*scudo*) which did not exist as a coin, but which signified 24 (silver) groats, Flemish currency" ("Chaucer's Merchants and the Foreign Exchange: An Introduction to Medieval Finance," *Studies in the Age of Chaucer* 2 (1980), p. 85).

19   For details of foreign merchants at Bruges living "en interaction fréquente et intense avec la société locale," see Peter Stabel, "Les marchands dans la ville," in *Les Marchands*, ed. André Vandewalle, pp. 85–97 (p. 94a); see further Jacques Paviot, *Bruges 1300–1500* (Paris: Editions Autrement, 2002), pp. 38–68.

20   See Stabel, "Les marchands," p. 86. The population of Bruges at this time is reckoned to be ca. 45,000.

21   See Vanessa Harding, "Cross-channel Trade and Cultural Contacts: London and the Low Countries in the Later Fourteenth Century," in *England and the Low Countries in the Late Middle Ages*, ed. Caroline Barron and Nigel Saul (New York: St. Martin's Press, 1995), p. 163. On the extraordinary mixing of Middle Dutch and Middle English terms that occurs in select fifteenth-century business documents, see Laura Wright, "Trade between England and the Low Countries: Evidence from Historical Linguistics," in ibid., pp. 169–79. Dutch terms for activities associated with beer-brewing and boat-building proved especially influential.

22 See *Chaucer Life-Records*, ed. Crow and Olson, p. 30 n. 5; these estimates are based on the study of more than 60 records.

23 Rhenish wine "could only pass to England through the markets or ports of the Low Countries" (Harding, "Cross-channel Trade," p. 156); the ships transporting this wine were often piloted by Flemish masters.

24 See *Chaucer Life-Records*, ed. Crow and Olson, pp. 29–66; Walter Prevenier, "Les perturbations dans les relations commerciales anglo-flamandes entre 1379 et 1407. Causes de désaccord et raisons d'une réconciliation," *Studia Historica Gandensia* 182 (1973), pp. 477–97; Pierre Chaplis, *Some Documents Regarding the Fulfilment and Interpretation of the Treaty of Bretigny 1361–1369*, Camden Miscellany 19 (London: Royal Historical Society, 1952), esp. pp. 6–8 (on Article 12, dropped from the ratified treaty, which proposed that the King of England should renounce claims to the sovereignty of, *inter alia*, Flanders).

25 Caroline Barron, "Introduction: England and the Low Countries 1327–1477," in *England and the Low Countries*, ed. Barron and Saul, p. 2.

26 See T. H. Lloyd, *The English Wool Trade*, pp. 209–10; David Nicholas, *Medieval Flanders* (New York: Longman, 1992), p. 290.

27 By 1127, traffic between the two regions was speedy enough for news of the murder of the Flemish count to reach London within two days; by the end of the thirteenth century, English wool was essential to the Flemish economy. See Lloyd, *The English Wool Trade*, p. 6; Marc De Laet, "De Vlaamse aktieve handel op Engeland in de eerste helft van de 14e eeuw, aan de hand van de customs accounts," in *Histoire économique de la Belgique: traitement des sources et état des questions. Economische geschiedenis van België: behandeling van de bronnen en problematiek. Actes du colloque de Bruxelles, 17–19 novembre, 1971, Ve et Vie sections*, ed. H. Coppejans-Desmedt (Brussels: Bibliothèque Royale, 1973). On Chaucer as Controller, see *Chaucer Life-Records*, ed Crow and Olson, pp. 148–270.

28 When Chaucer took office, Italians were still preeminent; the bulk of Italian exports was handled by Florentines. See Wendy Childs, "Anglo-Italian Contacts in the Fourteenth Century," in *Chaucer and the Italian Trecento*, ed. Piero Boitani (Cambridge: Cambridge University Press, 1983), pp. 65–87; Lloyd, *The English Wool Trade*, p. 255; Kathleen Biddick, *The Other Economy: Pastoral Husbandry on a Medieval Estate* (Berkeley: University of California Press, 1989), p. 3.

29 See Nicholas, *Medieval Flanders*, pp. 259–65; Wim Blockmans, "The Economic Expansion of Holland and Zeeland in the Fourteenth-Sixteenth Centuries," in *Studia Historica Œconomica. Liber Amicorum Herman van der Wee*, ed. A. Aerts, B. Henau, P. Janssens, R. Van Uytven (Leuven: Leuven University Press, 1993), pp. 48–50.

30 See Wim P. Blockmans, "Urban Space in the Low Countries, 13th–16th Centuries," in *Spazio urbano e organizzazione economica nell'Europa medievale, Annali della Facoltà di Scienze Politiche dell'Università di Milano* 29 (1993–4), p. 165. Equivalent figures for Ypres are 52% (in 1431) and for Bruges 25% (during the fourteenth century). As we shall see, different, capital-intensive enterprises

occupied a large percentage – perhaps 50% – of the professionally active population of Bruges.

31 See David Nicholas, *The Metamorphosis of a Medieval City: Ghent in the Age of the Arteveldes, 1302–1390* (Lincoln: University of Nebraska Press, 1987), p. 20; Nicholas, *Medieval Flanders*, p. 309.

32 The four oldest money exchanges of Bruges, for example, were hereditary fiefs of the count. See Nicholas, *Medieval Flanders*, pp. 231, 301.

33 There was considerable expenditure on public works, and city-dwellers owed a fierce primary allegiance to their cities (rather than to any larger territorial unit, such as "Flanders," or "Tuscany"). A delegation of Flemings, "de singulis villis Flandriae, qui majoris reputationis essent et fame," showed up at the English parliament in 1382, offering Richard II kingship of their country (the count of Flanders having run off to France): see Thomas Walsingham, *Historia anglicana*, ed. H. T. Riley, 2 vols. Rolls Series 28.1 (London: Longmans, Green, 1863–4), II.70–1. To judge from Walsingham, they met with a somewhat puzzled reception: could they be said to represent Flanders, or just its constituent cities?

34 See Alexandra F. Johnston, "Traders and Playmakers: English Guildsmen and the Low Countries," in *England and the Low Countries*, ed. Barron and Saul, p. 100. For a fine account of the involvement of London mercantile companies in dramatic performance, see Carol M. Meale, "*The Libelle of Englyshe Polycye* and Mercantile Literary Culture in Late-Medieval London," in *London and Europe in the Later Middle Ages*, ed. Julia Boffey and Pamela King (London: Center for Medieval and Renaissance Studies, Queen Mary and Westfield College, University of London, 1995), pp. 192–8.

35 Ethel Seaton, "Goode Lief My Wife," *Modern Language Review* 41 (1946), 196–202 (p. 201). The saint's cult spread quickly from Flanders to Boulogne and across the Channel; the name "Godelief" occurs quite frequently in Kent by the thirteenth century. There is a tableau representing scenes from her life in Onze Lieve Vrouwekerk, Bruges.

36 The great majority of fabliaux are of northern French and Flemish provenance; the analogues adjudged closest to the *Miller's Tale* and *Reeve's Tale* are both Flemish. See Peter G. Beidler, "*The Reeve's Tale*," in *Sources and Analogues of the Canterbury Tales*, vol. 1, ed. Robert M. Correale (Cambridge: D. S. Brewer, 2002), pp. 22–73 (p. 25); Beidler, "Chaucer's *Reeve's Tale* and its Flemish Analogue," *Chaucer Review* 26 (1991), 286–95.

37 See Wallace, *Chaucerian Polity*, pp. 125–81.

38 See David Nicholas, *Town and Countryside: Social, Economic, and Political Tensions in Fourteenth-Century Flanders*. University of Ghent, Publications of the Arts Faculty 152 (Bruges: De Tempel, 1971), pp. 138–41; Nicholas, *Medieval Flanders*, p. 228.

39 The text of the song, which opens by announcing "our" desire to sing of the churls, follows Louis de Baecker, *Chants historiques de la Flandre 400–1650* (Lille:

Ernest Vanackere, 1855), pp. 173–7. For a partial translation of this seven-stanza poem, see Nicholas, *Medieval Flanders*, pp. 253–4. The poem dates from ca. 1323–8 – a period in which rebellious peasants were staging their own public spectacles by forcing nobles to execute their own relatives (Nicholas, ibid. p. 215). Another such poem was composed at court, appealed to urban interests, and was housed in a monastery: see Walter Prevenier, "Court and City Culture in the Low Countries, 1100–1530," in *Medieval Dutch Literature in its European Context*, ed. Erik Kooper (Cambridge: Cambridge University Press, 1994), p. 23.

40 Including, as in London, a persistent division between victualling and non-victualling trades: see Nicholas, *Medieval Flanders*, p. 224. Such balancing has, of course, long been a specialty of the Low Countries: the European Union is based in Brussels, rather than in Paris or Berlin. Two days before Hitler came to power, Johan Huizinga – the most influential of apologists for Flemish culture (see Margaret Aston, "Huizinga's Harvest: England and *The Waning of the Middle Ages*," in Aston, *Faith and Fire: Popular and Unpopular Religion 1350–1600* [London: Hambledon Press, 1993], pp. 133–54) – was in Berlin, lecturing on the virtues of the Netherlands as cultural mediator between greater powers. See Bert F. Hoselitz, "Introduction" to Johan Huizinga, trans. James S. Holmes and Hans van Marle, *Men and Ideas: History, the Middle Ages, the Renaissance* (London: Eyre and Spottiswoode, 1960), p. 10. As in 1933, so in the Middle Ages, such mediatory skills were annulled when the great powers went to war with one another. Indeed, Flemings were often punished by one great power for showing allegiance to another: see Lloyd, *The English Wool Trade*, p. 99.

41 Lionel of Antwerp, Earl of Ulster, Duke of Clarence (and Chaucer's first master) had been born at Antwerp on November 29, 1338. Philippa, mother of John and Lionel, was daughter of the count and countess of Hainault (whose territory was located immediately to the south of Brabant and to the east of Artois). See T. F. Tout, "Lionel of Antwerp," in *Dictionary of National Biography*, 63 vols (London: Smith, Elder, 1885–1911), vol. 33, pp. 335–8.

42 See Nicholas, *Medieval Flanders*, p. 209; Lloyd, *The English Wool Trade*, p. 225.

43 See David Nicholas, *The van Arteveldes of Ghent: the Varieties of Vendetta and the Hero in History* (Ithaca, NY: Cornell University Press, 1988), pp. 120–59. This use of archives offers some instructive parallels with the English in 1381.

44 See Nicholas, *Medieval Flanders*, p. 307. Some Flemish textile workers emigrated to Brabant.

45 Walter Prevenier, "Les Perturbations," p. 494. In treaty negotiations of 1389, the Flemish ambassadors stated that if English cloths were to enter Flanders, "it would mean the destruction of our country" (quoted by John H. Munro, "Industrial Protectionism in Medieval Flanders: Urban or National?," in *The Medieval City*, ed. Harry A. Miskimin, David Herlihy, and A. L. Udovitch [New Haven: Yale University Press, 1977], p. 239).

46 The authority of these Flemish names could not be dispersed overnight: 50 years later, another English poet would complain "of cloth of Ipre, that *named* is better than oures" (emphasis mine; see *The Libelle of Englyshe Polycye: a poem [attributed to A. Molyneux] on the use of sea-power, 1436*, ed. Sir George Frederic Warner [Oxford: Clarendon Press, 1926], line 74).

47 Without a name, *creauncing*, credit-worthiness, is next to impossible: "We may creaunce whil we have a name, But goldlees for to be, it is no game" (7. 289–90).

48 See Margaret Aston, "The Impeachment of Bishop Despenser," *Bulletin of the Institute of Historical Research* 38 (1965), 127–48. Aston assesses the failed crusade and its aftermath as "the turning point in the foreign politics of the reign" (p. 127). In 1382, the English government was divided over which of "deux noble chymyns" to follow: intervention in Flanders or in Portugal. After the bishop's impeachment, the "way of Flanders" was effectively closed (*Rotuli Parliamentorum: ut et petitiones, et placita in Parliamento 1278–1503*, ed. John Strachey et al., 6 vols. [London, 1783], 3.133; Aston, pp. 132, 135).

49 See Herbert Hewitt, *The Organization of War Under Edward III, 1338–1362* (Manchester: Manchester University Press, 1966), p. 100; and see chapter 1 above, p. 46.

50 Poperinge was "no doubt selected by Chaucer," the *Riverside Chaucer* argues, "for its comic-sounding name and commonplace associations" (p. 918, n. to line 720; see further William Witherle Lawrence, "Satire in *Sir Thopas*," *PMLA* 50 [1935], 81–91).

51 In "Speke, Parrot," Skelton has much fun win the punning possibilities of "Popering" (as at line 70): "Popering" glances at Wolsey's ambition to be Pope; the association with pears leads to the phrase "Popering pear" becoming a figure for the phallus. See John Skelton, *Poems*, ed. Robert S. Kinsman (Oxford: Clarendon Press, 1969), p. 164.

52 See Nicholas, *Medieval Flanders*, pp. 280–3. Poperinge, 10 kilometers west of Ypres, was home to the largest textile industry in Flanders outside the Three Cities.

53 See Lloyd, *The English Wool Trade*, p. 12.

54 See *Chaucer Life-Records*, ed. Crow and Olson, pp. 32–40, esp. p. 38 n. 1. John de Mari's payments were made, apparently in March 1373, to Francis de Mari (possibly a relative), a leader of Genoese crossbowmen.

55 "Urban Space in the Low Countries," p. 166. Blockmans is speaking of Flanders and Brabant. Flemish non-nobility is further celebrated by the thirteenth-century *Prise de Nuevile* (in French, but spiced with Flemish borrowings) which describes how a large group of Flemings assembles in the industrial quarter of Arras and goes off to assault a castle. For excellent discussion of this burlesque poem, and of its possible bearing on *Sir Thopas*, see J. A. Burrow, "Chaucer's *Sir Thopas* and *La Prise de Nuevile*," *Yearbook of English Studies* 14 (1984), 44–55.

56 See Blockmans, "Urban Space in the Low Countries," p. 174; Nicholas, *Medieval Flanders*, p. 257; *Flemish Art: From the Beginning Until Now*, ed. Herman Liebaers et al. (New York: Arch Cape Press, 1988), pp. 61–3.

57 See Nicholas, *Medieval Flanders*, pp. 192–4. It is worth noting, with Juliet Vale, that the civic *festes* of Bruges and other Flemish cities often saw the urban elite tourneying with noble landowners (*Edward III and Chivalry: Chivalric Society and its Context* [Woodbridge: Boydell Press, 1982], pp. 25–41).

58 See chapter 1 above, p. 54.

59 Ballade 127.16. This visit, in which Deschamps was commissioned by Machaut to deliver the *Voir Dit* to the count, took place some time between 1365 (when Machaut completed the work) and 1377 (when he died). See Guillaume de Machaut, *Le Livre dou Voir Dit*, ed. Daniel Leech Wilkinson, trans. R. Barton Palmer (New York: Garland, 1998), p. lvii; I. S. Laurie, "Eustache Deschamps: 1340?–1404," in *Eustache Deschamps, French Courtier-Poet: His Work and His World*, ed. Deborah M. Sinnreich-Levi (New York: AMS Press, 1998), p. 3.

60 Prevenier, "Court and City Culture in the Low Countries," p. 18.

61 "*Sir Thopas*, a Satire," *Essays and Studies by Members of the English Association* 13 (1928), pp. 59–60

62 With French-leaning Hainault, yes, but not with Flanders.

63 "Introduction: England and the Low Countries," p. 21.

64 See Rita Copeland, *Rhetoric, Hermeneutics and Translation in the Middle Ages: Academic Traditions and Vernacular Texts* (Cambridge: Cambridge University Press, 1991); *The Idea of the Vernacular: An Anthology of Middle English Literary Theory, 1280–1520*, ed. Jocelyn Wogan-Brown, Nicholas Watson, Andrew Taylor, and Ruth Evans (Exeter: University of Exeter Press, 1999), pp. 314–30; *Medieval Dutch Literature*, ed. Kooper, *passim*; David Wallace, "Chaucer and the European *Rose*," in *Studies in the Age of Chaucer*, Proceedings, vol. 1, ed. Paul Strohm and T. J. Heffernan, pp. 61–7.

65 See *Chaucer Life-Records*, ed. Crow and Olson, p. 2; Derek Pearsall, *The Life of Geoffrey Chaucer: A Critical Biography* (Oxford: Blackwell, 1992), p. 16; McDonagh, *Belgium and Luxembourg*, p. 220.

66 See Lloyd, *The English Wool Trade*, pp. 116, 121.

67 See Scott McKendrick, "Tapestries from the Low Countries in England during the Fifteenth Century," in *England and the Low Countries*, ed. Barron and Saul, pp. 49, 51.

68 McKendrick, "Tapestries," p. 50. On Julius Caesar's use of *tessellata* (mosaic) and *sectilia* (intarsia) floors, reassembled for his fastidiously organized banquets, see Suetonius, *Divus Julius*, ch. 46–8, in *Suetonius*, trans. J. C. Rolfe, 2 vols., rev. edn., Loeb Classical Library (Cambridge, Mass.: Harvard University Press [1965–70]), I, 64.

69 *Sir Thopas*, 7.850; McKendrick, "Tapestries," p. 49.

70 See *Libelle*, ed. Warner, p. xxvi. Italian merchants were allowed to transport English wool from London to Calais, but were not supposed to seek direct access to Flemish markets.

71   See Lloyd, *The English Wool Trade*, p. 256.

72   Bryce Lyon, "Flanders," in *Dictionary of the Middle Ages*, ed. Joseph R. Strayer, 13 vols. (New York: Scribner, 1982–9), 5.80; Wim Blockmans, "The Social and Economic Context of Investment in Art in Flanders around 1400," in *Flanders in a European Perspective: Manuscript Illumination around 1400 in Flanders and Abroad*, ed. Maurits Smeyers and Bert Cardon. Proceedings of the International Colloquium, Leuven, 7–10 September 1993 (Leuven: Uitgeverij Peeters, 1995), p. 718.

73   See Blockmans, "Urban Space in the Low Countries," p. 174; Nicholas, *Medieval Flanders*, p. 296. Engelsestraat runs parallel to and a little east of Vlamingstraat; the house where English merchants weighed their commodities was in use by 1315 and was rebuilt in 1331.

74   See *Introduction to the Man of Law's Tale*, 2.122–5. The gambling intrinsic to merchant trade concerns not just the risky attempted business of buying cheap, traveling, and selling dear (see *Decameron*, 2.4), but all dealings with exchange of monies: see Raymond de Roover, "The Bruges Money Market around 1400," *Verhandelingen van de Koninklijke Vlaamse Academie voor Wetenschappen, Letteren en Schone Kunsten van België, Klasse der Letteren* 63 (1968), 32–7. Those of noble or royal blood should not feel the impulse to roll the dice, since they could hardly better the lot of their lineage. When "the kyng Demetrius" succumbed to gambling, "The kyng of Parthes, as the book seith us, / Sente him a paire of dees of gold in scorn, / For he hadde used hasard ther-biforn" (*Pardoner's Tale*, 6.621–4).

75   See Noël Geirnaert, "Universitas Mercature: Marchands, culture et religion à Bruges au Moyen Âge," in *Les Marchands*, ed. Vandewalle, pp. 151–63 (p. 156a).

76   See Blockmans, "Urban Space in the Low Countries," p. 174; De Roover, "Money Market," pp. 11–14; Philip D. Curtin, *Cross-Cultural Trade in World History* (Cambridge: Cambridge University Press, 1984), p. 6; Jacques Le Goff, *Your Money or Your Life: Economy and Religion in the Middle Ages* (New York: Zone Books, 1988).

77   For more exhaustive, technical description of these complex processes, see Kenneth S. Cahn, "Chaucer's Merchants," pp. 85–90; see also John M. Ganim, "Double Entry in Chaucer's *Shipman's Tale*: Double Entry before Pacioli," *Chaucer Review* 30 (1996), 294–305.

78   The wife of the *Shipman's Tale*, we should note, offers a clear rationale for her urgent need for capital accumulation: she needs must spend "on myn array, / And nat on wast" (7.418–19) since her primary social function is to image forth the status of a husband "That riche was" (7.2), but unpedigreed. Italian merchant wives showed a precocious grasp of their new symbolic role in the new commercial economy, leaving Italian merchant husbands – like chronicler Giovanni Villani – to recycle old forms of misogynistic lament. See Wallace, *Chaucerian Polity*, pp. 18–19; on prostitution, see Ruth Mazo Karras,

Common Women: Prostitution and Sexuality in Medieval England (New York: Oxford University Press, 1996), pp. 56–7; Richard Trexler, "La Prostitution Florentine au XVe siècle: Patronages et clienteles," *Annales: Economies, sociétés, civilisations* 36 (1981), 983–1015.

79 See Lloyd, *The English Wool Trade*, pp. 288–90; Randall Collins, *Weberian Sociological Theory* (Cambridge: Cambridge University Press, 1986), pp. 52–4.

80 For a fine account of Chaucer's Merchant (the tale-teller) as historical subject caught between aristocratic and Church-dictated terms of reference, set within a broader reading of "Chaucerian commerce," see Lee Patterson, *Chaucer and the Subject of History* (London: Routledge, 1991), pp. 333–44.

81 According to Massys' seventeenth-century biographer, the picture originally featured a citation of Leviticus 19: 36 on its frame ("Let the balance be just and the weights equal"): see Larry Silver, *The Paintings of Quinten Massys with Catalogue Raisonné* (Oxford: Phaidon, 1984), p. 136. Many objects in this painting, while maintaining their status *as* domestic objects, sustain religious associations: the water-filled crystal carafe; the candlestick; the prayer beads (useful for counting); the orange (betokening nuptial fertility or original sin). See Silver, pp. 137 and 152 n15.

82 See Silver, *Massys*, pp. 2–5, 137; Joel M. Upton, *Petrus Christus: His Place in Fifteenth-Century Flemish Painting* (University Park: Penn State University Press, 1990), pp. 7–11, 32–4; Zirka Zaremba Filipczak, *Picturing Art in Antwerp 1550–1700* (Princeton, NJ: Princeton University Press, 1987). Van Eyck died at Bruges in 1441; Christus purchased citizenship there in 1444. By 1560, according to Guicciardini, there were twice as many painters as bakers at Antwerp (some 300: see Filipczak, p. 3).

83 The snaking fabric on the counter aligning with the bride-to-be's body – another ambivalent sign – is a marriage girdle. See Peter H. Schabacker, *Petrus Christus* (Utrecht: Haentjens Dekker and Gumbert, 1974), p. 87.

84 On the banning of magnates from public office in Florence (and the consequent difficulties of finding a language for doing honor-bound business with northern Europe), see Wallace, *Chaucerian Polity*, pp. 15–16.

85 See the copies of Massys' *Banker and His Client* at Windsor Castle and at Paris, Cailleux collection (Silver, *Massys*, plates 120, 121); see Marinus van Reymerswaele, *The Banker and His Wife* (adapted from Massys), Musée des Beaux-Arts, Valenciennes (Vandewalle, *Hanze@Medici*, p. 35).

86 See Nicholas, *Medieval Flanders*, pp. 305–7. Ghent numbered about 50,000 people in 1357, but half that by 1385. At Tournai in 1349, the marrying or putting away of concubines was the first line of defense against the plague; sanitary measures came later. See *The Black Death*, trans. and ed. Rosemary Horrox (Manchester: Manchester University Press, 1994), p. 52. The Pardoner tells us that he has a wench in every town (6.453); poisoning – another activity infamously connected to plague: see chapter 4 below, p. 186 – is a vitally enabling device of his tale.

87   See Nicholas, *Medieval Flanders*, pp. 230, 313.

88   See further Roger H. Marijnissen, with Peter Ruyffelaere, *Jérôme Bosch: Tout l'œuvre peint et dessiné* (Anvers: Fonds Mercator, 1987), *Le Jardin des délices*, pp. 84–153, esp. pp. 134, 139, 141. There is a drawing of this same motif at the Albertina, Vienna: see Ludwig von Baldass, *Hieronymus Bosch* (London: Thames and Hudson, 1960), plate 152 and p. 239.

89   See J. H. A. Munro, *Wool, Cloth, and Gold: The Struggle for Bullion in Anglo-Burgundian Trade, 1340–1478* (Toronto: University of Toronto Press, 1972), pp. 47, 53, 58; Lloyd, *The English Wool Trade*, pp 244–5; Nicholas, *Medieval Flanders*, p. 321.

90   See *Riverside Chaucer*, ed. Benson, pp. 904–5.

91   See Glenn Burger, *Chaucer's Queer Nation* (Minneapolis: University of Minnesota Press, 2003), pp. 140–59; Steven F. Kruger, "Claiming the Pardoner: Toward a Gay Reading of Chaucer's *Pardoner's Tale*," *Exemplaria* 6.1 (Spring, 1994), 115–39. For a strikingly unshadowed reading of the Pardoner, see Carolyn Dinshaw, "Chaucer's Queer Touches / A Queer Touches Chaucer," *Exemplaria* 7.1 (Spring, 1995), 75–92.

92   *La commedia secondo l'antica vulgata*, ed. Giorgio Petrocchi (Turin: Einaudi, 1975). Durling and Martinez point out, following Parodi (1920), that the Italian forms of the names in line 15.4 sound like the words for "flaming" (*fiammeggia*), "wriggling" (*guizzante*), and "burning" (*brucia*); puns and equivocal language are a striking feature of this canto. See *The Divine Comedy of Dante Alighieri*, ed. and trans. Robert M. Durling, introd. and notes by Ronald L. Martinez, vol. 1, *Inferno* (New York: Oxford University Press, 1996), p. 238.

93   As Gelre Herald, Claes Haynenzoon accompanied William I of Guelders to England in 1390; he bought heraldic flags for the fleet and (while in England) bought bells to attach to these flags. Later, as Bavaria Herald (herald-in-chief to Duke Albert of Bavaria at the court of Holland), he wrote a *Wereldkroniek* ("Chronicle of the World," 1405–9): see Frits Pieter van Oostrum, *Court and Culture: Dutch Literature, 1350–1450*, trans Arnold J. Pomerans (Berkeley: University of California Press, 1992), pp. 129–30, 134. On folio 75r–v he tells of "een stout ridder," Liedrijcke by name, who "was armed with gold and azure and bore a shield of gules. This knight," the Herald continues, "beheld that Flanders was very desolate and little inhabited, and was a wild forest, marsh, and wasteland . . . But God, from whom all virtue flows, gave him the grace to conquer and settle the desolate land so that from him sprang as many rulers as from David, who was a shepherd and later became a great mighty king in the land of the Jews" (Oostrum, p. 144). The suggestion here is that Flemings, like Jews, will only find salvation for their "woeste land" by recognizing the redemptive power of ancient and noble bloodlines.

94   Cited by David Nicholas, "Of Poverty and Primacy: Demand, Liquidity, and the Flemish Economic Miracle, 1050–1200," *American Historical Review* 96 (1991), 17–41 (p. 41, emphasis added); the Four Members of Flanders are addressing their count in 1473.

95 See Miri Rubin, *Gentile Tales: The Narrative Assault on Late Medieval Jews* (New Haven: Yale University Press, 1999).

96 See William Langland, *The Vision of Piers Plowman: A Critical Edition of the B-Text*, ed. A. V. C. Schmidt (London: Dent, 1978).

97 See *Piers Plowman: An Edition of the C-text*, ed. Derek Pearsall (London: Edward Arnold, 1978), V, 1–104 and note on "Cornehull" (p. 97). This passage is new in C.

98 *The Canterbury Tales* (London: George Allen and Unwin, 1985), p. 58. On the significance of Chaucer's placing himself as the sixth member of this six-person group, following precedents by Jean de Mean, Dante, Boccaccio, and his own prior text (*Troilus and Criseyde*, 5.1789–92), see Wallace, *Chaucerian Polity*, pp. 80–2.

99 On the Pardoner as rhetor, and all that implies, see Rita Copeland, "The Pardoner's Body and the Disciplining of Rhetoric," in *Framing Medieval Bodies*, ed. Sarah Kay and Miri Rubin (Manchester: Manchester University Press, 1994), pp. 138–59.

100 On the notion of "the ego's era," which "begins before the advent of capital, [but] is accelerated by it," see Teresa Brennan, *History after Lacan* (New York: Routledge, 1993), p. 3. The term *medieval* here indicates that which contains the germ of, yet can never be perfectly integrated into, the modern. See further the "Introduction" above, pp. 10–11.

101 Groeninge Museum, Bruges; this triptych is considered by Walter S. Gibson to be a workshop production, "a rather inept adaptation of Boschian motifs" (*Hieronymus Bosch* [London: Thames and Hudson, 1973], p. 163). See further (featuring all the same major motifs) the great Last Judgment triptych at the Akademie der bildenen Künste, Vienna (Gibson, pp. 48–68); Bruce W. Holsinger, *Music, Body, and Desire in Medieval Culture: Hildegard of Bingen to Chaucer* (Stanford, Calif.: Stanford University Press, 2001), pp. 253–8.

102 *The Mystic Fable*, vol. I, *The Sixteenth and Seventeenth Centuries*, trans. Michael B. Smith (Chicago: University of Chicago Press, 1992), pp. 49–72.

103 See Raoul C. van Caenegem, "La preuve dans l'ancien droit Belge des origines à la fin du XVIIIe siècle," in *La Preuve*, II, *Moyen âge et temps modernes*, *Recueils de la Société Jean Bodin* 17 (1965), pp. 399–403. "Avec le temps," van Caenegem observes, "la primauté de l'aveu dans le procès criminel est devenue telle qu'on en est arrivé à déclarer indispensable pour toute condamnation à mort" (pp. 401–2).

104 Text of Trevisa's 1387 rendering of Ranulph of Higden, monk of Chester, follows Basil Cottle, *The Triumph of English 1350–1400* (London: Blandford Press, 1969), p. 18. Trevisa's translation concedes that these Flemings speak "Saxonlych ynow"; other linguistic groups in England are said to employ "strange wlaffyng, chyteryng, harryng, and garryng grisbittyng," amounting to "apeyryng of þe burþtonge" (p. 19).

105 "The Flemyng seith, and lerne it if thee leste, / That litel janglyng causeth muchel reste" (9.349–50).

106   MS Cotton, Julius B II as edited by C. L. Kingsford in *Chronicles of London* (Oxford: Oxford University Press, 1905), p. 15. Kingsford dates this manuscript 1435 (pp. viii–ix). On the Flemish-managed Southwark brothel, see Karras, *Common Women*, pp. 56–7.

107   "Introduction: England and the Low Countries," p. 12. Barron prefaces this statement by noting that "London, and indeed other English towns, were at times turbulent, but . . ."

108   Rubin, *Gentile Tales*, p. 1.

109   Ibid.

110   For meditation on our knowing things that a text itself cannot know about itself, and on discussion of eucharistic discourse in the *Pardoner's Tale*, see Paul Strohm, *Theory and the Premodern Text* (Minneapolis: University of Minnesota Press, 2000), pp. 165–81. On the relationship of transubstantiation to emergent discourses surrounding the commodity, see D. Vance Smith, *Arts of Possession: The Medieval Household Imaginary* (Minneapolis: University of Minnesota Press, 2003).

111   See James A. Doig, "Propaganda, Public Opinion and the Siege of Calais in 1436," in *Crown, Government and People in the Fifteenth Century*, ed. Rowena E. Archer (Stroud: Alan Sutton, 1995), pp. 79–106 (p. 93 – quoting from British Library, Additional MS 14848, f. 190 – and p. 96). The original plan was for Henry VI to head the rescue mission: see J. L. Watts, "When Did Henry VI's Minority End?" in *Trade, Devotion and Governance: Papers in Later Medieval History*, ed. Dorothy J. Clayton, Richard G. Davies, and Peter McNiven (Stroud, Gloucestershire: Alan Sutton, 1994), pp. 116–39 (p. 125). And see now further Scattergood, *"Libelle,"* in *Nation, Court and Culture*, ed. Cooney, pp. 28–49.

112   "The Idea of Englishness," p. 21. Pearsall's greater thesis is that there was "no steadily growing sense of national feeling" in fourteenth- and fifteenth-century England (p. 15).

113   See Doig, "Propaganda," pp. 98–102; V. J. Scattergood, *Politics and Poetry in the Fifteenth Century* (London: Blandford Press, 1971), pp. 83–90; *Historical Poems*, ed. Robbins, pp. 83–6. Further anti-Fleming rhetoric is essayed by the poem edited as "A Ballade, in Despyte of the Flemynges" (a title derived from MS Lambeth 84, f. 201v. ["And in despyte of the Flemyng[es], an Englissh man made this English yn baladdys"]): see *The Minor Poems of John Lydgate*, Part II, *Secular Poems*, ed. Henry Noble MacCracken and Merriam Sherwood, Early English Text Society, os 192 (London: Oxford University Press for EETS, 1934), pp. 600–1.

114   Roberto Weiss, "Humphrey Duke of Gloucester and Tito Livio Frulovisi," in *Fritz Saxl: A Volume of Memorial Essays from his Friends in England*, ed. D. J. Gordon (London: Thomas Nelson, 1957), pp. 218–27 (p. 223); Doig, "Propaganda," p. 102. The unique manuscript containing the *Humfroidos* is Biblioteca Columbina, Seville, MS 7.2.23. Richard Firth Green notes that "Humphrey of Gloucester took far less interest in Hoccleve's scheme to chronicle his 'actes'

than he did in Frulovisi's sycophantic Latin 'epic'" (*Poets and Princepleasers: Literature and the English Court in the Late Middle Ages* [Toronto: University of Toronto Press, 1980], p. 173); this in part reflects the fact that "chronicles in English would have been little read in foreign courts" (p. 173).

115 Authorship of the *Libelle* is not at present known. Warner argues for Adam Moleyns, clerk of the Council (*Libelle*, pp. xl–xlv). Carol Meale suggests that John Carpenter, common clerk of the city (1417–38) and a close associate of mayor and mercer Richard Whittington, "is a plausible candidate to be investigated as the work's patron" ("Mercantile Literary Culture," p. 219). The poem survives in two editions (19 manuscripts), dated 1436–8 and 1437–41 (with further revised versions of the second edition): see *Libelle*, ed. Warner, pp. lii–lvi as updated, corrected, and augmented by Carol M. Meale, "*The Libelle of Englyshe Polycye* and Mercantile Literary Culture," pp. 206–8, 219–26, and "Appendix" (listing all known manuscripts, pp. 226–8).

116 See *The Debate of the Horse, Goose, and Sheep*, in *Secular Poems*, ed. MacCracken and Sherwood. When Philip "Cam befor Caleis with Flemynges nat a fewe," he was beaten back and "vnethe escapid with the liff" (lines 414–19). On the frustrated romancing of Duke Humphrey through Lydgate's *Fall of Princes*, see Wallace, *Chaucerian Polity*, pp. 332–4.

117 On Flanders' supposed exemplifying of "the evils of drinking and of cupidity," see Dorothy M. Norris, "Chaucer's *Pardoner's Tale* and Flanders," *PMLA* 48 (1933), 636–41 (p. 636).

118 The passage quoted below is indebted to the Pardoner's animadversion against drinking Spanish wine ("This wine of Spaigne," which spreads "fumositee" to the brain; the drinker believes himself "Nat at the Rochelle," but "in Spaigne" [6.565–71]). The *Libelle* poet imitates not only items of vocabulary, but also the Pardoner's brilliant rhetorical technique.

119 *Rubia tinctoria*, madder, used for dying cloth.

120 The lord "of ful grete astate" (763) who proposed this plan for financing the conquest of Ireland is identified in the texts of three fifteenth-century manuscripts as the Earl of Ormond. James Butler (1392–1452), fourth earl, served at Agincourt and in the continental campaigns of 1418 and 1419 before becoming Lieutenant of Ireland in 1420 (*Libelle*, ed. Warner, p. 90).

121 *Libelle*, ed. Warner, p. lv; my emphasis. This manuscript, formerly at Keswick Hall, Norwich, was sold in 1936 and is now Boston Public Library, MS 1519. The William Caston who gave the book in 1471 to William Sonnyng was once thought to be the celebrated William Caxton, governor of the Merchant Adventurers at Bruges: but see now Meale, "*The Libelle of Englyshe Policye* and Mercantile Literary Culture," p. 220. The copy of the *Libelle* that is now Oxford, Bodleian Library, Laud MS 704, written ca. 1440–1450, was indeed owned by William Laud, chancellor of Oxford and archbishop of Canterbury.

122 See Luke Gibbons, *Transformations in Irish Culture* (Cork: Cork University Press, 1996), pp. 151–2.

123 *Discourse of Western Planting*, ed. David B. Quinn and Alison M. Quinn, Hakluyt Society, ES 45 (London: Hakluyt Society, 1993), pp. xxiii, 32.

124 "Above all," write the Quinns of Hakluyt, "he was completely ignorant of the way of life of North American Indians" (*Discourse*, p. xxii).

125 See Hakluyt, *Principall Navigations (1589)*, introd. Beers and Shelton, pp. xxv–vii, l–lii..

126 *Voyages, Navigations, Traffiques, and Discoueries of the English Nation*, 3 vols. (London: George Bishop, Ralfe Newberie, and Robert Barker, 1598–1600), I.187–208. Some topical (post-Armada) marginal glosses have been added. For example, by "For aliance of Scotland and of Spaine" we find: "This is now to be greatly feared" (I.200; *Libelle*, ed. Warner, line 732).

127 The great ship of Henry V, the *Grace Dieu*, was built to battle French-allied Genoese carracks: see Rose, "Henry V's *Grace Dieu*," p. 3.

128 "A preface to the Reader," *Voyages*, vol. 1, unpaginated, 8th page.

129 Richard Hakluyt, "Preface" to *Diverse Voyages*, 1582, conveniently available in *The Original Writings and Correspondence of the Two Richard Hakluyts*, ed. E. G. R. Taylor, 2 vols., Hakluyt Society, second series, 76 (London: Hakluyt Society, 1935), I.175–81 (p. 178); Hakluyt is dedicating this, his first collection, to Philip Sidney.

130 *Sodometries* (Stanford: Stanford University Press, 1992), pp. 4, 180.

131 *Forms of Nationhood: The Elizabethan Writing of England* (Chicago: University of Chicago Press, 1992), p. 164. Hakluyt's first surviving work is "A Discourse of the Commodity of the Taking of the Straits of Magellanus" (1580). Jeffrey Knapp, in similar vein, writes that "the English were in fact remarkably slow to colonize America, and their first attempts were dismal failures" (*An Empire Nowhere: England, America, and Literature from* Utopia *to* The Tempest [Berkeley: University of California Press, 1992], p. 1).

132 The *explicit* to the *Libel of English Policie* in Hakluyt likewise extends concern from keeping the Channel – such is the concern of the fifteenth-century poem – to keeping "the sea enuiron": such a task, the *explicator* insists, "exhorting all England," is a matter of both "profit and saluation" (2nd edn., p. 207). See also Seamus Heaney, "Glenmore Sonnets," VII, which begins "Dogger, Rockall, Malin, Irish Sea" (*Field Work* [London: Faber and Faber, 1979], p. 39).

133 Hakluyt, *Voyages*, 1st edn., p. 747. Lane here alludes to "doings" associated with Robert Dudley, earl of Leicester, dispatched by Elizabeth to the Netherlands (to no great effect).

134 See *The Fortunes and Misfortunes of Moll Flanders* (London: Penguin, 1996); first published in 1722.

135 On "the urban galaxy dominated by Los Angeles [as] the fastest growing metropolis in the advanced industrial world," see Mike Davis, *City of Quartz: Evacuating the Future in Los Angeles* (London: Verso, 1990), p. 6; see further Peter Plagens, "Los Angeles: The Ecology of Evil," *Artforum*, December 1972.

CHAPTER THREE

DANTE IN SOMERSET

> They mai moeve a man from his place . . . but certes, thei
> mai nat al arrace hym, ne aliene hym in al.
>
> **Chaucer, Boece.**

> The one who has disappeared appears still to be *there*, and his
> apparition is not nothing.
>
> **Derrida, Specters of Marx.**

The last two chapters have moved outward to Calais, as the limit of English
territory, and then Flanders, as a frontier or border region. Each ends in a
retreat – with the "loss" of Calais and the absorption of Flanders by greater
powers – that nonetheless issues in grander historical trajectories (leading,
ultimately, to the New World). This chapter would seem to reverse such
outward movement by considering a deeply English place: Somerset. But
here again, retreat to insular space simultaneously engages with, presents a
particular face to, a greater world. A particular English location may be so
made or imagined, I shall argue, as to isolate certain elements that might cut
its skyline, rendering them "outlandish" or *entfremdt* (from *entfremden*, the
process of estranging, alienating, or rendering foreign).[1] And such a process
portends not just the marking of an object or person as "foreign" within the
familiar place, but (from the moment of its first identification) its (his or her)
disappearance from the field.[2] Place, in this process, is understood to be
possessed of certain immanent qualities (themselves mysteriously exempt
from historical process). And yet nobody – here Chaucer's brilliantly negated,

transitive usage of *alienen* (cited above, p. 139) points the way – can ever be
definitively moved without trace (so long as there is an historical place to
contemplate).[3] This chapter unfolds by following the fortunes of one Italian
immigrant, Dante, and of the place he came to.

The mystique of medieval Flanders, we have noted, has been lost,
migrated, or dispersed; recovery of its peculiar premodern resonances draws
us down through powerful historical overlays (still best emblematized, perhaps, by the poppies of Flanders fields).[4] "Somerset," today, is also a place-
name evocative of rural quietude, if not pathos; so the notion of "Dante in
Somerset" strikes English readers, or readers who have spent much time in
England, as incongruous and faintly comical. Why is that? And how did that
particular "structure of feeling" (finding it comic or incongruous) come to
be?[5] Perhaps the unassimilable largeness and foreignness of Dante (as an
urbane medieval Italian, Ghibelline and Roman Catholic) makes him seem
so unlikely a visitor, or a long-term resident, of such a quiet, deeply rural
locality. The landscape of Somerset in southwest England has never been
fully assailed by the energies of an industrial revolution nor hymned as a
site of natural grandeur. Although Coleridge and Wordsworth forged their
brilliant, epoch-making collaboration in Somerset – and Coleridge wrote
most of his greatest verse in the county – *Lyrical Ballads*[6] looks elsewhere for
its most evocative landscapes: the "grassy hills" and "sylvan coombs" of the
Quantocks are ideal for recollecting Romantic grandeur, but cannot be productive of it.[7] Even the names are funny: Cheddar and Wookey Hole, Porlock
and Nether Stowey cannot compete with Windermere, Derwent Water,
and Tintern Abbey. Bristol, assumed to share something of the drowsiness
of its rural hinterland, has never been able to sustain a decent football team;
its players still run on to the pitch to the strains of "drink up thee zider" as
sung by the rustic-rock Wurzels.[8] It is thus difficult to associate the quiet
charm of Wells, the poignant ruins of Glastonbury, with the furious energies of Dante, a man who pursues his vision of world government while
traveling through heaven, hell, and purgatory.

But we are inclined to forget that Wells and Glastonbury do bear the
impress of furious, world-changing energies, those of the Protestant Reformation, which destroyed or dispersed the cathedral library at Wells and the
physical fabric of Glastonbury Abbey. The violence at Wells has had more
drastic consequences for efforts to understand, to imaginatively reconstitute, the past than what transpired at Glastonbury, for it is easier to re-create
some understanding of communal life from the surviving stones of a
Benedictine abbey than it is to reconstitute the functioning of a library from
lost books. The dispersal of books implies the loss not just of individual

volumes, but of systems of knowledge and social relationship through which such books were acquired, indexed, cross-referenced, stored, shared, circulated, copied, and discussed. It is one of the lost books of Wells that supplies the "Dante" of my title.

In speaking of "Dante" here, then, I mean a text of Dante (a Latin translation of the *Commedia*, discovered at Wells in the 1530s), mindful that for medieval – as for classical – writers, authorial text is suggestive of physical presence: such is the conceit which brings Vergil to Dante in *Inferno* 1. This Dante, which (I will argue) had been in Somerset for more than 100 years, offered the first linear translation of the *Commedia* available in England before the nineteenth century.[9] This manuscript of the greatest ghost-story ever told (to steal from Pat Boyde)[10] is now itself but a ghost; the physical object has disappeared. The first half of this chapter attempts to recover some understanding of what that manuscript might have been and how it might have got there. Palaeographers, concerned with minute analysis of material texts, are naturally suspicious of attempts to pursue lost objects in a subjunctive mode. What I aim for here is not the raising of a phantasmic manuscript, but rather an understanding of the nexus of relations (social, political, educational, religious) implied by the phenomenality of a particular text. Having thus established the ways in which Dante is "at home" in Somerset – for longer than we might first suppose – I go on to consider how successive remakings of English landscape render him foreign to the very same physical spaces.

Bubwith at Constance: the Dante Circle

It was sometime after 1533 that John Leland, a devoted and ultimately tragic agent of Henry VIII, made the first of his visits to Somerset, armed with the royal document commissioning him "to make a search after *England's Antiquities*, and peruse the Libraries of all Cathedrals, Abbies, Priories, Colleges, &c. as also all places wherein Records, Writings and secrets of Antiquity were reposed."[11] Somerset held a particular attraction for Leland because of its Arthurian connections; he was to return to the county in 1540 and again in 1542.[12] It was very likely on his first visit in the 1530s, however, that he compiled a list of books seen in Wells Cathedral library.[13] At the time of its construction in the second quarter of the fifteenth century, this library was larger than any other in England: some 165 feet long, it far outstripped comparable new buildings at Durham, Christ Church Canterbury, New College and Merton College, Oxford.[14] Leland was to write with great enthusiasm of

14 Wells Cathedral Library (above east cloister), after 1424, with seventeenth-century stalls. Photograph by George Hall, Chapter of Wells Cathedral.

having found "immense treasures of venerable antiquity" in the Wells Cathedral library.[15] The volume of particular interest here is the fourth of the 46 items at Wells that Leland chose to record: "Dantes translatus in carmen Latinum." The first sudden imagining of Dante in this place compares (at least for me) with Hogarth's *punctum*-like experience at Calais, as an unanticipated vision of the past – demanding considerable mental rearrangement – floods in through a forgotten sign.

The *space* of Leland's encounter with Dante survives (figure 14), although Wells Cathedral library today hardly seems, in Michel de Certeau's terms, "a practiced place."[16] Very few manuscripts survive: at Wells, there remains a single Ordinale, two folios from an Obituarium, and some binding fragments;[17] just six manuscripts securely linked with Wells are to be found elsewhere.[18] There are also leaves of the part song "Somewhat musyng" by Robert Fayrfax, one of Henry VIII's favorite musicians, but these (ironically enough) arrived only in the late seventeenth century, cut down by a Bodleian binder to strengthen a book published in 1611.[19] Many Wells manuscripts may have been destroyed as a consequence of the Acts 3 and 4 Edward VI c. 10 (1549–50), commanding all superstitious works[20] to be given to the mayor (or his subordinates), who would pass them on to the bishop (or his subordinates), who would burn them; it might be assumed that our "Dantes translatus" perished in such a bonfire, or in some related catastrophe.

The arresting phrase "in carmen Latinum" allows us to deduce with some confidence just what text of Dante Leland encountered at Wells. In November 1414, Nicholas Bubwith, bishop of Bath and Wells, had left Dover as king's ambassador, bound for the Council of Constance. While at this council, Bubwith grew better acquainted with his fellow English ambassador, bishop Robert Hallum (from the neighboring diocese of Salisbury). Bubwith and Hallum were northerners – Bubwith from Yorkshire, Hallum from Cheshire – who had fashioned impressive careers from humble origins. Bubwith was a chancery clerk in 1380, a king's clerk by 1387, master in chancery by June 1399, and in 1407 Treasurer of England. Hallum, having made his reputation at Oxford, entered the service of John of Gaunt in the mid-1380s. He served archbishop Courtenay as principal registrar from 1389 to 1394, and from 1403 to 1406 was chancellor of the University of Oxford.[21] While at Constance, the two Englishmen befriended a Franciscan, Giovanni Bertoldi de Serravalle, bishop of Firmano, who was keen to share his enthusiasm for Dante's *Commedia*. There was evidently plenty of free time at the council, which unfolded in some 45 sessions from November 5, 1414, to April 23, 1418. In January 1416, Bertoldi began translating the *Commedia* into Latin; the following month, he began an accompanying commentary. The translation, clearly designed to serve those knowing little Italian, was finished in May 1416; the commentary was completed in January of the following year. In the *incipit* to his commentary,[22] Bertoldi declares that he set to work as expressly instructed and required ("ad preceptum et instantiam") by Cardinal Amedeo di Saluzzo and by Nicholas Bubwych and Robert Halam, "amborum episcoporum in provintia Anglie." Bertoldi had himself spent time in England (perhaps in 1398): in concluding his commentary to *Inferno* 20, he recalls sailing back to Italy through the narrow straits overlooked by "mons Giubelcar."[23]

The importance of Constance as an extraordinary center of pan-European intellectual and literary exchange – a four-year site for an internationalist seminar – has been strangely underestimated, even by scholars as distinguished as P. O. Kristeller and Roberto Weiss.[24] In bringing together "music and musicians from almost anywhere in Europe," the Council played a very significant role in the rise of European music. Musicians at Constance could "exchange material, perform together, switch employers and plan new careers."[25] There were certainly tensions at the Council to set nations apart: the French, we have noted, were unwilling to accord *national* status to the English (who should be considered a subordinate part of the German nation). English and German nations met (separately) in the Franciscan monastery in the heart of the city, whereas the French and Italians were accommodated by the Dominicans outside the walls.[26] None of this seems to have discouraged English and Italian clerics from meeting around the text of Dante under the tutelage of the Italian bishop.

Bertoldi, too, has been a neglected figure – mostly because Italian Dantists have been seriously unimpressed by the quality of his work: "il Serravalle," Giovanni Ferraù writes in the *Enciclopedia dantesca*, "makes no discernible progress in [the long and distinguished history of] glossing the *Commedia*."[27] His commentary achieved very limited circulation in Italy; most later readers preferred to seek out earlier commentators, ignoring Bertoldi.[28] And Bertoldi himself is the harshest critic of his own Latin translation: at various points in the Dedication – which again explicitly addresses itself to Bubwith and Hallum – he speaks of the rudeness, ineptitude, inadequacy, and presumptuousness of his attempted transferral of Dante (Bertoldi prefers the term *transferendum* to *translatandum*) from the idiom of Italian verse to that of rustic Latin prose.[29] But, he argues, time was short: it was important to get the job done before Council members dispersed to France, England, Spain, Germany, and Italy. And (we might add) the vital accoutrements of Dante scholarship were in short supply at Constance: Bertoldi was forced to draw on memories of his years of teaching at Florence (between 1393 and 1397) and, much further back, on his association with Dante lectures given by Benvenuto da Imola between 1374 and 1376.[30] Benvenuto, who attended the pioneering *lecturae Dantis* given by Boccaccio in Florence in 1373–4, is the most important Dante commentator of the later fourteenth century; Bertoldi clearly owes much to his work.

But although Bertoldi's writing has little to offer the illustrious history of Italian commentary on Dante – where it has been treated as no more than a minor footnote between Benvenuto and Landini – it is of considerable interest in its attempted northward diffusion and mediation of Dante's text. Bertoldi's text and commentary, Ferraù argues, represent "the first and fundamental moment of Dante's fortunes in Germany" (I.609a); and it was through Bertoldi that the legend was first decisively spread abroad that Dante had studied not only at Paris, but at Oxford. Bubwith, according to Emden, possibly studied at Oxford, but did not incept; Hallum, we have noted, was Chancellor of the University. Hallum never made it home from Constance: he died on September 4, 1417, and was buried in Constance Cathedral.

Bubwith had returned to England by August 1418. When he died six years later, on October 27, 1424, he left 250 marks for the celebration of masses by poor or unbeneficed priests studying at Oxford; and he left considerable funds for a new bell-tower at Wells, for an almshouse, and for the building of a new cathedral library.[31] Leland was to note, more than a century later, "the hospitale of 24. poore menne and wymen" at Wells founded by "Nicolas Budwith Bisshop of Bath";[32] and it was in Bubwith's cathedral library that Leland was to discover "Dantes translatus in carmen Latinum."

Constance to Wells; Latinities and Vernaculars

The phrase "carmen Latinum," I have suggested, points to the presence of Bertoldi's work at Wells, for his Latin translation has the character of a parallel text keeping tenaciously abreast of the Italian original, line by line, hence offering the physical appearance of a *carmen*,[33] a poem or song:

Nel mezzo del cammin di nostra vita	In medio itineris vite nostre
Mi ritrovai per una selva oscura,	Reperi me in una silva obscura,
Ché la diritta via era smarrita.	Cuius recta via erat devia.
Ahi quanto dir qual era è cosa dura	Hey quantum ad dicendum qualis erat est res dura,
Esta selva selvaggia e aspra e forte	Ista silva silvestris et aspera et fortis,
Che nel pensier rinova la paura!	Que in meditatione renovat pavorem.
Tant' è amara che poco è più morte;	Tantum est amara quod ea vix amarior sit mors.
Ma per trattar del ben ch'i' vi trovai,	Sed ut tractem de bono quod in ea reperi,
Dirò de l'altre cose ch'i' v'ho scorte.	Dicam de aliis rebus quas in eadem percepi.

(Inferno 1.1–9)

The fidelity with which Bertoldi's Latin keeps company with the Italian here and henceforward, clause by clause and line by line, is really quite striking. His fourth line is egregiously long, but all in the interests of keeping abreast with concise and compact Italian; his fifth is as close to the original as any non-Italian language could possibly be. Such Latin dare not speak its name among classicizing Italian humanists modeling themselves after Petrarch; its robust, straightforward qualities more closely approximate the kind of daily speech passing between French, English, Spanish, German, and Italian clerics at Constance. Such Latin, in short, assumes humble lineaments by way of

facilitating access – for readers otherwise excluded – to Dante's great illustrious vernacular poem: a generous gesture that might be welcomed in the spirit
of Dante's own *Convivio*, a text that takes a compassionate and helpful attitude toward potential readers who find themselves excluded – for reasons of
time and public commitment – from more leisured access to learning. Bertoldi
thus effects a neat reversal of the roles habitually accorded to vernacularity
and *Latinitas*: Latin here assumes the role of a vernacular (a language of
everyday speech) in shaping to serve an illustrious mother tongue.[34]

We cannot know whether or not Bertoldi's "Dantes translatus" came to
Somerset accompanied by its commentary. It seems likely, since Bubwith
was one of the dedicatees of the work, and Bertoldi would hardly have
wished to labor – from May to January – for nothing. Duke Humfrey's
Library, Oxford, once held a copy of this commentary (discovered by John
Leland in the course of a visitation): this work "super opera Dantis Aligerii"
was written, Leland notes, during the time of the Council of Constance and
dedicated "ad Nicolaum Bubwice, Bathon. et Wellensem episcopum, et
D. Robertum Halam, episcopum, Sarisbur."[35] There is a manuscript of the
same commentary in the British Library: Egerton 2629, a paper manuscript
of the fifteenth century whose main hand (and style of decorative initials)
appear to be English. This last manuscript also makes mention of "Nicolay
(*sic*) Bubwych" and "domini roberti" (dropping Hallum's surname).[36] And
there is also a manuscript in Eger, Hungary, containing a copy of Bertoldi's
preamble, his translation, and his *Inferno* commentary; this exemplar is
dedicated not to English prelates, but to the Emperor Sigismund.[37] These
manuscripts, and their interrelationships, require further study. For present
purposes, however, we may turn to the extraordinary edition of Bertoldi's
translation and commentary published by two Italian Franciscans in 1891.
This massive edition (1236 pages, $15\frac{7}{8} \times 10\frac{3}{4}$ inches, weighing in at 8.5 kilo-
grams [about 20 pounds] of calendered paper, dedicated to Pope Leo XIII)
is based upon Biblioteca Vaticana MS Capponiano 1 (now Vaticana 7566–
7568). This is clearly not an autograph manuscript: four hands took part in
writing the commentary; perhaps another hand again wrote the translation.
In the 1891 edition, the translation, the commentary, and the canto summaries have been broken up and rearranged in the interests of creating "un
tutto armonico e compito."[38] In the manuscript, however, translation, commentary, and canto summaries are separated from one another (and could
therefore have circulated separately). Used judiciously, then, the 1891 edition
provides the best current guide to what was available at Wells after 1418.

Readers of Bertoldi's commentary encounter a modern vernacular text,
Dante's *Commedia*, painstakingly approached through those categories of

medieval literary theory first developed for the analysis of Scripture.[39] Having promised to procede "ad divisionem libri," the *preambula* immediately launches into eight preambles, beginning with "intentio auctoris" (p. 7). Preamble four discusses Dante's use of three styles, "qui sunt tragedia, sathyra et comedia" (p. 12). Preamble five discusses why Dante should have made himself a disciple of Vergil (with extended discussion of Dante's childhood love of Beatrice and his ignominious falling for another girl in Lucca called Pargoletta, p. 15); preamble eight moves us back around to the question of *intentio auctoris* (p. 20). The *preambula* then concludes by following the good and praiseworthy habit of literary critics and commentators ("expositores librorum et postillatores") who consider the four causes of a work (effective, material, formal, and final), the part of philosophy to which it belongs, and its title. The agent or "causa effectiva" of the work is said to be its author, "scilicet Dantes, domini Aldigherii de Aldigheriis, theologi poete Florentini" (p. 20).

Bertoldi's *Paradiso* begins without any preamble, but his *Purgatorio* is accorded a *preambula*. This contains four subordinate preambles; the last of these contains an arresting comparison between the island of Purgatory and the island of England ("Anglia") and, more loosely and suggestively, between Oxford and the earthly paradise. Bertoldi is attempting to explain how Dante and Vergil manage to set foot on the island mountain of Purgatory – driven upwards from the ocean by Lucifer's fall to earth – without crossing water:

Et sicut Anglia, existens insula sicuti est, est sic circumdata mari, quod ad illam non est possibilis accessus sine adiutorio navis, nisi quis volaret, ita ad hanc terram sic elevatam sursum, ad istum montem, nemo venire potest nisi per mare, fultus adiutorio navis. Sed nota quod si de alio emispirio poli anthartici veniret versus nostrum emispirium per foramen terre perforate, sic et taliter quod foramen inciperet illuc in alio emispirio, et veniret per centrum terre, et postea terminaret illud foramen in Oxoniis, sive in alio loco medio insule Anglie, vel etiam in circumferentiis insule, dummodo esset infra insulam, ille veniens de alio emispirio per illud foramen, non indigeret navi ad intrandum insulam Anglie, quia iam esset in ea. (pp. 429–30)

And just as England, being an island, is surrounded by sea so that no possible access may be made to it without the aid of a ship (no matter who might wish to do such a thing), it follows that to this land that has risen so high, to this mountain, nobody is able to come except by sea, supported by the aid of a ship. But just consider if such a person were to come from the southern pole of the other hemisphere toward our hemisphere by means of an opening bored through the ground; and what if such an opening were to begin in the other hemisphere, were to pass through the center of the earth, and were then to end at Oxford, or in some other place in the middle of the island of England . . .

Bertoldi's vivid appreciation here of England as an island certainly draws from his own journey north and west from Italy; mention of Oxford might also reflect personal experience (since the university city was a likely destination for this teaching theologian). Of course, the singling out of Oxford here, as at other points in Bertoldi's commentary, is calculated to appeal to the interests and sentimental attachments of those English expatriates for whom, in the first instance, he is writing and translating. The learned American student of Dante, G. L. Hamilton, writing in 1901, roundly denounced Bertoldi for making "the most absurd statements to satisfy the college pride of his English colleagues," for exposing "the cloven foot of sly flattery."[40] And Ferraù, the Italian Dantist, complains that Bertoldi too often amplifies or renders explicit things that in Benvenuto remain half-hidden or subtly allusive; such amplifications sometimes blossom into genuine short stories ("a volte transformando in vere e proprie novellette," I.609a). Such *novellette*, Ferraù graciously concedes, are not without their own charm and vivacity ("non prive di una loro grazia e vivacità," I.609a): indeed, they often have much more in common with Boccaccian *novelle* than with the Latin Dante commentary tradition (which had, by the fifteenth century, fallen into serious decline). Bertoldi's *Comentum*, largely bypassed by medieval and modern Italian scholarship, merits further study as an impromptu attempt, born of very peculiar circumstances (a lengthy Church council in Germany) to mediate Dante to northern Europeans.[41]

The peculiar charm and vivacity which Ferraù finds in Bertoldi's *novellette* may be found in many passages of his Latin verse. Readers of this *carmen* find qualities of adventure, drama, and pathos as gripping as anything in medieval romance: in Bertoldi's hands, the *Commedia* becomes (again, dare one say, with due deference to the Latin commentary tradition) compellingly readable. The celebrated dialogue between Dante and Francesca in *Inferno* V retains much of the power of the original; those familiar with the Italian will hear Dante's vernacular just below the surface.[42] The last of Bertoldi's glosses to this canto further exemplifies novellistic tendencies: Dante empathizes so very strongly with Paolo and Francesca, Bertoldi suggests, because their relation puts him in mind of his youthful love for Beatrice.[43] In forcing this parallel – which rewrites or creatively misremembers *Vita nuova* XIV – Bertoldi touches heights of sentimentality that we might not expect from *postillatores* of Latin tradition.[44] Here then are three famous tercets of *Inferno* V as rendered by the "Dantes translatus in carmen Latinum" brought to Somerset by Bubwith in 1418 and available to Leland in the 1530s. Francesca speaks:[45]

> "Amor, qui cordi gentili ractus se apprehendit,
>   Cepit istum de pulchra persona
>   Que fuit michi rapta, et modus adhuc me offendit.
> Amor, qui nullo amato amare parcit,
>   Me cepit de isto placere tam fortiter,
>   Qui, prout vides, adhuc me non deserit.
> Amor conduxit nos ad unam mortem:
>   Cayna expectat illum qui nos in vita extinxit."
>   Ista verba ab eis nobis fuerunt porrecta.
>   **(Inferno 5.100–8)**

> "Love, which soon runs in the gentle heart,
>   seized this one for the beautiful form
>   that was taken from me; and the manner still offends me.
> Love, which pardons no one loved from loving in return,
>   seized me with pleasure for this one so strongly
>   that, as you see, it will not leave me even now.
> Love led us both to one death:
>   Caina awaits him who snuffed out our life."
>   These words were borne from them to us.

But such textual pleasures *in potentia* come freighted with ironies; the translation of Bertoldi's manuscript from Constance to Wells highlights the eccentricity of English textual practices, viewed within wider European perspectives. Bertoldi had employed everyday, "rustic" Latinity to make an illustrious Italian text – one that developed some highly challenging theological views – more broadly accessible to northern Europeans. Such a strategy implicitly upholds the logic of the General Prologue to the Wycliffite Bible: for "Latyn," chapter 15 reasons, looking back to the time of Augustine and Jerome, "was a comoun langage to here puple aboute Rome . . . as Englishe is comoun langage to oure puple."[46] Such increase of accessibility was not what Archbishop Arundel had in mind for the English reading public. Fortunately for Bubwith and Hallum, however, the Latinity which Bertoldi employed to popularize (among a clerical elite) could also serve as a veil to obscure the view of a wider English populace. The desire to peek beneath this veil was certainly current in Somerset (as elsewhere) at this time; a text of 1431 emanating from Bubwith's successor at Wells, Bishop John Stafford, threatens to excommunicate any persons bold enough to translate from Scripture, or any part of Scripture, into "li[n]guam Anglicanam, que nostra vulgaris esse denoscitur."[47] A year earlier, William Emayn of Bristol had been tried for Lollardy (unorthodox belief) at the Wells chapter house. Sixteen charges were leveled against Emayn. Some have particular resonance for Wells (such as the view that any priest who "singeth for a soule in church collage" should take no money for his pains), but most are familiarly and broadly generic; here is the last:

> Item Maister John Wyclif was holier and now is more in blisse and hier in heven glorified than Seint Thomas of Canterbury the glorious Martir. (p. 79)

Bishop Stafford's *Register*, in narrating this trial, switches from Latin to the vernacular as the charges are addressed to the accused since, of course, William Emayne understood nothing but English. A yet more complex interplay between Latinity and vernacularity is to be heard five years later, as Bishop Stafford attempts to promulgate a letter on the religious education of people in his diocese. Eager to combat lay superstition and ignorance and to communicate with clerics of imperfect Latinity, Stafford (following the precedent of archbishops who legislated in less troubled times) makes a timely switch to the vernacular:

> In quorum remedium discriminum etc. hic stilum mutamus ex causa premissa et propter leviorem apercionemque simplicum intellectum ad sermonem sive literam divertimus in vulgari. We ordeyne and commaunde that every curat and preest having cure of soule of the people iiij times in the year . . . declare openly in Englissh to the puple withoute curious sotiltee Furst the particules of the bileve . . .[48]

In detailing the particulars of his program, Stafford has frequent occasion to move between Latin and the vernacular. Here, for example, he lists the fifth of the ten Commandments:

> The v heest is Non loqueris contra proximum tuum falsum testimonium, Thow shalt bere noo fals witnesse ayenst thi neybour.[49]

Such trafficking between languages leaves Stafford awkwardly situated: in translating from Exodus, chapter 20, for example, he breaks his own earlier injunction against Scriptural translation. Such dilemmas further highlight the peculiar status of our Wellsian "Dantes translatus": a text translated *into* vulgar Latin that was designed to facilitate easier access to a vernacular text (but only for clergy possessed of basic Latinity).[50] Further vulgarization "in ydioma Anglicum" (*Register*, p. 107) was clearly not on the cards during the manuscript's early years at Wells. Certain Dantean scenes, such as the interview with one damned pope (Nicholas III) who – buried head-down in Hell, his legs waving in the air – mistakes Dante for another (Boniface VIII), acquire peculiar local resonances. William Emayn, the Lollard tried at Wells in 1430, might have deduced (erroneously) that Dante too was of the opinion that "the pope in dedly sinne is the Antecrist and not the viker of Crist."[51] Dante's association of friars with Hell and the notion that a layman could confess a pope might lead to further misunderstandings:

> Ego stabam sicut Frater qui audit in confessione
> > Perfidum assassinum, qui postquam est fictus,
> > Revocat illum, ut mors cesset.
> Et ipse clamavit: "Es tu iam ibi,
> > Es tu iam ibi, Bonifati?
> > De pluribus annis est michi mentita scriptura."
> > > **(Inferno 19.49–57)**

> I was standing like the friar who hears in confession
> > the treacherous assassin who, once fixed in the earth,
> > calls him back to delay his death.
> And he cried out: "Are you already [standing] there,
> > Are you already there, Boniface?
> > The writing lied to me by several years."

Ironies proliferate here if we consider that Hallum – one of the dedicatees of this translation – was a patron of Richard Ullerston, whose defense of "barbarous" English for Scriptural translation (a defense made in Latin) was soon Englished as a Lollard tract that was copied and elaborated well into the sixteenth century.[52] Hallum, further, authored a sermon that urged ignoring the literacy of priests as a criterion for promotion (since Christ and his apostles never went to school).[53] And in 1412, Hallum had ordained the celebrated Peter Payne (forger of Oxford University documents, and principal of St. Edmund Hall) as first subdeacon and then (six weeks later) deacon at Salisbury.[54] At about the time that Hallum was settling into the presidency of the English "nation" at Constance, Payne was arriving in Prague to begin an extraordinary 40-year career as "Peter Englis": Hussite envoy, diplomat, and champion of Wyclif. Hallum, for his part, joined a committee of the "nations" in the Franciscan convent at Constance, which urged the

Bohemian priest and university rector, Jan Hus, to recant; Hus was burned the very next day (July 6, 1415).[55] It seems that such exposure to Hussite ideas at Constance allowed certain members of the English delegation – such as Thomas Netter – to sharpen their understanding of (hence their ability to suppress) Wycliffite ideas.[56]

It may be that our "Dante translatus" arrived in Somerset just ten years too late: *after* Constance, and hence after Arundel's *Constitutions* of 1407/9 (which made new works of a challenging theological cast – such as *Piers Plowman* – more difficult to conceive). The text stood little chance of being further translated (into English) or of migrating beyond the library walls. Its robust Latinity – designed as a window onto a vernacular text for non-Italian clerics – would have functioned as a further wall against English non-clerical readers.[57] This remains true, I think, even though the walls of Wells proved (as we shall immediately see, and as its architecture still suggests) unusually porous.

Readership and Literacy at Wells

In attempting to profile potential readers at Wells we should recognize, first and foremost, that Wells was not – like its close neighbor, Glastonbury – a monastic community. Wells was served not by monks, but by canons who met in chapter and ministered in the cathedral, but otherwise lived separately, each on his income from his prebend. Absenteeism was endemic, so canons were required to supply a vicar who would fulfill their obligations in choir. Many canons lived in the town of Wells, which – with a flourishing cloth trade and related crafts – was the largest town in Somerset (almost twice the size of Bath or Taunton); there were frequent run-ins with the local population.[58] A statute of 1338 inveighs against vicars and chaplains who gossip together when they should be singing psalms, go on hunting, fowling, and fishing expeditions, take part in dances and masques, and prowl around the cities (by day and by night) singing and shouting ("cum cantu et tumultu," article 18).[59] Some vicars disguise their tonsures (13), carry swords (20), play backgammon in alehouses (19) and take part in competitive drinking bouts (34); others keep concubines (24), commit adultery with married women (33), or meet with prostitutes in the church (34). At Wells, as at other secular churches, it was very difficult to regulate the constant intermingling of clergy and laity. Vicars choral and the swelling body of chantry chaplains were conspicuous offenders; many evidently saw their posts as dead-end jobs.

At Wells, as at Oxford, considerable effort was made to segregate clergy from townspeople in the later Middle Ages. The famous Vicars' Close (adopted as the main street of Southwark in Pier Paolo Pasolini's film of *The Canterbury Tales*) was founded in 1348; the college of Monterrey was established to accommodate 14 chantry chaplains in 1399. Statutes and chapter acts from 1460, 1486, and 1513/14 see the chapter continuing to struggle with challenges of outrageous secular dress, concubinage, and absenteeism throughout the later period.[60] But this unruly clerical substratum – and here parallels with Oxford might be extended – was counterbalanced or complemented by more illustrious scholarly traditions.[61] The reform-minded bishop Thomas Bekynton, scholar of Winchester College, and Fellow of New College, Oxford, favored highly educated members of chapter: 14 of the 56 clerks he collated to prebends were doctors of theology and 22 had law or arts degrees. Of the 732 institutions made during his reign as bishop, 37 were conditional upon attaining sufficient understanding of Latin and the Scriptures. Clerics who fell short were required to undertake further study: one Richard Brice, for example, was required to study "for two whole years in the schools at Wells" on becoming rector of Weston-in-Gordano (Somerset).[62] Bekynton corresponded with other humanists and was a keen collector of texts, ancient and modern.[63] His friend Thomas Chaundler, humanist and sometime chancellor of Oxford, was a Wells native who became a canon and served as chancellor at Wells from 1452 to 1467. William of Wareham, scholar and friend of Erasmus, was precentor at Wells from 1493 to 1501.[64] And the royal historiographer, Polydore Vergil, who labored on his *Historia Anglicana* for almost 30 years, was made archdeacon of Wells in 1508 (an office he retained even after his return to Urbino in 1553).[65] This archdeaconry was no sinecure: Vergil took pride in discharging his duties as moral overseer and member of chapter; his historical writings show convincing familiarity with Wells and Bath.[66]

This rich and complexly variegated reading public was subtended by a general culture of literacy that was pervasive at Wells. There was a choir school and a grammar school for young vicars and others; much thought was dedicated to communal processes of learning. Teachers and more talented pupils were encouraged to respond intelligently and compassionately to the struggles of less talented boys; the acquisition of literacy was clearly seen as a communal activity.[67] The earliest extant example of academic drama in England was passed down (in a manuscript seen by Leland) from this educational milieu;[68] traditions of masked drama and boy bishops flourished, with and without official approval, for hundreds of years.[69] There are fragments of music, most notably a setting of *Gaude Virgo Mater Christi* by Richard Hygons, *informator* (master of choristers) from 1479 to 1507.[70] Such, then, was the culture that gave space to Dante for more than a hundred years; all levels of it find equivalences in Bertoldi's text. The medieval literary theory of the *comentum* was designed to engage the particular interests of Oxford-trained clerics. The simplicity of the *carmen*'s Latin – reminiscent of the straightforward Latinity employed by another Dante commentator, Guido da Pisa, in his attempt to bring the *Aeneid* to small boys – would not discourage younger scholars of middling abilities.[71] And the *carmen*'s more extravagant storytelling qualities – rivaling those of a Boccaccian *novella* that reached this part of the world ca. 1450 – would please audiences in places where romance, particularly Arthurian romance, proved exceptionally popular.[72] I make no claim here that Dante was read by anyone at Wells. I do claim that the text of Dante at Wells was perfectly congruent with the multivalent culture that housed it; I see nothing that might have flagged it as alien, foreign, or out of place.

Catholic and Protestant Dantes

On April 18, 1514, one Agnes Panter appeared before the consistory court at Wells, charged with witchcraft: she and certain female companions had used a girdle to intimidate a cow, cure a horse, and charm away vomiting. On the same day it was reported that John Panter, of the parish of Dultyng, was accustomed to go to the Mendip hills every eve of St. John the Baptist in order to consult with devils; he then recounted his findings at length to one William Joly of Shepton Mallet.[73] Such reports may be interpreted in differing ways: as the work of an oppressive clerisy that would stamp out all expressions of popular oral and medical tradition; or as evidence (talking with devils, meddling with animals) of an endemically superstitious Catholic culture that Protestant reform was soon to sweep away.[74] And one wonders what consequences this might imply for our "Dantes translatus"; here again, after all, we learn of a man who seeks out hills, meets with animals (*Inferno* 1.31–60) and converses with demons. It is worth noting, however, that the charge laid against Agnes was soon downgraded from witchcraft to superstition; her penance was to say (on the Friday and Saturday following) five Our Fathers, five Hail Marys, and one Creed on her knees (p. 157). It is not known what, if anything, happened to John. What happened to Dante, Boccaccio tells us (within the broad parameters of the commentarial tradition that passes directly to Benvenuto and Bertoldi), is that he was held in suspicion: certain women of Verona spoke of him as one who pops down to hell whenever he likes (thus accounting for his dark complexion and curly beard) and returns to tell tales – *novelle* – of the people he finds down there.[75] Dante, on hearing this, smiled a little and passed on ("sorridendo alquanto, passò avanti").

Such a smile acknowledges the difficulties, often humorous, of denying the superstitious while proclaiming the supernatural in Catholic culture; Agnes is found guilty, but her penance is light. Such humor and such latitude grew harder to find, on both sides of the Reformation divide, as the sixteenth century wore on. Boccaccio's *Decameron*, written by an author who fathered at least five illegitimate children (while advising the bishop of Florence on fine points of canon law), was discovered to be an affront to clerical dignity.[76] Works that had lain for decades or centuries in English libraries were suddenly deemed, by the likes of John Bale, to be full of "all kyndes of wicked superstycyons."[77] And conversely, texts deemed superstitious in earlier centuries might now be deemed resistant to – in pioneering or heroic fashion – superstitions that had pervaded an earlier age.[78]

In looking back at medieval Italian poets, one Protestant Englishman deplored "their unnatural and eccentric habits of mind and manners, their attachments to system, their scholastic theology, superstition, ideal love, and above all their chivalry," which "had corrupted every true principle of life and literature"; a Protestant Irishman characterized the *Commedia* as "a tissue of barbarisms, absurdities, and horrors."[79] But these are Protestants of the eighteenth century: the second is Martin Sherlock (who became chaplain to the bishop of Derry in 1777); the first is Thomas Warton (1728–90), appointed – like his father before him – Professor of Poetry at Oxford. Their condemnation of Dante and the culture that produced him form part of that anti-Catholic discourse which, particularly after 1707, helped yoke together the disparate localities of a newly united United Kingdom.[80] This discourse receives its most memorable expression in the words of Horace Walpole, later Earl of Orford: "Dante," he says in a letter of 25 June 1782, "was extravagant, absurd, disgusting, in short a Methodist parson in Bedlam."[81] This sublime one-liner, a genuine Protestant wrecking-ball, makes no effort to comprehend the edifice it would destroy; Catholicism, which comes before the establishment of the true Church, and Methodism, which comes after, meet and embrace in lunatic unintelligibility.[82]

Things in the sixteenth century are very different. Leland was moved and perhaps ultimately unhinged by seeing the literary culture of medieval English Catholicism systematically (or, perhaps more painful to behold, unsystematically) destroyed. And John Foxe's *Actes and Monuments* – which was to be placed in every cathedral church of Elizabethan England, by state decree – contains no word of condemnation for Dante. In 1559, just eight years after the 1551 Act against "superstitious" works, Foxe happened to be working in the printing office of Oporinus in the Lutheran stronghold of Basle when the *editio princeps* of Dante's *Monarchia* passed through the press.[83] In the same year the same press printed the first folio edition of Foxe's *Actes*. In the 1570 edition, printed after Foxe's return to England, Dante appears as "an hereticke": a heretic in the eyes of *Catholic* authorities, that is, for his writing "wherein he proveth the pope not to be above the Emperour," for his preaching against "the vayne fables of Monkes and Friers," for his condemnation of those who would feed Christ's flock "not with the foode of the Gospel, but with winde," and for characterizing the pope as a wolf: "The Pope saith he, of a pastor is made a woolfe, to wast the church of Christ, and to procure with hys Clergye not the word of God to be preached, but his own decrees."[84] Foxe here picks up a famous passage of *Paradiso* 9, which laments that sheep and lambs have gone astray as the shepherd is turned wolf ("che fatto ha lupo del pastore") by the Florentine florin. The passage (given below in Bertoldi's Latin) goes on to condemn canon lawyers who abandon the Bible in order to study the Decretals for financial gain; their frantic calculations (Dante suggests) may be read in the margins of manuscript pages:

Propter istum Evangelium et Doctores magni	For this the Gospel and the great Doctors
Sunt derelicti, et solum ad Decretales	are abandoned, and only the Decretals
Studetur ita, quod apparet suis vivagnis.	is studied (as its margins attest).
Ad istud intendunt papa et cardinales:	Pope and cardinals attend only to this:
Non vadunt eorum cogitationes ad Nazareth,	their thoughts do not go to Nazareth
Ubi Gabriel aperuit alas.	where Gabriel opened his wings.
Sed Vaticanum, et alie partes electe	But the Vatican, and the other elect parts
Rome, que fuerunt cimiterium	of Rome that have been cemeteries
militie quam Petrus sequutus est,	to the soldiery that followed Peter
Cito libere erunt de adulterio.	Shall soon be freed from adultery.

(**Paradiso** *9.133–42)*

The adulterous union of which Dante here speaks, picking up the prophecy of *Purgatorio* 33.37–45, is that of a corrupted papacy with the Church; the prophetic suggestion that Rome would be restored to a tradition derived from the early Christian martyrs ("the soldiery that followed Peter") must have proved pleasing to Reformation Protestants. It certainly did not amuse

Counter-Reformation Catholicism: in 1614, when the *Commedia* joined the *Monarchia* on the *Index Expurgatorius* of prohibited books, this passage was ordered expurgated from all editions (with or without commentary).[85] The *Commedia* and *Monarchia* proved especially popular with German reformers; the Frenchman François Perrot (1586) collected together passages from Dante to show Italians the corruption of the Roman curia.[86] The Sienese Catholic Bellisario Bulgarini (1539–1619), one of Dante's harshest critics, declared that Dante's "intera favola ha del poco cristiano" (Dante's "whole poem has very little that is Christian about it").[87]

In the 1570 edition of Foxe's *Monuments*, in which Dante first appears, Chaucer is featured as one who moved questions against "these superstitious sects of Fryers, and other such beggerly religions" by speaking "in the person of a certaine uplandish and simple ploughman of the countrey".[88] Foxe here grants Chaucer unwarranted credit for having written *Jack Upland*. There are, however, many passages of a pastoral cast in Chaucer which suggest linkages (for the sixteenth-century mind) both with a reform-minded tradition of English poetry and with those passages from Dante that Foxe cites elsewhere. The *General Prologue* portrait of the Parson contains an extended span of sheep, wolf, and shitty shepherd imagery (1.501–12) of the kind that proved congenial to Lollard polemic.[89] The *Parson's Tale* proves even more expansive in similar vein: "These been the newe sheepherdes," the Parson exclaims, "that leten hir sheep wityngly go renne to the wolf that is in the breres, or do no fors of hir owene governaunce" (10.721).[90] Leland, in his brief Latin life of Chaucer, suggests that *Piers Plowman* ("which by the common consent of the learned is attributed to Chaucer as its true author") was expelled from editions of the *Canterbury Tales* "because it inveighed against the bad morals of the priests." There is some evidence to suggest, then, that in the mind of Leland and other, later, sixteenth-century English Protestants, Chaucer, Dante, and Langland were (in the conflict that was coming to mean more than all others) on the same side. Leland's naming of Dante at Wells does not *necessarily* expose the *Dantes translatus* as a text for destruction. Indeed, Dante might have been numbered among the good when seen among so many English *auctores*, cited by Leland, associated with Wycliffite traditions of reform (or the persecution of them): Philip Repingdon, John Uthred, Roger Dymmok, William Woodford, John Sharpe, and Nicholas Radcliffe.[91]

We need not necessarily assume, then, that our Wellsian Dante was destroyed at or before 1551 as a superstitious work. Manuscripts at Wells, it seems, were gradually dispersed rather than summarily destroyed. The academic drama noted above (which Leland saw) was given to Trinity College, Cambridge, by Thomas Nevile (master of the college, 1593–1615). Sidney

Sussex MS 75 (also seen by Leland) also found its way to Cambridge via the hands of a master: Samuel Ward, third master of Sidney Sussex College, had been made a prebendary of Wells in 1615 and a canon residentiary in January 1616/17.[92] The medieval collections at Wells may well have remained substantially intact[93] until the mid-seventeenth century, until, perhaps, 1642, when parliamentarians smashed stained glass and "Cavaliers," according to *Exceeding Joyfull Newes From the Earl of Bedford*, "did £10,000 worth of damage in Wells."[94] In 1646, Walter Ralegh (Sir Walter's nephew), dean of Wells, was stabbed to death; in 1649, thieves were seen stripping lead from the roof. The cathedral clergy were dispersed and no new dean was appointed until the Restoration.[95] "These holy, prophane days, and blessed execrable Times of troublesome tranquility," the poet John Taylor sarcastically observed of Wells in his *Wandering, to see the Wonders of the West* (1649), "have spoyled and defaced one of the goodliest and [most] magnificent Cathedrall Churches in the Christian world. But [for] such pious workes," he continues, "as polution and abusing of Churches, wee neede not goe amongst Turkes for proofes."[96] On the same day, Taylor traveled "foure miles further" to see "the Ruines of an Abby" (p. 4). During the Commonwealth, in the immediate aftermath of the public beheading of Charles I, head of the Church of England, Wells must have seemed (to Taylor and others) destined for the same ruined status as Glastonbury. "Dantes translatus in carmen Latinum" might, then, have fallen victim at Wells not to the first Cromwell (himself dean of Wells, 1537–40), but to the second: not Thomas, but Oliver.

Loving Landscape and the Kingly Person

"Somerset" – to touch base with our point of origin – has come to be regarded, in recent English historical memory, as a backward, rural county famed for broad accents and the drinking of cider. It seems incongruous to associate such a place with matters intellectual, such as the reading of Dante or the performing of academic drama, but such incongruity has a history that does not extend back to the fifteenth and earlier sixteenth centuries. Wells, we have noted, possessed one of the great libraries of late medieval England and, surrounding it, a vibrant, heterogeneous, complex network of reading communities. This library and these communities formed part of an international culture that could send Bubwith to Constance or draw Polydore Vergil from Urbino, cultural contacts that narrowed markedly as England withdrew into Protestant isolationism. Throughout the 1520s and 1530s, the English monarch (later head of his own Church of England) came to take an ever closer, controlling interest in English textual cultures. Efforts to control such cultures were, however, increasingly frustrated by waves of foreign invasion: English texts, printed in Antwerp, Basle, Paris, and other continental cities, were hunted down and burned by the sackful.[97] The extraordinary acceleration of efforts to map and investigate the archaeology of England throughout the sixteenth and seventeenth centuries tacitly accepts these new pressures toward insularity. Leland's internal pilgrimages across England, which merge (through tortured erotics) devotion to details of landscape with love of the kingly person, pioneer the process of severing localities from wider cultural filiations (while laying them under centralized political authority). Somerset thus comes to be loved as a deeply rural, thus quintessentially English, county (speaking its own peculiar idiolect) that will struggle to cope with anything foreign to itself. And so it becomes implausible to think of Somerset coping with anything so foreign, and as intellectually complex, as Dante.

In 1649, we have noted, John Taylor set out to see "the Wonders of the West." He did this, he tells us, to make money (needing to "devise a painfull way for my subsistence").[98] Having served Charles I and his "Royall Father" for some 45 years, Taylor is denied a living when Charles is beheaded, on January 30, 1649. Soon after, "old, lame and poor, by mad contentions beggerd," Taylor heads west, hoping that his account of "travell, gravell, dust, durt, flint" will be rewarded by gentlemanly sympathizers.[99] Since Anglicanism has become internally schismatic ("we neede not goe amongst Turkes for proofes", p. 4), the integrity of the kingdom must stand in for the missing body of a king:

> Thus having traveld North, and South, and East,
> I meane to end my travels with the West.[100]

The second Charles landed in Scotland late in 1650 and was crowned at Scone on January 1, 1651. Following the terminal defeat of his army at Worcester, Charles *the younger* – according to the famous story retold to English children down the centuries – escaped his Cromwellian pursuers by hiding in an oak tree. The tale's potential was in fact readily grasped from the earliest moments of the Restoration. John Crouch waxes apostrophic before the tree which had "CHARLES lodg'd in thy Boughs,"[101] beginning

> Blest *Oake!* Thou *Monarch* of the *British* Grove,
> Sacred to CHARLES (thy Guest,) as once to *Jove*;
> Thou *Bulwark* of our little world! dost stand,
> Or *move*, impregnable, by Sea and Land.
>
> *(37–40)*

John Danvers, also pamphleteering in 1660, actually has tree and monarch become as one: he pictures Charles entering a Wood, "where finding a hollow Oak, he was now content to make it his Pallace, for here he for some days concealed himself."[102] Hundreds of hostelries quickly adopted the Royal Oak as their sign, and the anniversary of Charles' ascension – which is to say the restoration of monarchy to England, Scotland, Wales, and Ireland – was celebrated as Royal Oak Day.[103] Medieval monarchs had long laid claim to large tracts of forest, eroticizing the relation as intensely personal and private.[104] The royal oak, however, becomes – as Crouch's lines intuit – a more potent symbol of national and global intent, for it binds people both to the landscape that saved and sustained an imperiled king and to the oak-built ships – such as the *Royal Oak* – then nosing into every corner of the world.[105] English sailors, famously, have hearts of oak; and Englishmen *en route* to India (according to a comic opera sung at the Theatre Royal, Drury Lane, ca. 1823) declare themselves "firm as oak and free from care."[106] All this spectacularly fulfills the dream of the *Libelle of Englyshe Polycye*: that England might realize the symbolic promise of its coin, the *noble* (which sees the English monarch afloat in a ship of war).[107]

In this long and complex evolving tradition of imagining the English monarch mysteriously immanent in the landscapes he rules, the westward traveler we began with again seems of compelling importance: John Leland, who in 1546 declared himself to Henry VIII as someone "totally eenflamed with . . . love."[108] The object of this desire is the body of a kingdom that Leland can never tire of traversing, can never know well enough. Leland is perennially driven to connect what he has read in books (principally of historiography) with what he might find on the road.[109] He is (like Taylor after him) a pilgrim who aspires never to leave home, a crusader who finds Jerusalem without crossing the ocean, and a lover who never tires of enumerating every secret corner of his beloved's body:

> I have so traveled in your domynions both by the see coastes and the myddle partes, sparynge neyther labour nor costes by the space of these vi. yeares past, that there is almost neyther cape nor baye, haven, creke or pere, ryver or confluence of ryvers, breches, washes, lakes, meres, fenny waters, mountaynes, valleys, mores, hethes, forestes, woodes, cyties, burges, castels, pryncypall manor places, monasteryes, and colleges, but I haue seane them, and noted in so doynge a whole worlde of thynges verye memorable. (signature Div)

For Leland, love of learning and love of place conjoin most intimately; the loss of monasteries as preeminent sites of learning (and chief hosts of the historiographical tradition he so prized) must have proved – not to overstate the case – disorientating. In the commentary to his Latin verse *Swansong* (*Cygnea Cantio*, published in 1545), Leland lovingly enumerates English monasteries *as if they were still standing* (rather than, for the most part, standing in ruins, "with many of their literary treasures dispersed to the four winds").[110] Bale is similarly mindful, in *The Laboryouse Journey*, that the work of institutional destruction upon which he and Leland depend for their own creative endeavors has spun beyond their control. He is dismayed to discover, on returning from abroad, "dyvers most ruynouslye spoyled, broaken up, and dyspersed lybrayes" (Di); he is fearful that not all forms of institutional destruction adduce to the common good:

> If we lose the treasure of these authors herin contayned, by the malyce or els slouthfull negligence of thys wycked age, whych is muche geuen to the destruccyon of thynges memorable, we may wele lamente and saye wyth the noble clarke Erasmus of Roterdame. Wyth muche payne I absteyne from wepynge (sayth he in certen Eppstle) for oft as I in readynge the Cataloges of olde writers, do beholde what profyghtes, yea, what pusaunce, ayde, and confort we haue lost. (signature Diii–iv)

It is a matter of crucial, *nacyon*-making import, then, that those attempting to discriminate between hidden treasure and works of superstition – texts to redeem (Cii) and texts to destroy – judge rightly. For there are many "unprofytable cloddes," Bale argues, "whyche seketh not els but them selues in the destruccyon of thynges memorable and necessarye" (Cviii). By his actions, Bale had argued in opening *The Laboryouse Journey*, John Leland had proved himself *not* to be such a clod: he has "not shewed hym selfe [to be] a barreyne and unfruteful clodde of earthe wythin hys owne nacyon" (Bvii). But, as this odd clod-echo strangely suggests, Leland and Bale must have realized the burdensome responsibility incumbent upon those who, dividing faithful sheep from superstitious goats, singled out books at libraries. They can never know for certain whether, in passing judgment on a particular volume, they side with the forces of light or the clods of destruction. Such tortured self-doubt and self-guessing seems ironically appropriate for these early Protestant attempts to establish a canon of Protestant writing.

Leland is easier to like than Bale for his spectacular inability to reconcile the psychotic demands of his own revolutionary moment: to at once love landscapes (of both bookish and natural topography) *and* the monarch (who inspires their intimate mapping, yet prescribes their ruination).[111] Bale, in the strange duet of *The Laboryouse Journey*, commends Leland's efforts at saving "the profitable workes of many excellent wryters, which els had been loste," redeeming them "from dust and byrdfylynges, or private vse to no profyte" (Cii). Many such "good authors," Leland tells Henry, have by now been removed to "the most magnificent libraryes of your royall palaces. Part also," Leland continues, "remayne in my custodie" (Cii). From these accumulated texts, Leland intended to fashion for Henry "within the space of xii. moneths folowyng, such a descripcion . . . of your realme in wryttinge" that an engraver or painter might make a map from it (Dvi). But within these twelve months, Henry had died, the second Act for the Dissolution of Monasteries had passed into law, and Leland (as Bale puts it) "fell beside his wittes" (Dvi). In March 1551, Leland was found by mayoral inquisition to be "mad, insane, lunatic, furious, frantic, enjoying drowsy or lucid intervals, so that he cannot manage his affairs";[112] he died the following spring, on April 18, 1552.

Ghosts and Slaves: Dante and Coleridge in Somerset

Dante, it seems, has in every sense vanished from Somerset, both as physical object – the text imported by Bubwith and encountered by Leland – and imaginative possibility. He has, further, been constructed (alienated) as a poet of furious, un-English extremes (as furious, perhaps, as the energies that removed him from Wells). And yet English Anglican culture has never been able to sever ties with Dante, and with everything he represents. Spenser, most intensively in *The Faerie Queen*, Book I, ransacks Catholic sacramental and monastic tradition – while running vigorous anti-Catholic polemic – to remythologize an ancient English past. The Anglican T. S. Eliot, in wartime London, chose not to see Dante, his most significant source of poetic and religious inspiration, but a figure based upon a famous Dantean visualization. Where Irish poets have staged full-blooded encounters with Dante on Irish ground within a continuous terrain of European culture, English poets have been reticent or oblique.[113] The contradictoriness of such English encounters is captured to brilliant and comic effect by Max Beerbohm's "Dante at Oxford" (figure 15).[114] The tall figure of Dante is interpellated as alien by the stocky, native figure of an Oxford proctor, who demands: "What is your name and college?" We cannot help but notice, however, how naturally the upright figure of Dante harmonizes with the Gothic architecture of this scene; it is the squat, rubicund proctor who seems non-native, out of place. Dante is a medieval scholar in a medieval scholarly setting; the beadle, we realize, is a Hogarth's head (see chapter 1, p. 30 and

15 Max Beerbohm, "Dante in Oxford," from *Poets' Corner* (1904). Cambridge University Library.

figure 1). Beerbohm thus brilliantly connects this scene of would-be *entfremdung*, foreigner-spotting, with that most intensive phase of Channel widening: the eighteenth century.

Virulent anti-Dantism, we have noted, is first heard in the eighteenth century as a complement to that anti-Catholicism which would integrate, discursively, the new United Kingdom against foreign threats. By the eighteenth century, English anti-Catholicism had sunk deep roots in popular consciousness (gathering up some of the antisemitic energies of an earlier time). So it was that, in 1780, at least 285 people were killed in anti-Catholic riots; such riots inspired a Somerset mob to plan destroying "two or three poor houses" at Wells, "belonging to very obscure persons, supposed to be Roman Catholicks."[115] But such confusion of popular or visceral anti-Catholicism with anti-Dantism is hard to find before this time; it is not difficult to see, for example, that Milton was one of Dante's most diligent pupils.[116] During the immediate post-Reformation period, Dante, Langland, and Chaucer are actually assimilated to the same anti-papal cause. Before this, they may be read as part of contiguous Catholic cultures (containing, of course, elements of internal dissent and critique); Dante's Mendips lie 50 miles south of Langland's Malvern hills.

The hills of Somerset, we have noted, hosted the great literary collaboration between Wordsworth and Coleridge that was to lead to the printing of *Lyrical Ballads* at Bristol in 1798. Somerset thus proved a fruitful place for recollecting a Romantic sublime that it could hardly inspire or embody: Wordsworth writes of Tintern, not Glastonbury, abbey. There is no sense in Wordsworth or Coleridge that Somerset ever hosted a vibrant, internationalist, literary culture; nor that it was the destruction of that culture which provided the grassy, localized setting for their own, would-be revolutionary reflections upon rustic lives in low or middling style. The landscape of their Somerset is marked, however, not by one but by two revolutionary phases, neither of which seems to disturb the green curtain of their poetry. The first, as we have seen, is that of the Reformation; the second is the slave trade.

When Coleridge and Sarah Fricker married in 1795 they first lived at Clevedon, not far from the Clevedon Court estate that had been purchased by the first Sir Abraham Elton in 1717 and improved by his heirs up to 1788. The Eltons, whose founding father, Abraham I, was the son of a road scavenger, had prospered through the most intensive phase of Bristol-based slaving; most of the many grand houses or "green mansions" built around Bristol in this period were financed, in whole or in part, by the African and West Indian trade.[117] It might seem unfair to think that Coleridge was in any way compromised by this, for he spoke out against the trade in a famous quayside lecture at Bristol in 1795, and he had even (he was proud to recall) written a prize-winning poem in Greek against the trade while he was an undergraduate at Cambridge.[118] All this is true, but deserves only limited credit, for by the time Coleridge spoke out the most intensive, wealth-generating phase of Bristol slaving (ca. 1700–50) was long over, and many in Bristol civic circles were keen to distance themselves from the trade originally subtending their wealth and social prominence.[119] At Cambridge, too, an anti-slavery stance was fashionable rather than revolutionary by 1792, for in the year that Coleridge won the Greek prize for his poem against the trade, Samuel Butler won the Latin prize for a poem on the self-same topic.[120] And Coleridge's decision to compete for the prize was driven not so much by libertarian as by commercial considerations. His funding at Cambridge, and his standing with his family, was precarious. He shares his plans to compete in a revealing letter to his parson brother George, written in November 1791:

> After Tea (N. b / Sugar is very dear) I read Classics till I go to bed – viz – eleven o'clock. If I were to read on as I do now – there is not the least doubt, that I should be Classical Medallist, and a very high Wrangler – but *Freshmen* always *begin* very *furiously*. I am reading Pindar, and composing Greek verse, like a mad dog. I am very fond of Greek verse, and shall try hard for the Brown's Prize ode.[121]

Coleridge's Sapphic stanzas, which he declaimed to the Cambridge University Senate on July 3, 1792, exhibit some of the conventional gambits and blind spots of such anti-slaving poems. He begins by invoking Death: that it might repatriate the West Indian slaves by letting them "fly to the dear / Resorts of pleasure, and to their fatherland" (11–12).[122] As is usual even in anti-slaving writing of this period, the captive Africans are seen as an undifferentiated mass (a "race of slaves," 24); and as is conventional in *pro*-slaving arguments, they are seen as "children of Necessity" consigned to "loathsome labours" (28–9). Personal individuation in the poem only arrives, to the accompaniment of a Dorian lyre, with the voice of "Wilberforce" (63). From this point on, Wilberforce owns the poem: his words, found more desirable than the acclaiming shouts of the masses "round the / delayed chariot of Victory, on the day of / delightful Triumph" (91–3), take up most of the remaining space; the concluding lines envision Wilberforce being hymned or rocketed to his reward – "thy name shall dart to heaven" by "the blessings of / the sufferers" (98–100).

Although this poem exerted scant influence in the nineteenth century, its attitudes remain foundational, for still to this day talk of the English and slavery quickly moves to the safe ground (in England) of William Wilberforce. Indeed, it seems (from countless school texts and exhibitions) that the topic actually *begins* with Wilberforce (at the moment of abolition). Such amnesia, or failure of linkage, is enabled by the fact that ports such as Bristol saw raw materials arrive from the Americas and manufactured goods depart for Africa; slaves, carried across the middle passage, traveled the invisible side of the triangle. But there are, inevitably, traces of broken linkage to be found in texts such as Coleridge's poem. His Greek ode bears a Latin title that firmly localizes the trade in the Caribbean: "Sors misera Servorum in insulis Indiae Occidentalis" (p. 476). In denouncing those "who feed on the persecution of the wretched" (56), however, Coleridge forgets his own fondness for afternoon tea and his complaint – in the letter to brother George, quoted above – that "Sugar is very dear."[123] A more general blind spot is the failure to grasp that the whole apparatus of Greek and Latin humanist scholarship – as instantiated by the prizewinning performances of Coleridge and Butler in 1792 – had earlier helped rationalize slavery by reviving the absolute, mutually imbricated, classical notions of liberty and servitude: the former knows itself by viewing and enforcing the latter.[124] The clean, neoclassical lines of the dozens of grand houses built across Somerset throughout the eighteenth century thus recall, even as they would seek to forget, those who died far away.

In formulating *Lyrical Ballads*, Wordsworth and Coleridge struggle to develop a language that might achieve "a natural delineation of human passions, human characters, and human incidents"; to this end they reject "the gaudiness and inane phraseology of many modern writers."[125] Young Wordsworth and Coleridge, like their sixteenth-century English antecedents, are self-consciously bent on reformation and revolution; they remake language and, to a very considerable extent, landscape (or the way landscape is experienced). Both sets of reformers – and the second set, crucially, work within frameworks inherited from the first – effect certain breaks with the past which see certain ghostly figures – Dante, black slaves – fade from the scene. Somerset – to judge from the life's work of Richard Long – is a place that mysteriously continues to invite endless crossings and journeyings.[126] It is a landscape of secrets and lies, markers and fragments,[127] attesting – through the dispersed library of Wells, or the grave of Scipio Africanus at Henbury (young, black, classicized, whitened, and finally Christian) – to a culture that, strategically constructed as local and rural, contains the world.[128]

NOTES

1   "Alienation," Raymond Williams remarks, "is now one of the most difficult words in the language" (*Keywords: A Vocabulary of Culture and Society* [London: Fontana, 1976], p. 33). Its meanings were already complex in Old French and Middle English by the fourteenth and fifteenth centuries. I here favor the term *entfremdung* for its suggesting a deliberate process, imagined as immanent to particular landscapes, empowered to identify that which figures as foreign or

fremdt in its midst. On the history of *entfremdung* (as witnessed in Middle High German literature, and as variously employed by Hegel, Marx, Heidegger, and others), see Richard Schacht, *Alienation* (London: George Allen and Unwin, 1971).

2 In rewriting this chapter I am haunted and inspired by an exhibit I saw somewhere years ago in which a young black photographer pictured herself in the Lake District; I cannot remember her name.

3 The citation is from *Boece* I, prosa 6, 51–4.

4 The greatest of countless poppy poems was written by a Bristol-born poet in June 1916: see "Break of Day in the Trenches," in *The Collected Works of Isaac Rosenberg*, ed. Ian Parsons (London: Chatto and Windus, 1979), pp. 103–4.

5 I employ the term "structure of feeling" here by way of recognizing a debt to Raymond Williams, *The Country and the City* (London: Chatto and Windus, 1973; see, for example, p. 96): a brilliant work marred chiefly by its scant account of the medieval countryside. There are but two references to Langland, both dismissive (pp. 11, 44).

6 See William Wordsworth and Samuel Taylor Coleridge, *Lyrical Ballads*, ed. R. L. Brett and A. R. Jones, 2nd edn. (London: Routledge, 1991); *Lyrical Ballads, with a Few Other Poems* was first published at Bristol by Joseph Cottle in 1798.

7 *1805 Prelude*, 13.393–4 in William Wordsworth, *The Prelude: The Four Texts (1798, 1799, 1805, 1850)*, ed. Jonathan Wordsworth (London: Penguin, 1995). "Quantock's grassy hills" become "smooth Quantock's airy ridge" in the 1850 version (13.396). In both versions this is the landscape in which Coleridge and Wordworth "Together wantoned in wild poesy" (*1805 Prelude* 13.414; *1850 Prelude* 13.418). On the life of William and Dorothy Wordsworth, Samuel and Sara Coleridge at Nether Stowey and Alfoxden in 1797–8, see Stephen Gill, *William Wordsworth: A Life* (Oxford: Clarendon Press, 1989), pp. 119–51; Rosemary Ashton, *The Life of Samuel Taylor Coleridge* (Oxford: Blackwell, 1996), pp. 101–44; Tom Mayberry, *Coleridge and Wordsworth in the West Country* (Stroud, Gloucestershire: Alan Sutton, 1992). On Wordsworth as "the prophet of Lakeland," see Ernest de Selincourt, "Introduction" to Wordsworth, *Guide to the Lakes*, ed. de Selincourt (London: Henry Frowde, 1906), pp. iii–xxviii (p. ix).

8 England's most liberal, politically correct newspaper (as I first researched this chapter) found occasion to share a characterization of Somerset as a county of "two-headed sheep-shaggers on combine harvesters" ("Tour Match: Somerset v. Sri Lanka," *The Guardian*, July 15, 1998, p. 26).

9 "Until 1782," Gilbert F. Cunningham writes, "not so much as a complete canto of the Divine Comedy had been printed in English translation" (*The Divine Comedy in English: A Critical Bibliography, 1782–1900* [Edinburgh: Oliver and Boyd, 1965], p. 13). And after then, of course, the deluge.

10 See *Dante, Philomythes and Philosopher: Man in the Cosmos* (Cambridge: Cambridge University Press, 1981), p. 43.

11   Anthony Wood, *Athenae Oxonienses*, 2 vols. (London: Knaplock et al., 1721), I.83a. See further, for powerful discussion of periodization issues and the Bale/ Leland relationship, James Simpson, *Reform and Cultural Revolution. The Oxford English Literary History*, vol. 2, *1350–1547* (Oxford: Oxford University Press, 2002), pp. 7–33; see also T. S. Dorsch, "Two English Antiquaries: John Leland and John Stow," *Essays and Studies*, NS 12 (1959), 18–35 (p. 22). Wood tells us that Leland was at one time "Rector of Poppeling (sometimes written Popering and Pepling) in the Marches of Calais" (I.82).

12   See Lucy Toulmin Smith, *The Itinerary of John Leland in or about the Years 1535– 43*, 5 vols. (London: G. Bell, 1906–10). For a useful one-volume moderniza- tion, abridgment, and rearrangement of this standard edition, see John H. Chandler, *John Leland's Itinerary: Travels in Tudor England* (Stroud, Gloucester- shire: Alan Sutton, 1993).

13   See James Carley, "John Leland at Somerset Libraries," *Somerset Archaeology and Natural History* 129 (1985), 141–54 (p. 141).

14   See C. M. Church, "Notes on the Buildings, Books, and Benefactors of the Library of the Dean and Chapter of the Cathedral Church of Wells," *Archaeologia* 57 (1901), 201–28 (pp. 203, 209).

15   John Leland, *Commentarii de Scriptoribus Britannicis*, ed. Antonius Hall, 2 vols. (Oxford: University Press, 1709), II, p. 387; Carley, "Somerset Libraries," p. 141.

16   Michel de Certeau, *Practice of Everyday Life*, trans. Steven Rendall (Berkeley: University of California Press, 1984), p. 117; and see above, p. 14.

17   Wells Cathedral Library, X4/32 and X4/33. The remarkable range of frag- ments in different hands in these two guard books includes material on avarice (15th century), on law (with glossaries, 14th century), and on female disorders (from a major compilation of Salernitan texts, ca. 1275–1325); with- out additional knowledge of provenance, little should be made of them.

18   See *Medieval Libraries of Great Britain: A List of Surviving Books*, ed. N. R. Ker, 2nd edn. (London: Royal Historical Society, 1964), p. 195, and *Supplement to the Second Edition*, ed. Andrew G. Watson (London: Royal Historical Society, 1987), p. 67; Carley, "Somerset Libraries", p. 142; Vivien Law and James P. Carley, "Grammar and Arithmetic in Two Thirteenth-Century English Monastic Collections: Cambridge, Sidney Sussex College, MS 75, and Oxford, Bodleian Library, MS Bodley 186 (S.C. 2088)," *Journal of Medieval Latin* 1 (1991), 140–167 (pp. 145–7).

19   Wells Cathedral Library, Box X4/34. Fayrfax's name heads the list of lay clerks of the Chapel Royal in an impressive sequence of major events: the funeral of Henry VII (May 9, 1509), the coronation of Henry VIII (June 24, 1509), the burial of Henry, infant prince (February 27, 1511) and the Field of the Cloth of Gold just outside Calais (June 1520). The Wells fragments were found in 1877 in the binding of a 1611 edition of Mantica's *Tractatus de coniecturis*. The vol- ume was presented to Wells Cathedral by one of the canons, Dr. Selleck, who died in 1690; the binding has been identified as the work of Francis Peerse,

binder at the Bodleian Library from 1613 to 1622. See Nicholas Sandon, "Fayrfax, Robert (1464–1521)," in *The New Grove Dictionary of Music and Musicians*, ed. Stanley Sadie, 20 vols. (London: Macmillan, 1980), 6.443b–445a; David Fallows, "The Drexel Fragments of Early Tudor Song," *Research Chronicle* (The Royal Music Association) 26 (1993), pp. 5–18.

20 Specifically, "all Books called Antyphoners Myssales Scrayles Processionalles Manuelles Legends Pyes Portuyses Prymars in Latin or Inglishe Cowchers Journales Ordinales, or other books or writings whatsoever heretofore used for service of the Churche, written or prynted in the Inglishe or Lattyn tongue" (*Statutes of the Realm*, 11 vols. [London: Eyre and Strahan, 1810–28], IV.110); there were stiff penalties for non-compliance.

21 See A. B Emden, *A Biographical Register of the University of Oxford*, 3 vols. (Oxford: Clarendon Press, 1957–9): "Bubwith, Nicholas," I.294b–296a; "Hallum, Robert," II.854a–855b. For more on Hallum, see Michael J. Bennett, *Community, Class and Careerism: Cheshire and Lancashire Society in the Age of* Sir Gawain and the Green Knight (Cambridge: Cambridge University Press, 1983), pp. 141, 144, 147, 155–60.

22 As represented by Vatican Library, MS Capponiano 1 (Vat. 7566–7568): see Johannes de Serravalle, *Translatio et Comentum totius libri Dantis Aldigherii*, ed. Marcellino da Civezza, M. O. and Teofilo Domenichelli, M. O. (Prato: Giachetti, 1891), *incipit*. "Bubwych" and "Halam" are further mentioned in the *dedicatio* to the translation, in the *conclusio* to the translation, and in the *conclusio* to the commentary (pp. 5, 1214, 1215).

23 "Prope Sibiliam, forte per centum leucas, est mons Giubelcar, iuxta quem montem mare Oceanum per angustum spatium septem leucarum fluit et vadit, et ingreditur mare Mediterraneum; et ego iam transivi per illud angustum spatium, quando redibam de regno Anglie ad partes Ytalie per mare" (p. 259). Bertoldi's editors think the year 1398 likeliest for this voyage because he would have been too busy at any other time (earlier as scholar and later as bishop). He certainly made a pilgrimage from Florence to the Holy Land in that year. See *Comentum*, p. xvii.

24 See Christopher Nighman, "Reform and Humanism in the Sermons of Richard Fleming at the Council of Constance (1417)," University of Toronto Ph.D. dissertation (1996), pp. 203–4.

25 Reinhard Strohm, "The Council of Constance," in *The Rise of European Music, 1380–1500* (Cambridge: Cambridge University Press, 1993), pp. 106–24 (p. 106).

26 See above, p. 3; see further *The Council of Constance: The Unification of the Church*, trans. Louise Ropes Loomis, ed. John Hine Mundy and Kennerly M. Woody (New York: Columbia University Press, 1961), p. 108.

27 G. Ferraù, "Bertoldi, Giovanni (Giovanni da Serravalle)," *Enciclopedia dantesca*, 6 vols. (Rome: Istituto della Enciclopedia Italiana, 1970–8), I.608b–609b; see further A. Vallone, "Bertoldi, Giovanni (Giovanni da Serravalle)," *Dizionario biografico degli italiani* (Rome: Istituto della Enciclopedia Italiana, 1960–),

IX.574a–576a. Brief mention is made of Bertoldi in *Dante: The Critical Heritage 1314(?)–1870*, ed. Michael Caesar (London: Routledge, 1989), pp. 19 and 76 (n. 37) and by Robert Hollander, "Dante and his Commentators," in *The Cambridge Companion to Dante*, ed. Rachel Jacoff (Cambridge: Cambridge University Press, 1993), pp. 226–36 (pp. 228–9). Hollander observes that Serravalle's commentary "has not been attended to as much as it probably should be"; he further notes that the 1891 edition (held by few libraries) is now available "in anastatic reproduction" (p. 229).

28   One exception to this trend is the second preamble to Spaniard Juan de Mena's *Coronación* (1438). Mena borrows directly from Bertoldi's discussion of tragedy; a copy of Bertoldi's commentary had come into the possession of Pedro de Luna (the hold-out Spanish pope, deposed by the Council of Constance in 1417). See Henry Ansgar Kelly, *Ideas and Forms of Tragedy from Aristotle to the Middle Ages* (Cambridge: Cambridge University Press, 1993), pp. 206–7.

29   See *dedicatio, Comentum*, pp. 5–6. Although it is misleading to number Bertoldi among the stellar humanist talents who came to Constance, I would argue that the very intensity of his self-abuse as Latinist in the Dante project ("de rusticana latinitate, incompta et inepta translatione") bespeaks understanding of what those new standards of humanist Latinity implied. Those who wrote to Petrarch (exposing their Latin to the severest scrutiny) often indulged in comparable bouts of obbligato self-recrimination: see David Wallace, *Chaucerian Polity: Absolutist Lineages and Associational Forms in England and Italy* (Stanford, Calif.: Stanford University Press, 1997), p. 265. For consideration of Bertoldi among talented humanists at Constance such as Poggio Bracciolini, Vergerio, Salutati and Chrysoloras, see Paul Arendt, *Die Predigten des Konstanzer Konzils* (Freiburg im Breisgau: Herder, 1933), pp. 83–4.

30   See Benvenuto da Imola, *Comentum super Dantis Aldigherij*, ed. G. P. Lacaita, 5 vols. (Florence: G. Barbèra, 1887).

31   See Emden, *Biographical Register*, "Bubwith, Nicholas," I.295–6; C. M. Church, "Notes on the Buildings, Books, and Benefactors of the Library of Wells," pp. 204–5. Bubwith's will is at Lambeth Library, Register Chichele, 378 (1414).

32   *Leland's Itinerary*, ed. Toulmin Smith, II.145. The hospital was actually founded after Bubwith's death (from the residuum of his estate).

33   Dante refers to his own "carmi" at *Paradiso* 17.111.

34   The Latin of Constance thus seems to straddle the concepts of "vernacular" and "vehicular" language as elaborated by Gilles Deleuze and Félix Guattari, "What is a Minor Literature?," in *Kafka: Toward a Minor Literature*, trans. Dana Polan (Minneapolis: University of Minnesota Press, 1986), pp. 16–27 (pp. 23–4). For a sustained, timely, and exemplary refusal to pit vernacular *against* Latin cultures, see Christopher Baswell, "Latinitas," in *The Cambridge History of Medieval English Literature*, ed. David Wallace (Cambridge: Cambridge University Press, 1999), pp. 122–51.

35   William Dunn Macray, *Annals of the Bodleian Library, Oxford*, 2nd edn. (Oxford: Bodleian Library, 1984), p. 400. It is worth noting that Thomas Bekynton, a

later bishop of Bath and Wells, had entered Duke Humphrey's service as
chancellor in 1420. Bekynton later recognized Humphrey as a life-long bene-
factor. See Arnold Judd, *The Life of Thomas Bekynton. Secretary to Henry VI and
Bishop of Bath and Wells 1443–1465* (Chichester: Regnum Press, 1961), pp. 9–14,
84–6, 162–3.

36   "Explicit commentum super totum librum dantis . . . hoc exposicio facta fuit
      et compilata a dicto domino Johanne . . . ad instanciam . . . domini Nicolay
      Bubwych dei et appostolice sedis gracia bathonientis et wellensis Episcopi
      necnon et domini roberti eiusdem sedis appostolice gracia Saresbinensis Episcopi
      qui ambo episcopi sunt de regno anglie in quo suas sedes habent completo
      libro reddantur gracie christo amen" (London, British Library, Egerton 2629,
      fol. 387r; abbreviations expanded).

37   See G. L. Hamilton, "Notes on the Latin Translation of, and Commentary on,
      the *Divina Commedia*, by Giovanni da Serravalle," *Twentieth Annual Report of
      the Dante Society*, 1901 (Boston, 1902), pp. 30–1.

38   *Comentum*, ed. da Civezza and Domenichelli, p. xxx.

39   See A. J. Minnis, *The Medieval Theory of Authorship: Scholastic Literary Attitudes
      in the Later Middle Ages*, 2nd edn. (Aldershot: Scolar Press, 1988); Rita Copeland,
      *Rhetoric, Hermeneutics and Translation; Medieval Literary Theory and Criticism
      c. 1100–1375: The Commentary Tradition*, ed. A. J. Minnis and A. B. Scott with
      the assistance of David Wallace, rev. edn. (Oxford: Clarendon Press, 1991);
      Rita Copeland, "Medieval Literary Theory and Criticism," in *The Johns Hopkins
      Guide to Literary Theory and Criticism*, ed. Michael Groden and Martin Kreiswirth
      (Baltimore, Md.: Johns Hopkins University Press, 1994), pp. 500a–508a.

40   Hamilton, "Notes on the Latin Translation," pp. 20, 22.

41   Bertoldi's *Comentum* also needs to be considered within the complex politics
      of the Council itself: Dante has much to say about papal authority and
      imperial power. On the significance of Constance in the history of conciliarist
      and papal monarchist ideas, see Antony Black, *Monarchy and Community:
      Political Ideas in the Later Conciliar Controversy* (Cambridge: Cambridge Uni-
      versity Press, 1970), pp. 1–7; Black, "The Conciliar Movement," in *The Cam-
      bridge History of Medieval Political Thought c. 350–c. 1450*, ed. J. H. Burns
      (Cambridge: Cambridge University Press, 1988), pp. 574–87. The Baslean
      conciliarist John Torquemada developed political ideas congruent, in certain
      important respects, with those of Dante: see Black, *Monarchy and Community*,
      pp. 77, 172.

42   Try this, for example:

> O animal gratiosum et benignum,
>   Qui visitando vadis per aierem perditum
>   Nos qui tinximus mundum sanguine nostro;
> Si essemus amici regis universi,
>   Nos rogaremus eum da tua pace,
>   Postquam compateris nostro malo perverso.

43   See the gloss appended to *Inferno* 5.140 (where Paolo weeps and Dante faints), which begins: "It is worth noting that this really happened to Dante. Dante, captured by love of Beatrice (or Bice), his lover [amasie sue] . . ." (p. 84).

44   The Dante commentaries of Boccaccio, Benvenuto, and Bertoldi are all more colorful and anecdotal than the more austere tradition exemplified by Pietro Alighieri (see *Medieval Literary Theory*, ed. A. J. Minnis and A. B. Scott with Wallace [Oxford: Clarendon Press, 1991], pp. 450–8, 476–91). Bertoldi clearly follows Benvenuto da Imola's lead in his glossing of *Inferno* 5 while adding further touches of dramatic detail: compare Benvenuto da Imola, *Comentum*, ed. Lacaita, I.184–216 (esp. p. 216); Johannes de Serravalle, *Translatio et Commentum*, pp. 76–84 (esp. p. 84).

45   This rendition from the printed edition is offered as an approximate guide to the lost Wells manuscript.

46   *Selections from English Wycliffite Writings*, ed. Anne Hudson (Cambridge: Cambridge University Press, 1978), pp. 67–72 (p. 70).

47   *The Register of John Stafford, Bishop of Bath and Wells, 1425–1443. From the Original in the Registry at Wells*, ed. Thomas Scott Holmes, 2 vols. (continuous pagination), Somerset Record Society 31–2 (1915–16), p. 107.

48   *Bishop Stafford's Register*, ed. Holmes, p. 174; compare *The Lay Folks' Catechism, or the English and Latin Versions of Archbishop Thoresby's Instruction for the People*, ed. T. F. Simmons and H. E. Nolloth, Early English Text Society, os 118 (London: K. Paul, Trench, Trübner, 1901), esp. p. 7 (Peckham, lines 15–19).

49   *Bishop Stafford's Register*, ed. Holmes, p. 176; compare *Lay Folks' Catechism*, ed. Simmons and Nolloth, p. 53 (Peckham, lines 98–9).

50   For stimulating meditations upon kindred complexities, see *The Idea of the Vernacular: An Anthology of Middle English Literary Theory, 1280–1520*, ed. Jocelyn Wogan-Brown, Nicholas Watson, Andrew Taylor, and Ruth Evans (University Park: Pennsylvania State University Press, 1999), pp. 311–78.

51   *Bishop Stafford's Register*, ed. Holmes, p. 78. Emayne was said to have characterized friars as "the childre of sathan" (p. 78).

52   See H. Leith Spencer, *English Preaching in the Late Middle Ages* (Oxford: Clarendon Press, 1993), pp. 176 and 430 n. 142; Anne Hudson, *Lollards and Their Books* (London: Hambledon Press, 1985), pp. 74–84. Ullerston is better known (from his other writings) as an adversary of the Lollards and defender of orthodoxy: see Hudson, *Lollards*, p. 75; Spencer, *English Preaching*, p. 163.

53   See Margaret Aston, *Lollards and Reformers: Images and Literacy in Late Medieval England* (London: Hambledon Press, 1984), pp. 193–217.

54   See Anne Hudson, *The Premature Reformation: Wycliffite Texts and Lollard History* (Oxford: Clarendon Press, 1988), p. 101; Emden, *Biographical Register*, "Payne, Peter," III.1441a–1443a.

55   See R[eginald] L[ane] P[oole], "Hallam or Hallum, Robert," *Dictionary of National Biography*, 63 vols. (London: Smith, Elder, 1885–1911), 8.983a–985b.

56   Hudson notes that Netter "had collected, doubtless primarily from the Council of Constance, a fair knowledge of the Hussite movement and its divisions"

(*The Premature Reformation*, p. 54); see further Kantik Ghosh, *The Wycliffite Heresy; Authority and the Interpretation of Texts* (Cambridge: Cambridge University Press, 2002), p. 175.

57 On the importance of Arundel's *Constitutions*, see Spencer, *English Preaching*, p. 163; Nicholas Watson, "Censorship and Cultural Change in Late Medieval England: Vernacular Theology, the Oxford Translation Debate, and Arundel's Constitutions of 1409," *Speculum* 70 (1995), pp. 822–64; Watson, "The Middle English Mystics," in *The Cambridge History of Medieval English Literature*, ed. Wallace, pp. 539–65 (pp. 559–64).

58 See Antonia Gransden, "The History of Wells Cathedral, c. 1090–1547" in *Wells Cathedral: A History*, ed. L. S. Colchester (West Compton House, near Shepton Mallet: Open Books, 1982), pp. 24–51 (pp. 37–8); Nicholas Orme, *Education in the West of England, 1066–1548* (Exeter: University of Exeter, 1976); Orme, *English Schools in the Middle Ages* (London: Methuen, 1973), pp. 121, 122. The 1377 poll tax recorded about 100 clerics in the cathedral close at Wells, another 22 in the city, and 901 lay taxpayers (Orme, *West of England*, p. 78).

59 See Aelred Watkin, *Dean Cosyn and Wells Cathedral Miscellanea*, Somerset Record Society 56 (1941), pp. 21–4.

60 See Gransden, "Wells, c. 1090–1547," pp. 38–9, 43; Warwick Rodwell, "The Buildings of Vicars' Close," in *Wells Cathedral*, ed. Colchester, pp. 212–26.

61 It would be foolish to try and separate these clerical strata entirely; an unruly cleric might still be a brilliant Latinist. It is perhaps worth noting that Bishop Stafford, who issued edicts "contra clericos concubinarios," was himself born out of wedlock; his birth defect was annulled by papal dispensation (*Bishop Stafford's Register*, ed. Holmes, pp. xvii–iii, 108).

62 See Helen Jewell, "English Bishops as Educational Benefactors in the Later Fifteenth Century," in *The Church, Politics and Patronage in the Fifteenth Century*, ed. Barrie Dobson (Gloucester: Sutton, 1984), pp. 146–67 (p. 148). For further discussion of clerics sentenced to reeducation at Wells, see Judd, *Life of Bekynton*, pp. 129–30.

63 On the celebrated "Bekynton anthology," see Baswell, "Latinitas," p. 150.

64 See Gransden, "Wells, c. 1090–1547," pp. 41–3; Jewell, "English Bishops," p. 158.

65 At some point in 1553 Vergil paid the communar at Wells his share in an obit; he died at Urbino in 1555. See Denys Hay, *Polydore Vergil: Renaissance Historian and Man of Letters* (Oxford: Clarendon Press, 1952), pp. 20–1. John Leland, who noted "Polydorus Armes in the cloths hanging over the stallus in the Quier" at Wells (Hay, p. 8), found the signal success of this Italian in England hard to swallow. "His enemies," Anthony Wood writes of Leland in 1722, "or such that cared not for him, as Pol. Virgil . . . did use to say that he was a vainglorious Person, and that he promised more than ever he was able to perform; and others, that his Poetical Wit made him so conceited, that it was the chief reason of his Frensy" (*Athenae Oxonienses*, I, 83).

66 Vergil did ordinarily live in London, "where the Wells chapter" (Hay argues) "clearly found it convenient to have a resident representative" (*Polydore Vergil*, p. 9).

67 See Watkin, *Wells Cathedral Miscellanea*, pp. 102–3 (translating from an ordinance of 1459); Orme, *West of England*, pp. 81, 83–8. On musical education at Wells, see Frank Llewellyn Harrison, *Music in Medieval Britain* (London: Routledge and Kegan Paul, 1958), pp. 179–81.

68 Cambridge, Trinity College MS R. 14.5 (881), fol. 9–34; see Carley, "Somerset Libraries," p. 152.

69 See *Records of Early English Drama: Somerset*, ed. James Stokes, 2 vols. (Toronto: University of Toronto Press, 1996), I, 236–56 (spanning the period 1327–1538).

70 Wells Cathedral Library, X4/34. This box also contains a mass fragment from the Octave of Pentecost. Hygons spent his whole working life, some 50 years, at Wells; his five-part setting of *Salve regina* in the Eton Choirbook, written "in all probability for his own choir," testifies "to the high musical standards which prevailed at Wells Cathedral in the later fifteenth century" (Nicholas Sandon, "Hygons, Richard, c. 1435–c. 1509)," in *New Grove*, ed. Sadie, 8.835b–836a).

71 See Guido da Pisa, *I Fatti di Aenea*, ed. Franceso Fòffano, new introduction by Franca Agena, Biblioteca Carducciana 15 (Florence: Sansoni, 1957).

72 See James P. Carley, "A Fragment of *Perlesvaus* at Wells Cathedral Library," *Zeitschrift für Romanische Philologie* 108 (1992), 35–61; Carley, "The Glastonbury Legends and the English Arthurian Grail Romances," *Neuphilologische Mitteilungen* 79 (1978), 359–66; Carley, "A Grave Event: Henry V, Glastonbury Abbey, and Joseph of Arimathea's Bones," in *Culture and the King: The Social Implications of the Arthurian Legend. Essays in Honor of Valerie M. Lagorio*, ed. Martin B. Shichtman and James P. Carley (Binghamton: State University of New York Press, 1994), pp. 129–48. Carley suggests that Edward III's enthusiasm for things Arthurian may be traced back to his visit to Glastonbury in 1331 ("Grave Event," pp. 142–3n11). Leonardo Bruni's Latin translation (ca. 1436–8) of *Decameron* 4.1, the terrible Ghismonda and Tancredi story, forms part of what is now Trinity College, Cambridge, MS O.9.38 (written ca. 1450, "overwhelming" in its Glastonbury associations): see A. G. Rigg, *A Glastonbury Miscellany of the Fifteenth Century* (Oxford: Oxford University Press, 1968), pp. 9, 89–90.

73 See Watkin, *Wells Cathedral Miscellanea*, p. 157 (translated from the proceedings of the consistory court).

74 Such cases were not, of course, unique to the sixteenth century. In 1438 one "Agnes Hancok, mulier," was accused of practising what we might now term folk medicine and of talking to fairies (spirits of the air, "quos vulgus 'feyry' appellant"): *Bishop Stafford's Register*, ed. Holmes, pp. 225–7 (p. 226). Two other women – Johanna Bruther and Alicia Bell – faced similar charges at the same time (p. 227).

75 *Trattatello in laude di Dante*, ed. P. G. Ricci, in Giovanni Boccaccio, *Tutte le opere*, ed. Vittore Branca, 12 vols. (Milan: Mondadori, 1965–), vol. 3, red. I, 113.

76 As may be deduced from the Florentine edition of 1573, "emendato secondo l'ordine del sacro Concilio di Trento" (cited in Achille Tartaro, "Boccaccismo e AntiBoccaccismo," in *Boccaccio: Storia della Critica*, 6 [Palermo, 1981], pp. 37–61 (p. 47)).

77 John Leyland and John Bale, *The Laboryouse Journey and Serche of Johan Leylande for Englandes Antiquitees, geuen of hym as a Newe Yeares Gyfte to Kynge Henry the VIII in the XXXVII yeare of his Reyne, with declaracyons enlarged by Johan Bale* (London: S. Mierdman for John Bale, 1549), signature Ci. This volume is available in facsimile form (from Oxford, Bodleian Library, shelfmark Wood 134) as John Leyland, *The Laboryouse Serche for Englandes Antiquitees* (Amsterdam: Theatrum Orbis Terrarum, 1975).

78 It is instructive to note that in his injunctions against Lollards of August 1431, Stafford characterizes those who would seek to English the Bible as false prophets and as "supersticiosi" in league with the devil (*Bishop Stafford's Register*, ed. Holmes, p. 104). Stafford directs his ire not just against Lollard texts, but (potentially) against anything in English: "Mandatum contra sortilogos, falsos juratores sive perjuros, vel libros lollardie vel alios in lingua vulgari conscriptos" (p. 103).

79 See *Dante Heritage*, ed. Caesar, pp. 404, 398.

80 See Linda Colley, *Britons: Forging the Nation 1707–1837* (New Haven: Yale University Press, 1992). It is worth noting that Anthony Wood begins his account of Leland (1721) by hailing him as "that singular light and ornament of Great Britain" (*Athenae Oxonienses*), I.82. The 1707 Act of Union did not, of course, *create* anti-Catholic discourse by Act of Parliament. Such discourse has a long and complex history: important dates in this process would include November 5, 1688 (the "Gunpowder Plot"), 1715 and 1745 (the "Jacobite rebellions"), 1780 (the Gordon Riots). See Colin Haydon, *Anti-Catholicism in Eighteenth-Century England* (Manchester: Manchester University Press, 1993); John Stevenson, *Popular Disturbances in England 1700–1832*, 2nd edn. (London: Longman, 1992); Daniel Szechi, *The Jacobites: Britain and Europe 1688–1788* (Manchester: Manchester University Press, 1994). Xenophobic aspects of English anti-Catholicism usefully diverted attention from the fact that, after 1714, the United Kingdom was governed by a new German-speaking dynasty.

81 *Dante in English Literature: From Chaucer to Cary (c. 1380–1844)*, ed. Paget Toynbee, 2 vols. (London: Methuen, 1909), I, 340.

82 Early Methodists, sometimes fiercely anti-Catholic, were themselves often characterized as crypto-papists: see Haydon, *Anti-Catholicism*, pp. 10, 63–6.

83 See *Dante Heritage*, ed. Caesar, pp. 273, 278.

84 John Foxe, *Actes and Monuments* (London: John Daye, 1570), p. 485b. This passage on Dante is indicated in the right-hand margin thus: "Dantes an Italian writer against the pope."

85 Three passages were to be expurgated: *Inferno* 19.48–117 (Dante's interview
with Nicholas III, discussed above); *Purgatorio* 29.106–18 (Pope Adrian V,
punished for avarice); *Paradiso* 9.136–42. See Luciana Martinelli, *Dante: Storia
della critica*, 4 (Palermo, 1966), p. 75. The *Monarchia* was placed on the *Index
Librorum Prohibitorum* at the close of the Council of Trent in 1564; it had been
publicly burned by the papal legate in Lombardy during the papacy of John
XXII. See *Dante in English Literature*, ed. Toynbee, I.56–7.

86 See Martinelli, *Dante*, p. 88.

87 As cited from Bulgarini's *Antidiscorso* in Martinelli, *Dante*, p. 89. See further the
entry "Bulgarini, Bellisario" (by F. Agostini), *Dizionario biografico degli italiani*,
15.40a–43a; this contains a good account of Italian anti-Dantean polemics in
the sixteenth and seventeenth centuries.

88 Text given as conveniently available in *Geoffrey Chaucer: The Critical Heritage*,
ed. Derek Brewer, 2 vols. (London: Routledge, 1995), I.107–9 (p. 107).

89 See *The Riverside Chaucer*, ed. Larry D. Benson (Boston: Houghton Mifflin,
1987), 1.501–12. Compare the Lollard sermon on Matthew 23 – "Crist biddith
us be war with thes false profetis that comen in clothing of scheepe and ben
wolues of raueyne" – as edited by Anne Hudson from British Library, MS
Royal 18. B. ix (G), folios 191v–194v in *Wycliffite Writings*, pp. 75–83 (p. 75).

90 Further animadversions against "the develes wolves that stranglen the sheep
of Jhesu Crist" begin at 10.768.

91 For an informative account of these authors, following a transcription of the
46 items at Wells as listed by Leland in his autograph notebook, see Carley,
"Somerset Libraries," pp. 147–52.

92 See Carley, "Somerset Libraries," p. 152; Law and Carley, "Grammar and
Arithmetic," pp. 146–7.

93 See Law and Carley, "Grammar and Arithmetic," p. 147; Robert Birley, "The
Cathedral Library," in *Wells Cathedral*, ed. Colchester, pp. 204–11 (p. 206).

94 John R. Guy, "From the Reformation until 1800," in *Wells Cathedral*, ed.
Colchester, pp. 148–78 (p. 159).

95 See Guy, "From the Reformation," pp. 158–60.

96 John Taylor (The Water Poet), *Wandering to see the Wonders of the West* (1649),
Mr Ashbee's Occasional Facsimile Reprints 8 (London: E. W. Ashbee, 1869),
p. 4. Wells was reportedly further damaged in the course of the Monmouth
rebellion of 1685: see William Dugdale, *Monasticon Anglicanum*, 6 vols. (London: Longmans Green, 1817–30), II.284.

97 See Brian Cummings, "Reformed Literature and Literature Reformed," in *The
Cambridge History of Medieval English Literature*, ed. Wallace, pp. 827–33.

98 *Wonders of the West*, title page.

99 "The Bil of John Taylor, or a Taylors Bill, without wither Imprimis or Items,"
a poem in couplets (with one irregular short line) advertising the contents
of the *Wonders* to come; printed on the reverse of the title page, Ashbee
Facsimile Reprint.

100 "Bil," concluding couplet, lines 42–3 (*sic*). John Taylor (1580–1653) was apprenticed to a London waterman before being press-ganged into the navy; by 1603 he had made 16 voyages in the queen's ships. "Although Taylor complacently styled himself the 'king's water poet' and the 'queen's waterman,'" Gordon Goodwin notes acerbically, "he can at best be only regarded as a literary bargee" (*Dictionary of National Biography* [London: Smith, Elder, 1885–1911], 55.431a–438a); his output was vast.

101 *TO HIS SACRED MAJESTIE: Loyall Reflections, Upon His Glorious Restauration, Procession and Coronation; Not forgetting the ROYAL OAKE* (London?: 1660?), a pamphlet of 4 leaves (8 pages), Cambridge University Library, Sel. 3.162 (9), line 47.

102 *The Royal Oake, or An Historicall Description of the Royal Progresse, wonderful Travels Miraculous Escapes, and Strange Accidents of his Sacred Majesty Charles the II* (London: Printed by J. C. for J. J., 1660), p. 2. This is the fourth edition of this six-page pamphlet.

103 See Charles Mosley, *The Oak: Its Natural History, Antiquity, and Folklore* (London: Elliot Stock, 1910), pp. 48–52. This handsome, small green book actually has an oblong sliver of oak glued to its front cover. It tells how on Royal Oak Day, May 29, ploughing horses and railway trains (in the late nineteenth century) were decked with sprays of oak leaves (pp. 49–50).

104 "It is in the forests," remarked Richard fitz Nigel, treasurer of the Exchequer under Henry II, "that the King's chambers [*penetralia regnum*] are, and their chief delights" (*Dialogus de Scaccario*, as cited by William Perry Marvin in the course of his brilliant, pioneering essay "Slaughter and Romance: Hunting Reserves in Late Medieval England," in *Medieval Crime and Social Control*, ed. Barbara A. Hanawalt and David Wallace (Minneapolis: University of Minnesota Press, 1999), pp. 224–52 (p. 243).

105 See A. J. Holland, *Ships of British Oak: The Rise and Decline of Wooden Shipbuilding in Hampshire* (Newton Abbot: David and Charles, 1971), pp. 65–98. In April 1678 Henry Teonge kissed the hand of Charles II at Whitehall; in January 1679 he sailed with the *Royal Oak* as chaplain from Minorca to England (burying some 60 sailors *en route*): see Henry Teonge, *Diary, 1675–1679*, ed. G. E. Manwaring (London: Routledge, 1927), pp. 202–3, 234–58. On May 29 the *Royal Oak* and accompanying ships, plus guns at Sandown, Walmer, and Deal castles "fired all together, so that for an hour's space it seemed like a sea-fight" (p. 255). Battle honors for ships named *Royal Oak* extend from Lowestoft (1665) to Jutland (1916). On October 14, 1939, *HMS Royal Oak* was sunk in Scapa Bay with the loss of 833 men and boy seamen: see Gerald Snyder, *The Royal Oak Disaster* (London: William Kimber, 1976). See further "Tot time in HMS Royal Oak," which pictures sailors from the doomed ship drawing their daily rum ration from an oaken barrel bearing the inscription "God Save the King" (*Royal Oak*, plate after p. 64).

106 See *Hearts of Oak: A Collection of Royal Naval Anecdotes*, ed. P. McLaren, foreword by Admiral Sandy Woodward (Brighton: Fernhurst Books, 1994);

Sir Henry Rowley Bishop, *Englishmen in India. Oh, firm as oak. Vocal score* (London: Goulding and D'Almaine, ca. 1823). Cambridge University Library, MR290.a.80.117, p. 2.

107   See chapter 2 above, p. 118.

108   Leyland and Bale, *Laboryouse Journey*, Div. For an excellent account of this complex text, see Simpson, "Ageism." For a sympathetic and influential account of Leland's spending "more than six Years in rambling to and fro in this Nation, and in making researches into the bowels of antiquity," see Wood, *Athenae Oxonienses*, I.82–5 (p. 83).

109   The collapse of Leland's grandiose schemes for producing a vast body of writing that would image forth Henry's kingdom, a collapse that may have imperilled his mental health, seems connected with one particular delusion that is worth pondering further: that the act of seeing, or of having seen, somehow guarantees the viability of a written account that will fully recall and preserve such a sight (or site). In such a fantasy, the labor of generating or writing such an account is forgotten or concealed from the would-be author, who characteristically or symptomatically represents himself (Dvi) as a purveyor of pictures.

110   James P. Carley, "Leland's *Cygnea cantio*: a Neglected Tudor River Poem," *Humanistica Lovaniensia* 32 (1983), 225–41 (p. 233). See also Wood, *Athenae Oxonienses*: "At the time of the dissolution of Monasteries, he [Leland] saw with very great pity what havock was made of ancient Monuments of learning, and if no remedy should be taken, they would all perish" (I.83).

111   Psychosis implies, above all, an unwillingness to form linkages; the linkage refused here is that between a new socio-religious order and those furious acts of textual and institutional destruction that bring it to be. See Simpson, *Reform and Cultural Revolution*, p. 17; Teresa Brennan, *History after Lacan* (London: Routledge, 1993), esp. p. 36.

112   *Calendar of the Patent Rolls preserved in the Public Record Office* (London: H.M. Stationery Office, 1901–), Edward VI, IV.1553, 181.

113   See Seamus Heaney, "Envies and Identifications: Dante and the Modern Poet," *Irish University Review* 15 (1985), pp. 5–19; David Wallace, "Dante in English," in *The Cambridge Companion to Dante*, ed. Jacoff, pp. 237–58 (pp. 251–4).

114   *Poets' Corner* (London: Heinemann, 1904).

115   P.R.O, W.O. 34/104/110, as cited in Haydon, *Anti-Catholicism*, p. 222 n. 85; Stevenson, *Popular Disturbances*, p. 102.

116   See Wallace, "Dante in English," pp. 241–4.

117   See Richard Holmes, *Coleridge: Early Visions* (London: Hodder and Stoughton, 1989), pp. 101–4; Rosemary Ashton, *The Life of Samuel Taylor Coleridge* (Oxford: Blackwell, 1996), pp. 74–81; Madge Dresser, *Slavery Obscured: The Social History of the Slave Trade in an English Provincial Port* (London: Continuum, 2001), pp. 101–16 (the phrase "green mansion" is from Dresser, p. 111).

118   See *Lectures 1795: On Politics and Religion*, ed. Lewis Patton and Peter Mann, Bollingen Series 75 (1971), pp. 231–51. Coleridge is heavily indebted to works

checked out from Bristol's Public Library the day before the lecture; it owes much to Thomas Clarkson's *An Essay on the Impolicy of the African Slave Trade* (1788). Coleridge's address, delivered on June 16, 1795, at the Assembly Coffeehouse on the Quay, Bristol, offers a lurid evocation of the middle passage and ends audaciously by equating the conditions of English peasants and African slaves. For the Greek text of the ode, winner of the Browne Gold Medal for 1792, see *The Poetical Works of Samuel Taylor Coleridge*, ed. James Dykes Campbell (London: Macmillan, 1893), "Appendix B" (pp. 476–7). For a translation, see Samuel Taylor Coleridge, *The Complete Poems*, ed. William Keach (London: Penguin, 1997), "Appendix 1" (pp. 419–21). Coleridge reviewed his credentials as an abolitionist in a letter to Clarkson dated March 3, 1808; he did not, however, devote any poem to the subject (with the exception of the Greek ode: see *Lectures 1795*, p. 232).

119 In 1823, some stanzas Englished from Coleridge's Greek ode against the slave trade appeared in the *London Magazine*; they were translated by Sir Charles Abraham Elton, son of the Reverend Sir Abraham Elton (and scion of a family that had prospered through slaving). He was later lieutenant-colonel of the Somerset militia. See Coleridge, *Poetical Works*, ed. J. D. Campbell, p. 654. Arthur Henry Hallam, the beloved "A.H." of Tennyson's *In Memoriam*, was a grandson of the same Sir Abraham Elton. Hallam, who revered Coleridge, was buried in the chancel of Clevedon church in 1833.

120 Butler, a distinguished classicist, was later bishop of Lichfield. The abolitionist Thomas Clarkson, from whom Coleridge freely borrowed in fashioning his 1795 lecture, had also been a prizewinner at Cambridge, in his case for a Latin essay against the trade: see *Lectures 1795*, ed. Patton and Mann, p. 232.

121 *Collected Letters of Samuel Taylor Coleridge*, ed. Earl Leslie Griggs, 6 vols. (Oxford: Clarendon Press, 1956–71), I, 16–17.

122 On the concept of the spirits of African slaves returning to their homelands at death, see the discussion of *Oroonoko* in chapter 6 below (p. 264).

123 In the 1795 lecture, delivered at Bristol's Assembly Coffeehouse on the Quay, Coleridge remembers the origins of everyday commodities in denouncing "the evils arising from the formation of imaginary wants." "We receive from the West Indias," he argues, "Sugars, Rum, Cotton, log-wood, cocoa, coffee, pimento, ginger, indigo, mahogany, and conserves—not one of these are necessary" (*Lectures 1795*, ed. Patton and Mann, p. 236).

124 See further chapter 4 below, pp. 190–4.

125 "Advertisement" to *Lyrical Ballads*, ed. Brett and Jones, p. 7.

126 "The medium of my work is walking (the element of time) and natural materials" (Richard Long, *Mirage* [London: Phaidon, 1998], unpaginated).

127 Fragments from a center bifolium of *Le Haut Livre du Graal, Perlesvaus*, copied by a fourteenth-century Anglo-Norman scribe, survive as pastedowns in the register of William Cosyn, dean of Wells from 1499 to 1525. See Carley, "Fragment of *Perlesvaus*"; Watkin, *Wells Miscellanea*, pp. ix–xxxv.

128   Scipio Africanus, servant to the Earl of Suffolk, died aged 18 in 1720; his
      tombstone at Henbury churchyard, Bristol, reads: "I who was born a PAGAN
      and a SLAVE / Now sweetly sleep a CHRISTIAN in my GRAVE / WHAT
      tho' my hue was dark, my SAVIOUR'S sight / Shall change this darkness into
      radiant Light" (as quoted in Dresser, *Slavery Obscured*, p. 80). For other African
      residents of Bristol ca. 1700–50, see Dresser, pp. 72–81 and table 5. Hortense
      Cumberbatch, the long-lost and forgotten black daughter of Mike Leigh's film,
      Secrets and Lies, shares a name with a family of long-standing Bristol connec-
      tions; portraits of Cumberbatches hang in the plantation house of St. Nicholas
      in Barbados (one of only three Jacobean buildings still standing in the New
      World).

CHAPTER FOUR

GENOA

> Having put foot ashoare in *Genoa*, I will not wish him to stay
> long there, in regard the very worst *Italian* dialect is spoken
> there, and besides, as it is proverbially said, there are in *Genoa*,
> *Mountaines without wood, Sea without fish, Women without Shame,*
> *and Men without conscience,* which makes them to be termed
> the *white Moores:* And when a *Jew* (and the *Jews* are held
> the most Mercuriall people in the World, by reason of their
> so often transmigrations, persecutions, and *Necessity*, which is
> the *Mother* of *Wit*) [I say when a Jew] meeteth with a *Genoway*,
> and is to negotiat with him, he puts his fingers in his eyes,
> fearing to be over-reached by him, and outmatched in
> cunning.
>
> **James Howell, Instructions for Forreine Travell.**

> Dic, dic Janua, quid fecisti.
> **Gabriele de' Mussis, Historia de Morbo.**

On the quayside at Bristol, not far from where Coleridge lectured against
the slave trade in 1795, the *Matthew* lies moored. This is a working replica of
the ship that carried John Cabot across the Atlantic in 1497, enabling him to
become (as the 1997 BBC tie-in book tells us) "the first European of his age
to land on the continent of North America and claim it for the English
monarch, Henry VII."[1] This was a momentous achievement, for while
"Columbus and his crew were still exploring the Caribbean islands and
no Spaniard landed on the North American continent proper until 1513,"

John Cabot of Bristol was securely setting foot on northern Newfoundland (or possibly southern Labrador, Nova Scotia, or even Maine) on June 24, 1497.[2] "The significance of the voyage of the *Matthew*," HRH Prince Philip argues, "is that it took John Cabot to the mainland of North America and which eventually led [*sic*] to the migration of many English-speaking people to the countries of that continent."[3] John Cabot himself, however, was no more English than Columbus was Spanish; both were in fact "Genovesi." Sebastiano Caboto, son of the illustrious Giovanni or Zuan, proved himself ignorant of this grand English-speaking destiny by spending the better part of his mature life (from 1512 to 1548) in the service of Spain.[4]

Premodern Flanders, chapter 2 has argued, was a place both admired and reviled, imitated and repudiated: a place built upon unfruitful soil that nonetheless generates a vibrant and distinctively urban culture. At heart, it seems, there is something empty or denatured "in Flaundres" – as imaginatively embodied and eloquently voiced by Chaucer's Pardoner – that is nonetheless fabulously alluring; something that holds us spellbound, that we could hardly do without. Premodern Genoa, this chapter will argue, arouses feelings of equivalent contradictory intensity, for it too connotes persons and practices at once valued and disparaged, at once audaciously expansive, yet indicative of something alien within. Our first epigraph, from a work of 1642 dedicated to Prince Charles (Howell became Historiographer Royal in 1661),[5] recycles centuries of popular feeling about Genoa: that its language (by implicit comparison with the gold standard of Florence) is crude; that it is of scant natural resources (no wood or fish); that is hardly a place at all (as mountains crowd it down to the sea); that its men and women are, in differing ways, immoral; that its people are white Moors (more of that anon) and gentile Jews, or rather that they outreach and outface Jews in their signature activities of diasporic travel and hard bargaining.[6] *Genovesi* reach and measure the limits of the navigable world, from Tartary in the far northeast to the Fortunate Islands, or the Canaries, in (just beyond) the west. Ultimately, the most famous Genoan of all moves directly from these westernmost isles to isles yet further west, adjoining a new-found continent. And yet in extending everywhere, in the service of anyone and everyone, Genoa itself seems nowhere, all at sea. The most eloquent way of voicing this morass of contradictory emotions, indicating our continuing complicity in and resistance to the project of Genoa, would seem to be the mighty bellow of Dante's *Inferno* 33: "Ahi Genovesi."

Late in 1372, Geoffrey Chaucer left London and traveled to Florence, where (so literary history tells us) he decisively encountered the writings of Dante, Boccaccio, and Petrarch that were to revolutionize his poetry. But before he got to Florence, in 1373, Chaucer did the king's business in Genoa (seeking support for the interminable war with France).[7] While negotiating with the Genoese – with whom he had daily dealings in London as controller of customs – Chaucer crossed the lines of a slave trade. Visitors to Genoa, as Iris Origo so memorably puts it, encountered "whole shiploads of bewildered, half-naked men, women and children, unable even to understand what was said to them . . . unloaded upon the quays and then – after being prodded and paraded like cattle at a fair . . . sold by auction to the *sensali* (brokers) who forwarded them to their clients inland, according to their requirements."[8] Chief of these inland destinations was Florence.

The question of what Chaucer and slaves thought or did in coming face to face is unknowable and perhaps unthinkable; meditation upon such a space of encounter took up much of the life of Emmanuel Levinas.[9] But we can ask why, as with "Dante in Somerset," certain locational propositions – such as "Chaucer among slaves" – resonate so strangely, generating eloquent resistances of laughter or blankness. In coming to Italy and encountering the great Trecento writers, the story runs, Chaucer finds new forms of expressive freedom associated with the vocation of *poeta* (a title of defining importance for Dante, Boccaccio, and Petrarch).[10] But the reviving classicism which helps articulate such new poetic identity coincides with, meshes with, and, I shall argue, decisively sustains the westward movement of slaving across the Mediterranean.

The Genoese, we have noted, form a network throughout northern Europe: they are settled at London and have designs on Southampton; they are prominent at Bruges. All manner of cargoes are carried in Genoese ships, or in ships manned by the Genoese: wool, finished fabrics, spices, troops (*en route* to the Anglo-French wars), crossbowmen (a Genoese specialty), and slaves. The fusion of Mediterranean and North Sea/Baltic sailing technologies will eventually extend Atlantic colonization and enslavement practices from the Canaries to the Americas. In this movement – such is the theme of these last three chapters – things played out in European places (as in chapters 1–3) get carried over. And conversely, news or *novelle* from newly discovered islands get carried back and disseminated in Latin and vernacular forms that meet long-established European expectations. All this leads me to doubt Todorov's assertion that "the discovery of America, or of the Americans, is certainly the most astonishing encounter of our history."[11] For so many aspects of this encounter – including the astonishment – had long been rehearsed before Columbus set sail.

Todorov's highly influential *The Conquest of America* has a dozen subdivided index entries under "genocide" and none under "Genoa." Perhaps this is fitting, for in this long process of westward migration, it will be the place of Genoa to be essentialized and scattered, employed and disowned, hidden (as Giovanni becomes John, Cristofero Christopher, and Colombo Columbus and Colon) and decried. But even as the legacy of humanism cannot fully be disowned – since, as well as abetting slavery, it shapes the philology needful for books such as this – so Genoa cannot be forgotten, for it brings slowly into being the transatlantic world, the black and white Atlantics, where many of us still live.

Merchants of Death

Dante, in the downward progress of his *Inferno*, has unflattering things to say about many Italian cities,[12] but his address to the Genoese is reserved (we have noted) for the lowest point of all. "Ahi Genovesi," he says,

> . . . uomini diversi
> d'ogne costume e pien d'ogne magagna,
> perché non siete voi del mondo spersi?
> *(33.151–3)*

> Ah, men of Genoa, foreign to every decency,
> full of every vice, why have you not been
> scattered from the face of the world?

The condition of being "del mondo spersi" that Dante wishes on Genoa is precisely chosen (from the verb *sperdere*: to disperse, scatter, or drive away): for the Genoans were indeed prone to scatter themselves throughout the known world, and beyond. "Genoans are dispersed through the world," an anonymous medieval Genoese poet writes, "and wherever they go and dwell a new Genoa takes shape."[13] The Genoese were imagined to be, literally and figuratively, all at sea, for the chief business of their tottering republic *was* the sea. "Our ancestors," says an anonymous Genoese debater in 1613, "understood that the narrowness and sterility of our homeland" would not allow the city to thrive; they thus elected "to cultivate the ample fields of the sea" ("in coltivare l'ampie campagne del mare").[14] Here again, in its willingness to improve upon meager gifts of nature, Genoa reminds us of Flanders. Such presumption in cutting the furrows of the sea proves just as perilous, in Dante's cosmos, as building the infernal walls of Sodom.[15]

Rather than relying on any large-scale manufacturing operations (such as weaponry at Milan, cloth at Florence), the Genoese trafficked the wares (and sometimes the crusaders or soldiery) of other nations from place to place. They thus developed instincts for seeking out and connecting pockets of scarcity and surplus; for discovering new territories and new commodities; for pushing out the limits of the known or navigable world. It was this restless, inquistive/acquisitive spirit that induced the Genoan Vivaldi brothers in 1291 to sail westward beyond the Mediterranean into uncharted Atlantic waters: a famous episode of unfinished voyaging tracked in *Inferno 26*, where Dante's Ulysses urges *his* brothers ("frati") to sail into the sunset. Dante clearly finds the presumption of such voyaging disastrous. It is worth noting, however, that the unknown Genoese poet cited above sounds positively Ulyssean in his navigational imagining: "all men are sailors," he says; "ogn omo tegno marinar / chi non cessa di navigar."[16]

There is no doubt that Genoese navigational and trading networks helped the Black Death of 1347–9 to spread with unprecedented efficiency, and that European chroniclers were well aware of this fact. Commentators generally agreed that the plague had spread westward from Cathay and Tartary.[17] Gabriele de' Mussis, who provides our second epigraph – "speak, speak Genoa of what you have done" – tells how the Genoese slaving stronghold of Caffa in the Crimea was besieged by Tartars who, dying in their thousands, resorted to biological or bacteriological warfare:

Quod Tartari, ex tanta clade et morbo pestifero fatigati, sic defficientes attoniti et undique stupefacti, sine spe salutis mori conspicientes, cadavera, machinis eorum superposita, Intra Caffensem urbem precipitari Jubebant, ut ipsorum fectore intollerabili omnino defficerent. Sic sic proiecta videbantur Cacumina mortuorum, nec christiani latere, nec fugere, nec a tali precipicio liberari valebant, licet deffunctos, quos poterant, marinis traderent fluctibus inmergendos.[18]

The dying Tartars, stunned and stupefied by the immensity of the disaster brought about by the disease, and realizing that they had no hope of escape, lost interest in the siege. But they ordered corpses to be placed in catapults and lobbed [them] into the city in the hope that the intolerable stench would kill everyone inside. What seemed like mountains of dead were thrown into the city, and the Christians could not hide or flee or escape from them, although they dumped as many of the bodies as they could in the sea.

De' Mussis goes on to describe refugees from Caffa wandering from port to port, spreading pestilence "as if they had brought evil spirits with them" (p. 19; "ac si maligni spiritus comitatantes," p. 158). Bristol, according to the Yorkshire *Anonimalle Chronicle*, is the first port of entry for the disease in

England (as carried "par marchaundz et maryners"); according to Augus-tinian canon Henry Knighton, the plague travels by sea first to Southampton and then Bristol, "where almost the whole population of the town per-ished."[19] Calais, another frequent port of call for Genoese sailors, is hit early and helps spread the disease by sending the dead body of its captain to London for burial.[20] Diseased Genoese merchants carry the plague to Lom-bardy; a sick Genoan taken in by a friend at Piacenza kills the whole fam-ily.[21] The Genoese themselves drive three of their infected galleys from Genoa by bombarding them with flaming arrows and other instruments of war. Driven from port to port, one galley puts in at Marseilles (which, duly infected, spreads the plague to Avignon – seat of the papacy – where mortal-ity is especially severe).[22] The Genoese galleys – according to this anonym-ous Flemish chronicler – conceive a plan to head for the Atlantic ("ad Oceanum") in order to offload their merchandise. By thus "wandering about the sea" ("per mare errantibus") they infect all parts of their long route: first Greece, then Sicily, Italy, Marseilles (and hence Avignon and the whole of Languedoc).[23]

It was, of course, the Jews who were accused of coordinating an inter-national conspiracy of well-poisoning and breeding poisonous toads; con-fessions extracted under torture at Savoy – testifying to a complex Jewish network of letter-writing and poison preparation – were widely circulated.[24] In his mandate of September 26, 1348, attached to the reissued bull *Sicut Judeis*, Clement VI denounces persecution of Jews, averring that Christians are plagued by God for the sins of Christians.[25] Sins of the Genoese soon came to mind: their willingness, for example, to man or hire out ships for any cause (including that of Turks and Saracens warring against Christians).[26] At Messina, Sicily, in 1347, according to the Franciscan Michele da Piazza, Genoese arriving in galleys are said to be fleeing divine vengeance, carrying punishment for their sins ("pro eorum iniquitatibus") in their bodies. To speak with one of the Genoans was to die; the Messinese (but too late to avoid infection) drive them back onto the waters whence they came.[27] If wandering Jews seem to bear the mark of divine disfavor, it is wandering Genoans (all Europe seems to notice) who bring on disaster. But of course, all Europe depends on the movement of Genoese ships.

Nobody in medieval Europe ever thinks that a plague spread from a Genoese slaving colony might signify divine disapproval of slavery. The spreading of disease will, of course, prove to be the most ruinous Genoese legacy of all to natives of the New World.

Boccaccio's *Decameron*, which opens with the Black Death that has spread from the east, characterizes Genoans as men naturally and voraciously driven by attachment to money ("uomini naturalmente vaghi di pecunia e rapaci," 2.4.14); in *Decameron* 1.8 it takes a Florentine to teach a Genoese nobleman the basics of "cortesia."[28] "Genoa scarcely comes within the range of our task," Jacob Burckhardt argues in his landmark *Civilization of the Renaissance in Italy*, "as before the time of Andrea Doria [the early sixteenth century] it took almost no part in the Renaissance."[29] Burckhardt here rehearses the familiar psychotic split intrinsic to "Renaissance" paradigm-making, which would divide the cultural from the political and economic. The study of Genoa continually confronts us with historical practices (enslavement, forced conversion, colonization) upon which cultural history has chosen not to dwell. If Florence – with its glorious efflorescences of painting, building, humanism, and literature – represents the superego of an emergent Renaissance, Genoa – always present, if out of sight – forms the id.

Passage through Genoa, in the *Decameron*, often opens out into storytelling scenarios of vast geographical compass; 4.3 begins at Marseilles (a rival seafaring and slaving city) and passes through Genoa *en route* to Crete and Rhodes (two islands pioneering plantation-style, slave-based colonization in the fourteenth century).[30] *Decameron* 2.9 begins with a Genoese merchant boasting of his wife's virtue in a Parisian inn and ends in Alexandria (which was, in fact, Genoa's chief trading partner).[31] The second Day of the *Decameron* features two *novelle* in which Genoans are encountered on the high seas as agents of piracy and enslavement. The first of them, 2.4, tells how a young Amalfitan pirate is himself pirated by "due gran cocche di genovesi" (14), two great Genoese carracks (ships of the kind that were too large to sail up the Thames, hence docked at Bristol and, later, Southampton).[32] And *Decameron* 2.6 features equivalent acts of piracy, this time (most notably) the snatching of children and their nurse from a Mediterranean island; they are taken to Genoa and bought as household slaves by the famous Genoese house (the only one deemed worthy of mention by Burckhardt) of Doria.[33] Dante, in *Purgatorio* 20, recalls the ways that pirates haggle over the price of slave girls.[34] In *Decameron* 2.6, madonna Beritola, Boccaccio's distraught heroine, goes half-wild alone on her island, breast-feeding two young roebucks (in lieu of her enslaved children) as her skin color changes from white to dark ("bruna," 20).

In August of 1373, following his return from Genoa, Chaucer was commissioned to deliver *La Seinte Marie et Seint George*, a Genoese tarit (or tarette: a large cargo ship) under arrest at Dartmouth, to the Genoese merchant "Johannes de Nigris"; this "John" was very likely the same man who, ten years earlier, had transported goods between London and Genoa for John de Mari (Chaucer's traveling companion on the Genoa mission) in a ship

called *La Seinte Marie*.[35] During the next few years, as London controller of
customs, Chaucer heard much talk of Genoese plans to make Southampton
(in Steven Epstein's phrase) "a Caffa or Pera of the north."[36] In 1379, a
Genoese ambassador arrived at London, charged to bring this about. This
man, Janus Imperiale, was the master of a Genoese tarit called, *encore une
fois, La Seinte Marie*. This Genoese John had secured a royal-sponsored agreement allowing him to trade directly with London, bypassing the staple at
Calais established three years earlier (and thus swelling royal coffers). This
agreement, plus the ambitious plans to turn Southampton into the leading
port of Europe, posed a direct threat to the leading merchant capitalists of
the newly-formed London–Calais axis. On August 26, 1379, Imperiale was
stabbed to death outside his London residence. This murder, as Paul Strohm
memorably tells it, was achieved and covered over through an extraordinary alliance of English apprentices, merchant capitalists, royal appointees
(like Chaucer) and magnates: a group determined to beat the Genoese at
their own game by treating the streets of London as the high seas by other
means.[37] Once again, the indispensable Genoese, like the Jews who are their
imaginative shadow, are subjected to violent and lawless treatment that
supposedly imitates their own *modus agendi*: "Yvele shal have that yvele wol
deserve."[38]

Tartar Girls and Mediterranean Slaving

The long history of medieval Genoese slaving moves from west to east
to west again between ca. 1150 and 1500. Saracens from Spain make up
the majority of slaves at Genoa until the Genoese negotiate their way
into the Black Sea and the Crimea in the later thirteenth century. By the
later fourteenth century there are Greek, Russian, Slav, Turkish, Bosnian,
and Circassian slaves at Genoa and Florence, but the great majority are
described as "Tartars." With the fall of Constantinople in 1453 and then of
Caffa in 1475, the focus of trade swings back to the west (which includes
the North African coastline).[39] After about 1500 the cost of obtaining a
slave becomes prohibitive to all but the richest and most powerful, popes
and dukes, cardinals and *grandes dames*.[40] Portraiture from this later period
is misleading, in that slave children are often deployed almost as exotic pets
or (in more modern American currency) Websters in the houses of the
great.[41] In the earlier period, however, slaves were a serious commodity
to which value – in successive stages – might be added. Plucked or sold
from her family in the Crimea, a young girl might spend a period at Caffa

(absorbing Christian values) before being shipped to Genoa. There she might be bought by a prosperous artisan, who would teach her a craft like silk-working, before selling her on for further transportation, say, to Aragon.

The overwhelming majority of these slaves were young teenage (and often not quite teenage) girls. In a list of slaves sold in Florence between July 4, 1366, and March 2, 1397, for example, 329 of the slaves are women or little girls; only four of the 28 males are over 16.[42] Some 98 percent of Florentine domestic slaves in this period, it has been argued, were female.[43] There have been various explanations for this: for example, that an impoverished Tartar father might be more willing to sell his daughters than his sons.[44] But it is worth noting that prices paid for pubescent girls generally exceed those paid for boys, men, or women. It is worth noting, further, that the famous foundling hospitals of Tuscany begin to flourish at this time.[45] One deed of sale commends the exceptional ugliness of a 12-year-old female slave (she is said to have the face of a *tavolaccio*, or badly made table) on the grounds that the master's wife "no[n] ne pigliera gielosia." The presence of such young women inevitably undermined the authority of wives, who were no doubt referred to another familiar Pauline injunction, that wives should obey their husbands as slaves their masters.[46]

Many features of later European colonialism – as the slaving Mediterranean prepares to enter the black Atlantic – are clearly forming throughout this earlier period. To say this is not to suggest seamless continuity with later, full-blown plantation slaving in the Americas; differentiation of human experience will stem, above all, from questions of scale.[47] Nonetheless, certain discursive and material practices of slaving, familiar from more recent times (familiar from the present), are becoming well-established, such as, for example, racial profiling. Deeds of sale do not yet feature skin color as an absolute criterion of worth or enslavement, but figure it rather as one aesthetic criterion among many.[48] Toward the end of the period, however, "Ethiopian" begins to stand in for Africans of any provenance and "black" begins to be deployed as a racial term.[49] The marking, scarring, and tattooing of enslaved bodies is commonplace; there are complex arrangements for the recovery of runaways. There are widespread practices of *locazione* or loaning out of female slaves, often for periods of breast-feeding. There are fears in the white population of being poisoned by slaves, or of being overwhelmed by sheer numbers. There are the little-known terrors of the middle passage (insurance claims make it clear that slaves threw themselves overboard).[50] There are traces, also, of the secret language of slaves, preserved in literary fragments[51] and (a subject needing more investigation) in the palpably eastern-inflected style of certain western paintings (slaves sometimes served artisan-painter masters).[52]

In 1396, a ship traveling between "Roumania" and Genoa contained 191 pieces of lead, 80 slaves, and 17 bales of pilgrims' robes.[53] It was an embarrassment for Christians to enslave Christians, or those who had converted, but compromises were found; for example, it was ruled that a person's fitness for enslavement might be determined not by her or his current religion, but rather by culture of origin. So it is that slaves often arrived with their names intact (at least as transcribed by semi-literate Tuscan traders) and were given Christian names only once they were sold and baptized: thus Cotlu, Jamanzach, Tholon, Charactas, and Sarumbieh become Maria, Caterina, and Marta. Such evolving refinements, I shall argue, were paralleled or sustained by discourses of an emergent humanism, particularly through its recuperation of classical texts and classical values. The whole mélange is neatly summarized by a transaction that took place in Genoa, in which a slave is sold for 40 pounds ("livres"): 25 of the pounds are paid in the form of two books, the *Office of Our Lady, the Virgin Mary* and Seneca's *Letter to Lucilius*.[54] Such a range of Christian and classical interests, thoroughly imbricated in this commercial nexus, brings us to the extensive meditation upon this slave-crossed Mediterranean space offered by Francesco Petrarca (or, as some manuscripts call him, "Franciscus Patriarca"), founding father of European humanism.[55]

Petrarch and Scythia; Spenser and Ireland

Seniles 10.2, written from Venice in 1367, is Petrarch's longest autobiographical letter and takes the form of a geographical survey featuring places where Petrarch himself has lived.[56] There are strong Golden Ageist elements here as Petrarch pits recollections of his halcyon youth against images of embattled and degraded contemporary Europe. The heart of the letter evokes Petrarch's first visit, as a boy, to Vaucluse, accompanied by the boyhood friend to whom, more than 50 years later, he now writes: Guido Sette, archbishop of Genoa. In writing from Venice to Genoa, Petrarch is encompassing the whole space of the Mediterranean and its slave trade, for if Genoa is the chief slaving power of this period, Venice is its only significant rival. Genoans had their chief Crimean beachhead at Caffa, the Venetians at Tana. Both were intensively involved, as Petrarch wrote, with commerce in slaves; the decade 1360–9 was actually the busiest period for the sale of young Tartars at Venice.[57] This, then, is Petrarch's view from the quayside in 1367:

Nam Grecie calamitas vetus est, sed Scitharum recens. Ut, unde nuper ingens annua vis frumenti navibus in hanc urbem invehi solebat, inde nunc servis honuste naves veniant, quos urgente fame miseri venditant parentes. Iamque insolita et inextimabilis turba servorum utriusque sexus hanc pulcerrimam urbem scithicis vultibus et informi colluvie, velut amnem nitidissimum torrens turbidus inficit; que, si suis emptoribus non esset acceptior quam michi et non amplius eorum oculos delectaret quam delectat meos, neque feda hec pubes hos angustos coartaret vicos, necque melioribus assuetos formis inameno advenas contristaret occursu; sed intra suam Scithiam cum fame arida ac pallenti lapidoso in agro, ubi Naso illam statuit, raras herbas dentibus velleret atque unguibus.[58] Et hec quidem hactenus. (pp. 1116–8)

The downfall of Greece is ancient, that of the Scythians recent. As a result, from where until recently huge quantities of grain would be brought every year by ship into this city, today ships come from there laden with slaves, sold by their parents under pressure of hunger. Already, a strange, enormous crowd of slaves of both sexes, like a muddy torrent tainting a limpid stream, taints this beautiful city with Scythian faces and hideous filth. If they were not more acceptable to their buyers than they are to me, and if they were not more pleasing to their eyes than to mine, these repulsive youths would not crowd our narrow streets; nor would they, by jostling people so clumsily, annoy foreign visitors, who are accustomed to better sights. Instead they would [still] be hungrily plucking the scanty grass with their teeth and nails on the stony soil of their Scythia, which Ovid once described. But enough of this.[59]

This passage, framed between references to Greece and Rome, is humanism, hard-core. Trecento Italian classicists, the next chapter argues, tend to imagine the extreme west as a structuring limit to all that is civilized. Here Petrarch develops a complex polarity more familiar to Greek and Roman thinking: between south and far north (but shading off into west and east). Scythia, for ancient Greeks, was antithetical to all things Hellenic, including its Asian vastness of scale; the grasslands of the Scythian steppes might go on forever. Hercules himself was more or less raped on this territory; fear of the all-consuming Scythian landscape, in Greek imagining, found expressive form in Scythian warrior women, the Amazons.[60] Ovid, evoked here by Petrarch, wrote home to Rome from his exile or "relegation" in Tomis of "a land gripped fast in frost"; "Beyond me lie the Don," he says, "and swamps of Scythia / And a few places, names scarce known at all. / Further just cold, defying habitation – / The world's end now, alas, how near to me!" Ovid's deeper fear, at this extreme physical limit, is of losing his authentically Roman voice: "Believe me," he says, "I'm afraid amid my Latin / Sintic or Pontic words you'll find I use."[61] Which is to say, he has a fear of cultural contamination, the same fear that grips Petrarch as he stands on the quay-side at Venice, fantasizing about repatriation.

And yet, of course, the influx of slaves reinforces and confirms *the* bino-mial most fundamental to classical consciousness (one already invoked by Petrarch earlier in this letter): liberty and servitude, Pozzo and Lucky; I know that I am free, knowing and seeing that you are not.[62] Civic debate at Genoa was clearly conditioned by awareness of 5,000 slaves in its midst: Genoa should not agree to be ruled by outsiders, according to one speaker at the 1396 assembly, "so that *we* are not shown to be slaves" (emphasis added).[63] Petrarch thus wastes his breath in measuring his superior aesthetic judgment against that of slave-traders, for these are the true purveyors of the revived classical package. Deeds of sale suggest, in fact, that the posses-sion of a slave functioned as a marker of prestige, of classicizing chic, for notaries (the class of intellectuals most dedicated to the development of humanist techniques); in fifteenth-century Genoa, notaries possessed four times as many slaves as all other liberal professions combined.[64]

Slavery prospers at faith frontiers. Perhaps, then, it is not surprising to find tales of Tartary and Scythia in the *Canterbury Tales* assigned to the warfaring class whose *modus agendi* defines frontiers, near and far. Fascina-tion with Tartars had been high in England since the time of Edward III. In 1331, some of the noblest and most beautiful women of the kingdom ("dominae de nobilioribus et pulcrioribus regni") had been processed through Cheapside, led on silver chains, by knights wearing Tartar masks ("ad similitudinem Tartarum larvati").[65] Chaucer's Squire, who has fought along the nearer frontier of the Hundred Years' War, duly tells a tale of Tartary that turns charming and exotic, but opens with notice of warfare and death:

> At Sarray, in the land of Tartarye,
> Ther dwelte a kynge that werryed Russye,
> Thurgh which ther dyde many a doughty man.
> *(5.9–11)*

The Squire's father, the exemplary Christian Knight, has himself "werryed Russye" in sustaining the more distant frontiers of Christendom; in fact, he has fought with Prussians, Russians, Lithuanians, Moroccans, Grenadians, Alexandrians, you name it.[66] He tells a tale of Greece and Scythia, featuring conquered and deracinated Amazons. Scythia, early on in his tale, is identi-fied with "the regne of Femenye" (1.877) and the enslaved Ypolita is termed "The faire, hardy queene of Scithia" (1.877, 882). Explicit opposition between Scythia and Greece – along the lines that Petrarch worked hard to revive – is underscored by the Latin epigraph to the *Knight's Tale* that appears in many manuscripts of all groups.[67] All of this percolates its way down to Edmund Spenser and (once again) to representations of Ireland as a wild western frontier in need of English intervention.[68] Spenser is clearly indebted to Chaucerian romancing of Christian English chivalry, although his commitment to monumental epic – a classical genre vigorously revived, as Maureen Quilligan observes,[69] as a complement to classical habits of slaving – rivals that of the Petrarchan *Africa* (the text for which he was crowned laureate at Rome). But it is worth noting how neatly Petrarch's division of Scythians from Italians in *Seniles* 10.2 meshes with Spenser's division of Irish from English[70] in *A View of the State of Ireland*; and how the identifying of Ireland with Scythia saves England from being likewise classed – as in Petrarch's *De vita solitaria* – as a nation beyond civilized geographical limits.[71]

The Scythian Irish, Spenser maintains, derive their strange and wasteful "boolying" (itinerant grazing) habits "from the Tartarians and the people about the Caspian sea, which are naturally Scythians."[72] The notion that eastern and western extremes might meet – which, we have noted, haunted Hakluyt – allows Spenser to suppose that the Irish are too western and too eastern at one and the same time; it also allows him to identify with Ovid as a poet of the imperial center translated to Scythia, the end of the world.[73] Ireland and Scythia even look alike, Spenser maintains, in that they are both "waste deserts fulle of grasse" (p. 55). Petrarch and Spenser devise pretty much the same strategy for their Scythian neighbors, namely, slow starvation.[74] The innate cannibalistic tendencies of the Irish, as noted above by Strabo and Petrarch, will speed the process of self-destruction, "for," according to Spenser's Irenius, "although there should none of them fall by the sword, nor bee slaine by the souldiour, yet thus being kept from manurance, and their cattle from running abroad, by this hard constraint they would quickly consume themselves, and devoure one another" (p. 101). Irenius goes on to equate such desperate scenes of slow starvation and cannibalism with events he had himself witnessed in the course of the Munster famine accompanying the Desmond rebellion (which began in 1579): "Out of every corner of the woods and glynnes they came creeping forth upon their hands, for their legges could not beare them; they looked like anatomies of death, they spake like ghosts crying out of their graves; they did eat dead carrions, happy where they could finde them, yea, and one another soone after"; this diet is varied by "water-cresses or shamrocks" (pp. 101–2).

In 1632, Thomas Morton observed that "the natives of New England are accustomed to build their houses much like the wild Irish"; not surprisingly, he refers to their dwelling places (wigwams) as "booleys."[75] As we shall soon see, the Genoese and Spanish map their way to the Americas and their native inhabitants via distinctive Atlantic island experiences in the Canaries; the English, similarly, imagine their way westward via the Atlantic island they have long claimed as their own.

We might well look to Chaucer with some desperation for moments resistant to these imperious Ovidianisms, these lethal remappings of premodern places from classicizing models. In Cambridge University Library MS Hh.4.12, a poem flowers suddenly from a crack in Chaucer's Boethius translation. "A blisful lyf, a paisible and a swete," the poem begins, "Ledden the peples in the former age."[76] The bliss of such a past, however, can only be imagined as antithetical to the ways of a ruinous present which, by the end of the poem, overshadows everything:

> For in our dayes nis but covetyse,
> Doublenesse, and tresoun, and envye,
> Poyson, manslawhtre, and mordre in sondry wise.
>
> *(61–3)*

The rueful self-recognition of this poem, albeit imagined across time rather than space, recalls that of Horace's sixteenth epode: to escape current civil strife, Horace proposes, we should cross "Oceanus" to seek "the Happy Fields and the Islands of the Blest, where every year the land, unploughed, yields corn, and ever blooms the vine unpruned."[77] Throughout its course, however, the poem is dogged by the thought that these islands will be much less blest or fortunate once "we" show up. Horace is writing in the long and extensive tradition of "Insulae Fortunatae" poems, dreaming of "Fortunate Islands" of perfect climate and idyllically simple life at the end of, just beyond, the western world. By the time of Chaucer, amazingly, such islands have been found. How will Europeans and their attendant literatures step through this magical boundary, one that has structured their world for so long? Once again it will be the Genoese, sailing boldly and calculatedly beyond the pillars of Hercules, who lead the way.

NOTES

1   Peter Firstbrook, *The Voyage of the Matthew: John Cabot and the Discovery of North America* (London: BBC Books, 1997), p. 12. The tiny but full-size replica *Matthew* did make the transatlantic crossing in 1997; some terrifying video film can be seen on board in Bristol.
2   Firstbrook, *Voyage of the Matthew*, p. 12.

3 Personal letter prefacing Firstbrook, *Voyage of the Matthew*, p. 7. "There is also circumstantial evidence," HRH Prince Philip remarks, "that fishermen from Bristol were fishing for cod on the Grand Banks off Newfoundland in the early fifteenth century." See further Ian Wilson, *The Columbus Myth: Did Men of Bristol reach America before Columbus?* (London: Simon and Schuster, 1991); Stephen J. Summerhill and John Alexander Williams, *Sinking Columbus: Contested History, Cultural Politics, and Mythmaking during the Quincentenary* (Gainesville: University Press of Florida, 2000).

4 See David B. Quinn, *Sebastian Cabot and Bristol Exploration*, rev. edn. (Bristol: Bristol Branch of the Historical Association, 1993), pp. 1–2.

5 James Howell, *Instructions for Forreine Travell (1642), collated with the second edition of 1650*, ed. Edward Arber (London: English Reprints, 1869), p. 41. The second edition of 1650 supplements the 1642 accounts of western European traveling with "An Appendix of Som Directions for *travelling* into *Turky* and the *Levant* parts." Howell was exceptionally proficient in languages (beginning with his native Welsh). See Sidney Lee, "Howell, James" (1594?–1666), *Dictionary of National Biography*, 63 vols. (London: Smith, Elder, 1885–1911), 28.109a–114b.

6 "Genuensis ergo mercator," as the widespread Latin proverb says.

7 On Chaucer's Italian journeys, see *Chaucer Life-Records*, ed. Martin M. Crow and Clair C. Olson (Austin: University of Texas Press, 1966), pp. 32–40, 53–61, 148–270. The mission to Genoa was led by John de Mari (a royal agent employed to hire Genoese mercenaries); he arranged to travel (with Chaucer in tow) accompanied by two Genoese crossbowmen, *balistarii* (pp. 37–8). On John de Mari's hiring of Genoese crossbowmen and galleymen at Bruges, see chapter 2 above, p. 100.

8 "The Domestic Enemy: The Eastern Slaves in Tuscany in the Fourteenth and Fifteenth Centuries," *Speculum* 30 (1955), 321–66 (p. 329).

9 See, for example, *A l'heure des nations* (Paris: Les Éditions de Minuit, 1988), especially the discussion of "propension au dehors" ("a propensity for the outside": "exigence remarquable d'une entrée en rapport avec toutes les nations, avec toutes les familles de l'humain" (p. 10)).

10 The association of "freedom" with certain modes of writing is assumed by a title such as Harriet Hawkins, *Poetic Freedom and Poetic Truth: Chaucer, Shakespeare, Marlowe, Milton* (Oxford: Clarendon Press, 1976). And the strong derivation of such an assumption from the consolidated *classicism* of the *tre coroni* is apparent from the book's opening sentence: "Their magnificently successful efforts to embody in poetry the truth as they knew it have given 'immortal glory among mortals' to Chaucer, Shakespeare, Milton, and some of their great contemporaries" (p. xi).

11 "D'abord la découverte de l'Amérique, ou plûtot celle des Américains, est bien la rencontre la plus étonnante de nostre histoire," Tzvetan Todorov, *La conquête de l'Amérique: La question de l'autre* (Paris: Éditions du Seiuil, 1982), p. 12; *The Conquest of America: The Question of the Other*, trans. Richard Howard (New York: Harper and Rowe, 1984), p. 4.

12   Mention of Italian cities is common in the Malebolge and there are explicit
     condemnations of Bologna (18.58–63), Lucca (25.10–15), Pistoia (25.10–15),
     Siena (29.121–32) and (lower than Malebolge) of Pisa (33.79–90) and Genoa
     (33.151–7). See *The Divine Comedy of Dante Alighieri*, vol. 1, *Inferno*, trans. and ed.
     Robert M. Durling and Ronald L. Martinez (New York: Oxford University
     Press, 1996), p. 406. Citations from the *Inferno* follow this text; translations are
     adapted from it.

13   *L'anonimo genovese e la sua raccolta di rime*, ed. F. L. Mannucci (Genoa: Muncipality
     of Genoa, 1904), as cited in Iris Origo, "Domestic Enemy," p. 325: "E tanti son
     li Zenoexi / E per lo mondo si destexi / Che unde li van e stan / Un atra Zenoa
     se fan."

14   Cited in Luciana Gatti, *Navi e cantieri della Republica di Genova (secoli XVI–XVIII)*
     (Genoa: Brigati, 1999), p. 13. Fernand Braudel, noting how the Genoese are
     effectively crowded down to the sea by sterile and mountainous terrain, suc-
     cinctly makes much the same point about the city: "Elle fabrique, mais pour les
     autres; elle navigue, mais pour les autres; elle investit, mais pour les autres"
     (*Civilisation matérielle et capitalisme* [*XVe–XVIIIe siècle*], 3 vols. [Paris: Armand
     Colin, 1967–79], 3.134).

15   See *Paradiso* 33.94–6 (in which the astonished Neptune sees the first-ever
     ship, captained by Jason in pursuit of the golden fleece); *Inferno* 15.4–6 (and
     chapter 2 above, p. 111). Jason is pointed out among the damned at *Inferno*
     18.86.

16   *L'anonimo genovese*, ed. Mannucci, p. 200 ("Tutti sono marinai . . .").

17   See Klaus Bergdolt, *Der Schwarze Tod in Europa: Die Grosse Pest und das Ende des
     Mittelalters* (Munich: C. H. Beck, 1995), pp. 33–5.

18   Latin text extracted from the *Historia de morbo* follows Heinrich Haeser, *Lehrbuch
     der Geschichte der Medicin und der epidemischen Krankheiten*, 3rd edn., 3 vols. (Jena:
     Hermann Dufft, 1875; Gustav Fischer, 1881–2), III.157–61 (pp. 157–8); trans-
     lation follows *The Black Death*, ed. and trans. Rosemary Horrox (Manchester:
     Manchester University Press, 1994), pp. 14–26 (p. 17). De' Mussis was a lawyer
     from Piacenza; he died in 1356.

19   See *The Anonimalle Chronicle, 1333 to 1381. From a MS. Written at St. Mary's Abbey,
     York*, ed. V. H. Galbraith (Manchester: Manchester University Press, 1970),
     p. 30; *Knighton's Chronicle 1337–1396*, ed. and trans. G. H. Martin (Oxford:
     Clarendon Press, 1995), p. 99.

20   See *Chronicon Galfridi le Baker De Swynebroke*, ed. Edward Maunde Thompson
     (Oxford: Clarendon Press, 1889), p. 99.

21   *Historia de morbo*, ed. Haeser, p. 159.

22   See *Breve Chronicon Clerici Anonymi* in *Recueil des Chroniques de Flandre*, ed. J.-J.
     De Smet, vol. 3 (Brussels: M. Hayez, 1856), pp. 14–17; *The Black Death*, trans.
     and ed. Horrox, pp. 42–3. This anonymous clerical chronicler speaks of the
     plague carrying off half the population; some 7,000 houses at Avignon stand
     empty.

23 *Breve Chronicon*, ed De Smet, p. 15; *The Black Death*, trans. and ed. Horrox, p. 42.

24 See J. F. C. Hecker, *The Epidemics of the Middle Ages*, 3rd edn., trans. B. G. Babington (London: Trübner, 1859), pp. 39–44, 70–4; *Strassburg Urkundenbuch* in *The Black Death*, trans. and ed. Horrox, pp. 211–19, esp. p. 212; Miri Rubin, *Gentile Tales: The Narrative Assault on Late Medieval Jews* (New Haven: Yale University Press, 1999).

25 See Shlomo Simonsohn, *The Apostolic See and the Jews. Documents: 492–1404*, Texts and Studies 94 (Toronto: Pontifical Institute of Medieval Studies, 1988), item 373 (pp. 397–8). The Pope has heard "quod nonnulli Christiani pestem, qua Deus populum Christianum ipsius peccatis populi provocatus affligit, Iudeorum falso tossicationibus, seducente dyabolo, imputantes" ("that the plague with which God is afflicting Christian people because of the sins of these very Christians, is being falsely represented by numerous Christians as the work of Jewish poisoners seduced by the devil"). On the long history of *Sicut Judaeis*, first used as an *incipit* by Pope Gregory I in 591 (writing against forced baptism of Jews in southern France), see Simonsohn, *The Apostolic See and the Jews: History*, Texts and Studies 109 (Toronto: Pontifical Institute of Medieval Studies, 1991), pp. 39–93 (esp. pp. 40, 64–5).

26 See Philip Ziegler, *The Black Death* (Godalming, Surrey: Bramley Books, 1998), p. 6

27 Michele di Piazza, *Historia Sicula ab anno 1337 ad annum 1361*, in *Lehrbuch der Geschichte der Medicin*, ed. Haeser, pp. 177–9 (p. 177). For comparable interactions with Genoese galleys at Pera and Constantinople, see *Chronicon Estense, Gesta Marchionum Estensium Complectens*, in *Rerum Italicarum Scriptores*, ed. Ludovico Antonio Muratori, vol. 15 (Milan: Ex Typographia Societatis Palatinae in Regia Curia, 1729), cols. 294–548 (col. 448). This section of the *Chronicon* dates from the 1350s (see p. 298).

28 Citations follow the edition of Vittore Branca in *Tutte le opere di Giovanni Boccaccio*, ed. Branca, 12 vols. (Milan: Mondadori, 1964–), vol. IV. On Genoa being "the Scotland of Italy" in its reputation for miserliness, see Victoria Kirkham, "A Pedigree for Courtesy: Or, How Dante's 'Purser' Cured a Miser (*Decameron* 1.8)," *Studi sul Boccaccio* 25 (1997), 213–38 (p. 215).

29 "Indeed," Burckhardt continues, "the inhabitant of the Riviera was proverbial among Italians for his contempt of all higher culture" (*The Civilization of the Renaissance in Italy*, 15th edn., trans. S. G. C. Middlemore (London: Harrap, 1929), p. 106). Burckhardt assigns Genoa only part of a paragraph at the tail-end of his chapter on the republics of Venice and Florence; both German and English editions feature a photograph of the Palazzo di San Giorgio ("formerly the headquarters of the Bank of Genoa," figure 48 caption).

30 On the prominent part paid by islands in Mediterranean slaving, see Peregrine Horden and Nicholas Purcell, *The Corrupting Sea: A Study of Mediterranean History* (Oxford: Blackwell, 2000), pp. 388–91; on attitudes carried forward to islands beyond the Mediterranean, see chapter 5 below, pp. 274–8.

31 In 1376, the top five trading partners (as a percentage of the value of Genoese trade) were Alexandria (24.6%), Spain (18.1), Flanders (16.4), Provence (15.4), Cyprus (8.70). See Steven A. Epstein, *Genoa and the Genoese* (Chapel Hill: University of North Carolina Press, 1996), p. 231.

32 See Wendy Childs, "Anglo-Italian Contacts in the Fourteenth Century," in *Chaucer and the Italian Trecento*, ed. Piero Boitani (Cambridge: Cambridge University Press, 1983), pp. 65–87 (p. 67). The Genoese experimented with Bristol until 1383 before settling on Southampton as their main shipping center.

33 *Decameron* 2.6.27. In 1456, more than a century later, the Doria were still a major slave-owning household (possessing 86 slaves, second only to the Spinola): see Domenico Gioffrè, *Il mercato degli schiavi a Genova nel secolo XV* (Genoa: Fratelli Bozzi, 1971), pp. 74–5.

34 This by way of evoking the manner in which King Charles II of Naples haggles over his own daughter's bride price ("come fanno i corsar de l'altre schiave," 20.81: see Steven A. Epstein, *Speaking of Slavery: Color, Ethnicity, and Human Bondage in Italy* [Ithaca, NY: Cornell University Press, 2001], p. 43).

35 See *Chaucer Life-Records*, ed. Crow and Olson, pp. 40–2.

36 Epstein, *Genoa*, p. 231.

37 See "Trade, Treason, and the Murder of Janus Imperial," in Paul Strohm, *Theory and the Premodern Text* (Minneapolis: University of Minnesota Press, 2000), pp. 112–31.

38 Thus the provost of the Asian city in Chaucer's *Prioress's Tale*, condemning Jews to be drawn "with wilde hors" (7.632–3).

39 Turks had crossed the Hellespont much earlier; they were well established at Gallipoli by 1356. See George Vernadsky, *The Mongols and Russia* (New Haven: Yale University Press, 1953), p. 205; and see now Epstein, *Speaking of Slavery*.

40 See Charles Verlinden, *L'Esclavage dans l'Europe médiévale*, 2 vols., I: *Péninsule Ibérique – France* (Bruges: De Tempel, 1955), II: *Italie – Colonies italiennes du Levant – Levant latin – Empire byzantin* (Ghent: Rijksuniversiteit te Gent, 1977); Robert Delort, "Quelques précisions sur le commerce des esclaves à Gênes vers la fin du XIVe siècle," *Mélanges d'archéologie et d'histoire. École Français de Rome* 78 (1966), 215–50; Michel Balard, "Remarques sur les esclaves à Gênes dans la seconde moitié du XIIIe siècle," *Mélanges . . . École Français de Rome* 80 (1968), 627–80; Gioffrè, *Il mercato*; Jocelyn Nigel Hillgarth, *The Spanish Kingdoms, 1250–1516*, 2 vols. (Oxford: Clarendon Press, 1978); John Thornton, *Africa and Africans in the Making of the Atlantic World* (Cambridge: Cambridge University Press, 1992); John Brian Williams, *From the Commercial Revolution to the State Revolution: The Development of Slavery in Medieval Genoa*, 2 vols., Ph.D. dissertation. University of Chicago, 1995; Epstein, *Genoa*, pp. 228–36, 262–70.

41 In the American TV situation comedies *Webster* (1983–7, starring Emmanuel Lewis) and *Diff'rent Strokes* (1978–86, starring Gary Coleman and Todd Bridges), exceptionally small male African-American actors (playing children) are adopted

by exceptionally tall, white, middle-class fathers. Mysteriously, the extended family, a resilient feature of African-American culture, is virtually absent. See Melbourne S. Cummings, "The Changing Image of the Black Family on Television," *Journal of Popular Culture* 22.2 (Fall 1988), 75–85 (p. 80); Robert R. Means Coleman, *African-American Viewers and the Black Situation Comedy: Situating Racial Humor* (New York: Garland, 1998), p. 99.

42 This list does not include all slaves sold in Florence at this period: see Origo, "Domestic Enemy," p. 336.

43 See Christiane Klapisch-Zuber, "Women Servants in Florence during the Fourteenth and Fifteenth Centuries," in *Women and Work in Preindustrial Europe*, ed. Barbara Hanawalt (Bloomington: Indiana University Press, 1986), pp. 56–80 (p. 68). See further Gioffrè, *Il mercato*, p. 23; Epstein, *Genoa*, p. 229; Susan Mosher Stuard, "Ancillary Evidence for the Decline of Medieval Slavery," *Past and Present* 149 (November 1995), 3–28 (p. 3).

44 See Delort, "Quelques précisions," p. 228. On Petrarch's understanding that desperate parents will sell their children into slavery, see *Seniles* 10.2 (discussed below, note 59).

45 See John Boswell, *The Kindness of Strangers: The Abandonment of Children in Western Europe from Late Antiquity to the Renaissance* (New York: Vintage, 1988), pp. 415–27; Klapisch-Zuber, "Women Servants," pp. 69–70; Origo, "Domestic Enemy," pp. 347–8.

46 According to Augustine, there is a natural order ("naturalis ordo") that compels those of lesser intellect to serve more rational beings; women should thus obey men (as children their parents and slaves their masters). "Est enim ordo naturalis," he writes, "in hominibus, ut serviant feminae viris, et filii parentibus; quia et illic haec justitia est ut infirmior ratio serviat fortiori. Haec igitur in dominationibus ut servitutibus clara justitia est ut qui excellunt ratione, excellant dominatione" (*Quaestionum in Pentateuchum, Patrologia Latina*, ed. J.-P. Migne, XXXIV, cols. 547–824 (col. 590); Verlinden, *L'Esclavage*, II.23. There is thus a clear justice in both domination and servitude. Paul's attitudes towards slavery and womanly obedience, while broadly derived from Senecan and Stoic ideas, are complex. 1 Timothy insists that women ought not to teach or tell a man what to do (2.12); all slaves "under the yoke" must have unqualified respect for their masters (6.1). 1 Corinthians urges all converts – including slaves – to remain in their station ("servus vocatus es? Non sit tibi curae," 7.20); women are to maintain silence in churches ("taceant") and remain subject ("subditas esse") according to the law (14.34: a verse now thought to be a post-Pauline interpellation). Paul's famous letter to Philemon, concerning the return of a fugitive slave known as "Onesimus" ("Useful"), maintains the master/slave distinction while modeling a more humane understanding – if such a paradox be considered intelligible – of ownership; in the Middle Ages, however, it was (Verlinden argues) exclusively employed to uphold the legitimacy of slaveholding (*L'Esclavage*, II.31–2).

47   At the time of Aphra Behn's visit to Surinam, the roughly equal number of
     blacks to whites (both relatively small) suggests working relations closer to
     the paternalistic, artisanal, and domestic models outlined in this chapter. In
     eighteenth- and nineteenth-century Surinam, however, slave labor worked on
     a massive scale with little differentiation of tasks over an almost unlimited
     working day; this bred fears in the white population of black people as an
     anonymous, endlessly replenishable, and potentially overwhelming mass. See
     further, chapter 6 below.

48   Non-white skin also begins to be interpreted – along with mutilation and brand-
     ing – as a *sign* betokening slavery; there were elaborate arrangements for the
     recovery of runaways, often involving cooperation between city-states that were
     otherwise mutually hostile.

49   See Charles Verlinden, "Le recrutement des esclaves à Venise au XIVe et XVe
     siècles," *Bulletin del L'Institut Historique Belge de Rome* 39 (1968), 83–202, esp.
     pp. 178–82; Gioffrè, *Il mercato*, pp. 33–6. For a study of ancient Greek references
     to *Aithiopes*, which are (it is argued) essentially free from color-based prejudice,
     see Frank M. Snowden, "Greeks and Ethiopians," in *Greeks and Barbarians:
     Essays on the Interactions between Greeks and Non-Greeks in Antiquity and the Con-
     sequences of Eurocentrism*, ed. John E. Coleman and Clark A. Walz (Bethesda,
     Md.: CDL Press, 1997), pp. 103–26.

50   See Origo, "Domestic Enemy," pp. 331, 337, 340–1; Philip P. Argenti, *The Occu-
     pation of Chios by the Genoese and their Administration of the Island 1346–1566*, 3
     vols. (Cambridge: Cambridge University Press, 1958), I.619–20.

51   See Mario Ferrara, "Linguaggio di schiave del Quattrocento," *Studi di Filologia
     Italiana* 8 (1950), 320–8. Ferrara edits and then analyzes slave language in
     a sonnet (featuring two female slaves and their mistress) by the Florentine
     poet and notary Alessandro Braccesi (1445–1503). He then discusses a second
     (anonymous) fifteenth-century sonnet, which presents a dialogue between two
     women slaves that makes no attempt to capture linguistic peculiarities. The
     first of the women declares that she comes "Da Schiavonia paisa," "from Slav
     country," thereby preserving the Slav/slave association. See further, on the
     language and textual remains of slaves, Epstein, *Speaking of Slavery*, pp. 16–61.

52   See S. Sobrequés, "La epoca del patriciado urbano," in *Historia Social y Economica
     de España y America*, ed. J. Vicens Vives, 5 vols. (Barcelona: Editorial Teide,
     1957–9), II.6–406 (p. 220); Gioffrè, *Il mercato*, p. 94. Gioffrè states the case quite
     strongly; Sobrequés is a little more qualified. There is firm evidence, however,
     of slaves teaching other slaves the art of painting. And in his will of January
     18, 1386, the Venetian painter Nicoletto Sernitecolo stipulates that his Tartar
     slave, Michele, should continue "l'esercizio dell'arte sua" (Gioffré, p. 90).

53   See Origo, "Domestic Enemy," p. 330.

54   Delort, "Quelques précisions," p. 241, n. 1.

55   See David Wallace, *Chaucerian Polity: Absolutist Lineages and Associational Forms
     in England and Italy* (Stanford, Calif,: Stanford University Press, 1997), p. 262.

56 Most conveniently available in Petrarca, *Prose*, ed. Martellotti et al., 1090–1125.

57 See Verlinden, "Le recrutement," p. 126. Of Tartar slaves imported at Venice between 1360 and 1399, 67.5% were women. Numbers dropped off markedly in the last two decades, probably as a result of campaigns (1387–96) by Timur i Leng (Timur the Lame, 1336–1405, better known in the West – following Marlowe's play of 1597 – as Tamburlaine the Great).

58 Petrarch undoubtedly echoes Ovid here: Ceres sends one of her rustic minions in search of Famine to the farthest border of frozen Scythia, "a gloomy and barren soil, a land without corn, without trees" (*Metamorphoses* 8.789); Famine is found "in a stony field, plucking with nails and teeth at the scanty herbage" ("quaesitamque Famem lapidoso vidit in agro/ unguibus et raras vellentem dentibus herbas" (8.799–800)). Citations follow *Metamorphoses*, ed. and trans. Frank Justus Miller, rev. G. P. Goold, Loeb Classical Library, 2 vols. (Cambridge, Mass.: Harvard University Press, 1984).

59 The translation is my own but owes something both to the Italian of Martellotti and the English of Francis Petrarch, *Letters of Old Age. Rerum Senilium Libri, I–XVIII*, trans. Aldo S. Bernardo, Saul Levin, and Reta S. Bernardo, 2 vols. (Baltimore, Md.: Johns Hopkins University Press, 1992), II.359–74. Bernardo et al. gloss "Scythians" as "Russians," which is quite wrong. Martellotti et al. note that "of this influx of slaves from the territories of the Black Sea there is no other report" (p. 1118 n. 1, my translation): an extraordinary statement which demonstrates, once again, the disciplinary gulf that would seem to divide expert philologists and students of humanism from the study of social and economic history.

60 See Pericles Georges, *Barbarian Asia and the Greek Experience: From the Archaic Period to the Age of Xenophon* (Baltimore, Md.: Johns Hopkins University Press, 1994), pp. xvi, 1–4, 203–4; Ludwig Edelstein, *The Idea of Progress in Classical Antiquity* (Baltimore, Md.: Johns Hopkins University Press, 1967), pp. 67–8; Frank M. Snowden, "Greeks and Ethiopians," in *Greeks and Barbarians*, ed. Coleman and Walz, pp. 103–26 (pp. 112–22); Renate Rolle, *The World of the Scythians*, trans. Gayna Walls (London: Batsford, 1989), pp. 11–18.

61 *Tristia*, trans. Melville, 3.14, lines 49–50 ("crede mihi, timeo ne sint inmixta Latinis / inque meis scriptis Pontica verba legas," *Tristia*, ed. Wheeler). On the medieval popularity of Ovid's exile elegies, see Ralph J. Hexter, *Ovid and Medieval Schooling: Studies in Medieval School Commentaries on Ovid's* Ars Amatoria, Epistulae ex Ponto, *and* Epistulae Heroidum (Munich: Arbeo-Gesellschaft, 1986), pp. 83–136.

62 "Hellenic liberty and slavery were indivisible," writes Perry Anderson: "each was the structural condition of the other" (*Lineages of the Absolutist State* [London: New Left Books, 1974], p. 23). See further Samuel Beckett, *Waiting for Godot* (New York: Grove Press, 1954).

63 "Ut non efficiamur sclavi": the words of Francesco de Aiguino of Voltri as cited by Epstein, *Genoa*, p. 249 and p. 357 n. 94. In 1381, the estimated number of

slaves at Genoa was 5056 (Gioffrè, *Mercato*, pp. 80–1 (n. 23). Numbers fell to around 1920 by the end of the century, which is to say that at the time of Chaucer's visit in 1373 the Genoese slave trade was near its peak.

64   See Gioffrè, *Il mercato*, p. 83.

65   See Vale, *Edward III and Chivalry: Chivalric Society and its Context, 1270–1350* (Woodbridge: Boydell Press, 1982), p. 62; see further p. 72.

66   See Terry Jones, *Chaucer's Knight: Portrait of a Medieval Mercenary*, 3rd edn. (London: Methuen, 1994). Jones notes that in *The Book of the Duchess*, Blanche of Lancaster is commended for *not* sending knights on quests, *inter alia*, "into Tartarye" (line 1025; Jones, p. 38).

67   "Iamque domos patrias, Scithie post aspera gentis/ Prelia, laurigero, etc." ("And now [Theseus, drawing nigh his] native land in laurelled car after fierce battling with the Scythian folk, etc."): *Riverside Chaucer*, pp. 37, 828.

68   On earlier English designs on Ireland, see chapter 2 above, pp. 119–20.

69   "On the Renaissance Epic: Spenser and Slavery," *South Atlantic Quarterly* 100 (2001), 15–39.

70   Linkage between the cannibalistic and incestuous inhabitants of Ireland and Scythians is explicitly made by Strabo, Petrarch's source, in the passage of his *Geography* cited below, pp. 233–4. This passage continues: "and yet, as for the matter of man-eating, that is said to be a custom of the Scythians also" (4.5.4, vol. II, pp. 260–1).

71   See above, p. 119.

72   Edmund Spenser, *A View of the State of Ireland. From the first printed edition (1633)*, ed. Andrew Hadfield and Willy Maley (Oxford: Blackwell, 1997), p. 55. It has to be said that this volume fails to deliver the promise of its title: "we have used," the editors explain in a footnote, "the 1809 reprint of Ware's edition, which contains some minor modifications in terms of punctuation and capitalization" (p. xxvi).

73   "Heu quam vicina," laments Ovid in *Tristia* 3.4b, "est ultima terra mihi!" (line 6 from the passage cited in my text above); on Hakluyt, see chapter 2 above, p. 120.

74   On Spenser's elaborate plans for the slow starvation of the Irish, corralled between four English garrisons, see *A View of the State of Ireland*, pp. 95–103.

75   Cited in Luke Gibbons, *Transformations in Irish Culture* (Cork: Cork University Press in association with Field Day, 1996), p. 151.

76   The poem survives in two manuscripts; the other is Cambridge University Library, Ii.3.21. See *Riverside Chaucer*, pp. 650–1, 1083, 1188; Rita Copeland, "Rhetoric and Vernacular Translation in the Middle Ages," *Studies in the Age of Chaucer* 9 (1987), 41–75 (pp. 62–66).

77   Horace, *The Odes and Epodes*, ed. and trans. C. E. Bennett, Loeb Classical Library (London: Heinemann, 1914): "arva, beata / petamus arva divites et insulas, reddit ubi Cererem tellus inarata quotannis / et imputata floret usque vinea" (lines 41–4).

CHAPTER FIVE

CANARIES (THE FORTUNATE ISLANDS)

here, in the Isles Canaries,
the scene of the crime.

Melba Joyce Boyd, **Transatlantic
Passages Revisited, Tenerife.**[1]

The discovery or rather rediscovery of the Canaries in the fourteenth century forms a perfect physical complement to the recuperative labors of humanist philology; for as Petrarch was discovering missing books of the *History of Rome* by Titus Livius (d. CE 17), so enterprising Genoese navigators were setting foot on territory described or imagined by Strabo, Pomponius Mela, Pliny, and (as we have just seen) Horace.[2] This western "discovery" was one, like many others, made long before by Phoenicians and other Africans. Pliny's chief source for the Fortunate Islands was the extensive geographical survey commissioned by King Juba of Mauritania, circa CE 7.[3] In CE 999, Ben-Farrouk, an Arab captain guarding the Portuguese coast against marauding Normans, visited Gran Canaria and was welcomed by the *Guanarteme* or chieftain Guanariga; the Nubian geographer Sharif-al-Idrisi writes of further Arab expeditions setting off from Lisbon in the eleventh century.[4] Ibn Khaldûn, born in Tunis on Ramadân 1, 732 (May 27, 1332), begins discussion of the Canaries in his *Muqaddimah* with Ptolemy; "we have heard," he adds, laconically, "that European Christian ships reached them in the middle of this century, fought with (the inhabitants), plundered them, captured some of them, and sold some of the captives" (I.117).[5] The best surviving mapping of the islands from this period (1374–6) is by Abraham Cresques, the Jewish cartographer from Majorca. The Canaries are accurately drawn

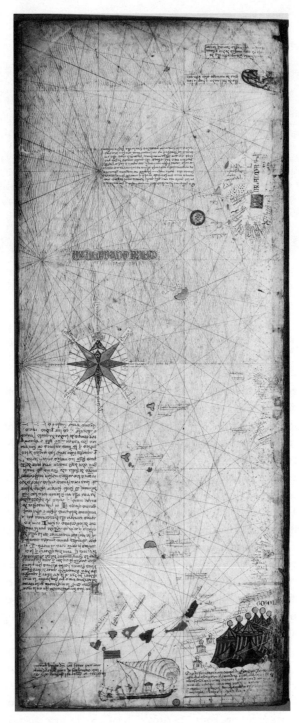

16 Abraham Cresques, detail from *Catalan World Atlas* (1374–6), showing Atlantic islands from the Canaries to Ireland. Bibliothèque Nationale de France, Paris.

and located, stringing out into the Atlantic (figure 16). A compass rose extends from the southwest corner of Lanzarote; from another such rose (northwest of this one) an inscription informs us that "The Fortunate Islands" are in the "great sea," bordering on the boundary of the west. Isidore of Seville, the map informs us, called these islands fortunate, since they abound in all commodities, grain, fruits, and trees.[6] Every inch of this colorful map, produced by a team, is extraordinarily playful, delighting in the diversity of humans and the places they choose to live in.

It is easy to see why, from Hesiod on, it was imagined that these islands of the extreme west would be dwelling places of the blessed, islands without seasons and hence beyond time. The Canaries, situated between 90 and 300 miles west of Saharan Africa, *are* in some senses without or beyond seasons, a place where the dew never falls; hence the winter trips to the island discovered by Genoan Lanzarotto Malocello, Lanzarote. In the Fortunate Islands, according to Pomponius Mela, fruits grow spontaneously, and there are two fountains (the stuff of much medieval and Renaissance myth), one of which enables the drinker to laugh himself to death.[7] Laughing drinkers abound on Tenerife today; many of them are English tourists, turning quickly pink on the white sands of the Playa de las Américas (specially flown in from Africa: Canarian beaches are, by nature, volcanic black).

Even the most egregious tourist experiences in the Canaries speak to a complex, deeply sedimented culture. At La Gomera, the Casa de Colón features miniature versions of Columbus' caravels[8] and a model of the Iglesia de la Virgen de la Asunción, a building begun in 1450, made entirely of sugar. At Santa Cruz de Tenerife you can drink at the Nelson café, named in honor of the naval hero whose right arm was blown off here in 1797, or buy fish at the market of Our Lady of Africa (figure 17): a vivid continuation of long-standing religious, commercial, and maritime experiences. Meanwhile, the bi-weekly English newspaper worries about suicide bombings in Morocco and tells of the decision to install Norwegian-built defensive missiles; Las Palmas is home to a squadron of F 18 fighter jets. In the first four months of 2003, state police at the Playa de las Américas deported 19 Senegalese, 12 Moroccans, 7 Romanians, 6 Nigerians (plus a few others from countries unnamed).[9]

At La Laguna, Tenerife's first major town, the Iglesia de la Concepción offers a beautifully intricate Gothic interior (figure 18), but no premodern refuge from contemporary complexities. At one end of the nave hangs a candelabra furnished by the Genoese merchants whose names are still found everywhere; at the other is a green-glazed font employed for baptizing *los Guanches* (the native people of Tenerife). By 1511, when building of the church began, there were few Guanche left to baptize; the great majority

17 Our Lady of Africa market, Santa Cruz de Tenerife. Photograph by David Wallace.

18 Iglesia de la Concepción, La Laguna, Tenerife. Photograph by David Wallace.

had either been enslaved or killed, resisting the Spanish.[10] It was the Canaries, famously, that Columbus chose as the point of departure for all four of his voyages to Cathay (or, as it turned out, the Americas): a fact which, as our epigraph suggests, has made them a site of prime importance in the African-American endeavor to recover the lost experience of the Middle Passage.[11] Before sailing west, however, the Genovese Colombo spent long years sailing and trafficking his way between the places featured in our first four chapters. As we shall see, by the time he set sail in 1492 *las Islas Canarias* had been complexly hymned, romanced, and chronicled in ways that would power-fully color his experience of islands further west.

The Humanist Atlantic

Giovanni Boccaccio is a figure of complex compound, mercantile, and intellectual authority: the son of a merchant, he trained under the Bardi as a merchant *discipulus* before toying with canon law (chiefly as a cover for reading much-loved Latin classics). While the first half of his career is taken up chiefly with works in Italian, culminating in the *Decameron*, the latter part sees him fall increasingly under the spell of Petrarch, authoring works of Latin encyclopedism, literary theory, and geography which were to prove vastly influential for more than three centuries. How would proto-humanists like Boccaccio and Petrarch react to news of classically attested, "re-found islands" ("isole ritrovate," as Boccaccio calls them) at the edge of the world? Boccaccio's account of the 1341 expedition to the Fortunate Islands, financed by King Alfonso IV of Portugal, develops a Latin humanist geography that never loses touch with its mercantile origins. As a former employee (like his father before him) of the Florentine Bardi company, Boccaccio was well placed to gather intelligence from merchant sources. Having procured access to the text between merchants that tells of the 1341 expedition (this has not survived), Boccaccio reworks it into his best humanist Latin and enters it into his literary compendium, the volume now known as the *Zibaldone Magliabechiano*.[12]

Boccaccio's account of the "Insulae Fortunatae" is a peculiar hybrid of rapacity and wonder, topography and the keeping of accounts. The expedi-tion, captained by a Genoese and crewed by Genoese, Florentines, Castilians, and other Spaniards, is clearly desperate to at least cover its costs. Boccaccio's account begins with accounting: the expedition brought back, he says, four men native to the islands, goatskins and sealskins, fish oil and fish fat, plus various materials that might work out as red dye (15–19). On the first, stony island (clearly on the Saharan side) they find an abundance of "goats and other beasts and naked men and women, savage in appearance and demeanor" ("capris et bestiis aliis atque nudis hominibus et mulieribus asperis cultu et ritu," 25); this careful marking of relative or absolute degrees of nakedness continues throughout. At the next island, known now as Gran Canaria, a large number of people are spotted. Almost all are naked ("fere nudi omnes," 30), but a few of the better sort wear goatskins dyed yellow and red. And now we have our first moment of cultural encounter, initiated by the islanders. The people on the island, Boccaccio says,

> instantly wished to communicate ["habere commertium"] with the people in the ship. But when the boats drew near the shore, the sailors, not understanding anything at all of what they said, did not dare to land. The natives' language, however, was polished enough and delivered Italian-fashion ["more ytalico"]. Some of the islanders, seeing nobody descending from the boats, then swam out; four of them were taken on board and afterwards carried away. But then, seeing nothing of use there ("nil ibi utilitatis"), the sailors move on. (35–41)

At the next island 25 sailors land and confront 30 men, "nudi omnes" (46), who run off through fear of their weaponry. The sailors, finding handsome houses, smash down the doors with stones (ignoring the cries of the householders). Nothing much of use or interest is found: just dried figs, high quality grain, and (in what appears to be an *oratorium* or temple) the stone statue of a man, naked but wearing a palm-leaf apron to shield his "obscena," holding a ball in his hand; this statue is shipped off to Lisbon (51–61).

This island-by-island account includes notices of fruits, trees, and remarkable geographical features, most notably the mysterious mountain on Tenerife (Teide, figure 19, the greatest volcano known to Europeans before 1778).[13] Boccaccio shapes the account to conclude by reiterating the point that these are not rich islands[14] and that the expenses of the expedition were barely covered. It is at this precise point that the account suddenly returns us to the four native swimmers: they are young, beardless, and of graceful countenance; they go about naked. They do, however, wear aprons of rushes or palm – covering all signs of puberty and obscenity, front and rear – which cannot be raised by puffs of wind or other causes (105–10). They are, moreover, uncircumcised and have long, almost navel-length fair hair (which also covers them); they go about barefoot. Physically, they are no bigger than us; they are decently proportioned, bold and strong and of considerable intelligence; they sing sweetly, dance like Frenchmen ("more gallico"), smile readily, and are more domestic-minded ("domestici," 119) than are many from Spain. And at this point the account blossoms into pure Golden Ageism. Once in the ship, these men ate figs and bread (which they seemed to like, tasting it for the first time): but they refused wine and drank only water. Gold and silver coins meant nothing to them; nor did spices ("aromata") of any kind, golden jewels, or swords. But they were seen to be of extraordinary faithfulness and judiciousness ("fidei et legalitatis," 129), for if one were given anything to eat he would divide it into equal portions to share with everyone else. At last, it seems, we are connecting with the ancient literary

19 Mount Teide, Tenerife. Photograph by David Wallace.

canons of the Insulae Fortunatae. But we are also queasily aware of another textual tradition at work here, that of those slaving deeds of sale considered in the previous chapter, with their careful observation of physical virtues and identifying traits (such as circumcision). These handsome boys, so full of domestic sense and natural virtue (and so lacking in avaricious instincts) will fetch a good price in Lisbon.

The very end of this extraordinary Boccaccian text features a supposed transcription of the islanders' number system, from 1 to 16 (10, 11, 12: "marava, vait marava, smatta marava . . ."). This Boccaccio must have dreamed up himself; he loved such listings, and opened one of his *zibaldoni* with various alphabets. But the penultimate paragraph also features perennial preoccupations: these people marry, Boccaccio says, and the married women wear aprons like the men. Young virgins, however, go about quite naked, without any sense of shame (132–4). Elsewhere, in his vernacular fiction, Boccaccio seems all in favor of nakedness. Here, however, it may additionally be read as inviting enslavement, for to be naked without shame is to be ignorant of the Fall, hence beyond the framework of Christian redemption.

In his *Esposizioni* or Dante lectures of 1373 (the year of Chaucer's visit to Florence), the now ageing Boccaccio fulminates happily in his Paolo and Francesca section against the foppish and lust-driven youth of today, especially their fondness for growing their hair long, "in forma barbarica," and for short tunics and bulging codpieces.[15] And suddenly his mind runs back more than 25 years to the Fortunate Islanders. Indians and Ethiopians, he says, take care to cover their privates, even though they live in excessive heat, but Indians and Ethiopians "have in them some humanity and sense of custom" ("hanno in sé alcuna umanità e costume," 36). "Those people who inhabit the re-found islands," however, "people one can describe as living beyond the circuit of the earth," possess "no form of speech, nor art, nor any kind of custom" conforming to the ways of "those who live civilly" ("civilmente vivono," 37). Boccaccio's immediate, polemical point is that even these folks cover their loins; but of greater moment here is the revisionary classicism of his account of the Canarians, this people beyond the pale of humanity and civility. Boccaccio's classicism hardens as he ventriloquizes the youth of Florence to say: "we are following the usage of other nations: this is how the English, the Germans, the French, and the Provençals carry on" (40). Boccaccio can thus provoke himself into fierce reminiscence of the days (before current effeminization) when such peoples "were our tributaries, our vassals, our slaves"; barbarous peoples who knew or could know nothing unless first taught by Italians ("Italiani," 41).

It is no accident that the English are here mentioned first as a nation of, if not quite beyond, the pale. Petrarch, in the geographical survey of his *De vita solitaria*, Book II, admits that the Fortunate Islanders enjoy a solitude exceeding that of almost all mortals, but since they are but beast-like keepers of beasts, and their solitude is natural rather than willfully chosen, this hardly counts.[16] Second in westward remoteness only to these islanders, according to Petrarch, are the Irish: a people with no interest in riches, politics, or agriculture, delighting only in *otium* and the enjoyment of *libertas*. "I'd call them a happy people," Petrarch continues, "were it not for another shameful and animalistic habit (if true)." The *infamia* and *malignitas morum* to which Petrarch alludes here derives from Strabo's account of Iernê, Ireland, which speaks of cannibalism, incest, and incestuous cannibalism.[17]

The extent to which European humanist attitudes toward western Atlantic settlements are essayed as early as the fourteenth century, and in ways that will endure, is remarkable (and so too, we see again, are the knock-on representational effects for Ireland). As proof of this we might run forward to 1494: that is, two years after Cristoforo Colombo, yet another seafaring son of Genoa in foreign employ,[18] had launched himself westward from the Canaries. It was in early October 1494 that the Nuremberg humanist, Hieronymus Münzer, encountered Canarians – men, women, and children – for sale in the slave market at Valencia.[19] The peoples of the islands had fought hard and very long against invasion and conquest: Gran Canaria was not officially conquered until 1483; Las Palmas and Tenerife held out until 1496.[20] Münzer uses the fact of Canarian rebellion against the King of Spain, their rightful overlord, as one justification for enslavement (p. 23); but his further reasoning adheres remarkably closely to templates laid down by slaving deeds and by Boccaccio more than a century before. The women are well-formed, he says, strong and long-limbed; but they are beasts (he says, in a rapid transition) in morals, since they live under no law ("sub nulla lege," p. 24). Living under law is then directly equated with living under clothes. The victorious King of Spain gives them a bishop and has a church built; and they are ready to take on our religion.[21] Before they were naked; now they wear clothes like us: "O quid facit doctrina et dilgencia, que bestias in humano corpore facit homines et mansuetos!"

Münzer, like Boccaccio, was a humanist of mercantile pedigree. A member of the Nuremberg humanist circle, he spent much of his share of profits in the family firm (run by his brother) on the latest humanist editions, procured by mercantile contacts, as they rolled from Italian presses. In 1483, some 11 years before the journey through Spain, he descended on Italy, toured classical and religious sites, and bought books. One of these was the

1481 Bottonus edition of Boccaccio's *Geneologiae Deorum Gentilium*, "bought by me at Milan when returning from Rome" (the inscription proudly proclaims) "and brought back by me to Nuremberg."[22] This volume also contains Boccaccio's geographical encyclopedia, *De montibus, silvis, fontibus, lacubus, fluminibus . . . maribus* (etc.). Münzer, like Boccaccio, was dedicated to mapping the world; in 1493 he got his chance as cartographer to the *Nuremberg Chronicle*.[23] Perhaps it is not so surprising, then, that in traveling through Spain the following year, his view of things shows strong Boccaccian filtration. The important point here is not literary influence, but rather how the compounding of cultural and commercial in Boccaccian humanism so suits it for catch-up migration to Nuremberg and points north.

Shortly after seeing the Canarians in Valencia (and describing local fruits and vegetation), Münzer turns his attention to "los marranos," "baptized Jews," he says, "or the children of baptized Jews who publicly confess the Christian faith while secretly living according to the Jewish rite" (p. 28). It is precisely at this period that young Jews, mostly girls, begin showing up in slave markets, some sold young by panicked parents.[24] E. P. Goldschmidt, from whom almost all my knowledge of Münzer derives, writes some spirited pages about what else Münzer might have seen in Valencia in 1494: garments taken from over a thousand "verbrannter" Jews, for example, decorating the walls of a church.[25] Goldschmidt, who actually discovered and catalogued Münzer's library, wrote this in German in a volume printed at Vienna in 1938.[26]

Such paradigms of a commercially minded Latin humanism, consolidated from Boccaccio to Münzer, offer powerfully predeterminative indications of how Europeans will come to represent and engage with the flora, fauna, and human beings of a New, or even a newer, World; it would not be difficult to extend such an authorial sequence into the sixteenth century. To do this, however, would be to drastically streamline and simplify the complex place from which the Genoan Columbus sets out. There are other discourses of and designs upon the Canaries at work in this period (some of them very "old world"); and there is also the challenge to retrieve some notion of a native viewpoint. This last consideration will rehearse, once again, issues attending the study of American encounters.

Norman Conquest and the Canarian Invasion of England

Following their discovery or rediscovery by Genoans, the Canaries were subjected to a series of attempted conquests, the most remarkable being that of Jean de Béthencourt, a Norman nobleman whose native patrimony was threatened by English incursions, and Gadifer de La Salle. This odd couple are adventurers every bit as extravagant and fanciful as those who, several generations later, were to head out further into the Atlantic. Béthencourt, whose name today lives on all over the Canaries, seems to have seen himself as a latter-day William the Conqueror; Gadifer, like other members of the La Salle family, bears a name from chivalric fiction and (like Chaucer's fictional knight) crusaded with other Christian "nacions in Pruce" (Prussia, 1.53). The two men first headed south as part of an expedition against the port of Al-Mahdiya, Barbary, organized by the Genoese in 1390; for two months they sat with French and English troops before the city considered by Froissart to be "an African Calais."[27] On May 1, 1402, they sailed for the Canaries, armed with a crusading indulgence from the captive pope Benedict XIII. As the English had repeopled Calais, Béthencourt – as told by the remarkable romancing chronicle *Le Canarien* – expelled the natives of Lanzarote, Fuerteventura, and Hierro, and moved in his own settler peasantry in what has been termed "the last Norman conquest of all."[28]

Le Canarien survives in two single-columned manuscripts.[29] The older one, now British Library, MS Egerton 2709, formed part of the duke of Burgundy's library by 1420 and favors Gadifer de La Salle (who is pictured in figure 20, sailing with his invading army under his personal sign of the Virgin). The second, Bibliothèque Municipale de Rouen, MS mm 129, retells the story in ways more flattering to Béthencourt (as ordered by his descendants, some 70 years later); it features 85 pen-drawn miniatures, beginning with two loin-clothed Canarians supporting the lion sable rampant of Béthencourt (folio 1v: looking forward to the armorial bearings of Elizabethan slaver, Sir John Hawkins).[30] As Jennifer Goodman suggests, these variant versions develop fantastical and magical elements of romance (especially those featuring islands) and the familiar themes of friendship and friendship betrayed.[31] But *Le Canarien* is much closer to Froissart than it is, say, to Mandeville's hallucinatory, armchair *Travels*; its narratives gloss very specific processes of colonization and resistance. Rebellious artisans, peasants, and *nativi* are killed by the thousand (without authorial compunction, and often as mere background to greater aristocratic themes) in Froissart; here too, the *Chroniques* form a strong precedent for the Canarian text.

The romance and chivalric elements of *Le Canarien* are not added *to* the historical business of conquering and colonizing islands; they represent modalities through which such business was conceived and executed. Chilling details, suggesting strange conjunctions of chivalry and slaving, need not be dismissed as pure fiction. Gadifer, for example, applies chivalric expertise

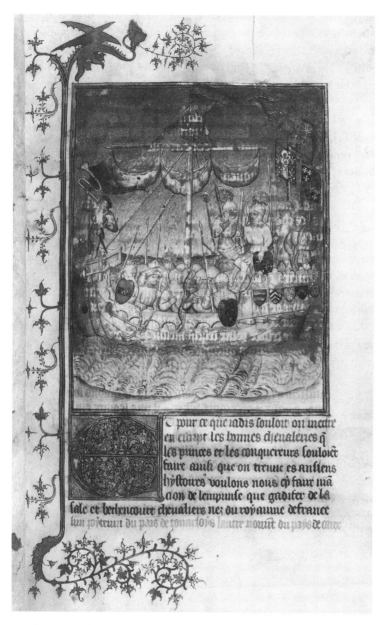

20 Crusade against the Canaries, from *Le Canarien*, British Library, MS Egerton 2709, folio 2r.

to hunting down first animal, then human, island-dwellers: first seals, then Canarians. He employs natives for translation duties and for perpetrating some of the more brutal acts of revenge. Much of this squares with accounts of Portuguese exploits in the islands in the 1440s (as the half-English Henry "the Navigator" attempted to winkle Jean de Béthencourt's Castilian descendants from their stronghold of Lanzarote).[32] People of "les isles de Canarie" were, as the Egerton *Canarien* observes, "de diverses loys et de divers langages" (folio 1v); Gomerans, as the *Crónica dos Feitos na Conquista de Guiné* notes, could be recruited to fight against the islanders of La Palma.[33] Premodern Europeans identify diversity only to exploit it, but in a sense, they know more than we do, for "the Canaries" were never a unified cultural space – a single place – for the original inhabitants of the islands (who had forgotten or never learned the art of sailing).

Quite how Canary islanders got to their islands, and from where, has long been a mystery. Early accounts often emphasize the fairness of their skin: a factor that, as *Le Canarien* observes, need not be viewed positively if one remembers how Jews are (for their sins) "descoulerez."[34] In the sale books of the Portuguese, however, Canarians are straightforwardly lumped together with slaves from West Africa and termed "Moors" and "Mooreses." Thus it is not entirely surprising that, in the Catalan romance *Tirant lo Blanc*, the Moorish invasion of England is led by the King of Canary:

Seguí's aprés que lo gran rei de Canària, jove fortíssim, ab la viril inquieta joventut de nobles esperances guarnida, sempre aspirant a honorosa victòria, féu gran estol de naus e de galeres, e passà a la nobla illa d'Anglaterra ab gran multitud de gents. Per ço com algunes fustes de corsaris havien robat un lloc seu, pres en si molt gran ira; e inflamat de gran supèrbia perquè algú havia tengut gosar d'enujar-lo, ab molt gran armada partí de la seua terra, e navegant ab pròsper vent arribà en les fèrtils e pacîfiques ribes d'Anglaterra, e en l'escura nit tot lo replegat estol entrà dins lo port d'Antona, e ab gran astúcia desembarcaren, en tota la morisma isqué en terra, sens que per los de l'illa no foren sentits.

It came about that the King of Canary, a virile and restless youth beset by noble aspirations, now ambitious as ever for glorious victory, assembled a large fleet of ships and galleys, and set sail for England with a huge force of men; and because some English corsairs had raided a site belonging to him. In a rage of wounded pride that someone had had the audacity to cross him in this way, he arrived speedily at the fertile and peaceful English shore. The fleet touched at the port of Southampton in the dark of night, and with great cunning all the Moors disembarked, unnoticed by the English.[35]

Published in 1490 and acclaimed by *Don Quixote* as "el mejor libro del mundo," *Tirant lo Blanc* would seem to take a remote and fantastical view of England: an island as exotic to romance imagining, perhaps, as *las Canarias*.[36] Its principal author, however, had actually spent time in England and was inspired by the texts he found there (particularly by the Anglo-Norman romance, *Guy of Warwick*). Born near Valencia in 1413 or 1414, Joanot Martorell issued a *requesta de batalla a ultrança* in 1437 against a fellow knight who had fooled with the affections of his sister; by the following spring he was in London, hoping that "the lord King of England and France," Henry VI, would help press his case for single combat to the death. Amazingly, the Lancastrian king complied and wrote to the Aragonese court.[37] Martorell thus moves within a multilingual but well-defined aristocratic European nexus; his fantastical romance, which sees the English saved from invading Moorish Canarians by the hermit king William of Warwick, trades in common European currency. Abraham Cresques's map depicting the Canaries, it is worth noticing, shows islands all the way up the Atlantic to England, Ireland, and the Orkneys as one continuous space.[38] And English "corsairs" did attempt to raid and invade Canarian sites throughout this premodern period. A pen drawing from the extraordinary cache of materials known as British Library, Cotton Augustus I.ii (figure 21) shows English men of war with designs on Lanzarote. As in the Rouen MS of *Le Canarien*, "Lancerotto" is seen as an island fortress; strange combinings of Edenic, Golden Age, and military scenes play out beneath its walls.

Given such powerful European overlays of these Atlantic island cultures, and given the extinction of the peoples themselves, it is difficult to know how to speak of or remember the Guanche and other Canarians. Many of their names, as with the "Tartars" in the last chapter, appear only as they vanish from sight (in deeds of sale). A slave arriving in eastern Iberia as Atturchayayne will soon be given a new "Christian name"; Isabel and Catalina, Fernando, and Juan (royal names) prove particularly popular.[39] *Meneceyatos* or local territories survive as modern place names, such as Tegueste, Tacaronte, and Güímar; it is possible to imagine islanders tending goats in these places (before and after conquest) or sugarcane (after it). Eventually, we resort to a museum such as (the best of its kind) the Museo Canario at Las Palmas de Gran Canaria. Here we may see remains of leatherworking, practiced across the archipelago: there are clothes, shoes, funeral shrouds, and even (somehow the most memorable) a glove. There are palm skirts worn by men (as noted by Boccaccio), hand mills, shell necklaces, needles, *pintaderas* (for making marks on skin), and *los ídolos*: humanoid figures, perhaps of the type carried off to Lisbon in 1341. And there are

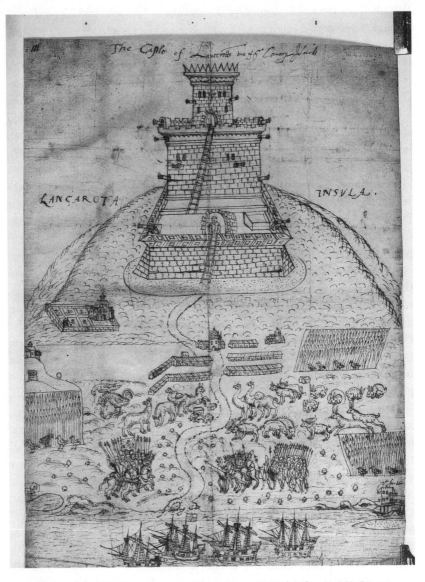

21 British warships before the castle of Lanzarote, British Library, MS Cotton Augustus I.ii.

scientific analyses of blood groups that strongly connect the ancient Canarians with Berber peoples (whose distinctive cultures have been similarly buried or overlaid by powerfully invasive cultures).[40] In the bookstore we find an exhibition catalogue dedicated to the scientific art of mummy analysis; the first photograph shows a mummified Canarian, now in Cambridge, England, taken from one of the islands (it is not known which one) by a Captain Young of his Majesty's sloop *Weesel* in 1722.[41]

Seeing Guanche mummies subjected to radiographical analysis helps little (at least for me) in understanding Guanches; the persistent application of the term "Stone Age" to these peoples, similarly, only widens the distance between them and us (and also, of course, from premodern encounters). But things are about to get much worse as we climb to the second floor of the Museo, for here we find, without warning, hundreds of Guanche skulls in glass cases. Neatly arranged in groups of three, the skulls rise from the floor in eleven lines of shelving; on top of these giant bookcases, just below the ceiling, is a row of white plaster, reconstructed heads (looking rather like classical busts); four full skeletons hang in one corner. One imagines a full-scale riot breaking out if something similar were discovered at the Smithsonian or in Australia; here, there are no descendants to reclaim ancestral remains.[42] But here again, such reactions may be missing something: it is quite a common sight (a friend from Lisbon tells me) to find skulls conserved in this way in Iberian churches.

More certain evidence of Guanche cultural practices framed by Catholic forms of display may be found on Tenerife, at the Basílica de Nuestra Señora de Candelaria. At some point in their pre-Catholic history (the Dominican Alonso de Espinosa estimates ca. 1400), Guanches found an image of a mother and child washed up on the eastern coast; it was placed in the cave of *mencey* Chinguaro at Güímar (site of the famous and mysterious pyramids). Catholic missionaries, on discovering Guanches already worshiping an image of the Virgin and Child, grasped their God-given opportunity "to begin the enlightenment of this fortunate people." A powerful cult of Our Lady of Candelaria soon formed, grew in intensity, and spread to Latin America (the Dominican de Espinosa first hearing about it in Guatamala).[43] Lope de Vega, prolific playwright of the Spanish Golden Age, drew upon much prior legendary and poetic material to fashion his *Comedia la Famosa de los guanches de Tenerife y Conquista de Canaria*; his third and final act opens with the discovery of the Virgin "con una candela en la mano," holding her son.[44] Perhaps the most impressive final act of this drama, however, came in 1826, when a tidal wave washed the image of the Virgin back out to sea. Today a simulacrum of the Virgin is worshiped in a fine new basilica (figure 22); a

22 Basilica of Our Lady of Candelaria, Tenerife, with statues of Guanche warriors. Photograph by David Wallace.

line of larger-than-life Guanche warrior statues stands by the margin of the black-beached ocean that delivered and then took back the mysterious image. This motif of the sea perpetually containing, occasionally returning, human treasures and travails resonates sympathetically with island legends and poetries still developing further out in the Atlantic. Then again, the Canarian statue also recalls the image of the Virgin found beached at Boulogne-sur-Mer and worshiped by Edward II, Henry VIII, and Chaucer's Wife of Bath; this, too, has disappeared.[45]

Old World Columbus

"We are all the direct descendants of Columbus," Tzvetan Todorov has written, "it is with him that our geneaology begins, insofar as the word *beginning* has a meaning."[46] Columbus, I would suggest, might better be seen as a figure of "our" genealogical middle: a man coming to cultural and commercial consciousness in the particular places and sea-lanes traced in this book. He sailed west from the Canaries not as Renaissance humanist or "new man," but rather as the son and grandson of wool-weavers, who had studied Latin and arithmetic at the traditional Genoese schools before training as an international merchant.[47] Rather than running directly forward to narratives of New World discovery, then, we should first connect Columbus to Old World practices in Old World places. We might then more fully grasp what carries over, in every sense, to his first sighting of the Orinoco River in 1498: a sighting to be shared, just over 150 years later, by the Englishwoman Aphra Behn.[48] What Behn and Columbus see are the same natural features and very different places: Columbus thought he was seeing the rivers of Paradise; Behn, in some respects just as extravagant in her imaginings, did not.

Chaucer's Mediterranean, as represented by his *Man of Law's Tale*, would seem to be profoundly pre-Columbian in every sense. And his solitary, God-fearing Custance, floating her way across and out of the *Grete See*, would hardly seem to cross paths (in any sense) with the solitary slave Costanza who, in 1400, sailed into and across the Mediterranean in a ship otherwise filled with sacks of wool.[49] Yet we notice, in Chaucer's narrative, that there would be no narrative at all without the crucial intervention, early on, of Syrian "chapmen" (2.135). These merchants, said to be "sad and trewe" (135), are valued both for the rare commodities that they carry from place to place – "spicerye" (136, a term covering a range of oriental goods), gold cloths, and richly colored satins – and for their intelligence gathering: a canny ruler, like the Sultan of Syria, will

Make hem good chiere, and busily espye
Tidynges of sundry regnes, for to leere   *learn*
The wonders that they myghte seen or here.
                                    (2.180–2)

The Syrian merchants, for their part, grasp both that they are esteemed and valued at all ports of call, from Syria to Rome, and that their predicament is precarious. If they are to escape the "heigh vengeance" (963) visited on Syrians by Romans at the end of the tale, they must perform that most characteristic of merchant-like acts, namely, disappear.[50] Genoans, as we have seen, were both revered and reviled for their prowess at sea, their daring, their commercial acumen; they are "white Moors" (in Howley's phrase) and more Jewish than the Jews. The hapless Genoan Janus Imperiale, murdered at London in 1379, thus travels the total Syrian trajectory of the *Man of Law's Tale*, from royal welcome to death in the street.[51]

A century later, and for 15 years preceding his first journey into the westward unknown, Columbus moved within those European trading networks – north, south, east, and west – that his Genoese ancestors had plied for hundreds of years. Eastward movement was becoming increasingly difficult for the Genoese; their last trading post in the Black Sea, Caffa, was captured by Ottoman Turks in the summer of 1475. At that time, Columbus was very likely on Chios, an island in the eastern Mediterranean where a Genoese consortium controlled all trade and shipping (and where domestic slavery had long been commonplace).[52] In August 1476, he sailed westward through the Pillars of Hercules before heading north for England. Having been sunk off the coast of Portugal by French pirates, Columbus and his fellow survivors were picked up on September 12 by a new fleet from Genoa (financed by Genoese merchants in London) to complete their journey. While wintering in the north, Columbus sailed to Ireland (very likely from Bristol) and possibly Iceland. A marginal annotation in his personal copy of the *Cosmographia . . . in Asiæ et Europæ . . . Descriptione* by Enea Silvio Piccolomini (Pope Pius II) records having seen "men of Cathay" washed up in Galway (perhaps Inuit Eskimos driven east by Atlantic storms).[53] Columbus continued to look west as a way of getting back east, the direction in which the Genoese had traveled with most profit since the time of Chaucer.

By the autumn of 1477, Columbus was back in Lisbon, and here, for the next decade, he became involved with the commodity that (like the late medieval Genoese) was tracking steadily across, and then beyond, the Mediterranean from east to west, namely, sugar. Cultivated along the eastern Mediterranean coast of Syria by Arabs as early as the seventh century CE, sugar plantations migrated west to Cyprus, Crete, Sicily, and, during the fourteenth and fifteenth centuries, reached their maximal extension in Portugal and southern Spain. By 1465, Madeiran sugar was available in London; the densely wooded and uninhabited islands had been cleared, and slaves from the Canaries and West Africa were working the plantations. Columbus traveled to Madeira in 1478 and 1479, and became an expert advocate of its prize commodity: "sugar syrup from Madeira," he declared, "is the best and most healthful sustenance in the world."[54] Following his marriage to Felipa Moniz y Perestrelo in 1479, Columbus acquired Portuguese citizenship and was thus able to participate in the Lisbon-based trading triangle that brought West African and Canarian slaves to Madeira and Madeiran sugar to the Mediterranean and northern Europe; he sailed one or more times to Guinea, the Portuguese name for that segment of the West African coast where, at São Jorge da Mina, they were building a fortified slaving colony.

Columbus and the New Canaries: 1341 Revisited

Following his transfer of business operations from Portugal to Spain late in 1485, Columbus was to set out on all four of his transatlantic voyages from Spain's first major Atlantic colony: the Canary Islands. The Gothic church of the Assumption on Gomera, first built in 1490, is still honored as the place where Columbus sought divine approval for the journey ahead.[55] Béthencourt failed in his ambition to invade, conquer, and colonize the more lush and populous Canaries lying further west. This was only achieved by the Spanish many decades later: conquistadors put down the last native uprising in 1489 (just three years before Columbus' arrival) and sugar plantations continued their westward march.[56] On his second voyage, Columbus (by royal command) duly brought along 20 experts in the cultivation of seeds and plants. Sugar-cane seeds collected at Gomera were thus planted at La Isabela on the north coast of Hispaniola (La Española, now divided between Haiti and the Dominican Republic). Although the Europeans left behind to tend the sugar canes sickened and died, the canes themselves grew prodigiously.[57] Thus in these first transatlantic steps, from the Canaries to the Caribbean islands, Columbus and company led where the Dutch and English would eagerly follow. But there is little sense here of discovering and acclaiming a New World, more a continuation of a long-established westward movement in search of more efficient growing conditions for Old World addictions.[58]

Before heading out on his first journey westward in 1492, Columbus spent a month at Gran Canaria and Gomera, effecting repairs to his frail fleet of three ships; Teide on Tenerife was observed in a volcanic state. Having left Gomera on September 6, the fleet was becalmed for three days in view of the Canaries; when the islands finally passed out of sight, many of the 87 crewmen wept.[59] Four weeks later, in his first encounter with the natives of Guanahani (renamed San Salvador), Columbus' mind ran back to the Canarian natives:

> All of them go around as naked [todos desnudos] as their mothers bore them; and the women also . . . Some of them paint themselves with black, and they are the color of the Canarians, neither black nor white [ni negros ni blancos].[60]

The next entry in Columbus' *Diario*, dated two days later, meditates further on the resemblance between these two sets of natives, the inhabitants of Guanahani and the Canarians:

> As soon as it dawned, many of these people came to the beach – all young as I have said, and all of good stature – very handsome people, with hair not curly but straight and coarse, like horsehair; and all of them very wide in the forehead and head, more so than any other race [generaçion] that I have seen so far. And their eyes are very handsome and not small; and none of them are black, but the color of the Canary Islanders [dla color dlos canaries]. Nor should anything else be expected since this island is on an east–west line [so vna linea] with the island of Hierro in the Canaries.[61]

Columbus here evaluates the natives with the same mix of rapacity and wonder, appreciation and mercantile calculation, that we witnessed in the Genoan encounter with Canarians in 1341. The unselfconscious nakedness of the islanders confirms ignorance of post-lapsarian salvation history; their youth, beauty, and physical stature, on full view, are to be admired both for their own sake and for their salability in European slave markets. And the concerted attempt at racial profiling perpetuates an ingrained Genoan habit now centuries old: non-blackness (corroborated by non-curly hair) augments value; so too, perhaps, the eyes that were "not small" (Columbus, thinking himself approaching the continent of Cathay, might have been expecting a different look).

Boccaccio, as we have seen, sought to monumentalize the discovery or "refinding" of the Canary Islands by translating the first-hand vernacular account of the Genoan expedition into humanist Latin. This process may be seen repeating itself in the *Epistola de insulis nuper inventis*, "translated from the Spanish tongue into Latin on May 29 1493," in which "the islands of India beyond the Ganges" are announced to the world. This text very soon inspired another vernacular version in the shape of an Italian poem in *ottava rima* by the Florentine poet Giuliano Dati.[62] The *explicit* to the poem's Florentine edition of Lorenzo Morgiani and Johannes Petri, dated October 26, 1493, speaks "of the discovery of the new Canary islands of the Indies" ("della inventione delle nuove isole di canaria indiane"). This designation of what we now know as Caribbean territories as "new Canary islands" suggests that for Florentines in 1493, these new Genoan discoveries represent variants of what Genoans have found before: not a surprising conclusion since, as we have just seen Columbus himself remark, the Canaries and these new islands lie on roughly the same line of latitude. Comparison of these three texts sees the imaginative and descriptive templates of 1341 enduring remarkably well; indeed, if we wished to press the case, it might be argued that Boccaccio's earlier account adheres more closely to supposed Renaissance humanist paradigms than do either of its successors.

The *Epistola de insulis nuper inventis*, translated by the noble and learned ("nobilis ac litteratus") Aliander de Cosco, remains in touch with the imagery and troping associated with the *insulae fortunatae* tradition without ever showing Boccaccian humanist classicist excitement at *inventio* (or *reinventio*: the discovery of what our reading of the ancients leads us to expect). There are, to be sure, moments of physical description evocative of Golden Age or earthly paradisiacal paradigms; there is, for example,

> a vast variety of trees which lick the stars and which never, I believe, lose their leaves, for I saw them as green and lovely as they are in May in Spain. Some of them were in flower, others carried fruit . . . Nightingales [garriebat philomena] and innumerable other birds of various sorts were chattering away in November, the time I was making my way through those parts. (p. 50)

But such poetic flight soon modulates to more practical topographical evaluation: Hispaniola, containing "fertile fields very suitable [aptissimi] for planting, pasture, or putting up buildings," plainly invites colonization (p. 50). As in the Trecento text, there is steady comparison between the naked and the clothed: the islanders, we are told, have never before seen "gentes vestitas." Communitarian instincts are also remarked: the willingness to share everything, especially food; the lack of any sense of private property ("bona propria"). Such qualities, celebrated as prehistorically European in poems such as Chaucer's *The Former Age*, here supply further arguments for colonial occupation. Lacking any sense of private property, these people have no sense that they themselves, or their territory, could be considered objects of desire. Hispaniola, we are told, is greatly to be coveted ("affectanda") and, once possessed ("affectata"), not to be given up. These people are amiable ("amabiles"), benevolent, benign; and (a sudden declaration this, as attention switches to slaving values) they are not black, like Ethiops ("nec sunt nigri velut ethiopes").

This fifteenth-century Genoan, like his fourteenth-century predecessors, is perennially aware that his patron expects to profit from his voyaging; thus his bottom line:

> Finally, to sum up in a few words the profit to be had from our expedition and speedy return, I undertake that I shall give our invincible Majesties as much gold as they have need of, as much spice, cotton and gum mastic [otherwise found only on Chios], as much aloe wood, as many pagan slaves as their majesties could wish [quantum eorum maiestas voluerit erigere]. (p. 54)

But below this bottom line, Columbus adds one more precious commodity, namely his own narrative, for things written or told about these islands before this time, he insists, are nothing but "ambages" and conjectures, the stuff of "fibula."[63] As a lifelong merchant, Columbus knows – as the Syrian merchants plying the Mediterranean in Chaucer's *Man of Law's Tale* know – that bearers of eyewitness intelligence are much in demand. The gold he claims to have found is not as plentiful as he claims, but the few natives he has violently seized ("violenter arripui") will, like the Canarians sent to Lisbon in 1341, prove a living pledge of the precious commodity of labor. And notice of his exploits – he speaks briefly of tailed natives and of cannibal males who mate with Amazon-like archer women – will surely render him *affectandus* and *affectatus*, much to be desired and not to be given up.

Of course, one crucial technological advance helped ensure that the 1492/3 expedition became rapidly famous, whereas word of the 1341 outing continued to languish in a literary scrapbook. Within months, Rome, Paris, Antwerp, and Basel each had their own printed editions of the Colombian *Epistola*.[64] It remains the case, however, that the *Epistola*'s content and literary modality remain comparable with, if not in some respects (strange to say) culturally anterior to, the Boccaccian text; and remarkably, the Italian poem by Giuliano Dati deriving from it, announcing discovery of "the new Canary islands of the Indies," slides further back in time, as far back, in fact, as the popular, piazza-singing *cantare* tradition from which Boccaccio fashioned his *Filostrato* and *Teseida* in the 1330s and 1340s. It is striking how easily the Colombian missive accommodates to the tropes and oral formulae of this narrative genre (which is an Italian cousin to the English tradition of popular romance).[65] The notion of a landscape of perennial blooming (the May in November passage quoted above) is, of course, a staple of romance and so easily adapted (stanza 32), although sparrows as well as nightingales are heard in the Italian version (31.5). News of fabulous abundance of precious metals, spices, and delicacies (such as rhubarb) is also a staple of the genre:

> De reubarbaro ce tanta abondantia
> e di cenamo [e] d'altra spetieria;
> l'oro e l'argento e 'l metallo ci avanza.
>
> *(33.1–3)*

> There is great abundance of rhubarb
> and of cinnamon of other spices;
> gold, silver, and metals are there in plenty.

News of nudity, and of encounters between the naked and the clothed, are teased out at some length (21–3); the "gente villana" of cannibals prove predictably popular (59–61), and the archer women they mate with are now accorded an island of their own as a fully independent nation ("questo popol tucto feminino," 61.5). Here again, these islands of the far west meet narrative expectations associated with the far east, in this case the fabulous Scythian Amazons. For it is, above all, a taste for thrilling spectacle that the poem rises to meet. These "women who do no women's work," it says, "really are a sight to behold [una grande fantasia] as they draw back their bows" (61.6–8). Craving for news, *novelle* (the basic units of the *Decameron*'s narration), *tidynges* (the equivalent Chaucerian term, featured over 20 times in *The House of Fame*) is an effect that poets of this long period both stimulate and satisfy; elaboration and embroidery of sources may be needed to retain the attention of sitters or bystanders ("circumstanti," as Dati calls them towards the end, 67.1).

Colombo's *inventiones*, then, are *buone novelle* for all levels of literary narration. Of course, there can be no confusing the kind of *ottave rime* written by Giuliano Dati with those later developed by Tasso and Ariosto. Dati was a priest (perhaps once married) who wrote a whole series of works for popular consumption (including one of the earliest accounts of the flying house of Loreto).[66] There was good precedent for professional religious taking up *cantare* narrative in this way: at least three of Catherine of Siena's male followers resorted to this medium.[67] Dati worked fast: his poem was published four days before the papal audience of June 19, 1493, in which the Spanish pope, Alexander VI, gave the Spanish monarchy legal title to the newly discovered islands. He was not (despite later claims) giving Spain custody of a New World (nobody in 1493 realizing that a new continent had been sighted), but rather applying the framework established by two bulls of 1091 (*Cum universae insulae; Cum omnes insulae*) that had awarded Ireland to

Henry II of England in 1155 and the Canaries to Don Luis de la Cerda of Castile in 1344.[68] The first 13 stanzas of Dati's poem are thus dedicated chiefly (with an aside on Ferdinand's prowess in torturing Marranos, 10.6–8) to the titles, territories, and lordships of the Spanish monarchy. Columbus, recast as a courtier, is sent smilingly on his way by Ferdinand; he claims at the end not to have discovered a New World, but simply to have extended the king's list of territories ("i' ho cresciuto . . . il vostro regno," 64.3). This impression is confirmed by the frontispiece to the 1493 Florentine edition (figure 23). Here, under the heading "The letter about the islands recently

23 Frontispiece to Giuliano Dati, *La lettera delle isole che ha trovato il re di Spagna* (Florence, 1493). British Library, London.

discovered by the King of Spain," Ferdinand points Columbus and company across a narrow channel (the Atlantic has already shrunk) toward one more island containing one more set of new and naked subjects.

Varieties of Atlantic Space

Another frontispiece or title page, this time dating from 1621 (figure 24), is also keen to shrink distances and emphasize continuities between eastern and western sides of the Atlantic world.[69] The book to follow tells of Columbus' adventures in the New World (now recognized as such) and of Catholic missionaries who followed in his train. The author, a Benedictine monk from the abbey of Seidenstetten in Lower Austria, delights in detailing flora, fauna, and popular customs (including a transcribed song, both words and music, to accompany a Caribbean dance). His narrative of discovery begins with an account of Columbus, which runs for just over ten pages before reaching "Insulas Fortunatas sive Canarias"; attention then shifts to the British abbot, Saint Brendan, "In Brittania S. Brandani Abbatis" (p. 12), the figure featured on the left of the title page (figure 24). We hear and indeed see (figure 25) how Brendan crosses the ocean with 14 monks and comes to the Canaries; how Brendan and Maclovius celebrate mass on the back of a whale; how they perform great works converting Canarians; how a Christ in the form of a young adolescent guides them to an island that some think to be in the Americas. And how, as the Venerable Bede relates, islands in the British seas used to contain thousands of holy monks and priests – Scots, English, and Irish – where now stinking Calvinism reigns. Thank goodness, at least, the islanders of the Canaries can be led back to the true faith (pp. 12–15).

The figure on the right of the title page is a Benedictine monk who, having crossed the Atlantic, is busily baptizing a native with holy water poured from a shell. Brendan points us across the page: we move from Canarian to Caribbean islands, but (the suggestion is) with no loss of religious continuity. The English crown, if not all the British, will tend to accentuate (as the Benedictine monk suggests) rupture rather than continuity in religious experience. In the course of their own belated incursions westward, the English will need to contend with (and ultimately disregard) those claims of Pope Alexander VI recalled in the 1621 frontispiece. They will need to sponsor forms of religious and cultural narrative that cannot, like this Benedictine representation, suggest such seamless continuity between past and future. Continuities will be urged, but only through strategic and

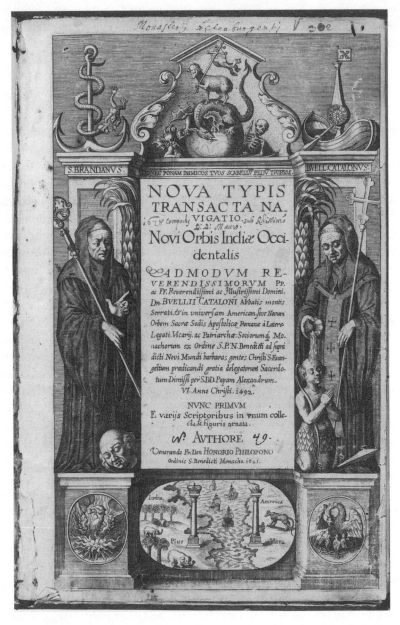

24 St. Brendan and a missionary Benedictine monk in the Americas, title page to Honorius Philoponus, *Nova Typis Transacta Navigatio Novi Orbis* (1621). British Library, London.

25 St. Brendan travels to the Canaries, celebrates mass on the back of a whale, Honorius Philoponus, *Nova Typis Transacta Navigatio Novi Orbis* (1621). British Library, London.

selective redisposition – as in the work of Hakluyt and Spenser – of ancient and medieval texts (newly gathered from places such as Wells). They will need, in short, to emphasize that the extension of European technologies, colonies, and addictions across first the Mediterranean and then the Atlantic really does bring us to a *New* World. But they will nonetheless need to begin this process with one more Genoan in foreign employ: Giovanni Caboto, who set off from Bristol in the *Matthew* on May 2, 1497.

NOTES

1   The poem is printed as an epilogue to *Black Imagination and the Middle Passage*, ed. Maria Diedrich, Henry Louis Gates, Jr., and Carl Pedersen (New York: Oxford University Press, 1999), pp. 305–6 (lines 53–4).

2   See Charles Verlinden, "Lanzarotto Malocello et la découverte portugaise des Canaries," *Revue Belge de Philologie et d'Histoire* 36 (1958), 1173–1209; Felipe Férnandez-Armesto, *The Canary Islands after the Conquest: The Making of a Colonial Society in the Early Sixteenth Century* (Oxford: Clarendon Press, 1982), pp. 1–3; Marcos Martínez Hernández, *Canarias en la Mitologia* (Santa Cruz de Tenerife: Centro de la Cultura Popular Canaria, 1992).

3   See Valerio Manfredi, *Isole Fortunate* (Rome: Bretschneider, 1996), pp. 56–7.

4   Salvador López Herrera, *The Canary Islands through History* (Santa Cruz de Tenerife: Graficas Tenerife, 1978), pp. 93–4.

5   *The Muqaddimah: An Introduction to History*, trans. from the Arabic by Franz Rosenthal, 3 vols. (London: Routledge and Kegan Paul, 1958), I.117. The Canaries, "from which Ptolemy began the determination of geographical longitude," are discussed by Ibn Khaldûn as "the Eternal Islands" (I.116).

6   This forms part of the extraordinary so-called *Catalan World Atlas* (which had migrated to Charles V's great library at the Louvre by 1380). Isidore of Seville (ca. 560–636) was a teacher and a tireless compiler of knowledge; his *Etymologiae* proved vastly influential.

7   See Mela, *De Chorographia*, ed. Piergiorgio Parroni (Rome: Edizioni di Storia e Letteratura, 1984), III.102; Frank E. Romer, *Pomponius Mela's Description of the World* (Ann Arbor: University of Michigan Press, 1998), pp. 129–30; Manfredi, *Isole Fortunate*, pp. 94–5.

8   On the crucially improved sailing capacities of the *caravela*, see J. R. S. Philips, *The Medieval Expansion of Europe* (Oxford: Oxford University Press, 1988), p. 230.

9   *Tenerife News*, 30 May–12 June 2003, pp. 1, 5.

10   The Guanche – a term properly applied only to the inhabitants of Tenerife, but customarily used to include all the native islanders – numbered only around 600 at Tenerife by 1513. See Fernández-Armesto, *Canary Islands*, pp. 5–12; Gilbert C. Din, *The Canary Islanders of Louisiana* (Baton Rouge: Louisiana State University Press, 1988), pp. 3–5.

11   "In February 1995," Diedrich, Gates, and Pedersen explain, "the Collegium for
      African American Research (CAAR), a Europe-based association of scholars
      working in the field of African American studies, hosted a conference in Puerto
      de la Cruz, Tenerife (Spain), inviting colleagues from Africa, the Americas, and
      Europe to discuss the history and the meaning of the transatlantic passage for
      African Americans" (*The Middle Passage*, p. 11). Melba Joyce Boyd, in the poem
      that provides the epigraph for this chapter (written for this conference), speaks
      of the Canaries as the place "where Columbus / traded Black Gold / and stole
      / nautical mythology / and encoded it onto / maps and an ocean grave"
      (p. 306, lines 55–9).

12   Florence, Biblioteca Nazionale Centrale, formerly II, II 327, now Banco Rari 50;
      the *De Canaria* section is at folios 123v–124r. For an edition and commentary,
      see M. Pastore Stocchi, "Il 'De Canaria' Boccaccesco e un *locus deperditus* nel
      'De Insulis' di Domenico Silvestri," *Rinascimento* 10 (1959), 143–56; for further
      commentary, see Giorgio Padoan, "Petrarca, Boccaccio e la scoperta delle
      Canarie," *Italia medioevale e umanistica* 7 (1964), 263–77. For a listing of the
      complete contents of this *zibaldone*, see Aldo Maria Costatini, "Studi sullo
      Zibaldone Magliabechiano. I. Descrizioni e analisi," *Studi sul Boccaccio* 7 (1973),
      21–58 (pp. 27–58).

13   That is, until Captain Cook and company caught sight of the Hawaiian islands.
      The peak of Tenerife's Teide rises 3,718 meters above the ocean (and some
      7,000 meters above the ocean floor); only Hawaii's Mauna Loa and Mauna
      Kilauea rise higher. Almost two-thirds of Tenerife is made up by the rugged
      slopes of Teide (which staged the last-stand resistance of the native Guanche).

14   With this declaration, "non dites insulas" (104), Boccaccio may be downplaying
      strict identification with the "divites . . . insulas" dreamed of by classical tradi-
      tion (see the citation of Horace's sixteenth epode above, p. 202, note 77).

15   *Esposizioni sopra la Comedia di Dante*, ed. Giorgio Padoan, in *Tutte le opere di
      Giovanni Boccaccio*, ed. Vittore Branca (Milan: Mondadori, 1964–), VI, 5 (ii),
      31–4.

16   Ed. Guido Martellotti, in Francesco Petrarca, *Prose*, ed Martellotti et al. (Milan
      and Naples: Ricciardi, 1955), 2.11 (pp. 522–4). Petrarch notes that these islands
      – celebrated by many poets, but above all by a lyric of Horace – were "pen-
      etrated" by an armed Genoan fleet "within the memory of our fathers."
      Petrarch's argument that Canarian remoteness does not qualify as true solitude
      (because it is natural, not willed) parallels that of contemporary friars against
      the poverty of peasants (who, similarly, do not "choose" to be poor).

17   See *De vita solitaria*, ed. Martellotti, 2.11 (p. 522 n. 5); *The Geography of Strabo*,
      ed. and trans. Horace Leonard Jones, Loeb Classical Library, 8 vols. (London:
      Heinemann, 1917–32), 2.5.8 (vol. I, pp. 442–3); 4.5.4 (vol. II, pp. 258–61). Strabo
      deems the inhabitants of Ierné "more savage than the Britons, since they are
      man-eaters as well as heavy eaters, and since, further, they count it an honorable
      thing, when their fathers die, to devour them, and openly to have intercourse,

not only with the other women, but with their mothers and sisters; but I am saying this only with the understanding that I have no trustworthy witnesses for it" (II.259–61).

18 On the Genoese lineage of Columbus, see *Columbus Documents: Summaries of Documents in Genoa*, ed. and trans. Luciano F. Farina and Robert W. Tolf (Detroit: Omnigraphics, 1992); *Christopher Columbus and His Family: The Genoese and Ligurian Documents*, ed. and trans. John Dotson and Aldo Agosto (Turnhout, Belgium: Brepols, 1998). The first surviving record, dated February 21, 1429, sees Giovanni Colombo, Cristofero's grandfather, take on an apprentice.

19 "*Itinerarium Hispanicum Hieronymu Monetarii, 1494–5*," ed. Ludwig Pfandl, *Revue Hispanique*, 48 (1920), 1–179 (pp. 23–4); see also Jerónimo Münzer, *Viaje por España y Portugal (1494–5)*, introd. Ramón Alba (Madrid: Ediciones Polifemo, 1991). Neither Pfandl nor Alba includes the preface in which Münzer speaks of his earlier journeying through Italy: see E. P. Goldschmidt, *Hieronymus Münzer und seine Bibliothek* (London: Warburg Institute, 1938), p. 27.

20 See J. N. Hillgarth, *The Spanish Kingdoms, 1250–1516*, 2 vols. (Oxford: Oxford University Press, 1976–8), II.576–7; Fernández-Armesto, *Canary Islands*, p. 3.

21 The first Christianizing missions to the Canaries had taken place more than a century earlier; the bishropric of Telde was founded on Gran Canaria in 1351. The missionary efforts of Catalan clerics and Majorcan hermits were spoiled by the slave-raiding of other Christians. See Hillgarth, *Spanish Kingdoms*, II.123.

22 Item 146, "Katalog von Münzers Bibliothek," in Goldschmidt, *Münzer*, pp. 115–45. On the well-established tradition of budding Nuremberg humanists traveling to Italy, see Guy Fitch Little, "The Renaissance, the Reformation, and the City of Nuremberg," in Jeffrey Chipps Smith, *Nuremberg, a Renaissance City, 1500–1618* (Austin: University of Texas Press, 1983), pp. 17–22 (p. 19).

23 See Smith, *Nuremberg*, pp. 90, 94–5; Smith, "The Transformation of Patrician Tastes in Renaissance Nuremberg," in Smith, *New Perspectives on Renaissance Nuremberg: Five Essays* (Austin: Archer M. Huntington Art Gallery, 1985), pp. 83–100 (p. 88); Ernst Ullmann, *Geschichte der deutschen Kunst 1470–1550. Malerei, Graphik und Kunsthandwerk* (Leipzig: Seemann, 1985), pp. 206–21 (esp. p. 211).

24 See the list of "Schiavi Ebrei," sold at Genoa between 1482 and 1498, appended to Domenico Gioffrè, *Il mercato degli schiavi a Genova nel secolo XV* (Genoa: Fratelli Bozzi, 1971), unpaginated; the first of these, seven-year-old "Tolosano," is sold "by her own father" for 12 ducats. The first ship of Sephardic refugees from Spain had arrived in 1478: see Rossana Urbani and Guido Nathan Zazzu, *The Jews in Genoa*, 2 vols. (Leiden: Brill, 1999), I, p. xxxii.

25 Goldschmidt, *Münzer*, p. 85.

26 Ernst Philip Goldschmidt (1887–1954) was a learned bibliographer and antiquarian bookseller, first in Vienna and from the 1920s in London and New York as well. See the obituaries by R. O. Dougan in the *Library*, 5th series, 9 (1954), 75–84, and by Jacques Vellekoop in the *Book Collector* 3 (1954), 119–24.

27 Jennifer Goodman, *Chivalry and Exploration, 1298–1630* (Woodbridge: Boydell Press, 1998), p. 108.

28 See Felipe Fernández-Armesto, *Before Columbus: Exploration and Colonisation from the Mediterranean to the Atlantic 1229–1492* (Basingstoke: Macmillan, 1987), pp. 175–83 (p. 184); Goodman, *Chivalry and Exploration*, pp. 104–30; John Mercer, *The Canary Islanders: Their Prehistory, Conquest, and Survival* (London: Rex Collings, 1980), pp. 160–79.

29 Both recently reproduced in a superb facsimile edition: *Le Canarien. Manuscritos, Transcripción y Tradducción*, ed. Berta Pico, Eduardo Aznar, and Dolores Corbella (La Laguna: Instituto de Estudios Canarios, 2003).

30 See Harry Kelsey, *Sir John Hawkins: Queen Elizabeth's Slavetrader* (New Haven: Yale University Press, 2003).

31 *Chivalry and Exploration*, p. 117.

32 See Goodman, *Chivalry and Exploration*, p. 125; Peter Russell, *Prince Henry "the Navigator"* (New Haven: Yale Nota Bene, 2001), pp. 264–90. Prince Henry of Portugal, Knight of the Garter, born March 4, 1394, was the third surviving son of John I and Philippa of Lancaster.

33 Russell, *Prince Henry*, p. 276.

34 Cited in Goodman, *Chivalry and Exploration*, pp. 119–20. On paleness, see Carolyn Dinshaw, "Pale Faces: Race, Religion, and Affect in Chaucer's Texts and Their Readers." *Studies in the Age of Chaucer* 23 (2001), 19–41.

35 Joanot de Martorell and Martí Joan de Galba, *Tirant lo Blanc*, ed. Víctor Gómez, 3 vols. (Valencia: Ediciones Alfons el Mangnánim, 1990), I, 18; trans. Ray La Fontaine (New York: Peter Lang, 1993), pp. 45–6.

36 Miguel de Cervantes Saavedra, *Don Quijote de la Mancha*, ed. Juan Ignacio Ferreras, 2 vols. (Madrid: Ediciones Akal, 1991), I.103 ("the best book in the world").

37 See *Tirant lo Blanc*, trans. La Fontaine, pp. 6–8.

38 See *Der katalanische Weltatlas vom Jahre 1375, nach d. in d. Bibliothèque Nationale, Paris*, ed. Hans-Christian Freiseleben (Stuttgart: Brockhaus, 1977), p. 12.

39 See Mercer, *Canary Islanders*, p. 229 (and pp. 190–1 above).

40 In this case, by pan-Arab Islam: see Antonio Arnáiz Villena and Jorge Alonso Garcia, *Egipicos, Berberes, Guanches y Vascos*, 2nd edn. (Madrid: Editorial Complatense, 2001).

41 *Momias. Los Secretos del Pasado. Catalogo*, 2nd edn. (Tenerife: Museo Arqueológico y Etnográfico de Tenerife, 1999), p. 9. The mummy was donated to Trinity College, Cambridge. Trinity in turn donated it to the Museum of Archaeology and Anthropology, University of Cambridge, in 1914; it has recently been transferred to the Department of Biological Anthropology at Cambridge.

42 There have been attempts to connect Guanche with present-day Canarian descendants: see, for example, José Luis Concepción, *Los guanches que sobrevivieron y su discendencia* (La Laguna, Tenerife: ACIC, 1982). Treatment of the Guanche has also been set within "human rights" frameworks: Antonio Pérez Voituriez,

Los aborigines canarios y los derechos humanos (Santa Cruz de Tenerife: Centro de la Cultura Popular Canaria, 1989).

43 Alonso de Espinosa, "The Origin and miracles of Our Lady of Candelaria" (published at Seville in 1594) in *The Guanches of Tenerife*, ed. Clements Markham, Hakluyt Society, 2nd series, 21 (London: Hakluyt Society, 1907). See further Mercer, *Canary Islanders*, p. 198; Fernández-Armesto, *Canary Islands*, pp. 188–91.

44 Lope de Vega, *Los guanches de Tenerife y Conquista de Canaria* (Santa Cruz de Tenerife: Museo de Historia de Tenerife, 1996), p. 49.

45 These floating Virgins might have begun their careers as the figureheads of ships; the Virgin at Boulogne, a major site of medieval pilgrimage (*Canterbury Tales* 1.465), disappeared during the French Revolution (see chapter 1, n. 145 above, p. 88).

46 *The Conquest of America: The Question of the Other*, trans. Richard Howard (New York: Harper and Row, 1984), p. 5.

47 As in Boccaccio's Florence, teenage sons of Genoa typically left home to look after family interests abroad, only returning to settle in the *patria* in their twenties or thirties. The legend of Columbus studying at the University of Pavia springs in part from the desire to align him with humanist educational paradigms.

48 This formed part of the third of Columbus' four transatlantic expeditions: see William Lemos, "Voyages of Columbus," in *The Christopher Columbus Encyclopedia*, ed. Silvio D. Bedini, 2 vols. (Basingstoke: Macmillan, 1992), II.693a–728b (p. 714); *Select Documents illustrating the Four Voyages of Columbus*, ed. Cecil Jane, 2 vols. (London: Hakluyt Society, 1930–3), map at II.70. Further references to the two Hakluyt Society volumes follow the slightly altered and corrected one-volume edition, ed. Jayne (Mineola, NY: Dover Publications, 1988).

49 See Origo, reporting on a document of September 1, 1400, "The Domestic Enemy: The Eastern Slaves in Tuscany in the Fourteenth and Fifteenth Centuries," *Speculum* 30 (1955), p. 331; David Wallace, *Chaucerian Polity: Absolutist Lineages and Associational Forms in England and Italy* (Stanford, Calif,: Stanford University Press, 2001) pp. 183–7.

50 Which they have safely accomplished by the ninth stanza of the tale. On the studied ability of merchants to disappear, see Wallace, *Chaucerian Polity*, pp. 187–90. Of the Merchant of his *General Prologue*, Chaucer observes: "But, sooth to seyn, I noot how men hym calle" (1.284).

51 On Imperiale, see chapter 4 above, p. 188.

52 Chios is the only place in Europe where the specific variety of acacia tree producing gum mastic (mixed with sugar as a thickening agent) is to be found; this commodity was so precious that the Genoese family controlling its exportation, the Giustiniani, limited fleets from Genoa to Chios to just one or two per decade (there were sailings in 1474 and 1475). They also employed large ships to carry their high-value cargo directly to England and Flanders. See

Helen Nader, "Columbus, Christopher: Early Maritime Experience," in *Columbus Encyclopedia*, I.167b–175a (p. 170a); Stuart B. Schwarz, *The Iberian Mediterranean and Atlantic Traditions in the Formation of Columbus as a Colonizer* (Minneapolis: Associates of the James Ford Bell Library, University of Minnesota, 1986); Philip Argenti, *The Occupation of Chios by the Genoese and their Administration of the Island 1346–1566*, 3 vols. (Cambridge: Cambridge University Press, 1958), esp. I.615–23. The earliest extant records of slave sales following the Genoese occupation of Chios date from 1359 and concern one Syrian and two Tartar women (I.616). For a spectacular exemplar of "crackpot Columbiana" (I borrow the phrase from Schwarz, p. 2), see Spyros Cateras, *Christopher Columbus was a Greek and His Real Name was Nikolaos Ypshilantis from the Greek Island Chios* (Manchester, New Hampshire: 48 Spruce Street, 1937).

53 See Luigi de Anna, *Le isole perdute e le isole ritrovate. Cristofero Colombo, Tile e Frislanda: Un problema nella storia dell'esplorazione nordatlantic* (Turku, Finland: University of Turku, 1993), pp. 14–20; Rebecca Catz, "Columbus, Christopher: Columbus in Portugal," in *Columbus Encyclopedia*, I.175a–187b (p. 175b).

54 Nader, "Early Maritime Experience," p. 173a (translating from a despatch of January 39, 1494, sent by Columbus to Ferdinand and Isabella); and see further Noel Deerr, *The History of Sugar*, 2 vols. (London: Chapman and Hall, 1949), I, 73–99, 117. See also Schwartz, *Columbus as a Colonizer*, pp. 5–6; Catz, "Columbus in Portugal," pp. 173b–174a.

55 See Kristine Edle Olson, photographer, with text and captions by Caroline MacDonald Haig, *La Gomera. Island of Columbus, Unspoilt Gem of the Canaries* (London: Thames and Hudson, 1989), p. 12; and photograph, p. 19.

56 This conquest brought death or disappearance by sword, enslavement or plague on a scale comparable with things to come in the New World: see Fernández-Armesto, *The Canary Islands*, p. 11; Hillgarth, *The Spanish Kingdoms*, II.44.

57 Deerr, *History of Sugar*, I, 116–17; Verlinden, *The Beginnings of Modern Colonization*, p. 22.

58 The first recorded bulk importation of sugar to England, according to Deerr, occurred as early as 1319, when Venetians sold "100,000 pounds of sugar and 10,000 pounds of candy sugar" in London, then bought wool and headed for Flanders. Ships and wool were captured by English pirates and the Italian merchant sailors killed (*History of Sugar*, I.97).

59 *The Diario of Christopher Columbus's First Voyage to America, 1492–1493. Abstracted by Fray Bartolomé de las Casas*, ed. and trans. Oliver Dunn and James E. Kelley, Jr. (Norman: University of Oklahoma Press, 1989), Saturday, October 13, 1492, pp. 22–9; William Lemos, "Voyages of Columbus," *Columbus Encyclopedia*, II.693b–728b (pp. 694a–695b).

60 *Diario*, Thursday, October 11, 1492 (pp. 64–7). The *Diario* survives as quoted and paraphrased by the colonist priest Bartholomé de Las Casas in the 1530s. Pedro de Las Casas accompanied Columbus on the second voyage of 1493; Bartholomé, his son, watched a procession at Seville on Palm Sunday 1493

featuring Columbus and his shipmates, followed by the first captured islanders from the Caribbean to set foot on European soil. Las Casas sailed to La Española in 1502 to manage estates granted to his father by Columbus. Ordained priest in 1507, he returned to Española and served as military chaplain to the conquest of Cuba. Although his admiration for Columbus never wavered, he later became an increasingly radical critic of colonization and native enslavement. See Benjamin Keen, "Las Casas, Bartolomé de," *Columbus Encyclopedia*, I.408b–412a; *Diario*, ed. Dunn and Kelley, pp. 4–5; Charles Gillen, *Bartolomé de Las Casas: Une esquisse biographique* (Paris: Cerf, 1995).

61   *Diario*, Saturday, October 13, 1492 (pp. 68–9).

62   Both texts are conveniently available in *Columbus in Italy: An Italian Versification of the Letter on the Discovery of the New World. With Facsimiles of the Italian and Latin editions of 1493*, introd. and trans. Martin Davies (London: British Library, 1991).

63   "Omnes per ambages et conjecturas"; Chaucer's *Troilus and Criseyde* glosses "with ambages" as "with double wordes slye" (5.897–8).

64   See *Columbus in Italy*, ed. Davies, pp. 15–16.

65   See David Wallace, *Chaucer and the Early Writings of Boccaccio* (Cambridge: D. S. Brewer, 1985), pp. 73–105.

66   See P. Farenga and G. Curcio, "Dati, Giuliano," in *Dizionario biografico degli italiani*, ed. Massimiliano Pavan (Rome: Istituto della Enciclopedia Italiana, 1960–), 33.31a–35a; Giuliano Dati, *La storia della inventione delle nuove insule di Channaria indiane*, ed. Mario Ruffini (Turin: Bottega d'Erasmo, 1957), pp. 8–10; *Columbus in Italy*, ed. Davies, pp. 10–12. The success of his *cantare* on the Indian Canaries inspired Dati to publish another on Prester John, *La gran magnificentia de Prete Ianni signore dell'India Maggiore e della Ethiopia* (1493–4) and then *I cantari dell'India cioè: delli huomini e donne e animali irrationali monstruosi* (1494–5). Other *cantari* include lives of saints, popes, and Scipio Africanus, a guide to Rome, and an account of recent Roman floods.

67   See David Wallace, "Mystics and Followers in Siena and East Anglia," in *The Medieval Mystical Tradition in England. Dartington 1984*, ed. Marion Glasscoe (Cambridge: Boydell and Brewer, 1984), pp. 169–91.

68   On the long history of this omni-insular doctrine, in which the papacy claimed the right to possess and dispose of islands lying in western Europe (and then beyond), see Luis Weckmann-Muñoz, "The Alexandrine Bulls of 1493: Pseudo-Asiatic Documents," in *First Images of America: The Impact of the New World on the Old*, ed. Fredi Chiappelli, 2 vols. (Berkeley: University of California Press, 1976), I.201–9.

69   Honorius Philoponus, *Nova Typis Transacta Navigatio Novi Orbis Indiae Occidentalis* (Linz, 1621). I refer to BL 493.i.21 (which, the British Library catalogue suggests, differs from other exemplars with the same frontispiece). The BL catalogue further suggests that "Honorius Philoponus" is a pseudonym for Gaspar Plautius; it is evident from the dedication, however, that "Plautius" is the author's abbot.

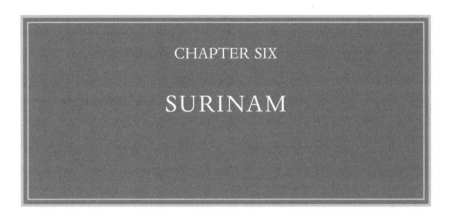

CHAPTER SIX

SURINAM

Adiosso Crobooy Mee de go dede me de go Na mee Gado.
John Gabriel Stedman, Narrative of a Five Years Expedition against the Revolted Negroes of Surinam.

C'est à ce prix que vous mangez du sucre en Europe.
Voltaire, Candide.

Nigra sum sed formosa, filiae Hierusalem.
Canticum Canticorum, 1:4.

"Surinam" possesses little resonance today for most people in the English-speaking world. It is a name associated, at least in Britain, with the signature blue label affixed to a Ffyfes banana, or with the recent fortunes of the Dutch national football team.[1] The territory was once in English hands, but only for sixteen years (1651–67). It was then traded away for the island of Manhattan; Dutch became the ruling language and the Netherlands the colonial power until Surinam achieved independence in 1975.[2] It may seem retrograde to cling to nation-state demarcations imposed by European powers (and largely ignored by peoples living deeper inland); it might be more relevant to speak of the Guyanas as a highly distinctive geographical area divided (and still contested) between Brazil, Venezuela, Surinam, Guyana (British Guiana until 1966), and "la Guyane française" (still accorded the status of a "département d'outremer").[3] But in earlier centuries, Surinam did resonate more powerfully as a place in the English-thinking imaginary. This was due in some measure to the national and international popularity of

Aphra Behn's *Oroonoko* – reprinted throughout the eighteenth century and translated into Dutch, French, and German – and to the popular play cobbled from it by Thomas Southerne in 1696. It also owed something to the importation of African slaves to work sugar plantations, massively accelerated between 1688 and 1738, and to tales of black flight to the bush; the Surinam Maroons have long been the hemisphere's largest maroon population.[4] English audiences were electrified by John Gabriel Stedman's accounts of his four years (his title claims five) in Surinam, where, as a soldier employed by the Dutch States-General, he fought escaped slaves (1774–7); engravers recruited to illustrate the printed editions included William Blake.[5] Surinam, the most prized and lucrative colony possessed by the United Provinces, became a byword for European cruelty and excess. In Voltaire's *Candide* (published simultaneously in five European capitals in 1759), the young hero definitively loses faith in Panglossian optimism as he enters Surinam.[6] Of the various fragments of slave and Maroon speech preserved by Stedman, the one given as an epigraph above seems most apposite: "farewell" (Stedman translates; it is painful to imagine the circumstances of his transcribing) "Good by I am Dying and Going to my God."[7]

Oroonoko, which tells how a white female colonist stranded in Surinam befriends and abandons an enslaved African prince, is assuming ever-increasing importance as the most widely read premodern Anglophone imagining of white/black relations.[8] Readers have long wondered what Behn, an Englishwoman with a Dutch name, brought back from Surinam (experiences for the memory bank; butterflies for "His Majesties Antiquaries"; feathers for the London stage; pp. 75–6). Here, while questioning this whole structuring logic of *to* and *from*, emphasis falls upon what, from the European repertoires explored in the last five chapters, Behn brings to such an encounter; and what (in the broadest sense) remains and endures. In beginning with Sranan, the language uniting the diverse ethnic groups inhabiting the country today, we grasp that Behn's precarious presence in Surinam[9] coincides with (participates in) the most crucial phase of language formation in the nation's history.[10] The chapter then maps the historical dynamics of Behn's Surinam along an extended temporal frame – proving more complex than issues of *before* and *after* – beginning with a scrap of a Hebrew love song and ending, again, with Sranan. Medieval exegeses of the verse *nigra sum sed formosa, filiae Hierusalem* explore attitudes to blackness, beauty, abjection, and being a woman (key issues for Behn) long before Mediterranean slaving extends out into the Atlantic; they implicitly comprehend "feudal mutuality," a concept whose dynamism declines as industrialized plantation logic pervades the Americas. Behn's *Oroonoko* sits on a cusp between losing the empathetic qualities of "feudal mutuality" and assuming the harsher logic of the later period (as chronicled and pictured by Stedman and Blake). Skin color, we notice, is migrating from an accidental trait of personhood to an absolute determinant of freedom and lack of freedom; differences of religion, considered in this greater scheme of things, no longer really matter much. The book ends by considering how prior times and places, explored in earlier chapters, haunt more recent, heterotemporal imaginings of this Caribbean space (of which Surinam and the Guyanas form the extreme western limit): the Reverend Isaac Teale is first paired with Evelyn Waugh, then David Dabydeen with the Sranan poet Trefossa.

Cuss, Buss, and Tref: Languages of Surinam

There are still places in Surinam with British names: the coast road westward from the capital Paramaribo, for example, passes through Inverness and Totness. But of more profound importance is the fact that English – specifically Behn's English – has passed into (is constitutive of) Sranan, the common language of Surinam. In 1693, a quarter-century after English withdrawal, a shipwrecked Dutch sailor encountering slaves in Surinam assumed them to be speaking English.[11] What he was actually hearing was a creolized tongue formed by the intensive fusion of English and West African usages. Such languages are formed through a pressing need for two-way communication between disparate parties (as experienced in Surinam's earliest colonial days); once established, the language develops its own distinctive and independent form as a language (while remaining open to relexification or expansion through contact with new tongues). English indentured and ex-indentured labor was of crucial importance in these earliest linguistic exchanges; the master's concubine or *sisi* also played a vital mediatory role.[12] English words can still be traced in current Sranan forms (*meki, wani, lafoe, hebi*: make, want, laugh, heavy). The Sranan terms *kosi* and *bosi* derive from the English *cuss* (cuss, curse) and *buss* (a kiss; a smack): terms more current in the English of Behn's time – and to their social uses in Surinam – than to our own.[13] The sentences Stedman chose to record – such as our epigraph – point back to creolizing Anglo-African encounters while suggesting continuing relations of extreme social imbalance. "Mee Saloby you langa alle Mee Hatty so langa mee leeby," for example, might be taken to record sentiments surrounding Stedman's long-term liaison with the slave Joanna.[14] At the same time, however, we remember his habit, from his earliest days in Surinam, of noting the fucking (his term) of "negro maids."[15] And the qualification "so langa mee leeby" – "so long as I live" – is further cause for disquiet in a society in which (following Stedman's own reckoning) slave deaths so greatly exceeded births that "the whole race of slaves . . . are totally extinct once every twenty years."[16]

Sranan, a name applied to both the tongue and the territory of Surinam, is today spoken by the greatest percentage of inhabitants (some 85–90 per-cent), followed by Dutch, Hindi, and Javanese.[17] Sranan itself has both accreted linguistic influences from later immigrant groups while preserving others from its earliest days, such as Portuguese, for example, brought to Surinam by Jews from Brazil and Cayenne in the 1660s. And they brought words from Hebrew too: the Sranan term *trefu/a* indicates a prohibition on certain kinds of food.[18] The complexity of Sranan – and the complex history of its social status – may be judged from the range of names by which it has been known: Krioro, Negro-English, Nengre-Engels, Nengre-Tongo, Taki-Taki, Sranantongo, Surinaams. The terms of its scholarly description are value-laden: Sranan and equivalent Caribbean languages are said to form through pidgins and creoles, whereas Middle English (a term we owe to Jacob Grimm) evolves through attendant *Mischsprächen*, interlanguages, and complex convergences of dialectal forms.[19] And yet for Deschamps, as we have seen (p. 57), Chaucer's late-forming native tongue is a bastard concoction in severe need of further French importation; if the word "creole" had been available to Deschamps, he would have applied it to "Middle English."[20]

"Wi nengre": The Black Sea

Sranan and equivalent Caribbean forms do not, of course, merely bear the impress of successive linguistic importations, but rather enfold them within complex cultural dialectics, now increasingly carried back to countries of origin. Recent championing of Sranan as a literary form owes much to the political radicalization of Surinamese students in Dutch universities in the 1960s.[21] The name chosen for their movement in Holland, Wie Eegie Sanie (Our Own Things), suggests parallels with the Irish Gaelic Sinn Fein ("We Ourselves"); the poem "Wi nengre" ("We Blacks"), by Michäel Slory, clearly riffs on "Wie Eegie Sanie" while refining analysis to matters of black and white. The poem finds the process of looking back most painful; but seeing the sea ("mi si a se") makes a confrontation with "historia" – while still questioningly resisted – inevitable:

> Fa wi musus luku
> na ini a spikri
> fu historia, di blaka, blaka?

How much we look
in the mirror of events,
which is black, black?[22]

This sea's immensity distinguishes it from any yet encountered in this book, although we have seen "Tartars" and "Ethiops," "Moors" and "Canarians" subjected to untold pains of terminal, sea-borne estrangement. White Europeans have been seen crossing from *patria* to new place, with thoughts of return always implicit; new places thus extend and enrich secure points of origin. For Slory, however, black history has disappeared beneath the sea's implacable surface; enslavement began as a one-way voyage from home place to (as Hortense Spillers puts it) *"nowhere* at all."[23] Analogous reflections upon the sea, viewed from the same coastal strip, inform David Dabydeen's *Turner* (1994), a poetic reworking of the English painter's *Slave Ship (Slavers Throwing Overboard the Dead and Dying, Typhoon Coming On)* (1840). This canvas, according to a famous chapter of John Ruskin's *Modern Painters*, features "the noblest sea that Turner ever painted . . . the noblest certainly ever painted by man." Dabydeen concentrates upon the shackled and drowning Africans that Ruskin – who actually owned this painting for 28 years – confines to a footnote.[24]

For Slory, Dabydeen, and other Guyanese and Caribbean poets, the sea holds a promise of oblivion or sea change, but also painful historical imaginings (that arise, unbidden, at any moment) of originating deracination. In Slory's "Wi nengre," the imperative to forget –"'Frigiti!'" – that which is over and done ("ben pasa") is challenged by the rolling of ocean foam, the abyss of black "historia." The drowned African slave of Dabydeen's *Turner*, craving "transfiguration or newness or creative amnesia," likewise finds that "although the sea has transformed him – bleached him of color and complicated his sense of gender – he still recognizes himself as 'nigger'" (p. x). The sea itself, or the crossing of it, both foments a hope of newness (the perennial great white hope, pursued throughout this book) and interpellates those who lose through negritude. Behn complies with this paradigm: her Oroonoko comes from no place (beyond the sea) to a new place that can never be his; and he is black. The facticity of blackness proves so fundamental to *Oroonoko* that one realizes an epochal marker has been crossed. For Behn (and this is a realization that her text, periodically, struggles to resist), the first and foundational difference is no longer a matter of religion, but of color, specifically of white/black.[25] Such a focus on skin brings her in view of Thomas Jefferson's ontological account of "the first difference":

The first difference which strikes us is that of color. Whether the black of the
negro resides in the reticular membrane between the skin and scarf-skin, or in
the scarf-skin itself; whether it proceeds from the color of the blood, the color
of the bile, or from that of some other secretion, the difference is fixed in
nature, and is as real as if its seat and cause were better known to us.[26]

Jefferson here labors to articulate a difference that is absolute, integral to the
body and not to be broken apart from it. Yet the need to break open black
bodies seems implicit in his terms of description by way of demonstrating
an irreducible "concentration of ethnicity" (Hortense Spillers' phrase) housed
in the flesh.[27] Such logic is alien to the medieval canons of servile description
considered in chapter 4, for there skin color formed just one taxonomic
element among many and the slave body was too precious a commodity to
be gratuitously broken. For the medieval slave traders (to think in terms
they might recognize), color was a matter not of substance, but rather accident; "the politics of melanin" were not yet all-consuming.[28]

Aphra Behn expends lavish physical description on the flora and fauna of
Surinam (none of it rivaling Maria Sibylla Merian's scientific picturing of
Surinam, following her visit in 1699–1701), but devotes no words at all to
the place from which Oroonoko is taken ("Coramantien, a country of blacks
so called," p. 78).[29] 'Biyi Bandele counters this by locating the greater part of
his two-part *Oroonoko* in a Yoruba setting; and Hortense Spillers, analogously, considers an African culture securely in place "before pious Cristobal,
Christum Ferens, the bearer of Christ, laid claim to what he thought was the
'Indies'."[30] We might complement such work of pre-Columbian contextual-
ization by considering the greater European *mentalité* that Columbus (picking up on Spiller's etymologizing) bears with him.

Peculiar cathections of woman, bondage, beauty, and blackness form
through the long, pre-Columbian history of *nigra sum sed formosa, filiae
Hierusalem*, our translated, displaced fragment of a Hebrew love song (Song
of Songs, 1:4). Abelard and Heloïse are chosen as the first exegetes because,
as white male and black woman (that is, woman in black) they offer particularly instructive points of comparison for the relationship between Oroonoko
and Behn. I first concentrate upon discourses of servitude, peasantry, and
antisemitism that get mapped onto blackness and thus travel (figuratively,
but with biting historical force) to Surinam. And then, secondly, I consider
what gets lost *en route*: interpersonal dynamics that must get mislaid as
relations paradigmatic of plantation slavery develop. Discourses of power (it
might be anticipated) are the province of Abelard, brilliant logician, systematic destroyer of intellectual opponents, heartbreaker, ultimate begetter of

exclusively masculine schools of study; Heloïse – singled out, beaten, sexually exploited, impregnated, shut up in a cloister – is thus left as their victim. But peculiarly medieval dynamics, sustained by the religion of which *nigra sed formosa* exegesis forms part, make this interpersonal *agon* more complex than moderns might expect.

"Nigra sum": Heloïse and Abelard

The Abelard and Heloïse relationship plays out between particular places, with a strong tension between national center – Paris, intellectual capital, home to young Heloïse – and geographical periphery: Abelard is a man of the far west, a Breton, who attributes his volatile temperament to "my native soil."[31] Heloïse, made pregnant in Paris, is dispatched to Brittany to give birth to their illegitimate child. Abelard, having been castrated, eventually finds his way back to Brittany to write the *Historia calamitatum* (as an outcast and wanderer, fearing death by poison or ambush, with a broken bone in his neck).[32] Having fallen foul of the world's most famous Churchman, Bernard of Clairvaux (1090–1153), Abelard is eventually condemned as a heretic; his books are to be burned, his followers excommunicated, and himself immured in perpetual silence.[33] Abelard manages to survive as a monk of Cluny, but dies 18 months later (April 1142). Abelard's late career, we might say, ends in or returns him to abjection, figured geographically: having fled to "the far ends of the earth," where, by the roar of the Ocean, "I could flee no further," he thinks of the Psalmist: "A finibus terre ad te clamavi, dum anxiaretur cor meum."[34] Heloïse, outliving him by some 21 years, ends as a much-loved abbess of the Paraclete (with six daughter houses). Heloïse, however, might not willingly concede deeper abjection to Abelard. As in the anguished erotic and ultimately religious *agon* of Lancelot and Guinivere, there seems something akin to competition between this couple for the status of the more abject, for abjection entails a power to command and oblige, a right to be loved and remembered.

In his second letter to Heloïse (the fourth of their surviving exchange), Abelard teases elaborate exegesis on the nature of whiteness and blackness from two verses of Scripture, beginning thus:

> De huius excellentia praerogativae sponsa in Canticis exsultans illa, ut ita dicam, quam Moyses duxit, Aethiopissa dicit: *Nigra sum, sed formosa filiae Hierusalem.* Ideo dilexit me rex et introduxit me in cubiculum suum. Et rursum: *Nolite considerare quod fusca sim* quia decoloravit me sol. (IV, p. 82)

The bride in the Canticles, an Ethiopian (such as the one Moses took as a wife) rejoices in the glory of her special position and says: "I am black but lovely, daughters of Jerusalem; therefore the king has loved me and brought me into his chamber." And again, "Take no notice of my darkness, because the sun has discolored me." (p. 138)

The ostensible issue of this section of exegesis is precedence: who, of Heloïse and Abelard, should come first (be named first), who last. Abelard had opened by arguing that Heloise, as *sponsa Christi*, deserves precedence. Following the passage cited above, however, Abelard argues that the Ethiopian woman, "nigra . . . sed formosa," represents contemplative souls in general ("generaliter"); but since Heloïse and her nuns wear black, the verses have particular application to them ("ad vos"). Having located Heloïse as a woman among women and identified them collectively with the Ethiopian, Abelard deepens his exploration of blackness and whiteness, exteriority and interiority, by speaking of skin, teeth, and bones. Whiteness is then read as signifying prosperity, blackness adversity.[35] This is soon developed into a discourse in which blackness and femaleness betoken an earthly life of willing abjection:

Nigra quoque est in exterioribus quia, dum in hac peregrinatione adhuc exsultat, vilem et abiectam se tenet in hac vita ut in illa sublimetur . . . (IV, p. 84)

She is black too in outward things because while she is still an exile on life's pilgrimage, she keeps herself humble and abject so that she may be exalted in the next . . . (p. 139)

The deformity of her blackness ("nigredinis deformitas") causes her to withdraw herself, reserving herself to her husband: she "would rather be known in bed than seen at table" (p. 140). Masculine eroticization of the recluse, the hidden woman,[36] is intensified by the thought of her blackness; and blackness suggests both tactile qualities and an availability for being touched (more marketplace than anchor-hold):

Et frequenter accidit ut nigrarum caro feminarum quanto est in aspectu deformior, tanto sit in tactu suavior; atque ideo earum voluptas secretis gaudiis quam publicis gratior sit et convenientior, et earum viri, ut illis oblectentur, magis eas in cubiculum introducunt quam ad publicum educunt. (IV, p. 85)

Moreover it often happens that the flesh of black women is all the softer to touch though it is less attractive to look at, and for this reason the pleasure they give is greater and more suitable for private than public enjoyment, and their husbands take them into a bedroom to enjoy them rather than parade them before the world. (p. 140)

Here Abelard strays from the first topic announced at the beginning of his letter (precedence: whose name should come first, his or hers) to address the second: Heloïse's demand that she be offered some remedy ("remedium") by way of comfort and consolation ("consolationis," IV, p. 83) for losing him.[37] Having identified Heloïse as a woman in black/a black woman (an identification analogous to that made by the author of *Ancrene Wisse*),[38] Abelard invites her to imagine the pleasures she might give in submitting to her master's touch. Of course, the saving and enabling supposition here is that the master is Christ; but, as Heloïse has already remarked (in the letter to which Abelard is currently responding), her mind often wanders – at the most inappropriate times – from religious devotion to imaginative recall of past erotic encounters.[39] Her imagining of herself as the black woman enclosed with her master is abetted by the fact that female slaves – before the large-scale development of plantations – were almost always identified with the domestic interior.[40] The term for a female slave – which remained constant from classical to medieval times – was *ancilla*: a term that might encourage a devout, enclosed woman to identify herself the more intensely as *ancilla Domini*, the handmaid of the Lord. Such a woman (the final part of the quotation above suggests) is the very antitype of those who would "parade before the world"; her devotions, her pleasures, are secret. In thinking of those who "ad publicum educunt," Abelard visualizes his fellow monks (making a grand display of their devotions, throwing open choir or cloister to parade in their finery, "ornamentis"; IV, p. 85; p. 141). "Better to keep silence," Abelard says,

... as it is shameful to speak of their wretched blindness that is wholly contrary to the religion of Christ which belongs to the poor. At heart they are Jews, following their own custom instead of a rule, making a mockery of God's command in their practices, looking to usage, not duty. (p. 142)

De quorum quidem caecitate miserrima et pauperum Christi religioni penitus contraria tanto est silere honestius quanto loqui turpus. Qui penitus iudaizantes consuetudinem suam sequuntur pro regula, et irritum fecerunt mandatum Dei propter traditiones suas, non quod debeat, quod soleat attendentes. (IV, p. 85)

Here, then, we pass from one racialized discourse to another: Heloïse is as the Ethiopian woman, "nigra . . . sed formosa"; the exhibitionist monks are

as Jews. One discourse envisions deep inwardness, the other excessive open-
ness. Neither discourse is *about* black women or Jews – each is about the
fantasies and anxieties of a white male cleric and logician – but each may
have consequences for its nominated group.[41] Each discourse is available for
social use; specific economic and political conditions will determine which
is activated, which remains latent. As we have seen, the first discourse is
fully realized at the far end of our period, although Abelard – we cannot
help but notice – appeals to the experience of feeling of black female flesh
("Et frequenter accidit . . .") as if to an established commonplace. The second
(antisemitic) discourse is already fraught with viciousness and danger as
Abelard writes (but things will get worse). Mobilization for the Crusades is
immediately accompanied by the massacring of European Jewish communities. Expansion of commerce dictates that the business of money-lending
be prised back from Jewish control (and that Christian theology hence be
rewritten, or, at least, ambiguated). Aristotle – first mediated to the West by
Jewish translators at Toledo – supplies scholasticism with tools of debate
that become the sharp instruments of anti-Jewish persecution. The discipline of logic – as pioneered by Abelard – feeds a rationalism that divides
those who see and acknowledge the truth (as derived from first principles)
from those who will not; tropes of blindness (as essayed by Abelard, above)
begin to attach themselves to Jews. And theologians such as Peter the Venerable – intimate friend and protector of both Abelard and Heloïse – begin
to lose patience: if Jews cannot or will not see the light and truth of Christian revelation, then they lie beyond the pale of reason, which is to say, they
cannot be considered human at all.[42] Such a proposition returns us to discourse on blackness, with analogous questioning of inside/outside status
(and the possibility of analogous conclusions). The "color wisdom of two
thousand years," according to Linda Van Norden, "confronted black as a
perennial mystery, a sphinx of three questions: 'What is the relation of black
to dark? Is black a primary color? Is black a color?' "[43]

Blackness, Peasantry, Villainy, Beauty

As we have seen, the notion of people beyond Christianity (and hence beyond the realm of the human) became an enabling formula for premodern
slaving. Conversion thus became problematic: could a Christianized slave
continue to be held in servitude? Enea Silvio Piccolomini, Pope Pius II, did
criticize a specific slave trade in a much-cited letter of October 7, 1462. But
this is to be read in the context of Italian and Portuguese rivalries; as both

Renaissance prince and scholar of antiquity, Aeneas Sylvius was not inclined to condemn slavery as such.[44] The same holds for the Stuart dynasty, heads of the Church in England. There is no evidence that the Stuarts ever mounted any serious effort at converting African slaves. There is, however, plentiful evidence of their involvement, or investment, in slaving. In 1660, the Royal African Adventurers were founded in London and granted a monopoly of the English African trade for a thousand years. The royalist general Prince Rupert – who traveled both to West Africa and the West Indies – was a leading light in this enterprise; leading investors included four members of the royal family, two dukes, a marquis, and five earls; the new queen, Catherine of Braganza, and the Queen Mother, Henrietta Maria, joined three years later. Between 1672 (when the Adventurers were relaunched as the Royal Africa Company) and 1689, just under 90,000 slaves were exported from Africa (many of them branded with the initials RAC).[45] In *Oroonoko*, Behn tells us that "the Christians never buy any slaves but they give them some name of their own" (p. 108). The conferral of a "Christian name" upon Oroonoko might prove awkward for the Christians. He is thus named Caesar: a name that both recognizes his exceptional virtue and affirms classical values (including slavery). No serious attempt is made to convert Oroonoko Caesar to Christianity.

The process of mapping othering discourses, sharpened and refined through scholasticism, neoclassicism, and anti-Jewish polemic, *onto* blackness is long and complex. It is of fundamental importance, however, to grasp that this is indeed a *process* (not an ontology), a historical development in the postclassical world; Greeks and Romans thoroughly endorsed slavery, but did not calibrate slave-like qualities by reference to "riffs of melanin."[46] The academic rationalism pioneered by Abelard and institutionalized by his heirs[47] could be employed to exile certain groups from humanity, declaring them brute-like; the profit-driven economic rationalism of later centuries – spearheaded by Genoese expeditions to the Canaries, and beyond – could prove just as uncompromising, with equivalent results. Blackness, as we encountered it in Abelard, is reportedly tactile, amenable to touch, willing to yield to its master's hand. It is also beautiful, "nigra . . . sed formosa" (or, in alternative translations of the crucial Hebrew conjunction, *nigra . . . et*: black *and* beautiful).[48] The discourse of beauty in blackness gets mislaid, or (better) overlaid in the centuries between Heloïse and Aphra Behn. It is never entirely lost,[49] although a discursive overlay of uglification and vilification intensifies during the centuries preceding and accompanying the African slave trade.

"Vilification," we have seen, is a process to which Abelard commits Heloïse in realizing her negritude ("Nigra quoque est," cited above): she is to keep herself "vilem et abjectam." The terms *vile* (on the one hand) and *villein*, *villain*, *villainy*, *village* (on the other) are etymologically distinct, although medieval texts are wont to conflate or aggregate them (as when, in *Piers Plowman* C 20.98, Faith curses the Jews for their "vyl vilanye").[50] To be a *vilein* (Old French) or *villanus* (late Latin) is to be bound to a master and work in the fields; it is thus to be the medieval successor of the Roman *servus* or slave. The moral character of this unfreedom, this bondage to the earth, finds physiological expression: the *camus* nose (so familiar from Chaucer and Bruegel); the piggy or bleary eyes, the stocky trunk, but also (in women, sexualizing them just enough to perk the master's interest) pert breasts and pretty hair and the urge to sing and dance.[51] Much of this will be mapped onto the blacks who succeed the whites as unfree field labor in New World plantations. Particular canons of medieval representation will facilitate this transition: first, and especially in France, the depiction of peasants as dark-skinned or black; and second, Biblical Ham's twin medieval roles as a founder of peoples, including black Africans, and as the forefather of European serfs. By the sixteenth century these traditions will conflate to make Ham the progenitor of black slaves.[52]

Changing permutations of *nigra sum* exegesis play out with equivalent complexity at the top end of sixteenth-century English society. As the black woman of the Canticles is read as typological predecessor of the Queen of Sheba (commonly referred to as an Ethiopian), so the white male beloved is tied to Solomon, a monarch enriched through trade in gold and spices, with whom Henry VIII, full of erotic and imperial ambition, was pleased to iden-tify.[53] Prayers, poems, and plays in the reign of Elizabeth yield fruitful com-plications of identity: she is at once, or by turns, Solomon and Sheba.[54] Fascinated apprehensions of intensified black/white interface pervade court performances of Ben Jonson's (and Inigo Jones') *Masque of Blackness* (1605), "a sumptuous shew" (according to a letter to Brussels) "represented by the Queen and some dozen ladies all painted like blackamoors, face and neck bare, and for the rest strangely altered in barbaresque mantles."[55] The spectacle of this elite court grouping of women "painted black" provoked another witness, Sir Dudley Carleton, to a more explicit contrast of black and white, for "it" (the ladies' blackness) "became them nothing so well as their red and white, and you cannot imagine a more ugly sight than a troop of lean-cheeked moors."[56] The masque itself prompts masculine imagining of encounters with feminine whiteness – familiar, but strangely different – beneath an enabling blanket of the dark, for the daughters of Niger, accord-ing to Jonson, once were white, but are now unalterably black.[57] Their one hope of deliverance from blackness lies in wandering from their homeland in search of a sun-like ruler, who turns out to be king of snowy-cliffed Albion (line 180: but no actorly surrogate for James appears).[58] The end of the masque sees Aethiopia pronounce a definitive separation of father Niger from his daughters (who are offered hope of whitening at some future date).[59] Such spectacles and such commentaries, purveyed to the social echelon that will most heavily invest in the project of enslaving Africans, play out almost as a prologue to English colonization of Bermuda in 1609 and of Barbados in 1625.[60]

Jonson's invitation to perceive pleasures associated with white feminine beauty beneath a cover of blackness maintains contact with Abelard's erotic imagining of the young Heloïse, yet to more devastating effect, for what was in the twelfth century largely a familiar fund of troping now approaches complex historical realization. It is not surprising to learn that the most often performed Shakespearian tragedy of the Restoration period was *Othello*.[61] Despite increasing vilification of black forms, cathections of blackness with beauty – as developed through medieval exegesis – live on. Around 1440, as African slaves become commonly available through Lisbon, the third of the Three Wise Men in Western art becomes black while remaining young, beautiful, and exotic (often sporting an earring).[62] Spenser, in parading his Seven Deadly Sins, deviates from Langland and Dunbar in coloring his Lechery black, but as a heraldic tincture – sable – blackness continues to signify positive traits (such as military prowess, illustrious lineage, wealth, and compassion).[63]

Abelard's gravitation to Heloïse seems almost paradigmatically expressive of a masculine need for subordinated and adulating women, a subordination figured through blackness. Heloïse is selected from among many women, or young girls, and then (almost literally) beaten into shape (lines 80–331; pp. 66–7). Her adulation reflects back an image of giant, almost imperial, size:

> What king or philosopher could match your fame? What district, town or village did not long to see you? When you appeared in public, who did not hurry to catch a glimpse of you, or crane his neck and strain his eyes to follow your departure? Every wife, every young girl desired you in absence and was on fire in your presence; queens and great ladies [*praepotens femina*] envied me my joys and my bed. (p. 115; I, p. 71)

And yet, there is a clear sense in which such discourse enlarges her while diminishing him. This is true not just for sappy modern readers, but also for our earlier counterparts (who understood the peculiar, time-specific dynamics of abjection). Abjection is to be understood here not as a state of being (or non-being) imposed upon women, but rather as a framework for complex, two-way negotiations in which each party owes something to the other. Strategies of and in abjection are developed with great subtlety and acumen by medieval women. What it means to be or be rendered *abjecta*, however, changes markedly with time. Absolutism brings new terrors for the subject free-falling *abjecte*; slavery, even considered as an absolutist reimagining of feudal social structure, renders the whole analytical framework problematic to the point of collapse.

Feudal Mutuality: White Male Abjection Envy

Recent historians have expressed considerable skepticism about the validity of *feudalism* as a historical category.[64] But even though it might prove difficult to pinpoint times and places ideally conforming to socioeconomic aspects of the feudal model, there can be no doubting its power and longevity as an imaginative proposition.[65] And since a reimagined feudalism became such an integral part of plantation slave management, it seems vital to reaffirm the distinctive lineaments of its medieval avatar. Medieval feudalism's most distinctive trait (compared with what comes later) is its understanding of mutuality: the sense that, however great the gulf between master and servant, Creator and creature, lesser and greater, each is bound in a relationship of reciprocal obligation (that characteristically, in a very real, physical sense, brings one to the other). Thus it is that Abbess Heloïse first writes to Abelard in the confident expectation that he is bound ("obligaveris") to respond. Indeed, the more God-like his power, the more tightly he is bound in obligation: "for you after God are the sole founder of this place," she says; "everything here is your own creation."[66] The fact that the "new plantation" of the Paraclete is seeded with feminine plants (nuns) requires Abelard to lend or surrender his masculine potency. Their claim by virtue of weakness – greater than that which male students and clerics can impose on him – is emphatically underscored through (almost rhythmic) repetition:

> While you spend so much on the stubborn, consider what you owe [debeas] to the obedient; you are so generous to your enemies but should reflect [debeas meditare] on how you are indebted to your daughters. Apart from everything else, consider the close tie by which you have bound yourself to me [quanto erga me te obligaveris debito], and repay the debt [debito] you owe [debes] a whole community of women dedicated to God by discharging it the more dutifully to her who is yours alone. (p. 112)

Such appeals to mutual obligation are intensified through inversions intrinsic to medieval religious discourse: for "ther the soule is hyest, noblyest and wurschypfullest," as Julian of Norwich has it, "yett it is lowest, mekest and mildest."[67] So it is that Heloïse, made abject by Abelard through physical violence and forced inclaustration, is thus (through this inversional logic) raised higher by Abelard and is hence able to mount even stronger claims upon him. And of course, the further a woman falls, or is thrown down, the more closely she imitates the sacred trajectory of ab-jection, the "throwing down" of incarnation and, ultimately, crucifixion. Imagining divine abjection to human masculinity falls short (Julian, and others, intuit) of measuring the true distances involved. One person of the Trinity wills, another conforms: "where of it folowyth," Julian argues, "that as verely as god is oure fader, as verely god is oure mother. Our fader wyllyth, oure mother werkyth" (p. 591). It was thus as "oure kynde moder, our gracious modyr" that Jesus "toke the ground of his werke full lowe and full myldely in the maydyns womb" (p. 594). And as "our very mother," Jesus is thus bound to share the best and most natural of maternal instincts: "The moder may suffer the chylde to fall some tyme and be dyssesed on dyverse manner, for the one profyte, but she may nevyr suffre that ony manner of peril come to her chylde, for love" (p. 604). Passages like these so enraged Clifton Wolters, Julian's first Penguin translator, that he branded her a heretic (for failing to imagine a Creator condemning his creatures to eternal torment).[68] But the internal logic (and historical survival) of Julian's imaginings bear powerful witness to the potency of abjection within feudalism as an imaginative and strategic resource for women. Julian, of course, is especially savvy. She realizes that imaginings of God must not reduce God to the terms of any specific covenant or agreement (a realization shared by contemporary nominalist theologians and by the poet of *Cleanness*).[69] God must not, in short, be boxed in like some contemporary landlord obliged to pay fixed wages. And so, as the third person of the Trinity, "he werkyth, rewardyng and gevyng. Rewardyng," Julian explains, "is a gyfte of trust that the lorde doth to them that hath traveyled; and gevyng is a curtesse werkyng which he doth freely of grace, fulfyllyng and ovyr passing alle that is deservyd of creaturys."[70]

Masculine meditations on God exercising his freedom to be God, hence exercising his *potentia absoluta*, tend to imagine the Creator visiting violent and precipitate acts (as in *Cleanness*) upon stupefied and terrorized creatures. In Julian's imagining, however, God asserts his freedom to surprise by slipping an unearned bonus into the pay-packet of the worker, "hym that hath travellid."

The inversional logic of religious abjection is alive and well at a more popular level in the dicta of Margery Kempe. "Sir," she tells the Archbishop of York's steward (who has opined that "holy folke shulde not lawghe"), "I haue gret cawse for to lawghe, for the mor schame I suffyr & despit, the meryar may I ben in owr Lord Ihesu Crist."[71] This reworks the punch line of the mini-sermon preached by Margery at Canterbury on the man who laughs at his abusers. For many days, he tells them, he has had to pay good money for men "to chyde me for remyssyon of my synne" (13, p. 28); now he can save his silver. "Rygth so." says Margery to her current abusers (keen to burn her as a Lollard), "whyl I was at hom in my owyn contre day be day wyth gret wepyng & mornyng, I sorwyd for I had no schame, skorne, & despyte as I was worthy." And now she has plenty: "her is a cartful of thornys redy for the," the crowd cries, "& a tonne to bren the wyth" (13, p. 28). Margery, trembling and quaking, prays and is soon rescued by two goodlooking (as usual) young men; she is thus abject, but not in despair. In fact, the only times of despair for Margery come when (as in the opening chapter) she fails to experience the mutuality of her relationship with Jesus, her lord and master. Bereft of this assurance, she bites and tears at her own body, denying all social ties. When reassurance comes, it is affirmed through one simple sentence that speaks to this crucial issue of mutuality: "Dowtyr, why hast thow forsakyn me, and I forsoke neuyr the?" (1, p. 8).

This paradigm of abjection within a relationship of feudal mutuality with Christ (the most exalted and the most abject) prompts Margery to scrupulous accounting of various humiliations suffered, as when, for example, her fellow pilgrims cut her gown short and dress her in white canvass, "for sche shuld ben holdyn a fool" (26, p. 62): a fool (Margery might reflect) much like the village idiot Jesus – "an ydiote & an ydul man & a fole" – of the *Meditationes vitae Christi*, who determines "to be hald as vnworthi & abiecte to the worlde"; to be held "*a worme & not a man.*"[72] This hunger for abjection can precipitate some strange social behaviors, as when Margery feels prompted by "owr Lord . . . for hys lofe" to give away not just all her own money, but also that of Richard, her broken-backed male companion. Richard, understandably, is "euyl plesyd" (which only adds to the economy of abuse and abjection; 37, p. 92).

Religious men could follow similar impulses with similar results; early Franciscans were especially keen to act out stupidity and folly in the spirit of their founder. Jacopone da Todi, for example, garnered generous abuse by showing up at his brother's wedding reception wearing nothing but honey and feathers.[73] But every priest, remembering himself flat on his face on the floor immediately before rising to receive his priestly powers at ordination,

understood these dynamics. Not surprisingly, then, we may discern masculine envy of female abjection experience, an experience which may bring a
woman closer to that of Christ on the cross than any man might envisage.
So it is that we sense the male author of *Ancrene Wisse* buzzing like a fly
around his female charges, urging them (in Part V, especially) to hoover up
every last trivial infraction in their outwardly uneventful lives and report
weekly to their confessor.[74] And yet, as we turn from Part V to Part VI, from
confession to penance, we see him backing off, from the very first sentence:

> Al is penitence ant strong penitence þet 3e eauer dreheð, mine leoue sustren;
> al þet 3e eauer doð of god, al þet 3e polieð, is ow martirdom i se derf ordre,
> for 3e beoð niht & dei up o Godes rode.[75]

> All you ever endure is penance, and hard penance, my dear sisters; all the
> good you ever do, all you suffer, is martyrdom for you in the most severe of
> orders, for night and day you are up on God's cross.

There is a clear sense throughout this chapter of a male author, as a man in
the world, essentially excluded from the most exalted, intimate, and terrible
experiences of the women for whom he writes. He seems, to borrow a term
from Caroline Bynum, to register the relatively pedestrian character of his
own experiential capacities *as* a masculine author. Medieval religious practices did tend, according to Bynum, "to produce symbolic usages in which
female was seen as below and above reason . . . whereas male was seen as
a rather pedestrian middle, incapable of direct contact either with angelic
or demonic power."[76] Midway through this section on penance, the *Wisse*
author does acknowledge peculiar affinities between these hidden women
and the incarnate Christ: "and was he not himself a recluse in Mary's womb?"
At the very end, however, he makes a sustained bid for an equivalent, even
surpassing, masculine abjection: "I know someone," he says, "who bears a
heavy coat of mail and a hair shirt, both at once, his middle thighs and arms
bound tight with iron in broad, thick bands, so that the sweat from it is an
agony to bear." This man "often asks me to teach him something with
which he can mortify his body. All that is bitter" (and here we have a
characteristic inversion) "seems sweet to him for our Lord's love"; the man
says that "God forgets him because he has not sent him any great illness."
There is something not just absurd but plain ridiculous about this man's
attempts to sink lower through self-enclosure in hair and metal: for however
low he gets, his body remains inferior as a vehicle for abject experience (of
the kind essayed by Julian at the beginning of her *Showings*) to that of these

women. His gratuitous intrusion[77] into the *Wisse* at a point where the male
author is feeling markedly inferior to his female readers might be taken as
a symptom of the "abjection envy" with which religious men viewed the
experiences of religious women.

Remarkable instances of white male designs on abject positions are
supplied by Bernard of Clairvaux's highly influential sermons on the *Song
of Songs*, particularly those excogitated from *Nigra sum sed formosa, filiae
Hierusalem.*[78] In Abelard's handling of this verse, Heloïse is imagined as the
woman in black (an enclosed nun) who stays within doors to serve and
pleasure her master and spouse. Bernard's strategy is to further eject the
abject, to displace the black woman and have men take her place. He sur-
veys the saints, so humble and abject ("abjectus") in outward appearance.[79]
His first candidate for the "person black and beautiful" – and here Bernard
emends Scripture in speaking of "animam et nigram, pariter et formosam" –
is St. Paul (an ironic choice, given the disabling, long-term effects of Pauline
strictures against female preaching). Paul, Bernard insists (evidently riffing
on the Latin *paulus*), was "blemished and ugly," a mere "runt of a man who
has suffered hunger and thirst, cold and nakedness, the hardship of constant
labor, countless beatings"; he is thus reputed "abject, dishonorable, black,
beneath notice, a scrap of this world's refuse" ("inglorius, ignobilis, niger,
obscurus, tamquam peripsema huius mundi"). Bernard's second candidate is
(implicitly) Bernard, for in the next sermon he launches into an extraordinary lament for his brother and fellow Clairvaux monk, Gerard. "You know
how I am situated," he tells his dead brother, "how dejected in spirit [ubi
iaceam], how your departure has affected me; there is none to give me a
helping hand" (26.6). This last claim is especially extravagant, since Bernard
speaks and pours his tears "before the eyes of my sons" (26.3); the disappear-
ing of woman (and hence of the heterosexual matrix that still governs
Abelard's imaginings) announces the arrival of a new and intense, all-male
affectivity. Bernard's sons should condole with their father, for he has been
harshly struck with God's rod of indignation ("virga indignationis"). God
strikes "justly because I deserve it," Bernard says, "harshly because I can
bear it" ("digne pro meritis, dure pro viribus"). This last phrase registers
another interesting claim for the superiority of male abjection, an abjection
machismo: men can endure more, so God beats them more soundly.

Such exegesis insinuates a distinction between human attributes considered essential (whiteness, manliness) and disposable (blackness, womanliness, and Jewishness: *filiae Hierusulam*). The first group, in effect, dresses
itself in the second to perform necessary but temporally delimited acts of

abjection. We thus see (recalling Stedman's exegesis of Lamentations) earlier avatars of a long-lived Christian tradition of spiritual blackface: as when, for example, God becomes man and darkens in the flesh ("nigrescat in carne," 28.2); thus "the blackening of one makes many bright" ("multos candidos facit unius denigratio"). In assuming this denigrated state, God also assumes the form of a slave (a new disposable term joins the list) to save slaves ("obnubiletur in forma servi pro vita servi"); Jesus is thus crucified as a deformed black man ("deforme et nigrum"), an object of laughter for the wicked, tears for the faithful ("risum malignatibus . . . fletum fidelibus," 28.4).[80] In Malory's *Tale of the Sankgreal*, Sir Bors must repudiate the white bird which enters his dreams and embrace the bird that is "merveylous blacke"; for "by the blak birde," he is later instructed, "myght ye understande Holy Chirche whych seyth, 'I am blake,' but he ys fayre."[81]

If blackness is an attribute to be assumed for specific abjecting experiences ("haec . . . quae denigrant Paulum," in Bernard's account, 25.5), it would seem that blackness is something to be shucked off once earthly life is over. Bernard, in fact, posits two species of blackness. The first is an enduring blackness, a blackness within and without, such as, for example, that of the Muslims against whom Bernard preached before and after the launching of the Second Crusade.[82] Such matching of infidel blackness against Christian whiteness, already well-developed in twelfth-century *chansons de geste*, later entangles with discourses of slavery, as in *Titus Andronicus*, for example, where Aaron (lover of Tamora, Queen of the Goths) acclaims his newborn son as a smiling "black slave," a "thick-lipped slave" (4.2.119, 174). Aaron himself, "the incarnate devil" (5.1.40), is dismissed with a succinct phrase that locates him beyond humanity, civility, and Christianity ("Away, inhuman dog, unhallowed slave," 5.3.14). This, then, is a blackness beyond abjection, a blackness not to be borrowed.

The second blackness, wherein and whereby heaven-sent or heaven-bound whiteness effects its abjecting or redeeming work on earth, is assumed only temporarily. The pilgrim soul, darkened by the endurance of penance, insult, persecution, or even by the very ardor of its longing, perceives and deprecates its blackness ever more keenly in light of the very brightness it apprehends at journey's end ("ex eo me obscuram deprehendo, nigram invenio, foedam despicio," 28.13). Finally, Bernard looks forward to the color and heat of the flesh being exterminated ("ad exterminationem coloris et caloris illius," 29.8); there is no blackness in heaven. And if there is nobody black, what then of the other disposable identities we have considered: the Jew, the slave, the woman?

Passages from Feudal to Absolute Imagining:
Oroonoko and Behn

Blackness may thus be viewed (used might be a better word) by whiteness as, alternatively, an eternal essence or a temporal phase; both options
are variously exploited up to 1689 and beyond.[83] Behn herself hesitates or
hovers between alternatives: her commitment to Oroonoko's nobility or roy-
alty finds expression in a desperate program of cultural whitening (achieved
chiefly through classical education: it was at court, Behn tells us, that
Oroonoko "learned so much humanity" from his French tutor).[84] Oroonoko
is thus accorded a blackness so dazzling that it (he) is almost white; his
countenance is as "perfect ebony, or polished jet" (pp. 80–1).[85] Behn's desperate yearning for whiteness in Oroonoko yields some strange details and
localized urgencies, such as her need to claim "that a Negro can change
color; for I have seen them," she insists, "frequently blush, and look pale,
and that as visibly as ever I saw in the most beautiful white" (p. 88). Ultimately, however, it is Behn's anxious acceptance that Oroonoko *cannot*
change color that estranges author from protagonist; the fear that the rebel
Oroonoko, "who had carried with him all the negroes," would "come down
and cut all our [white] throats" (p. 132). Behn even has Oroonoko himself
confirm (through the very failure of his classically modulated rhetoric) the
innate and enduring slavishness of the negroes he would command.[86] Slavery, he tells them, is "not for days, months, or years, but for eternity."
Slaves, "*villainous*, senseless men" (my emphasis), did not possess "the divine
quality of men, and were become insensible asses, fit only to bear" (p. 126).
The cathection of blackness to slavery (and of both to femininity) dooms the
rebellion to rapid collapse (as the male slaves are distracted by the women
and children hanging about their necks, urging surrender, p. 129).

Behn's ambiguous apprehension of blackness as something both permeable and perennial, relative and absolute, is to be associated with her understanding of femininity and womanliness (terms that, in contemporary
theoretical discussion, find themselves similarly divided between discourses
of essence and of accident or lack).[87] Womanliness that matters – that has
some determinative social force – is closely associated in *Oroonoko* with
beauty and youth:

> And certainly, nothing is more afflicting to a decayed beauty than to behold in
> itself [*sic*] declining charms, that were once adored, and to find those caresses
> paid to new beauties to which once she laid a claim; to hear them whisper as
> she passes by, "That was once a delicate woman." These abandoned ladies

therefore endeavour to revenge all the despites and decays of time on these flourishing happy ones. (p. 90)

Beauty is here assigned a powerful social role (determinative for men) in continually undermining any possible solidarity between women. Fear of its waning (as in "the heart of the antiquated Onahal") also renders women vulnerable to masculine flattery and manipulation.[88] Of Onahal (guardian of the Otan, and thus of Imoinda), Behn says: "though she had some decays in her face, she had none in her sense and wit" (p. 90). Behn thus posits the possibility of temporal migration within feminine identity: from youthful beauty to accumulated wit. In *Oroonoko*, the now ageing Behn marries the beauty of Oroonoko to her own practiced skill in the hope of producing something of enduring value, something "to survive to all ages" (p. 141). Such a transcendent phenomenon would, in essence, give us the whole of woman: beauty, forever conjoined with "sense and wit." It would also (at the same time) suggest how woman might complete herself by forging an alliance beyond her own kind. The amalgam Behn/Oroonoko thus bids for a transcendence hitherto reserved (in this long history) for white/masculinity.

At the end of Aphra Behn's last play, *The Widow Ranter* (set in Virginia), the English planter Timorous proposes to return "to my old trade again, bask under the shade of my own tobacco, and drink my punch in peace" (p. 324). His "trade" is to do nothing and owe nothing, while slave or indentured labor does everything. His aspiration is that of the Stuarts and of all the noble investors back in the old country; his *attitude* (of *otium* surrounded by *negotium*, studied idleness in the face of labor) is elegantly modeled by the white planter in Stedman's map of Surinam (figure 26). Oroonoko encounters the white world as one in which bonds of reciprocal obligation are first invoked (by the English slaving captain, p. 101) and then ruthlessly denied (by the captain, by the system of slavery itself). So when the rebel Oroonoko is promised that "all imaginable respect shall be paid you; and yourself, your wife, and child, if it be here born, shall depart free out of our land," he can but reply, from his own experience, that "there was no faith in the white men, or the gods they adored" (p. 130). Oroonoko testifies to the end of mutuality and to a society in which betrayal, local or systemic, has become (all the more shocking, for failing to shock or surprise) the way of the world.[89] He thus seems an archaic figure – in a global economy no longer prepared to honor oaths or oral agreements, but only written contracts, securities, and bonds – testifying to the passing of *trouthe*.[90] Since no vestige of reciprocity remains in such a world, he refuses to die abject (that is,

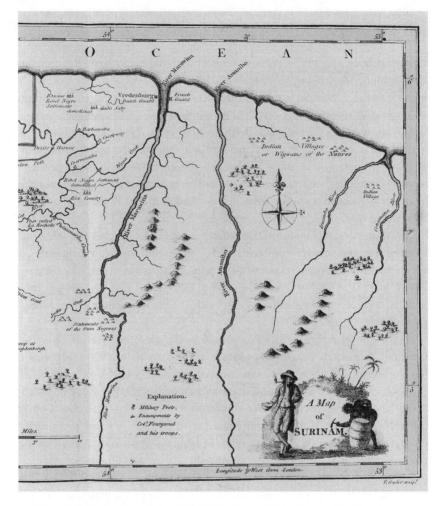

26 Map of Surinam, from John Gabriel Stedman, *Narrative of a Five Years'
Expedition against the Revolted Negroes of Surinam* (1796 edition), with modeling of
otium (left) and labor (right). British Library, London.

within such a world's own frame of reference). For to suffer abjectly – even
in Kristeva's peculiar understanding of *l'abjection* – is in some degree to
recognize an authorizing other without.[91] Oroonoko, rather, puts his mind
elsewhere, back to his West African homeland, perhaps, where (according
to his own theology) his spirit will soon follow.

Signifying frameworks and judicial pretensions left unrecognized by subjects they seek to destroy can find themselves seriously compromised: the

white society of *Titus Andronicus*, for example, seems never (in superior productions) adequately to interpellate Aaron by the values that hang him.[92] Oroonoko, refusing the peculiarly Christian framework of ethics that make abjection work, dies believing that "knowledge of the Christian gods" makes Africans "the vilest of all creeping things" (p. 131). It is a considerable achievement of Behn's text that it occasionally views Christian-sanctioned betrayals through the eyes of an incredulous outsider, as when, for example, Oroonoko leaves the English ship that has brought him to slavery: "Farewell, Sir!" he says to the English captain who has broken every civil convention of hospitality and honor to betray him. "Tis worth my suffering to gain so true a knowledge both of you and of your gods by whom you swear" (p. 106). There is, I think, a glimmer of empathy between Behn and her male protagonist at this point, which owes something to her experience specifically as a woman. For Behn, too, came all the way to the coast of Surinam at the bidding or command of men: perhaps her father, who was dead before the journey out was even completed (p. 115); more likely a man of some rank who took her along for the ride; quite possibly a sea captain who delivered her – and many women like her – to the Americas with no immediate prospects.[93]

No form of analogy or equivalence can equate the experience of a white English woman playwright to that of black enslaved Africans. Oroonoko, for Behn, might well pass as an extravagant figure for one of the "black Stuarts" (such as James II).[94] The name of Caesar, conferred upon Oroonoko at the slave plantation, was also conferred by Behn upon Charles II (in a poem on his passage to Ireland) and James II (as late as 1689);[95] the "frightful spectacles of a mangled king" that end her tale (p. 140) might move contemporaries to remember Charles I.[96] And yet, conversely, such allegorical cover might allow Behn to explore particular aspects of slave-like experience with which – as a talented and literate woman – she might empathize (if not identify); might allow her (as victim of the harsh economic logic informing European patriarchy) vicariously to explore the possibilities of gazing at this system, incredulously, from its outside.[97] The relationship between Oroonoko and Behn indubitably ends in bad faith; yet there are, in the narrative's duration, moments of rapprochement, imagined alliance, worth something. Such moments might almost be mapped as a history of pronouns (plural, first-person), the text's imagining of groups constituted as "we" and "us." We might begin at the point where Behn is acclaimed as Oroonoko's "Great Mistress" (p. 114). Here, already, the doom-laden end is in sight, for Oroonoko has just learned that Imoinda (now Clemene) is expecting a child; he knows that the English "will make a slave of that too, for all the breed is theirs to whom the parents belong" (p. 113). Traveler Behn is anxious as the white/ black divide widens; Oroonoko reassures her "that he would act nothing upon the white people" (p. 114). And then suddenly – immediately following Behn's famous "autobiographical" statement (p. 115) – the text enters or reenters an extraordinary, suspended space of utopian New World pastoral (there are no tigers in Surinam): "But to our sports," says Behn (p. 117).[98] Within the full economy of the text these "sports" might be read as funeral games, played out before the African protagonists are finally and definitively dispatched.[99] Locally, however, they enable Behn to infiltrate Oroonoko into the white, European "we":

> Sometimes we would go surprising, and in search of young tigers in their dens, watching when the old ones went forth to forage for prey, and oftentimes we have been in great danger, and have fled apace for our lives, when surprised by the dams. But once, above all other times, we went on this design, and Caesar was with us, who had no sooner stolen a young tiger from her nest, but going off, we encountered the dam, bearing a buttock of a cow, which she had torn off with her mighty paw, and going with it towards her den. We had only four women, Caesar, and an English gentleman, brother to Harry Martin, the great Oliverian. (p. 117)

Oroonoko's integration now enables more audacious encounters: it is deemed dangerous to visit an Indian town, but "for my part" (Behn tells us), "I said, if Caesar would, I would go" (p. 121). They are led to the Indians by a fisherman who,

> by long living there, [had] become a perfect Indian in color; we, who resolved to surprise them, by making them see something they never had seen (that is, white people) resolved only myself, my brother, and woman should go. (p. 121)

It is fascinating to note that, at the very moment that Behn and company are moved to white exhibitionism, the text is disturbed by the thought that whiteness may become blackness (or, at least, that skin color changes with time). Similar disturbance may be traced all the way back to Abelard, for his citation of the crucial "nigra . . . sed formosa" verse comes paired with the verse that follows it in the Song of Songs, namely "Take no notice of my darkness, because the sun has discolored me." Abelard dutifully cites the verse (p. 138), but never returns to gloss it. The notion of white migrating toward black will prove increasingly difficult to countenance as, with the passage of time, skin color is read as an absolute attribute. Behn and company certainly take no chances: "they were all naked," she says of the Indians, "and we were all dressed." This polarity is preserved even as the Indians lay hands on the English group, "feeling our breasts and arms, taking up one petticoat, then wondering to see another" (p. 121).[100] Behn and company evidently enjoy, for a moment, being the objects rather than the agents of anthropological discovery: "we suffered them to survey us as they pleased, and we thought they would never have done admiring us" (p. 122). This particular polarity is soon reversed, however, as the Europeans observe the contest of self-mutilation through which the Indians identify their next "Great War Captain" (p. 124). At this point, Caesar is fully integrated (never more so) into the European group, for he shares their collective wonder at the spectacle before them (which, Behn tells us, displays "a sort of courage too brutal to be applauded by our black hero," p. 124).

Soon, however, Behn peremptorily ends "this digression" by bringing us immediately back to the most intractable fact of "my story" (p. 125), namely Imoinda's advancing pregnancy. From this point on, as Oroonoko attempts to lead the slaves "to freedom, and glorious liberty" (p. 127), Behn pulls away: "we had by noon," Behn says, "about six hundred men, they call the militia of the county, that came to assist us in the pursuit of the fugitives" (p. 128). The migration of personal pronoun referents initiated here becomes more pronounced as white anxieties rise:

> You must know, that when the news was brought on Monday morning, that Caesar had betaken himself to the woods, and carried with him all the Negroes, we were possessed with extreme fear, which no dissuasions could dissipate, that he would secure himself till night, and then, that he would come down and cut all our throats. This apprehension made all the females of us fly down the river. (p. 132)

Having married Oroonoko to what, in white imagining, is the temporality native to his color – darkness, night – Behn sharply exits the scene and (in a sense) never stops running. She thus leaves the way clear for Imoinda, her sometime surrogate, to be decapitated by Oroonoko (p. 136); she even contrives to be absent for the final butchering of Oroonoko himself (p. 140). It is especially pusillanimous that she has herself taken "about three days journey down the river" (p. 139) to avoid this scene, and that she then invents three flimsy textual surrogates to cause and record it: "one Banister, a wild Irishman" (who has hitherto played no part in the narrative) expedites Oroonoko's capture, and Behn's "mother and sister," she tells us, "were by him all the while" throughout his dismemberment (pp. 139–40). And yet even here, in these last pages, Behn does contrive moments for Oroonoko to defy the European frame by suggesting solidarity with American peoples. The first comes as Oroonoko cuts "a piece of flesh from his own throat, and threw it at them" (the immediate referent for "them" here being simply "the English," p. 138). This self-mutilating reprises the warrior practices of the native village, originally assessed (we are told) as "a sort of courage too brutal to be applauded" by "our black hero" (p. 124). Oroonoko, in defying the Eurocentric logic of his own death, now honors such native "courage," strengthening the identification by assuming the American habit of smoking as the English hack him to death (p. 140).

It is in the time and space of Oroonoko's dying, unhappily and predictably, that Behn's text most clearly opens historical and imaginative lines of sight for Africans transported to the Americas. Two alternatives are posited: spiritual return to Africa (the Coramantiens believing that their spirits will so return after death); marrying African culture to that of the new continent (in the journey into the bush, Oroonoko emerges as a key mediator between ethnic groups).[101] This tension between Africanist and Americanist identifications has, of course, proved definitional for African-American political and cultural debate in the United States. *Oroonoko*'s Surinam, however, posits Afro-American possibilities not historically realizable in North America, for the vast, forested density of the continent inland from the coastal strip encourages flight from slavery and the development of adaptive and distinctive black cultures. As Behn notes, slave merchants took care to break national and cultural ties between Africans in selling them off (pp. 105–6); it was thus the synthesizing culture of the plantation that slaves took with them on escaping (along with axes, guns, pots, or anything else that might aid survival).[102] A century later, John Stedman and his fellow European mercenaries are still engaged in the hopeless historical task of containing and suppressing these Afro-American communities.[103] By then the Saramaka, one of the six Maroon tribes in Surinam, had already secured independence.[104] By then, too, life for black people who stayed on the plantation had sunk to levels of degradation and depersonalization undreamed of in *Oroonoko*.

Plantation Logic: Stedman and Blake

In traveling from El Dorado to Surinam, Voltaire's Candide takes a bizarrely improbable overland route. He does, however, retrace the successive, downgrading aspirations of Columbus and "le chevalier Raleigh": hoping for gold, they settle for sugar.[105] The slave encountered by Candide on entering

Surinam, missing a hand and a foot, bears the impress of plantation logic: any slave nipping a finger in the mill at the sugar-works shall lose a whole hand; any slave running off shall lose a foot. "This is the price," the unnamed slave observes, "at which you eat sugar in Europe." The price Europeans paid for their sugar was (and still is) low, relative to the human cost of its production. Surinamese plantations expanded massively in the course of the eighteenth century: by 1738 there were 591 plantations, with an estimated 50,000 to 55,000 slaves (accumulated at a rate of about 1,000 per year: mortality was high).[106] Plantations became self-enclosed systems, in which expendable labor was compelled by the harshest discipline to work almost unlimited days with little daily or seasonal variation of task. This has often, then and now, been imagined as a medieval feudalism, exported from the Old World to the New while exchanging white labor for black. There are, indeed, parallels: slaves, like medieval serfs, were regarded as extensions or instruments of the land they worked and could be sold along with it. There are thus also parallel forms of resistance.[107] But of course, crucial differences distinguish medieval peasants from eighteenth-century Caribbean plantation slaves. In Europe, work was seasonal and – as many a Book of Hours testifies – forms of labor were more varied and more localized in character (according to soil and climate). Landowners thus knew themselves to be in some sense indentured to the laborers working their land: peasants – as *nativi*, sons of the soil – knew much that lords did not (as explicitly acknowledged by texts such as Walter of Henley's *Husbandry* and Chaucer's portrayal of a peasant overseer, his Reeve). Recognition of lordly dependency upon local peasant intelligence concealed itself neatly within the ideal (socially archaic by 1381, but – as we have seen – still a powerful imaginative paradigm) of feudal mutuality: each of the three estates, owing something to each of the others, could expect something in return from both. By the time of Gervase Markham's *English Husbandman*, however, we see peasant labor implicitly denied any sense of special relationship to, understanding of, the land it works and inhabits; gentlemen farmers may acquire the same or better knowledge through bookish instruction.[108]

Such progressive ideological alienation of peasant from territory – accompanied by concrete acts of lordly enclosure, engrossment, and expulsion – might be figured as a shift from feudal toward absolutist paradigms (if it be remembered that absolutism effects not repudiation of feudal principles, but rather selective intensification of them).[109] The most crucial act of *deselection* here is the rejection of that spirit of mutuality intrinsic to medieval understanding (if not diurnal practice) of the feudal bond. Extreme emphasis is now placed upon the one-way, upward-ascending obligation of subject to sovereign, sinner to the Almighty.[110] The most extreme expression of this is the would-be feudal relationship of colonist owner to plantation slave: a bone-dry feudalism, from which every last drop of mutuality has been squeezed. The most extreme fantasies of monarchist absolutism, dramatically repudiated in England on January 30, 1649, might thus still be acted out in overseas, slave-based, plantation societies.[111] Compared with their Tudor forebears, the post-regicide Stuarts seem chastened in their absolutist imaginings; theirs are a matter of theatrical pretension, rather than political and economic conviction. It was thus only in Surinam that Behn might glimpse how a regime of absolute reimagined feudal polity might actually work.[112]

The most dramatic shift between the time of Behn's sojourn in and imagining of Surinam and the time of Voltaire and Stedman springs from matters of scale, namely the massive increase of African slaves and consequently of black to white ratios. A map of 1667 shows 178 plantations; Abraham Crijnssen, Zeeland naval commander, estimates that they were peopled in that year by about 4,000 inhabitants (an average per settlement of about 22.5).[113] Figures for 1688 (the year of *Oroonoko*'s publication) suggest, following English departures, only 23 plantations with 564 slaves counted (thus averaging about 20 per settlement).[114] But just 50 years later, as we have noted, some 50,000 to 55,000 slaves were recorded on just 591 plantations (establishing an average of close to 100 per plantation that was to continue, more or less, throughout the century). Such numbers suggest Behn's experience of slavery to be on a cusp situated between the more intimate, domestic, medieval model considered in chapter 4 (which valued a slave too highly for permanent maiming) and that of Voltaire and Stedman (in whose time slaves were viewed *en masse* as expendable chattels in large-scale economic enterprise).[115] We have seen flashes of white terror in Behn equivalent to those retailed by Stedman (as in his account of a "late Revolt" in which rebels make "no Scruple to Cut up Alive theyr European Mistresses Who were with Child in the Presence of their Husbands," p. 525). But we do not find Stedman's sense of black personality entirely subsumed by, assuming the shape of, labor (as when some slaves have their teeth smashed out "for Tasting the Sugar Cane Cultivated by themselves"; as when others commit suicide by leaping into "a Chaldron of Boiling Sugar," p. 532). There is, in short, an intimacy of scale in Behn's Surinam that, when read against the more massive, factory-like operations of the eighteenth century, seems (like Behn's hero) quite archaic.[116]

There is no doubt that Stedman delights to tell of the black miseries and joys of Surinam; his white audiences were clearly thrilled to hear about them. Before launching into an extended account, he attempts a sort of shuffling, semi-grammatical justification of slavery that echoes New and Old Testaments, and even *Hamlet*:

> That Slaves have been from the Earliest times / Witness Philemon & Onesima / need no Comment, indeed we are all Dependants in a Less or more Degree, but how to treat those Whom fate has Subjected to our Commands that is the Question, & how they are Treated in the Colony of Surinam Shall Presently be Seen –
>
> The Reader may Remember that I have introduced them in the 9th Chapter as Landing from the Coast of Guinea in a Lamentable State of Skin and bone, when
>
> > Their Visage is Blacker than a Coal they are not known in the Streets, their Skin Cleaveth to their bones it is Withered it is become like a Stick
> > *–Lament. 4th chapt. – Verse 8–*
>
> I have there Say'd that under the Care of Other Old Negro Slaves, they Soon become verry Fat and Sleek, learn the Language of the Colony, &c, When they are next Sent to Work in the Fields, to Which at first they Cheerfully Submit. (pp. 527–8)

Arrival in Surinam is here figured almost as a moment of salvation for black slaves: New World, new, albeit animalized bodies ("become verry Fat and Sleek"), new language, new opportunities for labor; the only perennially resistant factor here is the facticity of blackness. And it is the assurance that slaves cannot translate from blackness that rings in the white audience, allowing it to settle for spectacles to come. Such non-translatability runs only one way: the most crucial phrase in this passage (perhaps in this chapter) is "we are all . . . Less or more." If we are all more or less dependants and slaves, whites are all more or less capable of dipping into – not really empathizing with – the slave-like, black condition, for whites always already have the sanctuary of whiteness to return to. Blackness, as figured by the verse from Lamentations, is a condition perennially reproaching its wearer, a garment that the imaginative white reader might put on and cast off at will.[117] This impulse to assume blackness (or the place of blackness), albeit for a passing instant, has sunk deep roots in the white imaginary.[118] It rises unbidden to the surface (a strange, semi-conscious counterpart to Michäel Slory's black sea) of imaginary travels: when Hannibal Lecter crosses the Atlantic, the "hip room between armrests" in his 747 seat is said to be "twenty inches. This is two inches more space than a slave had on the Middle Passage."[119]

Before proceeding to describe the torturing of slaves in Surinam – the part of his lengthy work which proved most popular in England – Stedman

spends some ten pages celebrating the musical and poetical accomplish-
ments of blacks, including "Philis Wheatly's Soft and Elegant Manner of
Writing" (considered by Jefferson "below the dignity of criticism").[120] Stedman
thus strategically legitimates any flashes of empathy a white audience –
particularly a female one? – might feel in his ensuing account of black subjects. Immediately before purveying the most grisly passages, he promises to
balance them against more comforting images of black domestic life: "While
the one Picture," Stedman insists, "I am Almost Afraid will Occasion Such a
Shudder, that any further Perusal of this Work will be dropt & Laid Aside,
but I pledge my Word that the Other will make full and Ample Compensa-
tion" (p. 527). Here he protects his white audience from the suggestion that
their primary desire is to contemplate violence inflicted on fellow humans;
all this (the argument is entirely specious) is but a rough passage to a final
contemplation of domestic harmony.

Stedman's use of the term "Picture" suggests that he is already thinking of
producing a written text accompanied by visual images. When submitted to
his publisher, Joseph Johnson, his manuscript was accompanied by approximately 106 drawings and watercolors; Johnson engaged a range of engravers,
including the Royal Academician, Francesco Bartolozzi, and the young jour-
neyman, William Blake (16 plates). Blake's most famous illustrations follow
and indeed sharpen the differentiation by gender that is such a striking feature of Stedman's account of black suffering. Male slaves, according to
Stedman, typically die with composure, indifference, and contempt. The
negro Neptune, "no Slave, but his own master, & a Carpenter by trade"
(p. 546), is condemned for killing an estate overseer. Tied to a "Strong Cross,"
his left hand is amputated and his body broken "to Shivers," until "the
Splinters Blood and Marrow flew about the Field, but the Prisoner never
uttered a Groan, or a Sigh." Surprisingly undead, he asks for tobacco, mocks
"you Christians," sings "two Extempore Songs (With a Clear Voice)," asks a
Jew called De Vries to repay a debt, offers his detached hand as a snack and
laughs at his own wit. In Blake's illustration Neptune lies being broken on
the cross, staring imperturbably to where his left hand (now on the grass)
once was. Similarly impenetrable is the gaze of the male slave Blake depicts
hanging from a hook thrust through his ribcage; the viewer, finding nowhere to settle in this stark encounter, is offered a line of visual retreat by
two skulls on poles leading to a distant ship (about to sail beyond the frame
of the picture).[121] One early reader of this scene – in the King's Library copy,
now British Library 145.f.15,16 – signaled involvement by daubing red
watercolor blood-marks on the pure white ground in which Blake's Neptune hangs suspended.

This fantasy of black male indifference to pain is given most arresting expression in the authorial portrait engraved by Bartolozzi as the frontispiece to the 1796 edition. Stedman stands, like a big-game hunter, above a freshly bayoneted Surinamese African; a quatrain below the image, addressed to the dying man, ends with the line "Twas Yours to fall – but Mine to feel the wound" (figure 27).[122] Feeling the wound, however, is a role shared by

27 Francesco Bartolozzi, authorial portrait of John Gabriel Stedman as frontispiece to *Narrative of a Five Years' Expedition* (1796 edition). British Library, London.

Stedman with black females. Whereas black males remain – in the tradition of Behn's Oroonoko – impenetrable and inscrutable in their suffering,
deflecting the gaze like a closed continent, black females draw the viewer in.
In encountering "a truly beautiful Samboe girl of about 18, as naked as she
came to the World," tied to a tree after 200 lashes, Stedman is moved to ask
the overseer to untie her. His intervention only incites the overseer to
repeat the punishment, since it is his "unalterable rule" so "to prevent all
Strangers from interfearing with his Government" (p. 264). The overseer,
incensed at having his "loathsome Embraces" rejected, is thus able "to enjoy
his bloody-feast til he was Glutted" (pp. 266, 264). But Stedman, too, is
thereby licensed to view such sights purely as sexual spectacle (resolving
never again to communicate with overseers, p. 264).

Such license to spectate is transferred to the viewer by Blake's illustration
of this scene (figure 28). The four male figures, relegated to the background,
enact a tableau that guarantees perennial punishment for the black female
slave: Stedman, on the left, gesticulates his dismay; the overseer, on the
right, responds by recalling the two male flagellators who are returning to
their hut. The spectator, thus isolated and jammed up against the beautiful
female figure in the foreground, is thus assured that *nothing can be done*. No
shred of mutual obligation binds the viewer to the viewed. The female slave
is thus disposed for maximal spectating pleasure: her wounds are largely
hidden from us; her bonds, the tree supporting her and her lacerated loin-
cloth are all suggestively flimsy; her animation – down to the flexing toes –
differs markedly from the impassively immobile bodies of the tortured male
slaves.

Our involvement with this picture is intensely problematic. "Blake's
image," Marcus Wood argues, "teeters on the verge of pornography in
order to confront us with our own corruptibility," which it certainly does –
although it is not clear that Blake can thus be saved in this scenario through
arguments of pedagogical intent. Blake is further protected, of course, by his
reputation as a great humanitarian visionary: a title that nobody would
think to bestow upon the author of the 28-page, Cheapside version of
Stedman which feasts on his most sadistic scenes. This features a hand-
colored etching which, pulling out to three times the size of the book,
depicts a lascivious scene of whipping in which the woman, now naked and
in profile, has unaccountably become white.[123] This image intends to teach
us nothing, but we may want to ask to what forces, what appetites, it seeks
to respond. It dates from ca. 1805: the time of Trafalgar, when the victorious
British navy ensured domination of the sea-lanes for a century, secured
permanent access to India and Africa, and (as Joyce brilliantly perceived)

Flagellation of a Female Samboe Slave.

28 William Blake, "Flagellation of a Female Samboe Slave," from Stedman, *Narrative of a Five Years' Expedition* (1796 edition). British Library, London.

made its regimen of press-ganging, flogging, and violence in closed spaces part of national religion.[124] Cheapside internalization of this terrifying winning formula might thus be finding perverse emotional egress in the sixpenny etching. But Blake, too, forms part of this scenario. His flagellated "Female Samboe Slave" appeals to us both as a suffering individual and, iconograpically, as a continent, for she clearly finds a counterpart in the

Europe supported by Africa & America

London, Published Dec.r.1.1796, by J. Johnson, S.t Paul's Church Yard.

29 William Blake, "Europe supported by Africa and America," from Stedman, *Narrative of a Five Years' Expedition* (1796 edition). British Library, London.

"Emblematical Picture" (figure 29) with which Stedman chooses "to take my leave of Surinam" (p. 618). This "Picture" – also engraved and colored by Blake – shows blonde and demure "Europe Supported by Africa & America" (p. 618). In the history of slaving, black, naked, and female Africa moves from Europe's left hand to Europe's right (joining America). In Blake's

"Flagellation" image, Africa has moved center-stage, except that she is now flanked by a gesticulating Stedman on her right and the overseer and whipping African males on her left. Such is her condition, and all efforts of good-hearted people like Stedman are only making things worse, for as Stedman (anticipating Jefferson) remarks in the end, "we All only differ in the Colour," a difference that can never change (p. 618).

It is worth recalling, again, that the suppression of the revolt that Stedman records and Blake illustrates ended in failure; maroons still make up some 20 percent of the current Surinamese population. The allure of encounter with African-Americans who have, for some 350 years, sustained a culture beyond plantation slavery has thus proved potent. In 1972, two Harvard academics – S. Allen Counter and David L. Evans – traveled to the interior of Surinam, where "we discovered an experience, we discovered friends, we discovered ourselves." In 1976 a film was premiered at Harvard and then "in the deep Surinam rain forest"; two years later a new film entitled *I Sought My Brother*, fronted by Alex Haley, was shown on the Public Broadcasting Service.[125] Such ventures in part yearn for an encounter with survivors of the "African spiritual holocaust" that deprived slaves of their traditional belief systems and, according to Jon Butler, rendered them receptive to Christian conversion.[126] The eventual Christianization of plantation slaves accelerated loss of cultural memory while yet offering texts for New World resistance, the most resonant and long-lasting being perhaps Psalms 68:31, the foundation text of Ethiopianism ("Princes shall come out of Egypt, Ethiopia shall soon stretch her hands unto God").[127] Christianization of black slaves (as refused by Oroonoko) also raises the possibility that black subjects might be insinuated into the abjecting structure (also refused by Oroonoko) traced in this chapter through exegeses of the love song of the Ethiopian woman ("nigra sum"). Such a possibility is strengthened by the absolutist fantasy feudalism of the American plantation, a peculiar mix of "paternalism, violence, and sentimentalism."[128] In the domestic fiction of this society, most famously represented by *Uncle Tom's Cabin*, the infliction of violence or abuse upon "women's bodies and black bodies" is indeed offered, Nancy Bentley argues, "as a means by which the individual achieves a transcendent grace or enriched dignity and identity. But for the body of the white male," she continues, "this law does not hold." In such a world, "the idea that violence to a white man's body would enhance his selfhood is nonsensical or heretical – despite the fact that the model for the passive power of martyrdom, Jesus Christ, was a white man."[129] It is in this society, then, that the long trajectory of white masculine abjection envy traced in this chapter definitively dies.[130]

"Nigra sum": Teale's "Sable Venus"

This book began across a short strait of water from England and will end across an ocean, in Surinam. The idea of ending *out there*, in unfamiliar Caribbean space, was (as we shall see) quite terrifying for Evelyn Waugh. Desire to complete the "outward and return" paradigm powers the traveling of many English authors through unfamiliar places. The more reflective of them, however, realize that the final return crossing of sea or Channel cannot shuck off expanded awareness (through the very act of traveling) of a greater world. Wordsworth, pleasingly, stumbles at the Channel: for 40 years, following his return from Calais in 1802, he meditates on a fellow passenger who (in 1807) is "gaudy in array," a phrase recalling the "gaudiness and inane phraseology" that *Lyrical Ballads* finds reprehensible in "many modern writers."[131] By 1845, however, this same person is "spotless in array"; and whereas her 1807 avatar was a plain "Negro Woman," in 1845 she is still plain black, but now "white-robed."[132] Coleridge and Wordsworth, I have argued, deserve little credit for their belated embrace of anti-slaving causes (which, by the time they were Cambridge undergraduates, were fashionable enough to win poetry prizes).[133] But it is good to think of this unnamed black woman, about to enter England, haunting Wordsworth. By way of conclusion, then, I would like to keep us in the heterotemporal Caribbean space bordered, to the west, by Surinam.

In 1759, some 60 years before Wordsworth's sighting at Calais, Bryan Edwards (born at Westbury, Wiltshire, in 1743) is dispatched by an uncle of "liberal mind, and princely fortune" to the island of Jamaica. Here he is instructed by a clergyman, the Reverend Isaac Teale, who resides with the family. Since the pupil, Edwards, finds Latin grammar "insupportably disgusting," Edwards and Teale spend most of their time reading the poetry of Dryden and Pope and the plays of Molière.[134] In 1793, Edwards published his *History, Civil and Commercial, of the British Colonies in the West Indies*; in the third edition, 1801, Teale's "History of the Sable Venus: An Ode" appears, accompanied by an engraving (figure 30). Here, then, we encounter a startlingly different imagining of woman *nigra sed formosa*, for the Middle Passage that is bringing thousands of Africans to work Jamaican plantations here figures as a cavalcade piloted by a triumphal, unabjected black Venus. Engraver Grainger models her on Botticelli's goddess on the half-shell; poet Teale hovers between Virgilian eclogue and neo-Petrarchan triumph:

> Of iv'ry was the car, inlaid
> With ev'ry shell of lively shade;

The VOYAGE of the SABLE VENUS, from ANGOLA to the WEST INDIES.

30 W. Grainger, engraving illustrating Isaac Teale, "History of the Sable Venus: An Ode" (1801). British Library, London.

> The throne was burnish'd gold:
> The footstool gay with coral beam'd,
> The wheels with brightest amber gleam'd,
> And glist'ring round they roll'd.

Teale further objectifies the black Venus through a comparison with a Florentine Venus that allows further display of his own well-traveled learning:

> The loveliest limbs her form compose,
> Such as her sister Venus chose,
>   In Florence, where she's seen;
> Both just alike, except the white,
> No difference, no – none at night.
>   The beauteous dames between.

The salacious suggestions of those last lines are taken up later in the poem, as the arrival of the Sable Venus in Jamaica is acclaimed by the shouting of a crowd that is not all plebeian:

> No rabble rout, – I heard it said,
> Some great ones joined the cavalcade –
>   The Muse will not say who.

Which is to say: white masculine slave-owners, English persons of quality, look forward to having sex at night with newly bought, black female slaves. Such arrangements were by no means unusual among European men on long-term assignment to Africa or the Caribbean.[135] This, we should remember, is an ode written by a learned English clergyman who must have had at least a nodding acquaintance with the Song of Songs. But his frame of reference, beginning with his epigraph from Vergil, *Eclogue* 2.18 ("Alba ligura cadunt vaccinia nigra leguntur"), is thoroughly pagan: since black Venus dwells beyond the Christian frame, any English gentleman visiting her at night is just taking a brief holiday from Christendom.[136] And if one particular black Venus should defy his charms, there are others; the eclogue supplying the epigraph ends:

> invenies alium, si te hic fastidit, Alexin.
>   *(2.73)*

> You will find another Alexis, if this one scorns you.

The Reverend Isaac Teale's blithe versifying would seem to bring us far, in every sense, from the tortured rationalizing of Bernard and Abelard over woman *nigra sed formosa*. But again, it is important to emphasize that if some aspects of medieval poetics get lost in transit, others live on in European conceptualizations of far-western experiences. Here are just four examples arising from Teale's *translatio*, all of them suggesting a remarkable ease of slippage from medieval gendering of erotic discourse to the pragmatics of slavery. First, then, this stanza describing the "sable Venus":

> Her skin excell'd the raven plume,
> Her breath the fragrant orange bloom,
>   Her eye the tropick beam:
> Soft was her lip as silken down,
> And mild her look as ev'ning sun
>   That gilds the COBRE stream.[137]

This is tail-rhyme romance: Teale chooses it for himself (as Shakespeare chose it for Bottom) as suitable to convey eclogic, rustic, faintly clownish sentiments. Half of all surviving Middle English romances are written in this form, which (as brilliantly parodied by Chaucer's *Sir Thopas*) favors oral formulaic itemizing of female beauty. Such dissection of women into constituent parts – scattered women and scattered rhyme, in Nancy J. Vicker's felicitous characterization of Petrarch's poetic[138] – also recalls the description of slaves by bodily features in the Genoese slave markets; the genre travels well to the New World.

Secondly, when Teale approves of black Venus's nakedness –

> False dress deformity may shade,
> True beauty courts no foreign aid:
>   Can tapers light the sun? –
>   *(94–6)*

he is tapping ancient and medieval canons of masculine complaint, as voiced by Chaucer through his Wife of Bath. Oxes, asses, horses, hounds, basins, wash bowls, spoons, stools, pots, and clothing are all tried out before purchase,

> But folk of wyves maken noon assay,
> Til they be wedded – olde dotard shrewe! –
> And thanne, seistow, we wol oure vices shewe.
>   *(3.290–2)*

Chaucer is here translating from the *Liber aureolus de nuptis*, the great foundational misogynist chestnut of Theophrastus as preserved by Jerome, except that in Jerome the list of items thoroughly examined before purchase runs "horses, asses, cattle, even slaves of the smallest worth, clothes, kettles . . ."[139] Edwards celebrates the return of slaves to the list of chattels inspected before use or purchase; the arrival of his naked black female slave marks another return to classical values.

Thirdly, Teale (still in romance vein) represents the lady's yielding of her beauty as her masculine suitor's due reward:

> She smil'd with kind consenting eyes; –
> Beauty was ever valour's prize
>
> *(103–4)*

Her suitor, identified as "the pow'r that rules old ocean wide," assumes the person of a "tar" captaining an English man of war (97–101). Grainger represents this figure in mid-metamorphosis as a venerable masculine sea god bearing the ensign flag flown by British warships and merchant vessels from 1707 to 1801.[140] The suggestion that, in gifting her beauty to this figure, black Venus becomes his absolute possession is accentuated by her wrist and ankle bracelets (doubling, visually, as manacles).

Finally, Teale feels obliged to define his relation to the narrative of Venerian triumph ("Gay goddess of the sable smile!," 127) he has just composed. His tactic is Chaucerian: although he no longer – as an older man in clerical clothes – pays "allegiance to the Cyprian throne" (134), he still follows gratefully in her train.[141] He thus cheers her progress as a loyal if distanced retainer ("so staunch am I, so true," 144) from one Caribbean locale to the next: Phibia, Benneba, Mimba, Cuba, Quasheba (145–9). Which is to say a white clergyman acclaims the arrival of a black woman who has willingly and cheerfully surrendered herself to a life of sexual subjugation at the hands of English colonists far from her African home. Jon Butler's diagnosis of "startlingly lethargic Christian practice" among colonists seems here understated, if not (in the *longue durée* of this book) as startling as we might wish it to be.[142]

Waugh's White *otium*: Guyana to Bath

The second in this concluding sequence of Caribbean-based texts traces an English journey out through the inland landscape of *Oroonoko* and a grateful homecoming: Evelyn Waugh's *Ninety-Two Days* (1934). It opens thus:

OCTOBER 12TH, 1933

> At last, relentlessly, inevitably, the lugubrious morning has dawned; day of wrath which I have been postponing week by week for five months.[143]

The day of reckoning that Waugh has been at pains to avoid is that which must see him write, for "most Englishmen," he explains, "dislike work and grumble about their jobs and writers now make it so clear they hate writing, that their public may become excusably sympathetic and urge them to try something else" (p. 10). Waugh here honors the white *otium* modeled by Teale in Jamaica, by Timorous in the *Widow Ranter*, and by all the aristocratic investors in the Royal Africa Company and its successors. But, like Behn, he must earn a living by his pen and so sets sail (via Trinidad, where he has family connections) for British Guiana, which seemed "absurdly remote."[144] Once immersed in the rain forest, Waugh falls to wondering "whether there were any pleasures I had found in that country which I had missed in Europe" (p. 116). He can think of only two: washing and reading. The "sharp tang of the germicidal soap" allows him to erase "the dryness and disappointment of noon"; and reading *Nicholas Nickleby* "with avid relish" makes him begrudge anything "which kept me from this new and exciting hobby" (p. 116). As his title suggests, Waugh (rather like the bereaved royalist Taylor before him) sees his westward journey essentially as an act of penitential self-absenting for which his English audience will, in effect, pay by the day.[145] Here is his final paragraph:

> From Trinidad I took a comfortable Dutch ship to Southampton. There was some slight discussion at the Customs as to whether stuffed alligators were dutiable as furniture, but in the end these were allowed in as scientific specimens. After a change of luggage in London I went straight to Bath and spent a week there alone in an hotel. Spring was breaking in the gardens, tender and pure and very different from the gross vegetation of the tropics. I had seen no building that was stable or ancient for nearly six months. Bath, with its propriety and uncompromised grandeur, seemed to offer everything that was most valuable in English life; and there, pottering composedly among the squares and crescents, I came finally to the end of my journey. (p. 170)

Waugh's journeying brings him to the heart of Englishness; abroad proves only an evil necessary for due appreciation of English tenderness and budding purity. His stuffed alligator is at once an absurdity (the Guyanas are "absurdly remote") and an essential element of "furniture" (as Waugh insists), of English style, for English style consists not of Burberry raincoats, heavy drapes, and paisley wallpaper (as marketed to Americans), but rather the randomly assembled bric-à-brac of empire: black ebony Chinese cabinets, feathers (as collected by Behn), elephant's-foot waste-paper baskets (of the kind brought to Oxford by Sebastian Flyte), stuffed alligators.[146] All such impedimenta are abandoned, however, for the concluding solitary cloistering in a Bath hotel. Much of Bath's "propriety and uncompromised grandeur" is built on wealth accumulated through the slave trade: Bristol, ranking fourth on the world-wide list of transatlantic slave-ship departures (1662–1867), lies twelve miles down the road.[147] James Brydges, created First Duke of Chandos in 1719, was both a prime mover of the buildings Waugh admires and a leading shareholder in the Royal Africa Company. Loanable funds from West Indian and slave trades helped finance the Royal Crescent.[148] In 1759 the *Bath Journal* advertised a 13–year-old boy for sale, "quite black, well-built, intelligent, musical, trained as a footboy and skilled in waiting at table".[149] It is in Bath, seeking out buildings "stable or ancient," that Waugh regains the composure lost through foreign travel.

Eleven years later, Waugh's fictional, first-person surrogate retraces his steps in *Brideshead Revisited* to produce *"Ryder's Latin America."* His protagonist seeks out paintable scenes to match his own sense of inner devastation ("cities where no road led, and mausoleums where a single, agued family of Indians sheltered from the rains," p. 217). Waugh again pointedly emphasizes that his English protagonist remains untouched and unaltered: "I discarded the experiences of those two years with my tropical kit and returned to New York as I had set out" (p. 218). In *Ninety-Two Days*, Waugh waits until he can get to Bath to make love between himself (so to speak) and the essence of Englishness; in *Brideshead*, passions break out on ship as Ryder encounters the female surrogate of the young English aristocrat he had fallen for at Oxford. The paintings and drawings he brings back home, pitting *"his elegance and erudition"* against *"the maelstrom of barbarism"* (according to one review), beguile the English public while failing to deceive the cosmopolitan "nomad of no nationality" (p. 47), Anthony Blanche. But there is no consideration of any mark, trace, or influence that Ryder's passage through Latin America might have had on those who live there.

In *A Handful of Dust*, however, Waugh revisits the territory of *Ninety-Two Days* to imagine the unthinkable, that a conservative Englishman might be lured from dutiful upkeep of his crumbling ancestral home to enter the vast, uncharted territory of "Amazonas" (a place whose inhabitants have never heard "of the governments of Brazil or Dutch Guiana, both of which from time to time claimed its possession").[150] And that once drawn into this space, he be held captive by a Mr Todd, son of an "English" father (actually born in Barbados) who turned missionary, then gold-prospector. Todd himself lives in the savannah with Pie-wie women ("ugly but very devoted") and the numerous children he has had with them (p. 184). Mr Todd, although illiterate, is addicted to Dickens; the English visitor, Tony Last, is persuaded to serve this passion by reading to him every day. And there he stays; the cunning Mr. Todd convinces the outside world that Last has died. So rather than the "uncompromised grandeur" of Bath, the visiting Englishman contemplates "a palm thatch roof, breast high walls of mud and wattle, and a mud floor" where he is doomed to recite *Bleak House*, *Nicholas Nickleby*, and

Little Dorrit without respite, and with no hope of escape. Published in the same year as *Ninety-Two Days* (1934), *A Handful of Dust* reconfigures the elements of the travel narrative to imagine the ultimate "fear" ("I will show you fear in a handful of dust"): to be lost and forgotten *out there*, in a place "not marked on any map."[151] This, the ultimate or perennial border fear, echoes the lament at separation from Rome sounded throughout Ovid's *Tristia*: "heu quam vicina est ultima terra mihi!"[152]

Such fears of separation actually form part of a larger fantasy that there ever *could* be a clean separation between the imperial center and the geographical periphery, for each inhabits the other. This last proposition, generally axiomatic for postcolonial writers, is explored with particular acuity by David Dabydeen.

Dabydeen and Trefossa: Poetry and Being Absurd

Dabydeen's novel *The Intended* (1991) tells of a young "Indian West Indian Guyanese" boy from the savannah traveling to England, growing up in a London orphanage, and being educated in classrooms and in playground regroupings "of the Asian diaspora."[153] He then reads English at Oxford, thus reversing the movement of Waugh's Tony Last in moving from savannah hammocks to dreaming spires. This passage is far from easy: "we are mud, they the chiselled stone of Oxford that has survived centuries and will always be here" (p. 198). Premodern texts, particularly medieval ones, play significant roles in this *Bildungsroman*, ultimately allowing the savannah song to force its way through the polished surface of decorous modern English. Mastering the medieval at first seems a matter of academic advancement, although familiarity with Chaucer breeds both comic engagements with Mr. Ali, an Urdu-speaking, betel-nut-chewing landlord ("I got relatives in Canterbury," p. 97) and romantic complications with white English Janet (via *Troilus and Criseyde*). At Oxford, however, it is the effort "to master the alien language of medieval alliterative poetry, the sentences wrenched and wrecked by strange consonants," that mysteriously frees him up to write "in the broken way" of Joseph Countryman, his black friend and mentor, who lives in rubble and writes in mud.[154] And it was indeed *as* he grappled with this medieval alliterative tradition (an English alternative to Chaucerian verse and Chancery standard) that Dabydeen, so he tells me, first came to write the excoriating Guyanese poems that make up *Slave Song* (1984). Black fantasies of whiteness, white fantasies of blackness, are here voiced in the most viscerally expressive terms, their sado-masochistic imaginings always rooted

in the severe inequalities of sugar-plantation labor relations; Dabydeen inter-
sperses his poems with full-page illustrations from Stedman's *Narrative of a
Five Years Expedition against the Revolted Negroes of Surinam.*[155] Black men hack
and bundle cane all day in tropical heat; black women scratch at the recalci-
trant soil, plant and manure; white folks stop by to watch. Until recently,
the estates were owned by Bookers, providers both of sugar and an annual
literary prize ("Booker own me patacake, Booker own me pickni").[156] The
language tapped by these poems is angry, crude, energetic, and (to pick up a
key phrase from the novel) broken: "its brokeness," Dabydeen argues,

> no doubt reflecting the brokeness and suffering of its original users – African
> slaves and East Indian indentured labourers. Its potential as a naturally tragic
> language is there, there in its brokeness and rawness which is like the rawness
> of a wound. If one has learnt and used Queen's English for some years, the
> return to Creole is painful, almost nauseous for the language is uncomfort-
> ably raw, as I said, like a wound.[157]

Dabydeen further explores the difficulty of his own return to Guyana, following schooling in England, in "Two Cultures," the last poem of *Slave
Song*. His reception is bumpy, talking as he does "Like BBC!" Black trash like
you, he is told, "spoil dem good white people country"; should he "touch
me gyal-pickni," a jealous father tells him, "me go buss you yu backside."[158]
Toward the end of *The Intended*, the narrator is still powerfully attached to
Janet's room: "I longed for the calmness of it, the sense of place, the sense of
belonging" (p. 244). But it is precisely his displacement that allows him to
hear a powerful "song" through a medieval English poetry that, to most
English people, is a dead tradition. As postcolonial theory teaches us, the
"medieval" never dies in the modern; it remains as undigested fragments
and remainders, ready to trigger the kind of creative brilliance Dabydeen
shows in *Slave Song*. And this is a hardwon poetry that belongs neither here
nor there, England or Guyana, but to both these places.

I would like to end this long chapter called "Surinam" – the Guyanese
country next door, under the reign of Ffyfes, rather than of Bookers – with
another poetic record of return and with the language of Surinam itself.
Sranan, we have noted, was first forged at the time of Aphra Behn and the
historical surrogates of *Oroonoko*: 16 years of intense and unequal encounter between (primarily) English indentured laborers and African slaves.[159]
From the very beginnings, of course, it has accreted vocabulary from Amerindian, Portuguese, Hebrew, Dutch, and (later) Hindustani and Javanese
sources.[160] In the early twentieth century children were punished for speaking

Sranan in school; concerted efforts were made to supplant it with Dutch, the language of the colonial power. In the 1950s, however, Henny F. de Ziel, a native of Paramaribo radicalized by a period in Holland, began publishing poems under the pseudonym Trefossa.[161] His choice of name, apparently creolized from the hard-working "Tryphosa" acknowledged by Paul in Romans 16:12, announces not a bid for essential native identity (Paramaribo as Bath), but rather immersion in complex cultural currents. The poem below, written in 1973, observes this principle nicely in marrying the language of Surinam to the form of the European sonnet.

The poem divides into eight and six lines (following the original Italian, rather than the derivative English convention); its Italianate feel is furthered by deployment of both hendecasyllabics and caesura, plus the vowel suffixes (a feature of most Sranan words) that facilitate rhyming. With the aid of grammars and linguistic guides, Anglophone readers may discern English-derived items of vocabulary: the opening word *didibri* (an older form of *d'dibri*) means devil; *mofo* in lines 2 and 6 we can recognize (knocking off the final *o*) as mouth.[162] Having no grammatical gender, Sranan prefixes sex-indicators such as *man* or *uma* to nouns; man-p[i]kin in line 3 thus emerges as "male child," closely followed by a familiar *Gado* (God) and mysterious Tata, who much desires ("ben wani") something. *Libisma* in the next line breaks down as *libis-ma*, living person (human being); we can thus decode the second hemistich of the penultimate line, aided by the familiar Latin tag, as "living / life be unto you." Suitably encouraged, we learn that *fosi* in the last line derives from dialectal or vulgar English pronunciation of "first" as "fust"; we can then picture or hear the baby Jesus launching into his first cry.

Fishing in a Sranan poem for gobbets of English, like lumps in soup, renders us absurd, of course. But acceptance of absurdity, in the face of this text, is the beginning of wisdom, for we thus acknowledge ourselves peripheral to a cultural unfolding whose complexity and historical depth escape our grasp. The part of the world that produced this poem was for Evelyn Waugh, we have noted, "absurdly remote."[163] The English term absurd derives from Latin *absurdus*, which combines the intensifier *ab* with *surdus* to mean "deaf, inaudible, insufferable to the ear" (*OED*). The Guyanas remain absurd to Waugh because he remains defiantly deaf to them, contriving to keep them (in every sense) at a huge distance even when traveling through or making writerly capital from them. But in reading Trefossa's poem aloud before fully understanding it (as Dabydeen read *Sir Gawain*, or as Eliot recommends first reading Dante) we discover that which encourages further study and acquaintance, namely a distinctive music.[164] Certain English-derived terms of more recent vintage ("blèkout," "elèktrik powa") seem disruptive of poetic and, we might imagine, cultural rhythm.[165] But Trefossa's words neither straightforwardly assimilate nor flatly refuse all that leads to the complex and joyful moment of his writing here in Surinam.

Humor in èksèlsis

Didibri fir a fàrt tak bigi grani
byo psa grontapu her-es, mofo-yari.
A manpkin f' Gado, so Tata ben wani,
byo tron wan libisma. – Oh gran friyari!

"M' e por a prey, m' e blèkout alasani."
Na so didibri opo mofo bari.
"M' e kot den drât a tap a heri plani,
d' e tyar elèktrik powa gi den stari."

Ma . . . wruts! Syasroyti panya branti-faya.
Didibri kori hen krabyasi, baya!
A bron hen langa barba-kakumbe.

Èn engel singi: humor in èksèlsis!
Den lafu kwa-kwa: libi de pro vobis!
Èn beybi-Jesus krey a fosi: yè-è-è.[166]

NOTES

1 When Holland beat Germany in February 2000, Holland ended the game fielding no fewer than six players with roots in Surinam. See Ernst Bouwes, "Sur Thing," *WSC* 174 (August 2001), p. 29.

2 The colony was captured by the Dutch in 1667, recaptured from Barbados, but then handed back to the Dutch as part of the Treaty of Breda (signed July 1667). Groups of English planters left with slaves before handover to the Dutch; others followed in 1671 and 1675. In 1680 the last group of 102 Englishmen and slaves left, leaving just 39 Englishmen behind. The English retook Surinam during the Napoleonic period (1799–1802, 1804–16) but then ceded it to Holland following the Treaty of Paris. See "Geschiedenis" in *Encyclopedie van Suriname*, ed. C. F. A Bruijnig and J. Voorhoeve (Amsterdam: Argus Elsevier, 1977), pp. 233a–245b (pp. 233b–236a); Jul M. Dubois, *A Portrait of the Republic Suriname* (Paramaribo: Dubois and Dubois, 1978), p. 9; *Creole Drum: An Anthology of Creole Literature in Surinam*, ed. Jan Voorhoeve and Ursy M. Lichtveld, pp. 2, 275.

3   Jean-Claude Giacottino, *Les Guyanes* (Paris: Presses Universitaires de France, 1984), pp. 3–4.

4   The term *maroon*, applied to cover six ethnic groups in Surinam (speaking many variants of Saramaccan and Ndjuka, the two major languages), derives from Spanish *cimarrón*, a term originally applied to runaway domestic cattle in Hispaniola and later to native slaves escaped from the Spaniards. By the late 1530s the term had come to be applied primarily to escaped Afro-Americans. See Sally and Richard Price, *Afro-American Arts of the Suriname Rain Forest* (Berkeley: University of California Press, 1980), pp. 14 and 217, notes 2, 5.

5   *Narrative of a Five Years Expedition against the Revolted Negroes of Surinam. Transcribed for the First Time from the Original 1790 Manuscript*, ed. Richard Price and Sally Price (Baltimore, Md.: Johns Hopkins University Press, 1988), pp. xxxviii–xlviii.

6   Having heard Martin's account of his treatment as a slave on a Surinamese sugar plantation, Candide exclaims to Pangloss that "il faudra qu'à la fin je renonce à ton optimisme." On being asked what "optimisme" might be, Candide replies "c'est la rage de soutenir que tout est bien quand on est mal; et il versait des larmes en regardant son nègre; et en pleurant, il entra dans Surinam" (*Candide ou l'optimisme*, ed. Haydn Mason (London: Bristol Classical Press, 1995), p. 47 (and p. 98 n. 6). These two instances represent the only usage of the term "optimisme" in *Candide* (excepting its subtitle); the term is thus invoked only as its possibility disappears "dans Surinam."

7   Stedman, *Narrative*, ed. Price and Price, p. 516.

8   See *Oroonoko, or The Royal Slave. A True History*, ed. Janet Todd in Aphra Behn, *Oroonoko, The Rover and Other Works*, ed. Todd (London: Penguin, 1992).

9   In the course of *Oroonoko*'s first-person narrative, Behn tells how she came to Surinam: of how her father, appointed "lieutenant general of six and thirty islands, besides the continent of Surinam," died at sea *en route* to his new post; of how she and her mother and sisters lived without prospects in Surinam before returning to England (p. 115). It is very unlikely that Behn's father, probably a barber from Canterbury called Bartholomew Johnson, ever set sail for South America; the idealized father figure Behn invents for herself is clearly based on Lord Willougby, founder of a new colony growing sugar and tobacco along the Surinam river. Desperate women (many of them Irish) answered the call to service (perhaps even to marry) the men in the new Caribbean colonies: button-makers, orange wenches, "Crackt-Maiden-Servants," prostitutes, and transportable convicts. Behn may not have traveled in quite such unhappy company, but her days in Surinam (perhaps spent as a gentleman's mistress, or a lady's maid) may have brought her closer to the level of indentured labor than she cared to tell. See Janet Todd, *The Secret Life of Aphra Behn* (New Brunswick, NJ: Rutgers University Press, 1996), pp. 37–49 (p. 40); Margaret W. Ferguson, "Juggling the Categories of Race, Class, and Gender: Aphra Behn's *Oronooko*," *Women's Studies* 19 (1991), 159–81 (p. 166); Laura

Brown, "The Romance of Empire: *Oroonoko* and the Trade in Slaves," in *The New Eighteenth Century: Theory, Politics, Literature*, ed. Felicity Nussbaum and Laura Brown (London: Methuen, 1987), pp. 41–61 (pp. 55–6).

10 For the enslaved, this phase is especially acute: since the repeated dispersals of enslavement have destroyed familial and local linguistic ties, new horizontal forms of relatedness must be forged (beginning with language).

11 "De Engelse hebben hier een colonie gemaeckt," the Dutchman remarked, "en wort die taal daer nog meest bij de slaven gesproken" ("the English made a colony here, and that language is generally (or: mostly) spoken by the slaves"): as cited in Jan Voorhoeve, "Historical and Linguistic Evidence in Favour of the Relexification Theory in the Formation of Creoles," *Language in Society* 2 (1973), 133–45 (p. 140); for further discussion, see *Early Suriname Creole Texts: A Collection of 18th-century Sranan and Saramaccan Documents*, ed. Jacques Arends and Matthias Perl, Bibliotheca Ibero-American 49 (Frankfurt am Main: Vervuert, 1995), pp. 13–14. Voorhoeve considers three different Creoles spoken in Surinam: Sranan or coastal Creole, the language of the former slaves used on the plantations; Saramaccan, the language of the Matuari tribe along the Saramacca river and the Saramaccan tribe along the Suriname river; and Ndjuka, the language of the Paramaccan, Aucan, and Boni or Aluku tribe along the Maroni river and tributaries (p. 133).

12 See *Creole Drum*, ed. Voorhoeve and Lichtveld, pp. 4–5. The editors note that "as a slave language Creole remained relatively pure and did not undergo a destructive flux of Dutch lexical items and grammatical constructions" (p. 6). Processes of creolization in Jamaica (taken by Cromwell's expeditionary force in 1655) offer instructive points of comparison with developments in Surinam. In Jamaica, "the main contact" of African slaves was with indentured servants sent from Ireland and the west of England, "rather than with the planters themselves" (*Dictionary of Jamaican English*, ed. F. G. Cassidy and R. B. Le Page [Cambridge: Cambridge University Press, 1967], p. xli). In Surinam, there was a predominance of former indentured servants from Barbados which, following the 1650s sugar boom, was over-populated with whites: see Jacques Arends, "Demographic Factors in the Formation of Sranan," in *The Early Stages of Creolization*, ed. Arends (Amsterdam: John Benjamins, 1995), pp. 233–85 (p. 240).

13 See "Sranan Tongo," in *Encyclopedie van Suriname*, ed. Bruijnig and Voorhoeve, 573a–574a; J. J. M. Echteld, *The English Words in Sranan* (Groningen: J. B. Wolters, 1962), p. 9.

14 "I will Love you with All my Heart so long as I Live" (Stedman's translation, *Narrative*, ed. Price and Price, p. 516). Stedman's relationship with Joanna was actually accorded separate treatment in a German play (by Franz Kratter, 1804), in an anonymous English novel (1824) and in Eugène Sue's *Aventures de Hercule Hardi* (1840). The Guyanese black beloved of Hercule-Achille-Victor Hardi in this last work is called Jaguarette. See David Richards, *Masks of*

Difference: Cultural Representations in Literature, Anthropology and Art (Cambridge: Cambridge University Press, 1994), p. 104; Jean-Lois Bory, *Eugène Sue* (Paris: Hachette, 1962), p. 220 n. 4; *Joanna, or The Female Slave. A West Indian Tale. Founded on Stedman's Narrative of an Expedition Against the Revolted Negroes of Surinam* (London: Lupton Relfe, 1824). The 1824 volume was published by Constable and Co. (Edinburgh) and R. Milliken (Dublin); its preface declares that *"General Emancipation* must appear to every reflecting mind a measure neither practical nor advisable"; it then goes on to make familiar arguments for "the abolition of *cruelty*" (p. viii). The exhaustive, point-by-point description of Joanna's physical features, proving her "distinguished above all others of her species in the colony," suggests (again) overlapping canons of description as applied to women and (as in the deeds of sale considered in chapter 4) slaves (pp. 47–8).

For detailed analysis of Stedman's long relationship with Joanna (which included marriage to her), see Mary Louise Pratt, *Imperial Eyes: Travel Writing and Transculturation* (London: Routledge, 1992), pp. 92–102; Richards, *Masks of Difference*, pp. 100–7.

15 Stedman, *Narrative*, ed. Price and Price, pp. lix–lxi, 42–3.

16 Stedman as cited in Edward Dew, *The Difficult Flowering of Surinam: Ethnicity and Politics in a Plural Society* (The Hague: Martinus Nijhoff, 1978), p. 23.

17 *Creole Drum*, ed. Voorhoeve and Lichtveld, p. 11. Dutch, in a population survey of 1950, was spoken by 50–55% of the population, followed by Hindi (30–35%), and Javanese (15%).

18 Recruited by the English and sustained by the Dutch for their expertise in sugar production, the Jews of Paramaribo outnumbered their counterparts in any North American city and celebrated themselves with an extraordinary two-volume *Essai historique sur la colonie de Surinam* (1788). See *Historical Essay on the Colony of Surinam*, ed. Jacob R. Marcus and Stanley F. Chyet, trans. Simon Cohen (Cincinnati: American Jewish Archives, 1974); Echteld, *English Words in Sranan*, pp. 2, 181 n. 7; Dew, *Difficult Flowering*, p. 22; Richard Price, *Alabi's World* (Baltimore, Md.: Johns Hopkins University Press, 1990), p. 4.

19 For sophisticated meditation on these matters, see Thomas Hahn, "Early Middle English," in *The Cambridge History of Medieval English Literature*, ed. David Wallace (Cambridge: Cambridge University Press, 1999), pp. 61–91; *Early Stages*, ed. Arends; *Pidgins and Creoles: An Introduction*, ed. Arends, Pieter Muysken, and Norval Smith (Amsterdam: John Benjamins, 1995). On Grimm's coinage "Mittelenglisch" and the anxieties and confusions subtending such terminology, see David Matthews, *The Invention of Middle English: An Anthology of Primary Sources* (Turnhout: Brepols, 2000) and its accompanying volume *The Making of Middle English, 1765–1910* (Minneapolis: University of Minnesota Press, 1999).

20 In the *Legend of Good Women*, Chaucer picks and happily etymologizes the English daisy, *dayeseye*, as his flower of choice (albeit one owing its literary

pedigree to French *marguerite* tradition). Picking the dandelion (surely the
most English of flowers?) would invite further Gallic ridicule, with images of
English poets gazing unknowingly into the mouths of French royal beasts (le
dent de lion). See *Legend of Good Women*, F 185 ("the dayesye, or ellis the eye of
day"); the word descends from Old English, *dæƷes éaƷe*. On Deschamps' *ballade*
to Chaucer, see chapter 1 above, p. 57.

21   See *Creole Drum*, ed. Voorhoeve and Lichtveld, pp. 10–11.

22   *Creole Drum*, ed. Voorhoeve and Lichtveld, pp. 248–9. The preface to this
volume tells us that Jan Voorhoeve is Dutch, Ursy M. Lichtveld a Surinam
Creole, and Vernie A. February, the translator, South African (p. viii).

23   "Mama's Baby, Papa's Maybe: an American Grammar Book," now conveniently available in *The Black Feminist Reader*, ed. Joy James and T. Denean
Sharpley-Whiting (Oxford: Blackwell, 2000), pp. 57–87 (p. 70). "Those African
persons in 'Middle Passage'," Spillers argues, "were literally suspended in the
'oceanic' . . . these captive persons, without names that their captors would
recognize, were in movement across the Atlantic, but they were also *nowhere*
at all" (p. 70).

24   Dabydeen, *Turner: New and Selected Poems* (London: Jonathan Cape, 1994),
p. ix. For an extended account of Turner's *Slave Ship*, "the only indisputably
great work of Western art ever made to commemorate the Atlantic slave
trade, and particularly the English monopoly of this trade in the eighteenth
century," see Marcus Wood, *Blind Memory: Visual Representations of Slavery in
England and America 1780–1865* (Manchester: Manchester University Press, 2000),
pp. 41–68 (p. 41); see further Paul Gilroy, *The Black Atlantic: Modernity and
Double Consciousness* (London: Verso, 1993), pp. 13–17; Ian Baucom, "Specters
of the Atlantic," *South Atlantic Quarterly* 100 (2001), 61–82.

25   In *Oroonoko*, as Catherine Gallagher succinctly puts it, "the word 'black' distinguishes the bodies of those who can be bought and sold from those of people
who cannot" (*Nobody's Story: The Vanishing Acts of Women Writers in the
Marketplace, 1670–1820* [Oxford: Clarendon Press, 1994], p. 76). "Black" is thus
a word "used to describe a skin tone differing from all others that allows a
body to have an abstract exchange value independent of any of its other
physical qualities" (p. 76). This breaks decisively with earlier canons of slave
description described in chapter 4 above, pp. 188–90.

26   *Notes on the State of Virginia*, ed. William Peden (New York: Norton, 1972),
p. 138. Editions of the full-length text were first printed in Paris and London in
1785. A Baltimore printer produced an edition in 1800; five new American
editions appeared in 1801.

27   "Mama's Baby, Papa's Maybe," p. 62.

28   On "the politics of melanin," see Spillers, "Mama's Baby, Papa's Maybe,"
p. 68.

29   On Merian, see Natalie Zemon Davis, *Women on the Margin: Three Seventeenth-
Century Lives* (Cambridge, Mass.: Harvard University Press, 1995), pp. 140–202;

Kurt Wettengl, *Maria Sibylla Merian (1647–1717), Artist and Naturalist* (Stuttgart: Verlag Gerd Hatje, 1998); Maria Sibylla Merian, *The St. Petersburg Watercolours*, introd. Eckhard Hollmann (Munich and London: Prestel, 2003).

30 'Biyi Bandele, *Aphra Behn's Oroonoko in a New Adaptation* (Charlbury, Oxford-shire: Amber Lane Press, 1999) – this play was first performed by the Royal Shakespeare Company at The Other Place, Stratford-on-Avon, on April 7, 1999; Spillers, "Mama's Baby, Papa's Maybe," p. 65. It is striking how the imagination of Bandele's Oroonoko runs to the ocean even when wooing Imoinda in Coramantien: "I have burrowed my past, a / Bloodstained bundle wrapped in / Seaweed, into the cleansing salt-water vaults / Of the sea god-dess" (p. 39). See further, on the problematic status of "heritage" sites in West Africa, Theresa A. Singleton, "The Slave Trade Remembered on the Former Gold and Slave Coasts," in *From Slavery to Emancipation in the Atlantic World*, ed. Sylvia R. Frey and Betty Wood (London: Frank Cass, 1999), pp. 150–69.

31 *Historia calamitatum*, ed. Jacques Monfrin, 2nd edn. (Paris: Librairie Philoso-phique J. Vrin, 1962), line 11 ("sicut natura terre mee"); *Historia calamitatum*, in *The Letters of Abelard and Heloïse*, trans. Betty Radice (London: Penguin, 1974), p. 57. Citations and translations follow these editions. Citations from the Latin texts of the letters follow the editions of J. T. Muckle and T. P. McLaughlin, *Mediaeval Studies* 15 (1953), 17 (1955), 18 (1956).

32 *Historia calamitatum*, lines 1501–33, trans. pp. 102–3.

33 See M. T. Clanchy, *Abelard: A Medieval Life* (Oxford: Blackwell, 1997), pp. 6–9; *Letters*, trans. Radice, p. 41.

34 "From the end of the earth I have called to thee when my heart was in anguish" (*Historia calamitatum*, 1253–4, citing Psalms 61:2; trans. Radice, p. 95).

35 "Sicut enim candido prosperum, ita non incongrue nigro designatur adversum" (IV, p. 84).

36 Extreme attention is paid by the masculine author of *Ancrene Wisse* to regula-tion of windows: see *Anchoritic Spirituality: Ancrene Wisse and Associated Works*, trans. and introd. Anne Savage and Nicholas Watson (New York: Paulist Press, 1991), pp. 66–81, esp. p. 68: "Now, here comes a weak man . . . and he wants to see some young anchoresses. And he just has to see whether her looks please him, she whose face has not been burnt by the sun."

37 "But if I lose you," she pleads in letter 3, "what is left for me to hope for?" (p. 129; "Quid autem te amisso sperandum mihi superest?" III, p. 78).

38 The *Wisse* author, riffing on Canticles 1:5, argues that the black cloth in the anchoress' windows "symbolizes to the world outside that you are black and unworthy, and that the true sun has burned you outwardly" (trans. Savage and Watson, p. 66).

39 "In my case," Heloïse writes, "the pleasures of lovers which we shared have been too sweet – they can never displease me, and can scarcely be banished from my thoughts. Wherever I turn they are always there before my eyes,

bringing with them awakened longings and fantasies which will not even let me sleep. Even during the celebration of the Mass" (p. 133; III, pp. 80–1).

40 See chapter 4 above, p. 188, and Stuard, "Ancillary Evidence."

41 See Miri Rubin, *Gentile Tales: The Narrative Assault on Late Medieval Jews* (New Haven: Yale University Press, 1999).

42 On Peter the Venerable, abbot of Cluny, and his *Tractatus adversus Iudaeorum duritiem* ("A Tractate Against the Longstanding Insensibility of the Jews"), see Jeremy Cohen, *The Friars and the Jews: The Evolution of Medieval Anti-Judaism* (Ithaca, NY: Cornell University Press, 1982), pp. 28–30. Perhaps the most intimate of the many recorded transactions between Peter, Heloïse, and Abelard is that suggested by the "Absolution for Peter Abelard" (included in the 1614 edition of the letters): "I, Peter, Abbot of Cluny, who received Peter Abelard as a monk of Cluny, and gave his body, removed in secret, to the Abbess Heloïse and the nuns of the Paraclete, by the authority of Almighty God and of all the saints, in virtue of my office, absolve him from all his sins" (as translated in *Letters*, ed. Radice, p. 288); see further Christopher Baswell, "Heloïse," in *The Cambridge Companion to Medieval Women's Writing*, ed. Carolyn Dinshaw and David Wallace (Cambridge: Cambridge University Press, 2003), pp. 161–71 (pp. 161–3).

43 Linda Van Norden, *The Black Feet of the Peacock: The Color-Concept "Black" from the Greeks Through the Renaissance*, ed. John Pollock (Lanham, Md.: University Press of America, 1985), p. 3.

44 See Hugh Thomas, *The Slave Trade: The Story of the Atlantic Slave Trade, 1440–1870* (New York: Simon and Schuster, 1997), pp. 71–2. Thomas correctly exposes the wishful thinking of the *New Catholic Encyclopedia*, which argues that "the slave trade continued for centuries, in spite of its condemnation by the Papacy, beginning with Pius II on October 7, 1462" (vol. 13, 1967, p. 264; Thomas, p. 92).

45 Shareholders in the Royal Africa Company also included, between 1660 and 1688, 15 of the lord mayors of London and 25 sheriffs: see Thomas, *Slave Trade*, pp. 198–203; Moira Ferguson, *Subject to Others: British Women Writers and Colonial Slavery, 1670–1834* (New York: Routledge, 1992), pp. 11–12, 30–4.

46 Spillers, "Mama's Baby, Papa's Maybe," p. 66. Paul Freedman takes pains to note that "although they could be symbols of frightening savagery (as in *The Song of Roland*), black people since antiquity had been thought of more favorably as exotic, for example, the Ethiopians in the Isis cult and in Origen's commentaries" (*Images of the Medieval Peasant* [Stanford, Calif.: Stanford University Press, 1999], p. 93).

47 For detailed mapping of Abelard in relation to his academic antagonists and successors, see Randall Collins, *The Sociology of Philosophies: A Global Theory of Intellectual Change* (Cambridge, Mass.: The Belknap Press of Harvard University Press, 1998), pp. 464–8 and figure 9.3.

48 See for example St. Ambrose, *Commentarius in Cantica Canticorum, Patrologia Latina*, ed. Migne, vol. 15, 1553.24 (col. 1862): "*Nigra sum, et decora*"; see

further *A Hebrew and English Lexicon of the Old Testament*, ed. Francis Brown (Oxford: Clarendon Press, 1959), pp. 251–5. Brown explains that the Hebrew conjunction possesses an extraordinary range of possible nuances and meanings, according to context (including *and, but, or, then, therefore, notwithstanding, howbeit, so, thus, that*).

49 See Richard C. Trexler, *The Journey of the Magi: Meanings in History of a Christian Story* (Princeton, NJ: Princeton University Press, 1997), pp. 102–7.

50 *Piers Plowman. An Edition of the C-Text*, ed. Derek Pearsall (London: Edward Arnold, 1978). George Russell and George Kane emend to "[fou]l vilanye" (20.97); the reading "vyl" is attested by 12 MSS, "foul" by 4 (*Piers Plowman: The C Version*, ed. Russell and Kane (London: Athlone Press, 1997), p. 614.

51 See David Wallace, *Chaucerian Polity: Absolutist Lineages and Associational Forms in England and Italy* (Stanford, Calif.: Stanford University Press, 1997), pp. 131–2. In the time of Bruegel there was a vogue among aristocrats for visiting villages, dressed up (or passing) as peasants; peasantry was thus to be viewed (as in some Bruegel paintings) touristically, even anthropologically, as an exotic or foreign species.

52 By the eighteenth this has become, for white slaving societies, an enabling commonplace. See Freedman, *Images of the Medieval Peasant*, pp. 139–41, 91–3. Freedman offers an important caveat: "For the Christian Middle Ages, however, Ham was not exclusively associated with Africa, Africans were not thought of as exclusively black, and blacks were not thought of primarily as slaves" (p. 93).

53 See Kim F. Hall, *Things of Darkness: Economics of Race and Gender in Early Modern England* (Ithaca, NY: Cornell University Press, 1995), pp. 107–8; John N. King, *Tudor Royal Iconography: Literature and Art in an Age of Religious Crisis* (Princeton, NJ: Princeton University Press, 1989), pp. 81–8. Hall notes that "Solomon's story and his song became a key part of the 'typology of colonialism'" in this period; Solomon is "both an exemplar of the sage colonial ruler and an example of the dangers of erotic entanglements with foreign women" (p. 108).

54 See King, *Tudor Royal Iconography*, pp. 254–7. Shakespeare has Cranmer compare Elizabeth to Sheba in *Henry VIII* in terms also evocative of a cleaned-up Solomon: "Saba [Sheba] was never / More covetous of wisdom and fair virtue / Than this pure soul shall be" (*King Henry VIII*, ed. Gordon McMullan (London: Arden Shakespeare, 2000), 5.4.23–5 and "Introduction," pp. 88–91).

55 Letter of January 10, 1605, as cited in *Renaissance Drama by Women: Texts and Documents*, ed. S. P. Ceresano and Marion Wynne-Davies (London: Routledge, 1996), p. 169.

56 Letter of January 6, 1605, to Ralph Winwood as cited in *Renaissance Drama by Women*, ed. Ceresano and Wynne-Davies, p. 169. The women included three countesses, two Herberts, and the playwright Mary Wroth, née Sidney.

57 *The Masque of Blackness*, in *Ben Jonson: The Complete Masques*, ed. Stephen Orgel (New Haven: Yale University Press, 1969), lines 136–41.

58 "This land that lifts into the temperate air," says Oceanus, "is Albion the fair": an association not just of England (Albion) with identifying whiteness (from Latin, *albus*, white), but of Scotland too (named Albania in Latin sources): a useful doubling for King James I and VI.

59 *Masque of Blackness*, 300–25. Although the daughters of Niger are instructed to reassemble one year hence (322), the sequel masque (of Beauty) was not produced until 1608.

60 See Thomas, *The Slave Trade*, p. 174. On the growth of concomitant anxieties about the sexual allure of black men – of "delight in black-work" as Beaumont and Fletcher have it in *Love's Cure* – see Van Norden, *The Black Feet of the Peacock*, pp. 70–80.

61 See Janet Todd, *The Secret Life of Aphra Behn*, p. 444 n. 11. Todd notes that "the exotic erotic tie of black man and white woman was attractive in the seventeenth century but far less so in the eighteenth, when only the relationship of black woman and white man remained acceptable" (p. 444).

62 See Trexler, *The Journey of the Magi*, pp. 102–7; this trend begins in the 1360s.

63 See Van Norden, *Black Feet*, pp. 7, 72–3 (and *Faerie Queen*, I.4.24).

64 See, most importantly, Susan Reynolds, *Fiefs and Vassals: The Medieval Evidence Reinterpreted* (Oxford: Clarendon Press, 1994). Reynolds censures the tendency of medieval historians "to fit their findings into a framework of interpretation that was devised in the sixteenth century and elaborated in the sixteenth and seventeenth" (p. 2).

65 Boccaccio's impassioned imagining of the feudal south proved particularly influential: see David Wallace, *Giovanni Boccaccio, Decameron* (Cambridge: Cambridge University Press, 1991), pp. 53–61.

66 *Letters*, trans. Radice, p. 111. ("Huius quippe loci tu post Deum solus es fundator . . . Totum quod hic est tua creatio est," ed. Muckle, I, p. 69). And of course, once Abelard responds he becomes subject to the rules of what Marilynn Desmond terms "the epistolary contract" (*"Dominus/Ancilla*: Rhetorical Subjectivity and Sexual Violence in the Letters of Heloise," in *The Tongue of the Fathers: Gender and Ideology in Twelfth-Century Latin*, ed. David Townsend and Andrew Taylor (Philadelphia: University of Pennsylvania Press, 1998), pp. 35–54 (p. 46); see further Baswell, "Heloïse," pp. 164–5.

67 *A Book of Showings to the Anchoress Julian of Norwich*, ed. Edmund Colledge and James Walsh, 2 vols. (Toronto: Pontifical Institute of Mediaeval Studies, 1978), "The Long Text," vol. II, p. 590.

68 Julian of Norwich, *Revelations of Divine Love*, trans. Clifton Wolters (Harmondsworth: Penguin, 1966), pp. 36–8, esp. p. 38 ("Julian's heresy"). Julian's new Penguin editors, while not evading the issue of Julian's unwillingness to countenance a damning God, are more thoughtful, less incendiary than Wolters: see Julian of Norwich, *Revelations of Divine Love (Short and Long Text)*, trans. Elizabeth Spearing, introd. A. C. Spearing (Penguin: London, 1998), pp. xxiv–xxvii.

69 See David Wallace, "Cleanness and the Terms of Terror," in *Text and Matter: New Critical Perspectives of the "Pearl" Poet*, ed. R. J. Blanch, M. Youngerman Miller, and J. Wasserman (Troy, NY: Whitston Press, 1991), pp. 95–106.

70 "Long Text," ed. Colledge and Walsh, p. 587. Their text, edited from MS Bibliothèque Nationale Fonds Anglais 40 (and collated with other manuscripts) differs interestingly from that of British Library, Sloane 2499, where "trust" is "trewth": "Rewardyng is a large gevyng of trewth that the Lord doth to hym that hath travellid; and gevyng is a curtes workyng which he doith frely of grace fulfill, and overpassand al that is deservid of cretures" (*Women's Writing in Middle English*, ed. Alexandra Barratt [London: Longman, 1992], p. 122).

71 *The Book of Margery Kempe*, ed. Sanford Brown Meech and Hope Emily Allen, Early English Text Society, os 212 (London: Oxford University Press for EETS, 1940), chapter 54, p. 135.

72 Nicholas Love, *Mirror of the Blessed Life of Christ. A Critical Edition Based on Cambridge University Library Additional MSS 6578 and 6686*, ed. Michael G. Sargent (New York: Garland, 1992), lines 41–4, p. 61. Love's translation of the Franciscan *Meditationes* – a text that much influenced Margery – offers extended meditation on Christ's desire to make "him self foule & abiecte," on how he "coueyteth fully to be despised, & hald as foule, vnworthi & abiecte" (lines 3–4, 11–12, p. 62). See further lines 25–43, p. 62, where meditation on abjecting dynamics briefly widens to consider questions of class ("*Is not he that wrightes sone Joseph?*" lines 42–3). The factor that crucially underpins Christ's displays of abjection, however, as in the Franciscan choosing of poverty, is the power of choice itself ("& so it was his wille to be hald as vnworthi & abiecte," line 42, p. 61).

73 See George T. Peck, *The Fool of God: Jacopone da Todi* (Tuscaloosa: University of Alabama Press, 1980), p. 54.

74 His catalogue of "common sins" includes (and there is more) "too much or too little food or drink, grumbling, a grim face, broken silences, sitting long at the window, hours badly said without the heart's attention or at the wrong time, lying about something, swearing, fooling, roaring with laughter, spilling crumbs or beer, letting things go mouldy, rusty or rotten, leaving clothes unmended, rained on or unwashed, breaking a cup or dish. . ." (*Ancrene Wisse*, trans. Savage and Watson, p. 174).

75 *Ancrene Wisse, Parts Six and Seven*, ed. Geoffrey Shepherd, rev. edn. (Exeter: University of Exeter Press, 1985), lines 4–5, p. 3; translations follow *Anchoritic Spirituality*, trans. Savage and Watson.

76 "Why All the Fuss about the Body? A Medievalist's Perspective," *Critical Inquiry* 22 (Autumn 1995), 1–33 (p. 17). Elsewhere Bynum offers vital historicization of this notion of women empowered through being "below and above reason." The broad history is of increasing misogyny and decreasing tolerance by church authorities. "By 1500," Bynum writes, "the model of the female saint, expressed both in popular veneration and in official canonizations,

was in many ways the mirror image of society's notion of the witch" (*Holy Feast and Holy Fast: The Religious Significance of Food to Medieval Women* (Berkeley: University of California Press, 1987), p. 23.

77 The *Wisse* author immediately acknowledges that he might have chosen a female rather than male exemplar: "Ich wat ec swuch wommon þet þoleð lutel leasse" (p. 18); "I also know a woman of the same sort, who endures little less" (p. 188).

78 E. Ann Matter notes the survival of more than sixty commentaries on the Song of Songs dating from between the fourth and thirteenth centuries; six Cistercian versions were inspired by Bernard's text. See *The Voice of My Beloved: The Song of Songs in Western Medieval Christianity* (Philadelphia: University of Pennsylvania Press, 1990), p. 39 and Appendix (pp. 203–10, a listing of Latin commentaries to 1200).

79 *Sermones super Cantica Canticorum. S. Bernardi Opera*, vol. 1, ed. J. Leclercq, H. M. Rochais, and C. H. Talbot (Rome: Editiones Cisterciences, 1957), 25.5; translations follow *On the Song of Songs II*, trans. Kilian Walsh, The Works of Bernard of Clairvaux, vol. 3, Cistercian Fathers Series 7 (Kalamazoo, Mich.: Cistercian Publications, 1976).

80 It is interesting to note *Ancrene Wisse* developing an extended metaphor (ostensibly free of any reference to race or skin color) that establishes outward whiteness as an undesirable (indeed, damnation-worthy) quality (III, pp. 103–4).

81 Sir Thomas Malory, *Works*, ed. Eugène Vinaver, 2nd edn. (London: Oxford University Press, 1971), p. 566/11; p. 572/22–5. By white bird, a swan, "may men undirstonde the fynde [fiend]," for it is "whyght withoutefurth and blacke within" (p. 572/25–7).

82 See Bruce Holsinger, "The Color of Salvation: Desire, Death, and the Second Crusade in Bernard of Clairvaux's *Sermon on the Song of Songs*," in *The Tongue of the Fathers*, ed. Townsend and Taylor, pp. 156–86.

83 A tombstone commemorating (another) slave called "Caesar the Ethiopian," died January 15, 1780, sees him remain black throughout his long working life; but now, we are told, "His faithful soul has fled / To realms of heavenly light / And by the blood that Jesus shed / Is changed from Black to White" (Joseph R. Washington, Jr., *Anti-Blackness in English Religion 1500–1800* [New York: Edwin Mellen Press, 1984], p. 351).

84 See *Oroonoko*, ed. Todd, pp. 79–80. "Humanity" is employed as a synonym for "command of classical texts"; this is the same cultural program that upholds slavery as inevitable, defining and indeed structuring those civilized freedoms that no slave can possess.

85 See Gallagher, *Nobody's Story*, p. 67.

86 Following the failure of the rebellion, Oroonoko regrets "endeavouring to make those free, who were by nature slaves" (p. 130).

87 See, famously, Luce Irigaray, *Ce sexe qui n'en pas un* (Paris: Minuit, 1977); *This Sex Which Is Not One*, trans. Catherine Porter with Carolyn Burke (Ithaca, NY:

Cornell University Press, 1985). See further Toril Moi, *What is a Woman? And Other Essays* (Oxford: Oxford University Press, 1999): "The answer to the question of what a woman is, is not one. To say this, moreover, is specifically to deny that the answer is that woman is not one" (p. 9).

88 Aboan, male ally of Oroonoko, has "subdued the heart of the antiquated Onahal" through flattery (p. 90).

89 Of the slaving captain's "clapping great irons" on Oroonoko (having "besought the prince to honour his vessel with his presence"), Behn remarks: "Some have commended this act, as brave in the captain; but I will spare my sense of it, and leave it to my reader to judge as he pleases" (p. 102).

90 See Richard Firth Green, *A Crisis of Truth: Literature and Law in Ricardian England* (Philadelphia: University of Pennsylvania Press, 1999); on some of the deleterious effects occasioned by shifts from oral agreement to written law, see Firth Green, "Literature and Law," in *The Cambridge History of Medieval English Literature*, ed. Wallace, pp. 407–31 (p. 412).

91 Without and within, for Kristeva: see *Pouvoirs de l'horreur. Essai sur l'abjection* (Paris: Éditions du Seuil, 1980). Translation of the term *l'abjection* into English "may," Kristeva remarks, "be impossible" (*Julia Kristeva Interviews*, ed. Ross Mitchell Guberman [New York: Columbia University Press, 1996], p. 118). For an account of the Middle Passage employing Kristevan categories, see Claudine Reynaud, "The Poetics of Abjection in *Beloved*," in *Black Imagination*, ed. Diedrich, Gates, and Pedersen, pp. 70–85.

92 See, for example, the film version by Julie Tamor (2000).

93 Behn's play *The Widow Ranter* opens with the speculative landing of a penniless Englishman (Hazard) upon an American coast.

94 See Todd, "Introduction" to Aphra Behn, *Oroonoko*, ed. Todd, pp. 18–19. "Black" here betokens dark-haired and dark-complexioned.

95 See "A Farewel to *Celladon*, On his Going into Ireland," in *The Poems of Aphra Behn*, ed. Janet Todd (London: William Pickering, 1994) and "A Congratulatory Poem to Her Sacred Majesty Queen Mary upon Her Arrival in England," in *The Uncollected Verse of Aphra Behn*, ed. Germaine Greer (Stump Cross, Essex: Stump Cross Books, 1989). The latter poem finally commends Mary Stuart not for her marriage to William of Orange, but for being "Great Cesar's Offspring," namely daughter to the now exiled James II (line 107).

96 See Laura Brown, "The Romance of Empire: *Oroonoko* and the Trade in Slaves," in *The New Eighteenth Century*, ed. Nussbaum and Brown, pp. 41–61 (pp. 57–60).

97 Behn's first attempt to exploit her Surinam experience – as a spy in Holland – left her destitute when her English spymasters refused to pay up.

98 This space was adumbrated at the very beginning of the novel, where it is claimed that the English colonists live "in perfect amity" with the natives of the place, caressing them "with all the brotherly and friendly affection of the world" (p. 75). These natives are naked, but unconscious of being naked: very

like "our first parents before the Fall" (p. 76). The language employed to describe these peoples, who "understand no vice, or cunning" (p. 77), compares with the Golden Ageism earlier applied to Canarians (see chapter 5 above, pp. 209–10).

99 Analogously, it is only the certainty of death to come, bracketing racial and homophobic fears, that "allows" the bonding of black warriors the night before battle in Edward Zwick's 1989 film *Glory*.

100 For fine analysis of this encounter, see Richards, *Masks of Difference*, pp. 70–3.

101 "In this voyage Oroonoko begot so good an understanding between the Indians and the English, that there were no more fears" (p. 124); he thus momentarily assumes central position in the alignment of continents (see figure 29).

102 See Price and Price, *Afro-American Arts*, p. 19.

103 The Maroons of Surinam and their arts, Sally and Richard Price argue, "represent a unique balance of continuity in change that make them, in the fullest sense, Afro-American" (*Afro-American Arts*, p. 194).

104 This was in 1762, a century before the general emancipation of slaves in Surinam. See Richard Price, *First-Time: The Historical Vision of an Afro-American People* (Baltimore. Md.: Johns Hopkins University Press, 1983), pp. 167–81; Price, *Alabi's World*, pp. 34–8.

105 *Candide*, ed. Mason, p. 42. "The agricultural history of Surinam during the 17th century," R. M. N. Panday writes, "was sugar" (*Agriculture in Surinam, 1650–1950* [Amsterdam: H. J. Paris, 1959], p. 11). Prior to the arrival of Europeans, there was a stable agriculture based chiefly on corn.

106 See Waldo Heilbron, *Colonial Transformations and the Decomposition of Dutch Plantation Slavery in Surinam*, Caribbean Centre, Occasional Publication (London: Goldsmiths' College, University of London, 1993), p. 14.

107 Voltaire's slave, informed by the Dutchmen who convert him that "nous sommes tous enfants d'Adam, blancs et noirs," retorts that servitude is thus a very strange way to treat relatives ("parents," p. 47). Here he looks backwards and forwards at once: to the English peasant couplet of 1381 – "When Adam delved and Eva span,/ Who was then the gentleman?" – and to a citation of Byron's *Childe Harold* ("Hereditary bondmen! know ye not / Who would be free, themselves must strike the blow?") in Alfred Douglas, *My Bondage and My Freedom* (New York and Auburn: Miller, Orton and Mulligan, 1855), pp. xxiii, 153.

108 Compare Dorothea Oschinsky, *Walter of Henley, and Other Treatises on Estate Management and Accounting* (Oxford: Clarendon, 1971); Markham, *The English Husbandman* (1613), conveniently available in facsimile form (New York: Garland, 1982).

109 See Wallace, *Chaucerian Polity*, pp. 392–3.

110 The poet laureate of this theology is Mary (Sidney) Herbert: see her brilliant and terrifying Psalm translations, conveniently sampled in *Women Writers in Renaissance England*, ed. Randall Martin (London: Longman, 1997), pp. 311–36.

111 On the counterpoised yet cathected claims of subject (insisting on an absolute right to dispose of his own property) and monarch, see Gallagher, *Nobody's Story*, pp. 78–87.

112 Behn, it is worth noting, chooses to imagine her royal protagonist – clearly in some ways a "black Stuart" surrogate – as victim rather than master of such a place.

113 See "Crijnssen, Abraham" (p. 140b) and "Plantages" (pp. 479b–484a, esp. 480b) in *Encyclopedie van Suriname*, ed. Bruijnig and Voorhoeve; Heilbron, *Colonial Transformations*, p. 15.

114 See Heilbron, *Colonial Transformations*, p. 14. Arends calculates black-to-white ratios in Surinam as 1:1 (1652), 2:1 (1661), 3:1 (1671), 5:1 (1684), 12:1 (1700), 20:1 (1744), 24:1 (1783), 18:1 (1830). See "Demographic Factors," p. 260 and table 8.

115 Between 1650 and 1815, about 200,000 Africans were shipped by the Dutch to Surinam; at emancipation in 1863 the black population numbered only ca. 36,000. See Jacques Arends, "The Socio-historical Background of Creoles," in *Pidgins and Creoles*, ed. Arends, Muysken, and Smith, pp. 15–24 (p. 18).

116 The former indentured white servants who came to Surinam from Barbados in the 1650s were too poor to buy more than a few slaves each (Arends, "Demographic Factors," p. 240). And the great majority of slaves shipped to Surinam were adults, immediately able to work a full day: in the period 1680–1749, only 13.8% were children (3–15 years), a marked contrast to the preference for pubescent slaves in medieval Genoa (Arends, "Demographic Factors," p. 255 and table 5; and see chapter 4 above, pp. 188–90).

117 To say this is not to underestimate the transformative effects of putting on clothes (an experience of depth as well as surface): see Ann Rosalind Jones and Peter Stallybrass, *Renaissance Clothing and the Materials of Memory* (Cambridge: Cambridge University Press, 2000).

118 It is there, familiarly enough, in white "coverings" of black music (from Pat Boone to Eminem via the Rolling Stones).

119 Thomas Harris, *Hannibal* (London: William Heinemann, 1999), p. 247.

120 Stedman, *Narrative*, ed. Price and Price, p. 520; *Notes*, ed. Peden, p. 140.

121 I abbreviate discussion of these images because of the excellent recent account by Marcus Wood, *Blind Memory: Visual Representations of Slavery in England and America, 1760–1865* (Manchester: Manchester University Press, 2000), pp. 38–40, 234–6.

122 Reproduced in color as frontispiece to Stedman, *Narrative*, ed. Price and Price. Stedman claims credit for painting this scene, with Bartolozzi as engraver.

123 *Curious Adventures of Captain Stedman, during An Expedition to Surinam, in 1773; including the Struggles of the Negroes, and the Barbarities of the Planters, Dreadful Executions, The Manner of Selling Slaves, Mutiny of Sailors, Soldiers, &c. And various other Interesting Articles* (Cheapside, London: Thomas Tegg, ca. 1805). The title page features a wild array of typefaces (the phrase "Dreadful Executions"

is in Gothic script) and boasts "Price Only Sixpence." I follow the dating of the British Library catalogue (BL 1507/1830); for reproduction and discussion of this title page and image, see Wood, *Blind Memory*, pp. 237–8. The frontispiece to the 1735 edition of Thomas Southerne's play *Oroonoko* turns Imoinda white: see Ferguson, "Juggling," pp. 168–70.

124   "They believe in rod, the scourger almighty, creator of hell upon earth, and in Jacky Tar, the son of a gun, who was conceived of an unholy boast, born of the fighting navy" (*Ulysses*, ed. Hans Walter Gabler, 3 vols. [New York: Garland, 1986], vol. II, p. 709 (1354–6)).

125   S. Allen Counter and David L. Evans, *I Sought My Brother: An Afro-American Reunion* (Cambridge: Massachusetts Institute of Technology, 1981), pp. xix, 272, 276.

126   "Slavery and the African Spiritual Holocaust" is the title of the fifth chapter of Butler, *Awash in a Sea of Faith: Christianizing the American People* (Cambridge, Mass.: Harvard University Press, 1990), pp. 129–63.

127   On Ethiopianism in African-American thought and imaginative fiction, see Eric J. Sundquist, *To Wake the Nations: Race in the Making of American Literature* (Cambridge, Mass.: Belknap Press of Harvard University Press, 1993), pp. 551–63; John Cullen Gruesser, *Black on Black: Twentieth-Century African American Writing about Africa* (Lexington: University Press of Kentucky, 2000). Ethiopianism, Sundquist argues, "may generally be regarded as a set of beliefs, derived in the classical instance from a reading of Psalms 68.31 . . . that portrayed colonized Africa or enslaved Africans in the diaspora as prepared for providential delivery from bondage" (p. 553). Gruesser traces the rise of the concept through writers such as Maria W. Stewart (1833), W. E. B. DuBois, and Marcus Garvey, and its repudiation through Richard Wright's *Black Power* (1954) and Alice Walker's *The Color Purple* (1982).

128   Butler, *Awash in a Sea of Faith*, p. 129. "Anglican parish ministers," Butler argues, "forged a maudlin, self-pitying rhetoric about awesome and burdensome responsibilities that formed a . . . crucial characteristic of American planter paternalism" (p. 144). Slaves, it was argued, enjoyed considerable advantages over their masters, having nothing to worry about beyond their labor (Butler, p. 145; and compare above, p. 189, where equivalent arguments are essayed in Genoa some five centuries earlier).

129   "White Slaves: The Mulatto Hero in Antebellum Fiction," in *Subjects and Citizens: Nations, Race and Gender from Oroonoko to Anita Hill*, ed. Michael Moon and Cathy N. Davidson (Durham, NC: Duke University Press, 1995), pp. 195–216 (p. 196).

130   The belief that suffering draws the believer into a closer, more sympathetic relation to the Godhead, for so long a mainstay of Catholic Christianity, is rapidly receding in the West (most particularly in the religiously observant USA). When Cardinal John O'Connor of New York died on May 4, 2000, a church spokesman assured the faithful that their spiritual leader had not suffered: to which the medieval faithful might have replied, "what a pity."

131 See chapter 3 above, p. 164.

132 See Dominic Rainsford, "The English Channel: Romantic Insularities," *European English Messenger* 12 (Spring 2003), 21–4.

133 See chapter 3 above, p. 164.

134 *The History, Civil and Commercial, of the British Colonies in the West Indies*, 3rd edn., 3 vols. (London: John Stockdale, 1801), p. xii. The "Sketch of the Life of the Author" (p. ix) which prefaces the volume concentrates on his education in humane letters and says nothing at all of his business life in Jamaica; the "sketch" is written for posterity, since "it is not pleasant to think that misrepresentation or malice may fasten on my memory" (p. xiii). The volume is dedicated to the King, under whose "mild and auspicious Government" the West Indies have become "the principal source of the national opulence and maritime power."

135 See Pratt, *Imperial Eyes*, pp. 95–6.

136 "The white privets fall, the dark hyacinths are culled" (Vergil, *Eclogues, Georgics, Aeneid I–VI*, trans. H. Rushton Fairclough, rev. G. P. Goold, Loeb Classical Library [Cambridge, Mass.: Harvard University Press, 1999]). The poem, which concerns itself with black / white love ("niger . . . candidus," 16), concerns the love of a shepherd for the beautiful ("formosum," 1) boy Alexis. It thus further hints at – beneath the veil of Latinity covering Teale and Edwards, master and pupil – possible vacationing from heterosexual norms. Teale, in the manner of an eclogue, explicitly addresses "dear Bryan" in his final line.

137 "History of the Sable Venus; an Ode. Written in Jamaica," in Edwards, *History*, II.32–8, lines 79–84. The "Cobre" is glossed as "a river so called in Jamaica."

138 "Diana Described: Scattered Women and Scattered Rhyme," in *Writing and Sexual Difference*, ed. Elizabeth Abel (Chicago: University of Chicago Press, 1982), pp. 95–109.

139 *Chaucer Sources and Backgrounds*, ed. Robert P. Miller, p. 412.

140 See Whitney Smith, *Flags Through the Ages and Across the World* (Maidenhead: McGraw-Hill, 1975), pp. 182–4.

141 Chaucer consistently portrays himself as an outsider to love; the early author portraits have him in clerical dress. Petrarch, at a crucial juncture in his career, elected to abandon his courtier's clothes for clerical garb (see Wallace, *Chaucerian Polity*, p. 348).

142 *Awash in a Sea of Faith*, p. 7.

143 *Ninety-Two Days* (London: Penguin, 1986), p. 7.

144 *Ninety-Two Days*, p. 13. "Dutch Guiana conveyed nothing," Waugh notes, "but that is scarcely surprising since no normally educated Englishman knows anything about Dutch colonies" (p. 13).

145 On Taylor's journey and his subsequent publication, see chapter 3 above, pp. 158–9.

146 The point is more politely put by Terence Conran: "one of the clues to English style comes from our maritime inheritance. We were the great travelers

and traders of the world, and wherever we went we brought back artifacts and influences" ("Foreword" to Susan Slesin and Stafford Cliff, *English Style* [London: Thames and Hudson, 1984], pp. viii–ix [p. viii]). This luxurious volume was originally published in the USA (by Clarkson N. Potter, Inc., One Park Avenue, New York, NY 10016) and in Canada; it was manufactured in Japan. For the "elephant's-foot waste-paper basket," part of "a strange jumble of objects" in Sebastian Flyte's room, see Evelyn Waugh, *Brideshead Revisited* (London: Penguin, 2000), p. 33.

147   David Eltis, David Richardson, and Stephen D. Behrendt, "Patterns in the Transatlantic Slave Trade, 1662–1867. New Indications of African Origins of Slaves Arriving in the Americas," in *Black Imagination*, ed. Diedrich, Gates, and Pedersen, pp. 21–32 (table 1, p. 23).

148   See Graham Davis and Penny Bonsall, *Bath: A New History*, pp. 29–31, 52; R. S. Neale, *Bath 1680–1850: A Social History, or A Valley of Pleasure Yet a Sink of Iniquity* (London: Routledge and Kegan Paul, 1981), pp. 119–30, 166. Despite its title, Peter Borsay's hefty *The Image of Georgian Bath, 1700–2000: Towns, Heritage, and History* (Oxford: Oxford University Press, 2000) offers no discussion of slavery-related aspects of Bath's heritage.

149   As cited in Davis and Bonsall, *Bath*, p. 52. See further Trevor Fawcett, "Black People in Georgian Bath," *Avon Past* 16 (Spring 1993), 3–9.

150   *A Handful of Dust* (New York: Barnes and Noble, 2001), p. 181.

151   *A Handful of Dust*, p. 181; the novel's title and its epigraph are taken from T. S. Eliot, *The Waste Land*.

152   See *Tristia* 3.4b and chapter 4 above, p. 191.

153   *The Intended* (London: Vintage, 2000), p. 5.

154   *The Intended*, pp. 195, 197.

155   Dabydeen chose to make the eighteenth century his scholarly specialty: see *Hogarth, Walpole and Commercial Britain* (London: Hansib, 1987); *Hogarth's Blacks: Images of Blacks in Eighteenth-Century English Art* (Manchester: Manchester University Press, 1987).

156   Dabydeen, "Song of the Creole Women," in *Slave Song* (Mundelstrup, Denmark: Dangaroo Press, 1984), p. 17, lines 3–14 ("Booker owns my cunt / Booker owns my children," trans. Dabydeen, p. 45). In the penultimate paragraph of *The Intended*, Dabydeen's Oxford-bound narrator is the recipient of language equivalently raw and uncompromising (spoken by Patel, his Hindu, Gujerati-speaking friend): "Just because you ain't got a mother don't mean that England will mother you, you stupid mother-fucker" (p. 246).

157   *Slave Song*, pp. 13–14.

158   "Two Cultures," in *Slave Song*, p. 42, lines 2,18, 23 ("you touch my girl-child, and I'll split your arse!", p. 71: note how the seventeenth-century English term "buss" flourishes in Guyanese as well as in Sranan; on the baby Jesus as "man-p[i]kin," see Trefossa's poem below).

159   "Sranan may be considered a Mischsprache of English and African, but it is quite wrong to select certain linguistic features and to say that they must be

one or the other. Each feature must be seen as part of a total linguistic structure. In fact, its phonemic and sentence structure points in both directions; its
morphology . . . however, is reminiscent of West African" (Echteld, *English
Words in Sranan*, p. 181 n. 6).

160 Edward Dew sees Surinam possessing "the most complex multi-ethnic population in the Caribbean" (*Difficult Flowering*, p. vii).

161 See Dew, *Difficult Flowering*, pp. 4–8; Dubois, *Portrait*, pp. 15–16; *Creole Drum*,
ed. Voorhoeve and Lichtveld, pp. 9–13, 195–7.

162 My analysis is indebted to Echteld, *English Words in Sranan*; Jan Voorhoeve,
Sranan Syntax (Amsterdam: North-Holland Publishing Company, 1962); Lilian
Adamson and Norval Smith, "Sranan," in *Pidgins and Creoles*, ed. Arends,
Muysken and Smith, 219–232. In their discussion of ideophones (an African-
derived feature of Sranan), Adamson and Smith note the collocational restrict-
iveness of certain terms, such as fAAN, employed only as an intensifier of
whiteness: "A weti so fAAN," "He is so *very* white" (p. 226; there is an equivalent term, pII, applied uniquely to blackness: "A blaka so pII").

163 *Ninety-Two Days*, p. 13. The phrase echoes the title (and attitude) of the travel
book written following Waugh's visit to Abyssinia in August 1930 for the
coronation of Haile Selassie, *Remote People* (London: Duckworth, 1931).

164 For the proposition that "genuine poetry can communicate before it is understood," see "Dante" in T. S. Eliot, *Selected Essays* (London: Faber and Faber,
1999), pp. 237–77 (p. 238). Eliot's prescription for reading usefully counter-
points the studied idleness of Waugh: "if from your first deciphering of it [the
Commedia; by extension, any foreign text] there comes now and then some
direct shock of poetic intensity, nothing but laziness can deaden the desire for
fuller and fuller knowledge" (p. 238).

165 In the 1960s, about half of the hard-won, traditional Saramaka territory was
flooded to provide electricity for the new Alcoa smelter near Paramaribo (the
capital and Trefossa's native city): see Price, *First-Time*, map as frontispiece
(unpaginated).

166 Text from *Creole Drum*, ed. Voorhoeve and Lichtveld, trans. Vernie A. February, pp. 206–9.

Humor in excelsis

The Devil got wind of some big happening
soon at the end of the year in the world.
The Son of God, so the Father willed it,
would become a child of man. Oh! What a ball!

"I'll be a spoilsport, cause a total black out."
Thus the Devil with his loud mouth.
"I'll cut the wires at the plant,
supplying electricity to the stars."

But . . . presto. A short circuit and the fire spreads.
The devil found the tables turned on him.
He scorched his beard, his whiskers, everything.

The angels started singing: humor in excelsis.
They guffawed: ha! ha! ha! Life be unto you.
And the baby Jesus gave its first squall: wah! wah! wah!

ACKNOWLEDGMENTS

This book owes more to great libraries and museums than to beach time on Tenerife. Thanks, then, to all who curate and inform, fetch and pour at the following places: Cambridge University Library (still ugliest and best of libraries); Van Pelt Library, University of Pennsylvania; Warburg Institute, London; Courtauld Institute of Art, London; the British Library; the Senate House Library, University of London; Wells Cathedral Library (Anne Crawford, Archivist); Museo Canario at Las Palmas de Gran Canaria; Municipalité de Calais; Museum of Archaeology and Anthropology, Cambridge (especially Tabitha Cadbury); Groeninge Museum, Bruges. The Department of English at King's College, London, and Clare Hall, Cambridge, proved perfect places for research and writing. The book is most peculiarly the product of Philadelphia and the University of Pennsylvania, especially the English Department's med/Ren group; the Center for Italian Studies; the Borders group (Classics and Comparative Literature, Medieval Studies, and Religion); and the Center for Africana Studies. Colleagues in all these areas have helped this far-flung project along; in particular I would like to thank Kevin Brownlee, Rebecca Bushnell, Joe Clarke, Stuart Curran, Joan Dayan, Margreta de Grazia, Toni Esposito, Joe Farrell, Barbara Fuchs, Vicki Kirkham, Ania Loomba, Penny Marcus, E. Ann Matter, Peter Stallybrass, and Emily Steiner. Rita Copeland, whose understanding of the Middle Ages is longer and deeper than mine, has shared the pressures and pleasures of a two-chair household; I remain fundamentally in her debt. Penn graduate students in English and Comparative Literature have often been my first and best respondents; I thank them for deferring their own projects to entertain mine. Daily life over the last three years, in chairing English, has been sustained by the companionship and hard work of Elizabeth Anderson, Stephanie Palmer, Ann Marie Pitts, Loretta Williams, and Miriam Mann Guerrero. My particular friendship with Margreta de Grazia has flourished within the bounds of the administrative suite; Deans Bushnell and Farrell proved expert in explaining the ways of English to our higher powers.

Friends beyond the Schuylkill and Delaware have provided both informed responses to this project and vital friendship: I think here particularly of Derek Brewer, Marina Brownlee, Jonathan Burt, Ardis Butterfield, Ann Cobby, Janet Cowan, Carolyn Dinshaw, Eamon Duffy, Penny Fielding, Cynthia Fowler, Elaine Freedgood, Simon Gaunt, Vanessa Harding, Claire Harman, Gerry Heng, Terry Jones, Robin Kirkpatrick, Clare Lees, Derek Pearsall, Paul Quinn, Miri Rubin, Larry Scanlon, Brent Shaw, Diane Shisk, James Simpson, D. Vance Smith, Gareth Steadman-Jones, Ian P. Wei, James I. Wimsatt, Nicky Zeeman, and Patrick Zutshi. Audiences at some thirty venues, from Los Angeles to Santiago de Compostella, have helped this project understand itself. The book is dedicated to the *troika* that has most to do with its final form. Paul Strohm's feared and famous editorial eye has again served me well; his friendship and exemplary *modus vivendi* continue to sustain and inspire. Bruce Holsinger also delivered a superb late critique that took an entire summer to be absorbed; I especially value his ear for music, his championing of work by younger scholars, and his willingness to urge me to do better. There are ideas, sometimes whole sentences, in this book that Paul and Bruce could claim as their own. My brother, Richard Wallace, proved an excellent, quick-witted traveling companion (figure 5), extraordinarily patient with the world's worst map-reader. Crystal Bartolovich has also provided invaluable commentary on this project; I can't think of a long e-mail from Crystal that has not forced (sooner or later) some form of textual surgery. Colin Thubron, somewhere on the Silk Road as I write, provides the priceless encouragement of the true traveler.

I am indebted to the following for permission to reproduce illustrations: Syndics of Cambridge University Library (1, 13, 15); Bodleian Library, University of Oxford (2, MS Gough Gen. Top. 16, detail); Bibliothèque Nationale de France, Paris (6, 16); Erich Lessing/Art Resource, New York (8); Metropolitan Museum of Art, New York (9); Scala/Art Resource, New York (10, 11); Bridgeman Art Library International (12); the Chapter of Wells Cathedral (photographer, George Hall, 14); British Library (20, 21, 23–30). Parts of some chapters – everything has been extensively rewritten – appear in the following publications: "Chaucer and Deschamps, Translation and the Hundred Years' War," in the *Medieval Translator* 8 (2003), pp. 179–88;

"Humanism, Slavery, and the Republic of Letters," in *The Public Intellectual*, ed. Helen Small (Oxford: Blackwell, 2002), pp. 62–88; "Dante in Somerset: Ghosts, Historiography, Periodization," *New Medieval Literatures* 3 (1999), pp. 9–38; "In Flaundres," *Studies in the Age of Chaucer* 19 (1997), pp. 63–91.

I would like to thank my inspirational editor, Andrew McNeillie, for helping think out this project; final thanks go to my sharp-eyed copy-editor, Sandra Raphael, award-winning indexer, Barbara Hird, Karen Wilson, and the team at Blackwell for making this book.

INDEX

Note: Primary sources are indexed by author and not by editor. References in italics denote illustrations.

Index